SALTWATER
FISHING
Made Easy

SALTWATER FISHING Made Easy

MARTIN POLLIZOTTO

International Marine / McGraw-Hill

Camden, Maine • New York • Chicago • San Francisco • Lisbon • London • Madrid • Mexico City
Milan • New Delhi • San Juan • Seoul • Singapore • Sydney • Toronto

The **McGraw·Hill** Companies

1 2 3 4 5 6 7 8 9 10 DOC DOC 0 9 8 7 6

Library of Congress Cataloging-in-Publication Data
Pollizotto, Martin.
  Saltwater fishing made easy / Martin Pollizotto.
     p.   cm.
  Includes index.
  ISBN 0-07-146722-X (pbk. : alk. paper)
  1. Saltwater fishing. I. Title.
  SH457.P65 2006
  799.16—dc22   2006000751

Questions regarding the content of this book should be addressed to
International Marine
P.O. Box 220
Camden, ME 04843
www.internationalmarine.com

Questions regarding the ordering of this book should be addressed to
The McGraw-Hill Companies
Customer Service Department
P.O. Box 547
Blacklick, OH 43004
Retail customers: 1-800-262-4729
Bookstores: 1-800-722-4726

Photographs and illustrations courtesy the author unless otherwise noted.
Permission is hereby granted to Martin Pollizotto by Seaguar, the inventor and leader in fluorocarbon line, to reproduce the images on pages 91–102 in connection with the book *Saltwater Fishing Made Easy* in its first and subsequent editions for no consideration.
Fish illustrations by David Kiphuth, Les Gallagher, and U.S. Fish and Wildlife Service.

DEDICATION

To my wife, Nancy, for all her understanding and support.

CONTENTS

Color illustrations may be found following page 182.

PREFACE

It's difficult for me to pinpoint exactly when my grandfather first exposed me to saltwater fishing. "Pop" was a marine carpenter, a master craftsman, and an avid saltwater angler whom I frequently visited at the boatyard where he worked on City Island in the Bronx.

When he could, Pop would position me on a dock at the boatyard and teach me the basics of fishing. I enjoyed sitting there with a rod and reel in hand, hoping a fish would grab hold of the baited hook. I don't believe I ever caught a fish from that dock. I was too busy getting into trouble.

I remember several occasions of hopelessly fouling the line on the reel and Pop cursing as he tried to straighten out the mess. All kids manage to foul fishing line, no matter how careful they are. But he seemed to enjoy taking me fishing, regardless of my childish behavior. Our fishing was restricted primarily to inshore waters for porgies, along the docks for winter flounder. When he stayed at our house the night before, that always meant an early start for an inshore party boat trip—after a big breakfast at Jack's Diner.

Me on top, Pop in the middle, and my brother on the bottom. (Courtesy Vincent Pollizotto)

While fishing at the docks, I occasionally saw other, older anglers fishing with fancy doodads, so I thought they were needed to catch fish. Pop advised me otherwise and kept our terminal tackle (that is, rigs) as simple as possible. I thought he was wrong: after all, I knew better than he did! But although I was frustrated by his insistence, I listened and did as he suggested. Now I realize that he knew what he was doing. And now I appreciate the encouragement and support he provided. He kept the spark alive.

When I was old enough, I ventured off on my own with the knowledge, skill, and love for saltwater fishing that Pop taught me. Soon I expanded my fishing exploits, heading for deepwater offshore fishing and surf fishing. I have fished the East and West coasts and the Gulf of Mexico on board party, charter, and private boats and along the surf. I completely enjoy it all.

Do you remember your first saltwater fishing trip? It's one of the most frequently mentioned early memories from childhood. Ask friends to tell you the story of their first fishing experience, and chances are it will be deeply personal and very meaningful in their lives—full of loving memories, relaxed good times, the family fishing together from a local pier or a rented small boat. Saltwater fishing held family and friends together years ago, and it still can.

Nearly fifty years ago, Pop gave me several rods and reels, and I still use them on occasion. I cherish that equipment and keep it in excellent condition, waxing and lubricating it once a year, even if I haven't used it. And I often bring my grandchildren to local docks for a couple of hours of fishing, just as Pop did with me. It's a thrill to see the expressions on their faces when they reel in a fish, no matter how small it is.

ACKNOWLEDGMENTS

Many people helped me write this book, providing advice, research assistance, and support. I especially want to thank Bob Dorian, for his continued encouragement; my brother Louis and his two sons, Louis Jr. and Adam, for their advice; William H. Harrison, a fellow angling buddy; John Quackenbush, for his fishing knowledge; Dave Connery, for his research along the Pacific coast; the High Plains Tackle Shop, for supplying me with dead bait for photos; and J&H Super Outlet, for allowing me to photograph some of their inventory. Thanks to my daughter Wendy Hart for her advice and support, and to my son Dennis for his support and assistance with some of the photos.

I also thank my parents, who always had faith in me and encouraged me to pursue my goals. Thanks to my many fishing buddies for their endless willingness to provide fishing companionship regardless of the hour. Finally, I'd like to thank my wife, Nancy, for her tolerance, and my son Martin Jr. for his medical advice while I wrote this book.

Be aware that no baitfish, eel, or worm was harmed for the photos in this book. All bait shown was already dead at the time the photos were taken.

INTRODUCTION: WHY FISH?

Humans have fished since prehistoric times, with bare hands, sticks used as spears, and crude handmade hooks made from bone. From these beginnings as a means of survival, fishing has progressed to a legitimate sport supported by a virtually limitless variety of gear—some useful, some superfluous. As individual sportsmen, we are always trying for that bigger and better catch, which continually fuels our interest in new equipment and more refined techniques.

Fishing has a reputation for being a sport for old men and women with lots of patience and lots of time on their hands. On the contrary, fishing offers excitement, thrills, and satisfaction every time a fish grabs your hook, whether it simply tugs at the line or jumps and does all kinds of acrobatics; or whether it makes long, powerful runs or darts around obstacles while attempting to free itself. It's possible to land small fish just by reeling them in with little or no effort, their strength easily overcome by good technique and the right equipment. Large fish and hard fighters require more in the way of skill and technique, more judicious use of the reel's drag setting, more patience—*maybe* stronger equipment, too, although for many anglers much of the fun comes from the challenge of using the lightest tackle possible while allowing the fish to fight. Regardless, each species reacts differently in its efforts to get away. It's your job to play the fish until it's landed.

Who hasn't gone to a fish market expecting to purchase fresh fish for a special occasion or an impressive recipe? The question is, just how fresh is the fish we want to purchase? We've all tasted "fresh" fish that had no flavor whatsoever. That was because the fish sat on ice for several days after being caught and was jockeyed from one ice pile to another. Pity the cook who spends a lot of time preparing a meal with that fish. Catching your own confers superior flavor and freshness to your meals at a reasonable cost. Then think about how delicious a meal could be with fish that you caught only hours earlier.

I wrote this book to help first-time anglers get off to a good start, and to help experienced fishermen and -women improve their skills. It provides the basic knowledge needed to catch the 89 species of saltwater fish that are described in Chapter 19.

Saltwater fishing is truly an enjoyable and relaxing sport, and an ideal break from busy modern-day schedules. And although exciting, it's not physically demanding or stressful, allowing fishing aficionados to continue past their prime.

Tight lines to you all!

PART 1

FISHING BASICS

CHAPTER 1

LUCK, THE LAW, THE MOON, AND DOING WHAT'S RIGHT

Saltwater fishing is not especially complicated, and fish are not terribly smart. Fish do, however, possess highly refined survival instincts—namely, they are ever vigilant in their search for food. You can take advantage of this vigilance as you pursue dozens of species on the East, West, and Gulf coasts of the United States.

Each species of fish has its own feeding habits and its own favorite habitats. Some can be caught almost anytime of year in certain waters; others are seasonal, visiting different places as they follow their food sources. Some fish are found only offshore—on open, or "big," water; others frequent inshore waters—harbors, bays, and estuaries. Some can be readily hooked by dropping a line off a pier or by casting from a rocky or sandy shoreline. Others remain in deep water and require boats for their pursuit. Some remain in the same general area year-round; others migrate hundreds or thousands of miles each year. The only thing complicated about fishing is keeping track of the preferences of many different species—knowing where and when to find them, what they like to eat, how they like it "served," and how to snag them while they're consuming it.

For example, fish that are considered excellent bait stealers don't analyze a baited hook. Instead, some instinct drives them to approach the hook from the side, and that just happens to mean that they grab the bait without swallowing the hook. It's your job to properly place the bait on the hook so it's not easily taken by a fish from any angle.

Because fish are constantly searching for food, their behavior is fairly predictable. The angler who has knowledge of the following is the most likely to catch fish.

1. The species' habitats. (For example, you won't catch bluefish along the northern Atlantic coast during February and March because bluefish simply aren't there at this time of year. On the other hand, offshore codfish are common in that area during that season.)

2. The species' behavior at a specific time of day and a given time of year, and any outside influences (such as weather conditions, noise, or unusual activity) that may affect that behavior.

3. What triggers a fish's feeding instinct.

4. Types of natural bait or artificial lures that attract a specific species.

5. How to "present" the bait or lure to the fish. For example, some fish that are known mainly as surface feeders also pursue food along the bottom. When a known surface-feeding species is not biting on the surface, try presenting the bait at or near the bottom.

Different species of fish have different diets, and they feed at different times of day or at different tidal stages. Most fish travel to different but specific areas within a bay or an ocean at different times of year in search of food or to spawn. It's this rotational cycle that keeps saltwater fishing interesting throughout the year.

Having said all this, I admit that luck can be involved in catching fish. The fish might actually be just where you thought they would be based on the above factors. Or through word-of-mouth reports from other anglers, boat captains, and bait-shop owners, you can find out where the fish are biting (or where they *were* biting a few hours ago, or yesterday).

Yet it's still a matter of skill to attract and hook them. Seasoned anglers match the size of the hook and bait to the size and preferences of the fish they are pursuing. For example, cod have a large mouth, allowing them to grab fairly large prey. That requires a large hook, along with an ample supply of bait to match. In contrast, winter flounder inhale food into their small mouths, which necessitates a smaller hook with a matching amount of bait.

In addition, be aware of state laws that dictate the type and size of fish that you may catch and keep, and when it is legal to do so. (See Appendix A, Fishing and the Law, for more information.)

Joining a saltwater fishing club is one of the best ways to move quickly along the learning curve. Some clubs focus on specific interests, such as surf fishing or offshore fishing; others cover the entire spectrum of saltwater fishing. Generally, all age groups are welcome.

Members of these clubs enhance their skills through talking with other anglers and participating in club activities. Fishing outings, beach barbecues, and contests often have a strong family orientation. Most clubs also hold formal business meetings at least once a month to discuss practical and political aspects of saltwater fishing in their region.

There are saltwater fishing clubs in every coastal state. Ask at your local tackle shop about clubs in your area, or search the Web for a club near you. Enter "Saltwater Fishing Club" + "(your state)" in your favorite search engine. There are also a few suggestions in Appendix E, Useful Fishing Websites, under Organizations.

UNDERSTANDING FISH

Mother Nature provides fish with extremely effective and extremely diverse feeding instincts. To choose the most effective fishing rigs, you need to know what your targeted species is likely to consume and how and when it consumes it. The preferred food sources for each of the species are explained in Chapter 9, Natural Bait, and in Chapter 19, 89 Popular Species and How to Catch Them. Here, let's look at an all-important influence on their feeding behavior: tides.

Tides

Understanding the tides helps you know when to fish. Just like people, fish have active periods and rest periods. Unlike people, fish's activities are determined by the tides. The tide tells fish when to be on the move for food and when to rest. Because fish do not have eyelids, they cannot close their eyes to rest. Instead, most species remain inactive during certain tides.

Tides are up-and-down movements of the oceans caused by the gravitational pull of the moon and sun on the Earth. As the tide rises and falls, water flows in and out of bays, harbors, and estuaries and along the shore, creating strong currents. These currents provoke feeding behavior in fish. Whereas tidal changes have little effect far offshore and are of no concern to anglers who venture there in boats, tides are of the utmost importance when fishing inshore waters.

In most locations, the tide changes four times a day, resulting in two high tides and two low tides. Low tide occurs roughly 6 hours after high tide. At the end of each rising and falling tide, there is a period called *slack tide*, when there is little or no current, or movement of water, in or out of the bays, harbors, and estuaries. Slack tide usually lasts 2¾ to 3 hours, although it varies with location.

Published tide tables, such as those found in local newspapers, are general approximations. A strong wind from offshore can create a high tide sooner than predicted. When the wind is blowing against the incoming tide, the opposite occurs.

During slack tide, most saltwater predator fish that frequent inshore waters rest and do not seek food. Slack tide, therefore, is usually an unproductive time to fish inshore—which isn't to say that it's not worth a try. For example, anglers who like to be on the water at the very beginning of a tidal change often find themselves on the water during a slack tide. By presenting the proper bait, along with chumming or chunking, it is possible to provoke fish into feeding during a slack tide. After all, fish are curious creatures and are always looking for an easy meal.

A rising tide is referred to as a *flood tide;* a falling tide is called an *ebb tide.* The change in water level is determined by the phase of the moon and the relative positions of the Earth, the moon, and the sun.

Each month, the moon goes through four phases: new moon, first quarter moon, full moon, and last quarter moon (sometimes called third quarter moon). The new moon and the full moon occur when the moon, sun, and Earth are in a nearly direct line with one another. This increases the overall gravitational pull on the Earth, which causes relatively high high tides and relatively low low tides. These extreme tides are called *spring tides,* which has nothing to do with the season.

During the first quarter moon and the last quarter moon, the moon, sun, and Earth form the points of a triangle, with the Earth at the apex. This arrangement generates less gravitational pull on the Earth, causing relatively low high tides and relatively high low tides. These more moderate tides are called *neap tides.* Naturally, currents are stronger during spring tides than during neap tides. As you'll see later, the strength of the current has an impact on where the fish are.

MORE ON THE MOON

As the moon revolves around the Earth, it appears to change shape. This optical illusion is caused by the different angles from which we see the part of the moon's surface that is illuminated by the sun. The moon passes through four phases during a cycle that repeats itself every 29½ days. The phases always follow one another in the same order, as follows:

New moon: The sun, Earth, and moon are almost in a straight line, with the moon between the sun and the Earth. The part of the moon seen from Earth is facing away from the sun, so it's very dark. A new moon causes a spring tide.

First quarter: We're seeing the moon from the "side." The right side is illuminated, and the left side is dark. During the time between the new moon and the first quarter, the part of the moon that appears lighted gets larger every day, and continues to increase until the full moon. A first quarter moon causes a neap tide.

Full moon: The Earth, sun, and moon are nearly in a straight line, with the Earth in the middle. The moon is entirely illuminated from our vantage point on Earth. A full moon causes a spring tide.

Last quarter: We're looking at the side of the moon opposite from the one we saw during the first quarter. The left half is illuminated, and the right half is dark. From the full moon to the last quarter, the illuminated area gets smaller every day. It continues to shrink until the new moon, when the cycle starts all over again. A last quarter moon causes a neap tide.

Atmospheric pressure has a subtle effect on the level of the tide. Low barometric pressure allows the tide to rise higher; high barometric pressure pushes it down. During hurricanes, when the barometric pressure is extremely low, tides can be dangerously high, resulting in wave damage and flooding in low-lying coastal areas.

Using the Tide to Catch Fish

When the tide begins to ebb, the current forces baitfish into deeper water, concentrating them into smaller areas and making them easy prey for larger predator fish. The ebb tide thus triggers the predators' feeding instinct. Flood tides also trigger the feeding instinct, and predator fish lie in wait for baitfish to flow into the mouths of inlets, bays, harbors, and estuaries or along the surf. Fishing action subsides during slack tides because baitfish disperse themselves, seeking shelter from predators. There are exceptions, but this is what happens with each ebb and flood tide for most areas on the East and West coasts and in the Gulf of Mexico.

As a rule of thumb, the best fishing takes place 1½ to 2 hours after the ebb and flood tides begin. Tide tables appear daily in many newspapers, and many tackle shops give them away.

Read them for the approximate times, but remember that weather conditions can make the tides occur earlier or later than "scheduled," and not *all* fish feed during a rising or falling tide. Exceptions are noted for some individual species in Chapter 19.

Fish Sense

Knowing *how* fish seek food is just as important as knowing *where* and *when* they do it. Fish use three of their senses: hearing, smell, and sight. Of these, hearing is the most important, especially for predator fish.

Hearing

Fish hear through their internal "ears" (fluid-filled canals with sensory hairs), and with the aid of their *lateral line* (also called a longitudinal line), a sensory device that runs along the sides of some fish and detects low-frequency vibrations, such as the sound of another fish swimming. Predator fish are especially attuned to the sounds that wounded and struggling baitfish make while swimming, and they respond to these sounds before they see their quarry.

You can take advantage of this behavior by using various noise-making artificial lures or by creating a commotion in the water while retrieving the lure. Surf anglers, for instance, use rattling lures to attract predators as they work (retrieve) the lure through the water. Certain flies are designed to push the water and make a burbling sound as they are worked. Jigs such as bucktails, rubber worms, or surgical tubes also move water, creating enough sound to draw the attention of predator fish.

However, surface or subsurface swimming fish tend to spook easily when they hear unfamiliar sounds from boats, a wading angler, or an artificial lure that haphazardly hits the water. Don't run your boat through a suspected area of surface-feeding fish, and avoid making noise while anchoring. And don't go splashing into the water like a charging rhinoceros, or the fish will flee.

Smell

Fish also rely on their keen sense of smell, so anglers often release food particles, or *chum*, into the water to entice any nearby fish to feed. You can also apply a couple of drops of fish oil on artificial bait or lures to encourage a fish to strike. *Natural* baits, such as mackerel strips, bunker strips, clams, sandworms, or bloodworms, should have a fresh scent of their own and need no additional fish oil unless you want to create a stronger aroma. Fish oils can be purchased at better tackle shops.

Wherever possible, avoid wearing hand cream, cologne, aftershave, and other fragrant concoctions before heading out to fish. Fish will avoid any bait or lure that has a non-bait-like odor. After applying sunscreen or bug dope, wash your hands thoroughly with mild soap before handling bait or lures.

Sight

Predator fish rely least on their sense of sight, at least until they are close enough to see their prey. Fish are nearsighted; they don't see distant objects clearly, and they lack the ability to judge distance. Fish can see clearly only up to about 2½ feet, and they cannot see directly behind them. However, their eyes are sensitive to movement, and a streaking artificial lure is often perceived as a fleeing baitfish—that is, an easy meal. Some saltwater fish species can differentiate color; others cannot. However, most fish can distinguish between dark and light shades.

LEGAL AND ETHICAL CONSIDERATIONS

Before you head out to fish, you should have a tide table, which tells the high and low tides for each day, familiarize yourself with the habitats and feeding habits of the fish you're after, and know the laws protecting the species. Fishing is an ethical sport, with standards of behavior to protect its participants, its future, and the future of the species. To that end, it is important to know how to properly release fish back into the environment without injury.

The Law

Many coastal states require a current saltwater fishing license. Bring it with you when you're fishing in case law enforcement personnel ask to see it. Most states also have laws specifying the minimum size and maximum number of saltwater fish you can keep. They also have moratoriums—times of the year when particular species may not be kept regardless of size—to give the species adequate time to spawn, help increase the stocks, and prevent the extinction of a species. All of these laws are strictly enforced, and hefty fines are imposed on anglers who ignore them. The regulations differ from state to state, and even within a state they change constantly, so check with the state's marine and recreational fishing agency. (For more information, see Appendix A, Fishing and the Law.)

Any fish you intend to keep must meet the legal size limits for the species. An accurate measuring device, such as a tape measure, will do, or you can use the large plastic rulers sold in most tackle shops. There is no room for guesswork here, such as using your arm or foot as a measuring device.

The law stipulates specific measuring guidelines. For example, some species must be measured from the tip of the nose to the fork of the tail, whereas others are measured to the end of the tail. Be aware of any stipulations that require the mouth of the fish to be closed while you're measuring. (If the mouth is open when you're measuring the fish, the measurement may read slightly longer.) If a state official happens to inspect your catch and finds one fish that's not long enough, or one fish too many, you may be fined. It's easier to comply with the laws than to pay fines, not to mention the legal fees involved if you elect to contest the fine in court.

Fishing Ethics

Most anglers take the ethics of the sport seriously—especially a commitment to protect and preserve the environment. Regardless of where you fish, consider what you bring with you. Use trash receptacles to discard empty wrappers or containers, and never discard anything in the water or on the dock, jetty, or beach. Not only does trash create an unsightly mess, it can threaten the well-being of wildlife and fish.

Most anglers fillet their catch after they get home and dispose of the remains responsibly. If you clean your catch in the field, be considerate of other anglers and the environment. Before you even begin, make sure there's a suitable refuse container handy. And be one of the good guys: tuck a plastic trash bag in your belt and collect any debris you stumble upon that's been left behind by inconsiderate anglers.

It is unethical to keep more fish than you plan to eat. Although there is nothing illegal about taking home a full limit of fish, day after day this adds up to more fish than most of us could comfortably consume. It unnecessarily stresses fish populations, reducing the number of fish that will have a chance to spawn, and limiting the number of fish for years to come.

So rather than taking the limit, please limit the take. Fish all you want, but release the fish you don't plan to eat. If you want to prove how successful you were, or just preserve the memories, bring an inexpensive camera on your fishing trips. Disposable cameras are ideal. As soon as you photograph the fish, you can release it to fight another day.

Releasing Fish

Most fish become stressed when hooked, and the stress can be fatal. The less you handle the fish, and the less you stress it by playing it for a long time, the greater its chance of survival when returned to the water.

If you catch an undersized fish, or plan to release the fish regardless of its legal size, try not to remove it from the water while you unhook it. If the fish must be brought out of the water, make sure it's for the shortest possible time. Don't allow the fish to thrash about; it can injure itself (and big fish can injure you and damage your boat as well). Instead, cover the fish's eyes with a wet cloth to help calm it. Avoid touching the gills, and never handle a fish with dry hands; use wet hands or wet gloves to avoid abrading the protective mucous coating on the fish's skin. Never yank a hook free from the fish's mouth; use a hook removal device instead. If you can't remove the hook without injuring the fish, cut the leader or the line as close to the hook as possible; the hook will eventually work its way out. To give the fish a fighting chance, place it back in the water and hold it gently, allowing water to flow through its gills before you release it.

CHAPTER 2

COMFORT AND SAFETY

Every year, newspapers publish stories about anglers who drown or otherwise lose their lives while fishing. In almost every case, the fatal fishing accidents could have been avoided if basic safety practices had been followed and common sense applied. No fish, regardless of its size, is worth a tragedy.

Any number of lesser mishaps can also just plain ruin a good day of fishing—cuts, bruises, sunburn, seasickness, food poisoning. Fishing safety addresses these issues too.

GENERAL SAFETY GUIDELINES

Here are some general guidelines regarding health and safety issues associated with fishing. For basic information on first aid, I recommend that you study an appropriate book on the subject. For medical emergencies, consult a medical professional.

First Aid

First aid can involve anything from dressing a small cut to controlling bleeding from major wounds to administering cardiopulmonary resuscitation (CPR) to a person whose breathing or heart functions have stopped. When every second counts, CPR is a lifesaving technique, especially for anglers fishing in remote locations. Contact your local Red Cross chapter or hospital to learn how to receive training in this valuable skill, as well as in general first aid. In all cases of interrupted breathing or heart stoppage, regardless of CPR training and regardless of its success or failure, call 911 immediately to obtain professional medical assistance.

Accidents happen, so carry a well-stocked first-aid kit every time you go fishing so you're prepared to handle minor injuries. The kit should include bandages of various sizes, gauze, antiseptic, antibiotic cream, painkiller (aspirin or other headache medication), a chemical ice pack, tweezers, and rubber gloves. Make sure to include any special prescription medications you may need. Inventory the kit frequently to keep it properly stocked, and replace items when they reach their expiration date.

Fishhook Dangers

Getting impaled by a fishhook happens too frequently. Although fishhooks can get lodged almost anywhere, the most common injuries are to fingers, arms, legs, and the head. Fishhooks are unsanitary and can easily lead to infection, not to mention that their barbs are painful and difficult to remove.

Even careful anglers occasionally get snagged due to a momentary lapse of attention, the carelessness of others, or perhaps just bad luck. So keep your tetanus vaccination up to date.

Don't try to remove a fishhook unless you have appropriate training or a complete understanding of the procedure. It's better to call 911 for professional medical attention; keep calm, and answer the dispatcher's questions clearly. If the impaled person must be moved, carefully immobilize the affected body part and the hook to prevent the hook from working its way farther in.

If the injured angler is taking Coumadin or another blood thinner, try to control the bleeding while awaiting medical assistance. Never give aspirin to the victim of a bleeding wound because it also acts as a blood thinner.

Sun and Heat

In the sun, wind, and salt air, dehydration is a common problem that can have serious, even life-threatening, implications. Keep your cooler stocked with nonalcoholic cold drinks and plenty of plain water and partake frequently. Keep a couple of extra bottles of drinking water somewhere other than in your cooler for emergencies. Make sure they stay there, and replace them periodically.

On hot, sunny days, beware of severe sunburn, heat exhaustion (heat prostration), and sunstroke (heat stroke). Dress properly, wear a hat, use sunscreen, and drink plenty of water. Never drink alcohol or beverages that contain caffeine such as coffee, tea, or colas on hot, sunny days, as they act as diuretics.

Light-headedness is a possible sign of heat exhaustion. Have the affected person sit in a shaded area of the boat, or get the person to shore and an air-conditioned environment, such as a car. Provide cool, fresh water and keep the person seated until medical assistance arrives. Always remain with the person.

Lightning

Aside from drowning, lightning presents the greatest risk to anglers because of their exposed position when fishing. When lightning strikes, it most often hits the highest object in the immediate area. In many cases, the highest object is an angler on a boat or standing on a beach. Fishing rods make excellent lightning targets—especially those fancy (and electrically conductive) graphite ones.

When a storm approaches, stop fishing immediately. Avoid being the highest object in the immediate area. If you're on a boat, head for shore. If you can, get out of the boat and find a well-covered or roofed shelter. If you're on a beach, head for your car or some other enclosure.

A good way to be aware of an approaching electrical storm is with a portable AM radio. If a storm is approaching, you will hear static on the radio. It's a good idea to seek shelter at this point. Of course, a weather radio, which is constantly tuned to National Weather Service broadcasts, gives more information.

While I'm on the subject of electrocution, beware of low-hanging electrical wires above the area where you fish. Otherwise, a nice overhead cast could have shocking results.

Self-Protection

The conditions on the shore or on the water are frequently completely different from those just a few miles, or even blocks, inland. So even if you're setting out on a calm, sunny day, it's wise to bring clothes for more than one type of weather condition.

Dress appropriately. On cold days, wear layered woolen clothing and bring along an extra sweater or two. On hot days, cotton garments will help keep you cool, but remember to cover up with long pants and sleeves to avoid overexposure to the sun. (Choose clothing that can be washed, as opposed to dry-cleaned, and clothes that you won't mind getting stained with fish blood.) Tie a rag to your belt so you have something to wipe your hands on to remove slime while handling fish or bait. Fishing can get pretty sloppy.

You'll likely be standing for hours on end, so choose comfortable shoes. Waterproof footwear can be a nice comfort on a cold, wet day.

Rain *can* make a fishing trip miserable, but it needn't. You should have a good set of raingear (including pants or overalls) that is vented to release perspiration. Otherwise, you may get soaked with sweat even though the raingear keeps out the rain.

The sun can be relentless and its rays can penetrate many fabrics. Apply water-resistant sunscreen anyplace the sun may reach—even under your shirt. Wear polarized sunglasses to protect your eyes from harmful ultraviolet rays and to prevent a glare-induced headache.

You'll need a hat. During the summer months, wear a white cotton baseball cap with small vent holes in the top. It should have a long bill with a dark-colored underside to keep glare out of your eyes. In cold weather, you lose a huge amount of body heat through your head, so during the winter months wear a woolen watch cap that can be pulled down over your ears. This can be worn under a baseball-type cap.

Fishing and insect pests go together. You'll become well acquainted with biting flies—especially those nasty green-headed horseflies that will harass you on the beach and manage to find you even on a boat in the middle of the bay. Mosquitoes and sand fleas will also be a nuisance. Although there is often a breeze that keeps pests to a minimum, you can't rely on it. Carry and use insect repellent.

Safety on Boats

Boating requires a great deal of specialized knowledge. This book doesn't intend to tell you everything you need to know about boating safety: that would require whole chapters on navigation, anchoring, the Rules of the Road (the steering and sailing rules, sound signals, and requirements for navigation lights and day shapes), man-overboard responses, and so on. But here are some tips on staying safe while you're fishing aboard a boat, based on my personal experience.

- Don't overload the boat. Check the boat's capacity plate for its load limits, and never exceed the weight limit or the number of people that can be safely and legally carried on board.

- Avoid sea conditions that the boat is not designed to handle safely, and conditions beyond the limits of your personal boat-handling skills. Be aware of waves, current, and wind conditions, and rocks and underwater obstructions. If conditions are foggy, wait until the fog lifts.

- Know the tide schedule, and carry up-to-date nautical charts. Also be aware of current weather conditions and the forecast.

- Know how to navigate. Know the Rules of the Road, and follow them.

- Know what to do in a man-overboard situation.

- Always wear a personal flotation device (PFD)—a life vest or jacket. Have appropriate-sized PFDs for everyone on board.

- Never allow anglers or other passengers to sit on the gunwale with their feet dangling over the side.

- Always look behind and to both sides of you before casting your line.

- Keep sharp objects, such as fishing knives, hooks, lures, and gaffs, securely stowed to prevent them from shifting in rough conditions.

- Don't leave fishing rods lying on the deck, where someone could trip on them; and don't lean them against the inside gunwales of the boat, where someone could lean on them and break them—with a possible injury resulting from the sharp ends. Keep them in the boat's rod lockers or rod holders.

- Have an appropriate means of communication. Cell phones can be handy, but it is easy to be out of satellite range on a boat. (If you do carry a cell phone, protect it from the elements in a waterproof bag.) Boats should be equipped with a VHF radio. The boatowner should know how to use it, and a second person should know, too, in case the owner is incapacitated. For that matter, someone besides the owner should know how to operate the boat.

- Tell someone on land where you intend to fish and about what time you plan to return. (If you're going to be away overnight or longer, file a written float plan, including information about your boat, its passengers and equipment, where you're headed, and when you plan to be back.) Tell him or her to call the Coast Guard if you don't return on time, but be sure to build in a margin of error. We don't want the Coasties wasting their time chasing down every boat that's half an hour late.

- Learn about boating safety by contacting the Coast Guard Auxiliary (www.cgaux.org) or the U.S. Power Squadrons (www.usps.org).

Seasickness

Seasickness is no laughing matter; it is extremely uncomfortable. Many fishing trips are cut short because of it. If you're seasick on board a party or charter boat, you won't have the option of returning to shore; you'll just have to live with it until the trip is over.

The best approach to seasickness is preventive. Avoid eating greasy foods and consuming alcohol and caffeine prior to your trip. On large vessels, avoid the bow and the stern areas, which are subject to more violent motion than the waist (middle) of the boat. Avoid exposure to exhaust fumes from diesel engines. And consider using antiseasick medications or devices.

Dramamine and Bonine are common over-the-counter motion-sickness drugs. When taken as directed, they can help prevent seasickness. Scopolamine is a prescription adhesive patch that is used transdermally—that is, the medicine is absorbed through the skin. The patch is applied like a Band-Aid. (People who can't swallow pills find this helpful.) And a bracelet called Sea-Band offers a nonmedicinal approach. The package contains two bracelets, which are worn on both wrists and work using the principle of acupressure. They are surprisingly effective.

A seasick angler is incapable of doing anything except—at best—leaning over the side of the boat. If you're the affected person, try to find a location out of everyone's way, on the leeward side of the boat (that's the direction the wind is blowing *to*, not the direction it's coming *from*). After the worst is over, try to get some sleep.

There isn't much you can do to help someone who is seasick except lend moral support. Because a seasick stomach can't keep down medication long enough for it to be effective, seasickness can't be cured once it develops.

No one is immune from motion sickness; it eventually catches up with everyone, regardless of their seagoing experience. I know, because I have hung over the rail trying not to rupture an internal organ or two. Believe me, it's a horrible experience, never to be forgotten.

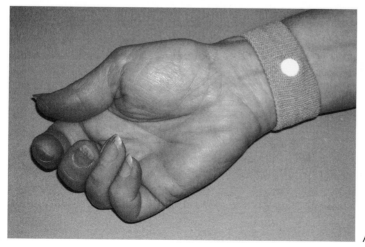

A Sea-Band is worn on the wrist.

Surf Fishing Safety

- Surf-fish with a buddy; avoid fishing alone. Good fishing beaches can be remote, and the surf can be hazardous. A lone angler is at risk.

- Check the water conditions when you arrive. Know the stage of the tide—whether it's flooding or ebbing. If the tide is high, ask other anglers what they observed

Wearing a headlamp, this surf angler is ready for evening fishing.

about the contour of the bottom when the tide was low. If the tide is low, ask about the behavior of the waves when it was high.

- On many beaches, waves arrive in definite sequences, such as seven small waves followed by two larger ones. Take some time after arriving at the beach to observe the sequence of waves before making any quick judgments about how close you can get to the surf.

- Pay attention to, and don't exceed, the limits of your strength, agility, and endurance.

- Be aware of the surf's undertow. Never wander far into the water.

- If you elect to enter the surf, wear a PFD. Although it can be cumbersome, it can save your life should you fall or be knocked over in the surf.

- If a wave or the current overcomes you while you're wading, get rid of your equipment. Reduce the weight you're carrying, and gain a free hand or two to grab hold of anything solid.

- Large rocks or boulders may be inviting places to stand on. Avoid them. They are often covered with slippery marine vegetation that can precipitate a fall into the water, coupled with cuts, abrasions, and broken bones.

- Footing can be hazardous on stone jetties. Wear aluminum- or steel-studded sandals, called Korkers, over your wading shoes for traction.

- Always carry a first-aid kit.

- Look behind and to both sides of you before every cast to prevent injury to others.

- Carry a flashlight with fresh batteries when you fish at night. Some anglers use a headlamp to keep their hands free for baiting hooks, tying knots, and attaching lures. (Avoid shining the light toward the water while you're fishing. It tends to scare fish away.) A headlamp will also help you avoid debris on the beach when you walk back to your car with both hands full of gear.

- Carry a cell phone. Let someone on land know the phone number, the location where you intend to fish, and the time you expect to return. Be aware of limitations of cell phone coverage.

Ciguatera

Ciguatera poisoning is caused by eating the flesh of certain subtropical and tropical fish, such as barracuda and greater amberjack, that have ingested toxic dinoflagellates. It generally takes years for affected fish to develop concentrations that cause problems for humans who eat the fish, and incidence is highly area specific. Cooking does not usually kill the bacteria.

Ciguatera is not usually fatal, but even a mild case is extremely unpleasant. In nonfatal severe cases, recovery can take months or even years. It causes nausea, gastrointestinal cramping, and vomiting. Neurological discomfort soon follows, with headaches, muscular aches, and weakness. There may be cardiovascular problems, and a numbing sensation of the lips, tongue, and mouth. To avoid ciguatera poisoning, it's best to avoid eating fish that frequent tropical reefs. If you do eat such fish and experience symptoms, consult a physician immediately. One resource, which also provides information on a test kit, is http://cigua.oceanit.com.

PART 2

FISHING EQUIPMENT

GETTING EQUIPPED

Well-stocked tackle shop.

Before you buy your equipment, you should know how you're going to fish. Some people prefer to sit or stand on a dock; others enjoy standing at the edge of the surf on a sandy shore. Still others prefer a day on a boat on the open water. These and other techniques of fishing are described in Part 3; each technique requires different equipment, and it usually takes two or three fishing trips before you know what you need for your style of fishing.

That said, there is a whole tackle box full of equipment that everyone needs, so I'll talk about some of that here.

There is much to choose from at tackle shops—enough to confuse even the most advanced angler. Some items are designed primarily to attract humans rather than fish. Just remember to keep it simple and stay focused on what's needed, and avoid large chain stores, whose sales depend on volume. You'll receive the best advice from mom-and-pop tackle shop proprietors, who do what they can to turn you into a regular customer by giving you good tips and local knowledge.

Freshwater fishing gear isn't recommended for salt water. It's too light for most saltwater species, and it corrodes quickly when exposed to the salt. You need equipment that is specifically designed for the rigors of a saltwater environment. So let's get started.

ESSENTIAL FISHING EQUIPMENT

Rods and Reels

For the beginning angler, a good choice of rod is a 6- to 7-foot moderate- to fast-action spinning rod. It is sufficient for just about every type of fish species, from scup to large bluefish or even striped bass. After you've gained experience and acquired definite opinions, you can increase your rod inventory judiciously.

You'll also need a versatile spinning reel to match the spinning rod. The spinning reel should be capable of holding at least 150 yards of 20- to 25-pound-test monofilament line. Most inexpensive spinning reels are acceptable for beginners. However, it's important that the reel fit snugly without side movement when fully tightened on the rod, and the combination of the rod and reel should feel comfortable. One way to avoid any question of properly matching the rod and reel is to purchase a rod and reel combination outfit. The manufacturer has already done the thinking for you.

Compared to most other fishing techniques, surf fishing requires more complex and specialized gear. A 10- to 12-foot or even a 14-foot moderate- to fast-action surf rod and matching spinning reel are acceptable choices. Bigger does not necessarily mean better, so buy a surf rod that you feel will be easy to work with.

See Chapters 4 and 5 for more on rods and reels.

For hooks and lures, it's best to learn the type of fish that are running and which species can be targeted in the area you intend to fish. The tackle shop owner will know what hook or lure size is best for the particular targeted species and the local fishing area.

Tackle Boxes and Backpacks

You will need a tackle box to carry and stow equipment. Tackle boxes come in various types, sizes, materials, and price ranges. They all have numerous compartments of different sizes suitable to house lures, jigs, sinkers, hooks, swivels, small tools, and other supplies. The choice is largely a matter of personal preference; no one type is decidedly better than another.

A well-organized tackle box will keep your gear reasonably dry, neatly consolidated, and readily accessible, and will enable you to accurately inventory its contents. A disorganized tackle box is a chamber of horrors. Tackle becomes tangled, you won't be able to find what you need—much less extricate it easily—and you'll likely poke yourself on hooks as you try to disengage them.

There is no need to purchase a tackle box big enough to hold a bulky reel because reels should never be stowed in a tackle box. Keep them secured to the rod and transport them together as a complete setup.

A standard student's backpack makes a convenient tackle box because it frees your hands to carry two or more rods and their attached reels and a cooler. A backpack is handy when you're fishing from a dock, jetty, or boat, and it's particularly helpful when you're surf fishing. Having to walk on a sandy beach while loaded down with equipment can be exhausting; a backpack makes the trek much easier. Almost everything you'll need at the beach—including a first-aid kit and your lunch—will fit in the backpack's numerous pockets and compartments. To prevent hooks and lures from snagging on the fabric, use the clear plastic compartmented (and inexpensive) containers that are sold at any tackle shop.

Small tackle box.

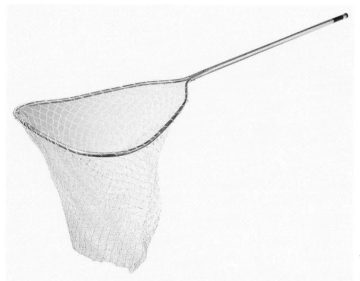

Typical large-mouth fishing net.
(Courtesy Frabill)

Gaffs and Nets

Gaffs and nets are used primarily when fishing from boats to pull fish out of the water, after which the hook can be removed. If the boat has low freeboard (the height of the sides above the water), a short-handled gaff or net will work fine. If the boat has high freeboard, a longer handle is needed to safely reach the fish. Regardless of gaff size, they're sharp; to avoid serious injury, stow them carefully.

Because a gaff will inevitably injure the fish, it should not be used if you practice hook and release. Instead, net the fish aboard the boat, or try to remove the hook while the fish is still in the water. If the hook won't come out easily, cut the leader close to the hook. The hook will eventually work its way out and will not harm the fish.

On the other hand, avoid using a landing net for sharp-toothed fish, which will play havoc with the nylon netting. Most sharp-toothed fish (considered desirable by anglers) can be gaffed aboard. If you plan to release a sharp-toothed fish, gaff it carefully under the lower jaw; this causes the least amount of injury, and most fish so gaffed will quickly heal. But be aware that it's hard to place a gaff accurately on a fish that's thrashing violently on the end of your line.

Gaffs and nets are usually not required—or practical—for fishing from piers, jetties, or beaches. High piers would require gaff or net handles so long as to be impractical, so you have to hope that your hook is well set, and depend on the strength of the line as you reel the fish up. In surf, you

HOW NOT TO LAND A FISH

Never attempt to "horse" a large fish over the gunwale of a boat by lifting its weight with the fishing line. Regardless of how low the boat's freeboard is, there is a good chance that the line will break or the hook will dislodge from the fish's mouth.

Instead, gently lead the fish into the waiting net or to the gaff. These tools are designed for lifting the fish's weight.

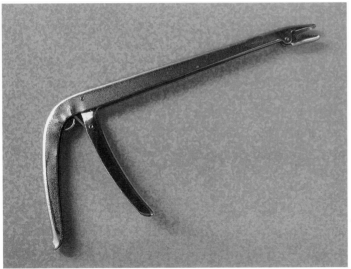

Hook removal tool.

can generally use the line to pull the fish onto the beach until it's close enough to grab. Avoid jerking the line unnecessarily.

Hook Removal Tool

A hook removal tool is a handy device to have in your tackle box. Hook removers keep hands and fingers at a safe distance from the fish's mouth. Also called a hook extractor, the tool is used to grasp the hook at its bend, providing the needed reach and leverage to twist and remove it. The tool is especially valuable when removing hooks from sharp-toothed fish such as bluefish, which would love to deprive you of a finger or two.

A pair of needle-nose pliers will also work; they should be made from stainless steel or titanium alloy to resist corrosion. Conventional household pliers will rust before you know it and make a mess in your tackle box.

Be aware that some fish will leap forward when you attempt to remove the hook, and could grab you on the hand or arm, or even your face. So never allow children to remove the hook from a sharp-toothed fish, even with a hook removal tool.

OTHER ESSENTIAL EQUIPMENT

A *cooler* (stocked with ice) keeps beverages and lunch cold and your catch fresh. Consider the cooler's weight, bulk, and durability when purchasing, as well as the size and quantity of fish you expect to keep in it. The cooler must be able to close completely without the fish's tails hanging out. Wheels can be a nice feature, but they're not very useful on soft sand or uneven jetties.

Fingernail clippers make clean cuts in fishing line. This essential piece of equipment is inexpensive and small enough to store in a tackle box compartment.

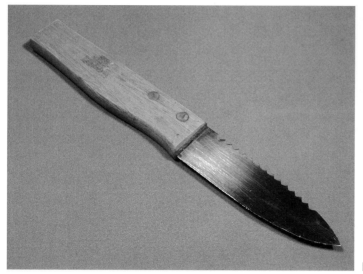
Inexpensive bait knife.

A *bait knife*, used primarily to cut bait, is a useful, inexpensive, multipurpose tool. Get one that is heavy duty and the right size to store easily in your tackle box. Some bait knives have a serrated edge, good for removing fish scales.

A *fillet knife* is fine bladed and very sharp and should be used only for filleting fish. Keep yours sharp and out of harm's way, in its own compartment in your tackle box.

Use a *chum pot* to disperse small, chopped-up bits of fish discards into the water to attract fish to the vicinity of your baited hook or lure. Most commercially made chum pots look like perforated cylinders (usually metal, often plastic coated; see photo page 116), but almost anything—a covered plastic pail, an onion sack—can serve the purpose.

A *finger cot* or *finger stall* is used to protect your index finger from the abrasive effects of the line when casting, particularly when surf fishing or using spinning equipment of any kind (see photo page 132). Finger cots can be purchased at better tackle shops. Adhesive bandage strips can be used instead, but they are a nuisance when wet.

A Few Pieces of More Specialized Gear

Alert bells (see photo next page) attach to the tip of a surf rod and let you know that a fish has hit your baited hook. The bells sound when a fish tugs on the line, so you don't have to constantly watch the tip of the rod while waiting for a bite.

A *fighting belt* (see photo next page) supports the butt end of your fishing rod and prevents it from poking in your abdomen when you're fighting a powerful fish. A fighting belt is advisable when you're fishing for any species weighing more than 8 pounds. Tackle shops stock a variety of designs. A fighting belt isn't heavy or uncomfortable, so you can wear it for the duration of a fishing trip.

Alert bells fastened to the tip of a rod.

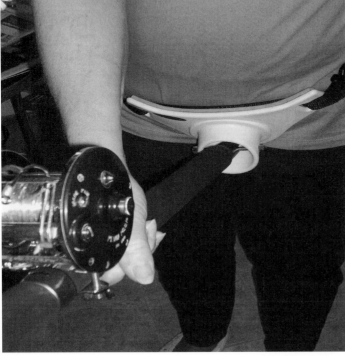

Fighting belt.

GATHERING YOUR EQUIPMENT

Regardless of the fishing technique you're using, you always want to have all the equipment you'll need—and none of the equipment you won't need. It's too easy to load yourself down with excess gear, so before you leave home, carefully consider the requirements of the trip. Keep your choices to a minimum. If you'll be fishing from a dock, leave the surf fishing equipment at home, and vice versa.

Always have an ample supply of hooks, sinkers, swivels, lures, natural bait, and bottled water, and your lunch. It's not necessary to carry extra spools of line, extra reels, more than two types of rods, or the kitchen sink.

Most situations call for something to sit on. Usually the cooler is adequate, but if you're not bringing one, consider a folding chair or camping pad.

Keep separate checklists of what to bring for each type of fishing you do. Gather the appropriate items together the night before the trip; if you intend to get an early start, load the car the night before. Keep a separate predeparture punch list of last-minute items to pack or buy.

If you'll be boat fishing, bring proper footgear, appropriate clothing for any type of weather you might encounter, a hat, sunglasses, sunblock, plenty of water, your lunch, a cooler, and a seasickness remedy or preventive.

Party boats provide most, although not all, of the gear you need, so check with the provider to find out exactly what you should bring. Some party boats provide the rod and reel for free; others charge a fee. Most party boats supply the right kind of bait for the fish they're pursuing, and many also provide the proper terminal tackle. You can usually bring your own rod, reel, terminal tackle, and bait. Bring an ice-filled cooler to store perishable items and the fish you catch.

Charter boats provide all the tackle and bait you'll need, but you'll still want to bring lunch or snacks and a cooler (with ice) to bring home your catch.

If you'll be fishing from a dock or jetty, bring one or two rods and reels; suitable attire; a tackle box or backpack; natural bait and/or artificial lures; an ice-filled cooler with bottled water, your lunch, and snacks; a supply of terminal tackle, including hooks, lures, and sinkers; a hat; sunglasses; sunscreen; and insect repellent.

For surf fishing, make sure the rod and reel are of the appropriate type, and add sand spikes (to hold your rod upright on the beach), waders, and a waterproof pullover parka. As mentioned earlier, a small AM radio is a handy safety device because increasing static can alert you to an approaching thunderstorm. When the reception starts to crackle and shriek, get off the beach and into your car.

More details on equipment for each style of fishing are given in Part 3.

C H A P T E R   4

SALTWATER FISHING RODS

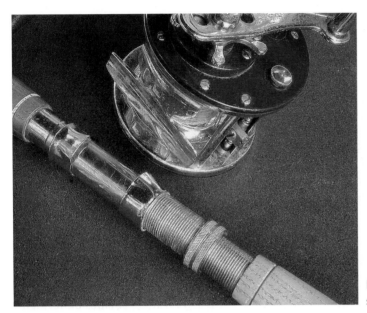

Bait-casting reel and rod reel seat.

The rod and the reel are the basic tools of fishing. Although the two must work together as a single unit for casting and retrieving a line and fighting the fish, they are usually bought and considered as separate items. We'll examine rods here, but be sure to look at the end of Chapter 5, Saltwater Reels, for important maintenance information that applies to rods as well.

ROD BASICS

Fishing rods have come a long way since the days of the old cane rods, which were made from bamboo, and "fencing" rods, which were made from tempered steel and looked like fencing swords. Compared to modern rods, cane rods were stiff, and the metal ones were heavy for their size.

Nowadays, fishing rods are manufactured from modern materials such as fiberglass, carbon fiber (also known as graphite), and graphite-fiberglass composites. Graphite rods are lighter and more sensitive for detecting fish; fiberglass rods are typically tougher and more durable. (The fibers of a fiberglass rod soften with use, making the rod more limber as it ages. Many advanced anglers like this.) Rods made from a composite of graphite and fiberglass combine these properties, and many anglers find that they offer the ideal balance of durability, sensitivity, and weight.

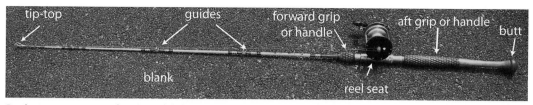

Basic components of a typical fishing rod.

Fishing Rod Components

Handgrip

Saltwater fishing rods have two grips, or handles: one above the reel seat and one below it. The forward grip is used when setting the hook—pulling back the tip of the rod to make sure the fish is well and truly hooked. It is also used to help support the rod while fighting the fish. The aft grip, located near the bottom of the rod, provides leverage and a secure handhold. This is the grip you hold when casting. When resting, most anglers support the rod by placing the aft grip under their armpit.

Rod grips are made of cork or plastic foam for comfort and a secure grip even when wet. The grip length and style vary according to the type and overall design of the rod (spinning rod, bait-casting rod, etc., discussed below.) For now, suffice it to say that most slow- and medium-action boat rods and spinning rods have lighter-weight cork grips, which transfer vibration better than foam for increased sensitivity. In contrast, fast- and extra-fast-action boat rods and spinning rods typically have an elongated foam grip, which provides better handling and leverage for fighting a fish.

When you're fighting a fish without the benefit of a fighting belt, the butt end of the fishing rod will often end up jammed into your gut. That's why the butt is covered by a plastic or rubber cap. On some rods these caps are removable, covering a recess that fits securely over a *boss* (protruding stud) in the gimbal of a fighting belt or a fighting chair.

Line Guides

Fishing rods have line guides (also known as rod guides) located at intervals along the rod blank to guide the fishing line in a straight course from the reel to the tip of the rod. The more guides on a rod, the better. When a rod bends under the strain of a hard-fighting fish, the line changes angle at each line guide. More guides mean a gentler change of direction, hence less strain on the line.

Large-looped guides are designed for long-distance casting and are compatible with spinning reels. The larger diameter reduces the amount of friction as the line passes through the guides at high speed during a cast.

Smaller-diameter guides are found on boat rods, which are used when dropping the baited hook straight down from a boat (as opposed to casting it) when bottom fishing, drifting, or trolling smaller game fish. Under these circumstances, where the line is not being pulled quickly

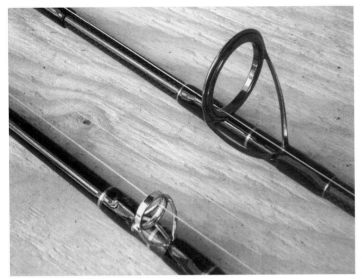

Small and large line guides fastened to their respective rods.

through the guides, friction is trivial. Smaller-diameter guides are cheaper to manufacture, and rods with smaller guides are easier to store and transport. Extra-fast-action rods, which are used for trolling larger game fish, are often equipped with *roller guides*, which reduce friction when the line is under heavy stress, as when fighting a large fish.

A *tip-top* is the special line guide located at the tip of a fishing rod. It allows the line to exit and enter smoothly at various angles. Most tip-tops are simple rings, but those used on big-game trolling boat rods often have rollers. Because tip-tops are subject to greater line wear than the other guides, some rod manufacturers use higher-quality materials for tip-tops than for the other guides on the same rod.

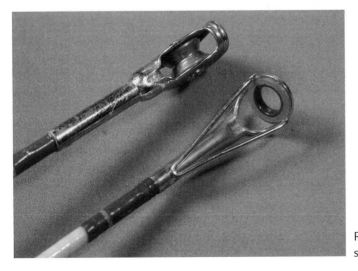

Roller tip-top and ring and support guide.

Most inexpensive guides are made from stainless steel, which is suitable for most applications and for monofilament line. However, stainless steel guides can be easily damaged if not handled properly. If the inside diameter of the loop becomes scratched or dented, the line will chafe, weaken, and eventually break. Stainless steel guides on some cheaper rods are prone to corrosion if the rod is not washed thoroughly with fresh water after each use.

Guides found on better rods may be made from anodized aluminum, ceramic, Monel, Carboloy, or carbide materials. These are not as easily scuffed and will resist corrosion better than most types of stainless steel. However, most of these materials are brittle and will crack if handled roughly.

Wire fishing line, which is used for trolling, rapidly wears grooves into softer materials. Rods used for trolling with wire line should have carbide, Monel, or Carboloy line guides.

To check the smoothness of the guides on rods that have seen some use, pass a piece of nylon pantyhose through them, one guide at a time. The nylon will snag on any roughness, indicating that the guide should be replaced.

Reel Seat

A reel seat securely fastens the reel to the rod. The slot of the forward retainer is fixed on most rods; the rear retainer is movable, and is held in place with a threaded retaining nut. Better rods have two retaining nuts, the second one serving as a jam nut or locknut. The reel must fit tightly with no movement whatsoever. If you can't get an absolutely solid fit, use a different reel with the rod (or vice versa).

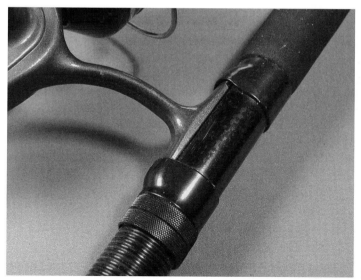

Reel fastened to the reel seat.

Hook Keeper

A hook keeper is a small wire loop attached just ahead of the forward handgrip. It's a convenient place to fasten your hook or lure to prevent it from swinging about dangerously when you're moving around, when the rod is in a boat's rod holder but is not in use, or when it's in storage. Many rods don't have a hook keeper. It's easy enough to use the base of a line guide for the same purpose, but the keeper will protect the guides from damage, and it's a nice accessory.

The hook or lure is placed on the hook keeper, and the reel is tightened enough to take up any slack in the line.

Rod Performance

The primary determinants of rod performance are length, action, and weight.

Rod Length

Longer rods cast farther than shorter ones, but shorter ones are easier to transport and store. Longer rods are capable of exerting greater leverage, but you have to be strong enough to apply that leverage. You may find that you can exert more power with a shorter stick.

Rod Action

Action, which is synonymous with taper, refers to a rod's flexibility. Rod action is broken down into four categories: extra fast, fast, moderate or medium, and slow. Extra-fast-action rods have the greatest taper, and most of the bending occurs in the top third of their length. Moderate-action rods bend readily to about their midpoint but are stiff below that point. Slow-action rods have the least taper, so they flex more consistently over their entire length. Some people find this terminology counterintuitive until they understand the following: a fast rod is usually more sensitive to vibrations than a slow-action rod. The moment a fish begins the tickle the hook, you can feel it. A slow-action rod absorbs the vibrations, so you don't notice the fish as quickly.

In general, saltwater fishing rods should have moderate to extra-fast action—for greater sensitivity and because their greater overall stiffness allows you to move the fish around more effectively. Slow-action rods may be used when fishing from docks for pan-sized fish such as snapper, bluefish, white croaker, or spot, but many slow-action rods are not suitable at all for saltwater fishing because they are too limber for most of the sought-after species.

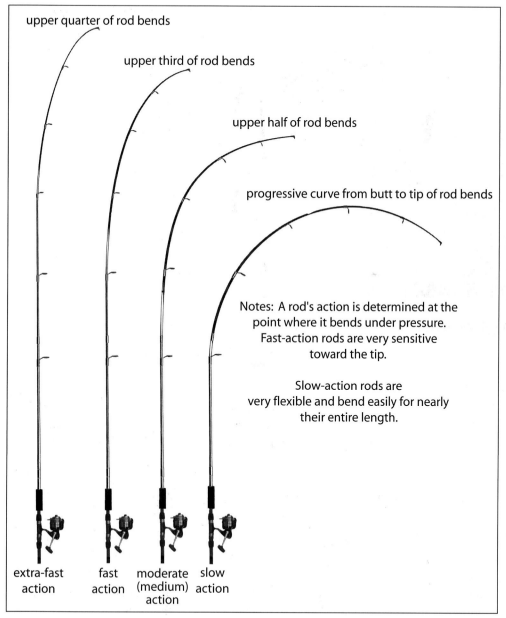

upper quarter of rod bends

upper third of rod bends

upper half of rod bends

progressive curve from butt to tip of rod bends

Notes: A rod's action is determined at the point where it bends under pressure. Fast-action rods are very sensitive toward the tip.

Slow-action rods are very flexible and bend easily for nearly their entire length.

extra-fast action

fast action

moderate (medium) action

slow action

Various types of rod action.

Rod Weight

Whereas rod action describes *how* a rod flexes, rod weight describes *how much*—in other words, its overall stiffness. Rod action is about sensitivity; rod weight is about power and strength. Heavier rods can cast heavier weights farther distances, and haul in heavier fish.

There are six rod weight classifications: ultralight, light, medium, medium heavy, heavy, and extra heavy. Although rods that weigh more in pounds and ounces tend to have heavier rod weight classifications, this is not an absolute. A "heavy" rod made of graphite could weigh less on the scale than a "light" rod made of cheaper materials.

Because heavier rods are intended for bigger fish, it should come as no surprise that heavier rods require heavier (stronger) fishing line. To choose the correct rod weight, first you must know the type, size, and strength of the fish you're targeting—which leads you to also consider the line strength, and the size of the bait rig or lure you'll be casting (see the Rod Weight table). Most general-purpose saltwater rods are classified as medium to heavy weight. Most rods for offshore sportfishing are heavy or extra heavy. See Chapter 6 for more on line weight considerations.

One Piece or Two?

Rods are available in one-piece and two-piece models. Two-piece rods are easier to transport and store, but some anglers feel that one-piece rods are more sensitive, allowing them to feel subtle taps as a fish plays with the hook or lure. The ferrule that joins a two-piece rod together may introduce some looseness or wiggle; even if the ferrule is tight when new, it may loosen over time. Most well-made two-piece rods have good, reliable ferrules, however, so the choice between a one- and two-piece rod is largely a matter of personal preference.

Rod Types

Different types of fishing rods are designed for use with different types of reels and different methods of fishing. No one rod can do it all, so give careful thought to your needs when selecting your first rod, or your next one.

Saltwater rods fall into two major categories: spinning rods (including most surf rods) and bait-casting rods (boat rods and trolling rods). A third category, fly fishing rods, is so distinct that it's addressed separately in Chapter 17.

ROD WEIGHT		
Weight or Power of Rod	**Adequate Line Test**	**Adequate Lure Weight**
Ultralight	1–4 lb. test	$1/64$–$1/16$ oz.
Light	4–8 lb. test	$1/32$–$1/8$ oz.
Medium	4–12 lb. test	$1/8$–$3/8$ oz.
Medium heavy	8–14 lb. test	$3/16$–$1/2$ oz.
Heavy	15–25 lb. test	Up to $1^1/2$ oz.
Extra heavy	25 lb. test and above	$1^1/2$ oz. and above

Spinning Rods

Spinning rods are designed to be used with spinning reels (see Chapter 5 for more on reels). Spinning rods have large-diameter rod guides mounted on the bottom of the rod shaft or blank. The rods range from 5 to 8 feet in length and are available in any type of action and weight. Used extensively by beginning and advanced anglers alike, spinning rods are the most popular type of saltwater rod. Their versatility strongly recommends them for most beginning anglers. Smaller spinning rods are most often used for fishing from docks, piers, jetties, and beaches.

Spinning rod quality ranges from very poor to extremely fine. Expect to spend around $30 for a pretty good one from a reputable tackle shop. You could spend more than $1,000 for a custom-built tournament rod, but that's totally unnecessary for a beginning angler.

Surf Rods

Surf rods are essentially large, heavy-duty, medium- to fast-action spinning rods. Because they are used to throw heavy sinkers (4 to 8 ounces) plus bait and other terminal tackle up to 100 yards into the surf—where the large predator fish hang out—they range in length from 9 to 14 feet. Surf rods are not suitable for boat fishing because of their excessive length.

Surf rods have a long handle, allowing you to use two hands to obtain the needed power and leverage during a cast. When shopping for a surf rod, look for the largest-diameter guides available, to limit the amount of line resistance when casting.

One-piece and two-piece surf rods are available. Two-piece rods can be transported and stored more easily, but some surf anglers argue that one-piece rods have better casting capabilities. Neither design is necessarily better; it's a matter of opinion, and the argument is bound to continue forever.

A good beginner's surf rod can range from 9 to 12 feet; it should have medium action and be capable of holding a reel of at least 200 yards of 15- to 25-pound-test line. Longer rods are better for fishing from jetties because they allow you to keep the line away from rocks at the base of the structure, thus preventing line chafe and reducing the chance of hang-ups on the retrieve.

Boat Rods

Boat rods are designed for use with bait-casting reels. Although they are available in an assortment of actions and weights, boat rods are usually heavier, stronger, and stiffer than conventional spinning rods (except surf rods), tend to be of higher quality, and are designed for use with heavy line to catch larger fish. As with other bait-casting rods, the reel seat and line guides are on the top of the rod.

Boat rods are used for most over-the-rail fishing techniques, including bottom fishing, drifting, and trolling. They range from 5½- to 8-foot lengths and have fairly small-diameter line guides that get progressively smaller toward the tip. Because of this, boat rods do not

Assortment of rods to choose from at a tackle shop.

cast well; but small-diameter guides do not hinder dropping the baited hook straight down over the rail, and they do provide better support and control of the line when you're fighting a fish.

Trolling Rods

Designed to fight the largest offshore game fish from large boats, trolling rods are bait-casting rods with fast to extra-fast action and medium-heavy to extra-heavy weight. They range from 6 to 8 feet in length and usually have roller-type line guides, which reduce friction while the line is under load.

Buying a Rod

For the beginning angler, shopping for a rod can be a confusing experience. There are dozens—perhaps hundreds—of rods on display at well-stocked tackle shops.

Before purchasing a rod, consider your general fishing interests. What method of fishing will you be doing: surf fishing? fishing from piers and jetties? bottom fishing from a skiff in a protected bay? What type and size of fish will you pursue, and what strength of line will you use? What kind of terminal tackle will you use, and will it be with natural bait or lures? How strong are you, and how's your stamina? Where will you store your gear, and how will you transport it? What's your budget? The answers to all of these questions will influence your decision of what rod to buy.

Fortunately, most rod manufacturers try to make rod selection easy. They print specific data on the tube of the rod just above the forward grip, usually including model number, rod length, action, material of construction, recommended line weight, and recommended lure weight. This data leaves little doubt as to the design of the rod and its fishing capabilities. (Although, as a beginner, you may have to ask the shop proprietor to steer you toward the right general type of rod: boat rod, surf rod, etc.)

Carefully inspect your prospective purchase for possible defects. Rods are usually displayed in a vertical rack, cheek by jowl with dozens of others. Customers pick up, handle, and return these rods to the racks, and may unintentionally mishandle and damage them. Make sure that the line guides on the rod you select are firmly attached, aligned with one another, and not bent, and that there are no cracks at the ring or loop supports. Inspect the rod tube (or tubes, if it's a two-piece model) for deep scratches. Take a close look at the female portion of the ferrule of a two-piece rod and look for chips or cracks. Check that the sections of a two-piece rod fit snugly, so they will not come apart easily when the rod is in use. Assemble and shake a two-piece rod; you should feel no vibration or looseness and it should feel as though it's a one-piece rod.

Make sure that the rod feels comfortable, the grip feels good in your hand and under your armpit, and the balance feels natural.

The length of the rod depends on the type of fishing you'll be doing and your personal preferences. Remember that you'll be holding the rod for hours at a time, so make sure it's comfortable and not too heavy. In the store, it may be helpful to hold a rod with a suitable reel attached and have someone gently apply a little downward pressure at the tip. This may give you some idea of what the rod will feel like with a fish on the end of the line (although, admittedly, that's a far cry from the feel of a real fish after hours of fishing). Trial and error may be the only solution. Luckily, most rods are not extremely expensive, and you may also be able to borrow some friends' rods to get a feel for a variety of models.

CHAPTER 5

SALTWATER REELS

There is a huge variety of saltwater fishing reels. Spinning, spin-casting, conventional bait-casting, and low-profile bait-casting reels come in different styles, quality, and price ranges. As with saltwater rods, you first have to determine the type of fishing you intend to do. From there, the choice becomes more manageable and logical.

Reels are designed to store fishing line on a spool conveniently, neatly, and tightly. A mechanism allows the line to come off the spool easily when casting, and a manually adjustable drag mechanism usually maintains line tension while allowing some line to gradually spool off the reel while you're fighting a fish. Without this, it would be too easy for the fish to break the line by giving it a good hard yank. Of course, there is a crank, or handle, that you turn to roll the line back onto the spool when retrieving the hook, lure, or fish.

REEL BASICS

Reel Construction

Fishing reels are manufactured from die-cast or forged aluminum alloys or from graphite materials. Many of the more expensive reels are manufactured from lightweight, corrosion-resistant, anodized aluminum alloys; these reels are a bit heavier than those made from graphite but are more durable. The light weight of graphite helps prevent arm and wrist strain.

The internal mechanisms rely on ball bearings or bushings for support, stability, and smooth operation. Better types of reels have sealed stainless steel ball bearings; these reels are more reliable and more durable than models with less expensive bushings.

Generally, the more ball bearings a reel has, the more smoothly it operates. Good reels have between four and six ball bearings; some newer, more expensive models have as many as twelve.

Retrieval Ratio

A reel's retrieval ratio refers to how quickly the reel puts line onto the spool for each turn of the crank. For example, a reel with a retrieval ratio of 5.5:1 wraps five and a half turns of line onto the spool for every complete turn of the crank. The amount of line wrapped in a single turn varies with the spool's diameter, and the length of line retrieved increases as more line is wrapped onto the spool, increasing the reel's effective diameter as the spool fills up. A good retrieval ratio for most new anglers is 3.0:1, providing adequate line retrieval at a lower cost. Reels with higher ratios tend to be more expensive, although they do allow you to reel in line faster, making it easier to keep slack out of the line and land fish more quickly.

Conventional bait-casting reel.

REEL TYPES

Conventional Bait-Casting Reels

Conventional bait-casting reels are used for most over-the-rail boat fishing and trolling, neither of which requires long-distance casting. These reels feature a spool mounted transversely to the axis of the rod. Line is wrapped around the spool, which spins when you release or retrieve line. Conventional bait-casting reels are sturdy and are available in a wide range of sizes. Smaller reels do not hold as much line as larger ones, although they are lighter and often less expensive. The size of reel you buy should be determined by the amount and weight of line you will need, which in turn is determined by the type of fishing you expect to do.

Conventional bait-casting reels impart a better feel of the line than spinning reels, which makes them superior for trolling and deepwater bottom fishing. Their inability to cast quite as far as spinning reels is not a liability because in these methods of fishing you often simply let the line drop straight down with the weight of the terminal tackle. If you're trolling, allow the boat's slow forward motion to pull the line from the reel; keep your thumb on the spool to prevent it from spinning too freely, and let the reel pay out about 200 feet of line before locking the spool by moving the lever.

Unlike spinning reels, bait-casting reels impart no twist to the line on the retrieve. Lures, however, can cause line twist regardless of the type of reel you use, so you still may need to use a swivel with a bait-casting reel to minimize twist.

Thumbing a conventional bait-casting reel.

USING BAIT-CASTING REELS

Most bait-casting reels have a push button or a lever to disengage the spool from the crank mechanism. To cast with a bait-casting reel, start by drawing in line until your bait rig or lure is dangling 3 to 6 inches below the rod tip. Place your thumb on the spool to hold it stationary, then disengage the spool using the button or lever. Draw the rod straight up overhead and slightly backward, until it is behind you at about 45 degrees from vertical. Then whip the rod forward until it reaches 45 degrees in front of you. Remove your thumb from the spool as the rod reaches this point to allow the weight of the lure or rig to pull line off the spool. Continue to apply subtle pressure with your thumb to control the speed at which the line pays out, then clamp down firmly as it slows to avoid backlash.

On most bait-casting reels, you must manually reengage the spool to the reel's drive mechanism with the button or lever, although some reels automatically reengage when you turn the crank to retrieve line.

Many better conventional bait-casting reels are equipped with a level line feature, which distributes the line evenly across the width of the spool as you crank it in. This feature does add internal friction, however, and some anglers prefer to do their line leveling manually.

Two types of drag systems are found on bait-casting reels: a star drag and a lever drag. With a star drag system, you simply turn the star-shaped wheel that is located between the reel's body and the crank handle to increase or decrease pressure on the spool. A star drag is easy to operate and is adequate for most fishing applications. A lever drag system permits more precise, incremental adjustments and typically offers smoother, more consistent performance. However, reels with a lever drag system are more expensive.

LINE BACKLASH

Conventional bait-casting reels are prone to line backlash because of the momentum of the revolving spool. Remember Newton's First Law of Motion: "An object at rest tends to stay at rest and an object in motion tends to stay in motion with the same speed and in the same direction unless acted upon by an unbalanced force." When you cast a lure or bait, its weight pulls line off the spool, which turns rapidly. As soon as the lure or bait hits the water, it stops pulling line off the spool. But the spool hasn't yet gotten the message, and it keeps spinning at high speed for a little while, feeding out more line, which is not getting pulled through the guides. The result is a mass of tangled line on the spool, and it can be a nuisance to straighten out.

If this happens to you, disengage the spool by putting the reel in the free spool mode (as if you're casting), then pull all the loose line from the spool until

Backlash on a conventional bait-casting reel.

you're down to the neat, tight layers of line. Hold the line snugly at the forward grip of the rod and turn the crank until the excess line is neatly and tightly back on the spool. Then you can resume fishing.

Low-Profile Bait-Casting Reels

Low-profile bait-casting reels are similar in design to conventional bait-casting reels, with the significant addition of an adjustable magnetic or centrifugal braking system. This system slows down the spool during casting, making the reel less prone to backlash. The system requires some getting used to, however, to operate reliably.

Low-profile bait casters also have a thumb-operated bar to disengage the spool, making casting quicker and more convenient. Like conventional bait casters, low-profile bait casters are stronger than spinning reels and allow you to cast heavyweight lures and baited hooks and sinkers. Most low-profile bait casters have a magnetic or centrifugal braking system, which automatically slows the spool's rotation to minimize backlash. Smaller than conventional bait-casting reels, low-profile models have more limited line capacity, making them inappropriate for deep-sea trolling. This doesn't compromise their use with most other fishing methods, however.

Low-profile bait-casting reel.

Spinning Reels

Spinning reels are also known as open-faced reels. They make it easy to cast a variety of terminal tackle, which makes them highly versatile for most types of saltwater fishing. They are not as sensitive to feel as bait-casting reels, however, and they can be cumbersome because they sit fairly high off the rod on a pedestal.

Unlike bait-casting reels, spinning reels are not prone to line backlash, because the spool does not rotate during the cast. Rather, the spool is mounted parallel to the rod's axis, and line is pulled straight off the end of the spool. (The only time the spool on a spinning reel rotates is when the drag is engaged and a fish is pulling line off the reel against the drag.) On the retrieve, a bail arm rotates around the spool, wrapping the line onto it. This system does impart line twist, however, because the line has to make a 90-degree turn when it winds onto the spool. This can generate excessive resistance on a cast because the twisted line has a hard time passing through the guides. The resistance can be a real nuisance, so a line swivel is virtually mandatory.

Spinning reel.

Two types of drag systems are available. Front drags are more reliable when you're fighting larger fish; rear drags are easier to reach and more convenient.

Regardless of which drag system you prefer, make sure that it can be tightened in small increments. Also the reel you use must keep the release pressure steady and smooth, allowing the reel to release line at any setting throughout its range until fully tightened.

Spin-Casting Reels

Spin-casting reels, also known as closed-face reels, are generally not used by serious anglers. Although they are stronger and less cumbersome than spinning reels, and are simpler and faster to cast, they are also less sensitive, have poorer casting accuracy, and, like spinning reels, are prone to line twist. Note that most children's rod and reel combination outfits include spin-casting reels.

Rod and Reel Deals

If you're new to saltwater fishing, combination rod and reel packages are an ideal way to start. Manufacturers match the reel with the rod. All you need to do is determine which method of fishing you'll be doing, and the species of fish you'll be targeting most often, then choose from among the packages that suit your needs.

SETTING THE DRAG

When adjusted properly, the reel's drag keeps line tension below a certain level, allowing you to concentrate on playing the fish without having to worry about letting out additional line to relieve the tension. The drag should be set strong enough to set the hook without giving up line.

It is relatively simple to set the drag on a reel. It helps to visualize what takes place inside the reel to understand how the drag system works.

Spin-casting reel.

Combination rods and reels stored vertically in racks at a tackle shop.

Combination rods and reels on display.

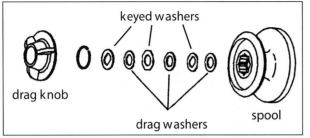

keyed washers

drag knob

drag washers

spool

Typical drag system of a spinning reel.

Most spinning-reel drag systems consist of an external drag knob, several keyed washers, and several drag washers. The drag knob is tightened by turning it clockwise. This applies pressure against the drag washers, which in turn apply friction to the spool. When the drag knob is fully tightened, there is enough pressure to prevent the spool from turning. When the drag knob is turned counterclockwise, the drag offers progressively less resistance, until it is backed out so far that the spool is completely free to rotate. In conventional bait-casting reels, the friction washers apply pressure to a gear, not directly to the spool. Otherwise, the same principle applies.

When you're on the water and about to present your lure or baited hook, consider the strength of the fish you are likely to encounter. Adjust the drag to provide just enough resistance to set the hook and slow a running fish. A rule of thumb states that you should set the drag to about 25 percent of the line's pound-test rating. But because few anglers bring force meters on their fishing trips, this is difficult to accomplish.

To adjust the drag, tighten the drag knob of a spinning reel—or the star of a bait-casting reel—turning it clockwise as far as it will go. Pull on the line with the reel engaged (that is, not in free spool mode); the spool should not turn. Now, while continuing to pull on the line, loosen the drag knob or star by turning it counterclockwise just until the drag begins to give a bit and the spool begins to turn. You should feel resistance with the reel engaged as the spool struggles to rotate. Turn the drag knob or star about another $\frac{1}{16}$ to $\frac{1}{8}$ turn, then check to see whether the adjustment appears reasonable by pulling on the line again with the reel engaged. This method of adjustment may seem crude, but it works. Remember that it takes only slight tweaking of the drag adjustment knob or star to adjust a drag system.

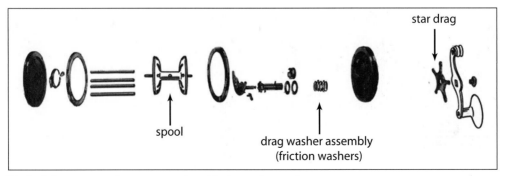

star drag

spool

drag washer assembly
(friction washers)

Typical drag system for a conventional bait-casting reel.

Star drag adjuster for a conventional bait-casting reel.

Typical drag adjuster for a front drag spinning reel.

FIXING A COMMON SPINNING-REEL PROBLEM

A common problem with spinning reels is having the bail arm flip over during a cast, resulting in a broken line and a lost terminal rig or lure. This is especially problematic with surf fishing, where the weight of the terminal tackle seems to play havoc with the bail. One solution is to remove the bail arm, leaving only the line roller assembly. Although this eliminates the problem, you must henceforth manually lift the line off the roller when you're ready to cast, then manually replace the line on the roller after the cast to prepare the reel to retrieve the line. Before removing the bail, check to ensure that you will not otherwise affect the reel's operation.

Some manufacturers sell bail modification kits, which allow the reel's bail arm system to be removed without impairing the reel's function. If you are not sure how to install this modification, have a reliable tackle shop do it for you.

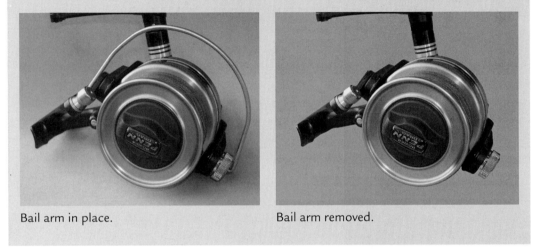

Bail arm in place.   Bail arm removed.

ROD AND REEL CARE

All rods and reels require preventive maintenance to hold corrosion at bay and remain in good working order. At the end of each fishing trip, rinse your rods and reels gently with fresh water from a garden hose. Avoid using high-pressure water on reels because it will force salt deposits deeper into the reel, causing problems later.

At the end of the fishing season, remove the reel from its rod. Discard about three-quarters of the line from the spool, keeping the remaining quarter as fill. (You never expect to actually play a fish on this "excess" fill line; its purpose is simply to provide bulk, placing the useful, new line closer to the edge of the spool, where it will pay out more easily.) Soak the reel in warm, soapy water for an hour or two, then remove any remaining salt deposits with a soft-bristle scrub brush. Rinse the reel in cool, fresh water, then allow it to dry.

Clean and lubricate all moving parts following the manufacturer's instructions. Clean the drag washers with a clean, dry cloth, but do not lubricate them. Most good bait-casting reels have lubrication points, which allow you to force in reel lubricant without having to take apart the reel. Spinning reels have relatively few major parts to disassemble. When you're done cleaning and lubricating the moving parts, apply a coat of good auto paste wax.

Annual lubrication is necessary for all fishing reels.

Splice on new line using a simplified blood knot if the new and replacement lines are the same diameter; use an improved blood knot if they differ. (See Chapter 12 for how to tie these knots.) Before storing a reel for the winter or for any length of time, loosen the drag so the line isn't under tension. Store the reel in a cool, dry place.

CHAPTER 6

LINE, LEADER, AND SWIVELS

Fishing line is among the least expensive items in your fishing inventory, and among the most important. It's what connects you to the fish. It just doesn't make sense to buy no-name, bargain-basement fishing line, or to use line after it has begun to age or show signs of wear. If a fish outfights you, so be it. But there's no excuse for losing a fish because you didn't put good line on your reel.

LINE BASICS

For such a seemingly simple item, fishing line has a wide variety of characteristics. Different weights and materials are the basic qualities to consider. Then there are different degrees of stretch and abrasion resistance, soft versus stiff line, and high- and low-visibility line.

Line Weight

All conventional fishing line is classified according to its rated breaking strength, usually expressed as *pound test*, and its diameter, measured in thousandths or ten thousandths of an inch. There is a general correlation between the two; a thicker line usually has a higher strength rating than a thinner line.

A 15-pound-test line will hold at least 15 pounds of weight before breaking. That's *static* weight. A 10-pound fish can easily generate more than 20 pounds of force and break your 15-pound line if you let the fish get a running start—hence the importance of keeping slack out of your line after you set the hook. The International Game Fish Association (IGFA) rates the strength of line in kilograms, or kilos (1 kilo is 2.2 pounds). If a line is labeled in pounds and kilos, the higher figure is the accurate one; the lower figure is approximate. For example, if a spool of 15-pound-test line has an IGFA rating of 7.5 kilos, the actual breaking strength is at least 16.5 pounds. (IGFA ratings apply mainly to monofilament line. The IGFA prohibits the use of wire line in tournaments, so it doesn't rate this line.)

In fact, most line exceeds its strength rating by 10 to 15 percent when it's new. All line loses strength with age and use.

Given similar materials, thicker line is obviously stronger than thinner line, but thicker line is not always preferable. Thinner line tends to cast farther, and it is less visible to fish. This makes a big difference to some fish and not so much to others, as you'll see below.

Line Types
Monofilament Line

Monofilament line, by far the most popular type of fishing line, is the best choice for general purposes. As its name suggests, it is manufactured as a single strand (of nylon). It is available in strength ratings from 2-pound test to more than 200-pound test and a variety of colors. For inshore saltwater fishing, the most common strengths range from 10- to 40-pound test.

Monofilament line is manufactured from nylon polymers that are heated to a fluid state. Chemicals are added to modify the material's stiffness, strength, stretch, toughness, and color. The mixture is then extruded through tiny holes in a die to form strands of line; the size of the holes in the extrusion die determines the diameter of the line. The extruded line is rapidly cooled and wound onto spools.

Under tension, monofilament line can stretch about 15 to 25 percent when it's dry and 20 to 30 percent when it's wet. The more stretch a line has, the better its casting characteristics and the less chance it will break when you're fighting a fish. However, more stretch makes it more difficult to set the hook efficently. Advanced anglers prefer line with little stretch, relying on their skill and a properly adjusted reel drag to prevent line breakage during a fight. Beginners should use more flexible line, which is more forgiving of improper drag settings and occasional inattention when fighting a fish.

After monofilament line is factory-wound onto the spool, it takes on a more or less permanent curve. This shape memory causes it to coil up when not under tension and twist during use, necessitating the use of a line swivel. In addition, monofilament line can be weakened by excessive exposure to direct sunlight or heat and should be kept in a cool, dry, shaded

Various types of monofilament line on spools.

place when not in use. Monofilament line has poor abrasion resistance and can be easily scored and damaged.

Before you begin fishing, always check monofilament line for nicks or abrasions by passing the first 10 to 15 feet between your lips—do I have to say this?—*without hooks on the line!* If you feel any flaws, that portion of the line should be replaced. Use a simplified blood knot to splice on a new length of line of the same diameter, or an improved blood knot if the new line has a different diameter (see Chapter 12 for how to tie these knots). Remember that using knots of any kind will reduce the strength of the line by about 20 percent at the knot.

During a cast, a knot can hang up on the rod's line guides. If casting is important to your fishing, as when fishing from a dock, pier, or jetty, or when surf fishing, consider the location of the knot to prevent the knot from inhibiting the distance of the cast. Avoid positioning the knot where it must travel through the line guides on a cast, even if it means cutting off and discarding a long length of line. The position of knots is not as critical with bait-casting rods and reels, which are rarely used for making long casts.

Fluorocarbon Line

Fluorocarbon line is fast becoming popular with anglers because it is almost invisible when submerged and will not spook line-shy fish. Fluorocarbon line has a hard finish, which makes it extremely abrasion resistant, and it does not absorb water, as does monofilament line, so its strength is not compromised.

Fluorocarbon line does have a few drawbacks, however. It is stiffer and has more shape memory than monofilament line, especially when it's cold. This can impair its casting performance and cause it to become unmanageable on a reel spool. Because it has a slick surface, you should take extra care when tying knots. The line tends to be brittle, requiring greater care in setting the drag on the reel to avoid breakage from overtension. It also costs more than monofilament line.

Braided Dacron Line

Braided Dacron line consists of mulitiple strands of polyester fibers that retain their strength when wet. This line stretches only 5 to 10 percent, so you can more readily feel bites. Braided Dacron line is not stiff, is easy to work with, and accepts a variety of knots. Within one season, it loses a small amount of line strength compared to that of monofilament line.

On the downside, braided Dacron line is highly visible in water. As such, it is used primarily for deepwater trolling or bottom fishing. It is used primarily with conventional bait-casting reels for trolling lures, jigs, or baited hooks.

Wire Line

Line made from stainless steel, Monel, bronze, or copper wire is designed for deepwater trolling. Wire line is available from 20-pound test to more than 60-pound test. The weight of the line allows it to sink deeper without the use of a *drail sinker*—a hydrodynamically shaped lead sinker that is often used to get the baited hook or lure deeper in the water. Wire line has almost no stretch, permitting effective *jigging*—that is, moving the rod up and down to make the bait or lure move. Lack of stretch also means that a hook can be set easily—so easily, in fact, that most times a fish will hook itself.

Wire line kinks easily, which work-hardens the wire and creates weak spots. This type of line cannot be spliced and should be replaced if kinked. Wire line will groove rod guides that are not made of Monel or carbide alloys. It is suitable only for use with larger conventional bait-casting trolling reels.

Lead-Core Line

Lead-core line has a flexible lead core that is sheathed with a tightly braided nylon sleeve. Lead-core line is used only for deepwater trolling without the use of drail sinkers. The exterior sheathing is usually color coded in 10-yard increments to allow you to determine the amount of line released. This is especially helpful when trolling at a precise depth.

As with wire line, lead-core line is suitable for use only with conventional bait-casting reels. Lead-core line is more flexible than wire line, but, like wire line, it cannot be spliced and must be replaced if kinked. It is available from 14-pound test to more than 60-pound test.

Line Appearance

Some fish are *line shy*—that is, they avoid a lure or baited hook if they see the line, which they recognize as unnatural. Small-diameter line is harder to see—a plus—but it's not as strong as thicker line; as line diameter decreases, so does the strength of the fishing rig. For your leader, select the least visible, smallest-diameter line that will still bring in the fish without breaking. Consider snelling your own hooks with a fluorocarbon transparent leader to minimize the line's visibility close to the hook. (Leaders are discussed below; for more on snelled hooks, see Chapter 7.)

Line Color

There are times when you'll need to see the line on the surface of the water, and other times when you'll want to prevent the fish from seeing the line. Monofilament line is manufactured in pink, gold, yellow, coffee, moss green, red, and light blue, plus fluorescent green, blue, and yellow. You can readily see fluorescent colors on the surface, but fish can see them pretty well too. For line-shy fish, pale pink or clear line works well. (One manufacturer claims that its red line is virtually invisible to fish.)

Monofilament line comes in a variety of colors. (Courtesy Pure Fishing America)

Some anglers buy different pound-test lines in different colors for ease of identification. As long as they keep their colors straight, they always know what strength line is on their reel simply by looking at the color.

Spooling Line onto Reels

When you buy a new reel, the tackle shop will gladly load it for you with whatever kind of line you wish to buy. However, there will soon come a time when you have to do it yourself.

To remove old line, it's possible to just pull it off the reel and let it gather on the floor. I prefer to take an empty line spool (the kind that new line comes on), pass a long bolt through the center hole, tighten the spool to the bolt with a couple of flat washers and a nut, then place the end of the bolt in the chuck of a variable-speed electric drill. I tie the line to the spool, turn on the drill, and voilà!—not only is the line removed from my reel spool in a matter of seconds, it's wrapped tidily and is easy to discard.

Spooling Bait-Casting Reels

If your reel is equipped with a level-wind system, feed the new line through the rod guides or directly onto the reel. If you don't have a level-wind reel, don't go through the guides. Instead, tie the line to the reel's spool using an arbor knot or a uni-knot (see Chapter 12). Insert a pencil through the center hole of the spool of new line and hold it so that the line feeds off the top of the spool, as shown in the photo. Have a helper hold the pencil while you apply light pressure to the sides of the spool, allowing it to turn easily but not freely.

If the reel is equipped with a level-wind system, your helper needs only to maintain the proper resistance while you turn the crank and draw line onto the spool. If your reel is not

Spooling new line onto a conventional bait-casting reel.

correct   incorrect

Note how the line is poorly distributed and bunched on the reel on the right. Avoid this—line stacking—when spooling new line onto your reel.

equipped with a level-wind mechanism, the helper should move the spool slowly from side to side to avoid *line stacking*—having the line bunch up higher on one part of the spool than another. Wind the line to within $\frac{1}{16}$ to $\frac{1}{8}$ inch of the reel spool's lip.

Spooling Spinning Reels

Line stacking is not a problem with spinning reels. They are, in effect, self-leveling, because the spool moves in and out as the bail circles around it.

Feed the new line so it travels through the rod guides or directly to the reel—making sure that it travels over the bail roller—and attach it to the spool using the arbor knot or uni-knot (see Chapter 12).

Because the reel spool does not rotate on a spinning reel, the spool of new line should not turn either. The line should be drawn straight off the top of the line spool. Place the plastic line spool, with the label facing up, on a flat surface. Place a heavy book (such as a telephone book) next to it. Pull the line straight off the spool and place it between the pages of the book (toward the middle or bottom so the line is weighted down). Take ten to fifteen turns on the reel handle, then lower it to release the tension and create some slack. If the line lies in gentle, neat coils, continue filling the reel spool. If the slack line shows severe twists, turn the plastic line spool over and continue to wind the new line onto the reel spool. Fill the reel spool no closer than $\frac{1}{8}$ inch from the spool lip, or rim.

Discarding Old Fishing Line

Line on a reel should be changed at least once a year or when it becomes worn, whichever comes first.

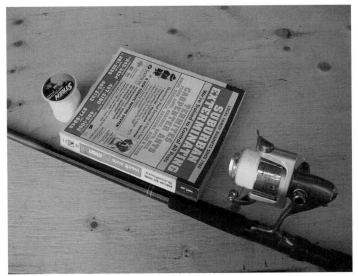

Spooling a spinning reel.

When discarding worn fishing line, do not toss it into the water or onto a pier, dock, jetty, or beach. Even in trash cans, bunches of tangled line can still ensnare seabirds and other wildlife, leading to a slow and agonizing death. So before you throw out old line (in a trash can), cut it into 12-inch lengths, making sure that there are no loops. Wildlife and your fellow anglers will appreciate it.

Leader

A leader is a length of monofilament or fluorocarbon line or flexible wire positioned between the main line and the hook or lure. A leader can serve two purposes: prevent line-shy fish from seeing the more visible main line, and prevent sharp-toothed fish from biting the line in two. Monofilament leaders are usually between 1 and 3 feet long; most wire leaders range from 6 to 24 inches.

Monofilament and fluorocarbon leaders usually have a greater pound-test rating than the main line. A swivel should be used between the leader and the main line to keep the main line from twisting.

Because of its transparency, fluorocarbon leader is best for particularly line-shy fish, such as albacore and bonito. Black flexible wire leader is also almost invisible and is effective for sharp-toothed fish, such as mackerel, bluefish, and barracuda.

Snelled hooks are hooks with leader material already attached. See Chapter 7 for more information.

If a wire leader becomes kinked when you're fighting a fish, it has been seriously weakened and should be replaced.

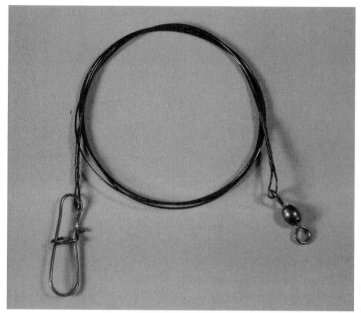

Wire leader equipped with a
clip and a barrel swivel.

Swivels

Terminal tackle—such as baited hooks, lures of any kind, and sinkers—rotate while they're being retrieved through the water, causing the main line or leader to twist. A twisted line will soon present its ugly face in the form of short casts, tangles, kinks, impaired lure performance, and lost terminal rigs. A swivel keeps the main line or leader from twisting on the retrieve. Like fishing line, swivel strength is rated in pound test. Your swivel's strength should match that of your line.

Some lures are designed to spin rapidly, and these require an especially effective swivel to avoid line twist. For this reason, I recommend ball bearing swivels. I also prefer swivels with

An assortment of swivels.

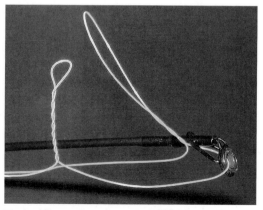

Typical line twist when a swivel is not used.

Interlocking snap swivels.

a dull black finish and avoid those with a shiny brass or chrome finish. The latter can be so attractive to some fish that they hit the swivel and miss the lure or baited hook.

There are three basic types of swivels, and you should have all three in your tackle box. Versatile interlocking snap swivels (also known simply as snap swivels) are used to attach lures or snelled hooks to the main line; they allow quick and easy changes. The barrel end of a snap swivel is tied to the main line; the lure or snelled hook is attached to the swivel's snap mechanism.

A barrel swivel is usually tied between the end of the main line and the leader when you want to keep the terminal end of the line simple. The barrel swivel has an in-line design, so it does not get hung up on obstructions as readily as other types of swivels. It is good for fishing over *structure* (rocks and other debris on the sea floor) and with trolling rigs.

Three-way swivels are used with drifting rigs. The main line is attached to the center eyelet, and the sinker and the snelled hook are attached to the other two eyelets. This type of swivel can easily get hung up on obstructions, so avoid using it over structure.

Barrel swivels.

Three-way swivels.

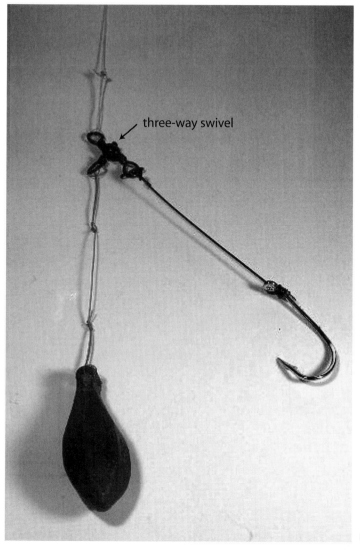

three-way swivel

Use of a three-way swivel.

CHAPTER 7

HOOKS

When you're fishing on salt water, you never know what species of fish you may encounter. You might be fishing for fluke when suddenly a school of feeding bluefish arrives. If you have a decent assortment of hooks in your tackle box, it's a small matter to change your terminal rig to "accommodate" the bluefish.

Hooks are chosen according to the size and species of fish targeted, the type of bait used, and the method of fishing. There is no formula for selecting the right hook because there are many variables, including the size of the fish's mouth, its strength as a swimmer, its method of fighting, and the way it goes about grabbing bait. But as a rule of thumb, the larger the fish, the larger the hook. Most anglers do just fine with a few hooks of different sizes that are appropriate to the most common species of fish in the area where they're fishing. Don't be shy about asking at the tackle shop what kinds of hooks work well.

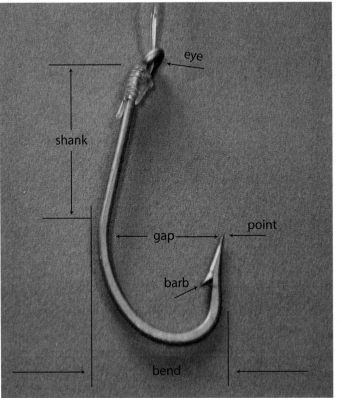

Parts of a hook.

HOOK SELECTION

Consider the size of the fish's mouth when selecting a hook. The fish has to be able to get the bait into its mouth, and the bait should be large enough to cover most of the hook. A hook that is too large means too much bait for the fish, or a lot of exposed metal that the fish may not like the looks of. On the other hand, small hooks don't hold big fish very well. Conversely, if the hook is too small, the fish may swallow it, making its removal almost impossible.

The correct hook is the smallest one that is strong enough to land the desired fish. The smaller and lighter the hook, the less visible it will be to the fish and the more likely it will present the bait in a natural manner.

Hook Size

Fishhook size is designated numerically. Below a certain size, the larger the number, the smaller the hook. A number 10 hook, therefore, is smaller than a number 4 hook of the same style. Hooks larger than number 1 use a different system, however. A number followed by a slash and a zero indicates a large hook, and the numbers *increase* with hook size. Thus, a number 5/0 hook is larger than a number 2/0 hook, which is larger than a number 10 hook.

The thickness of the hook in any given size should also be considered. A thin hook will penetrate more easily than a thick hook. If you're having trouble setting the hook, chances are that the hook is too thick for the targeted species, so use a thinner hook of the same size.

Hook Designs

There are three basic hook designs: conventional J hooks; circle, or C, hooks; and treble hooks. J and C hooks are used primarily with bait; treble hooks are found on most saltwater plugs and lures. J and C hooks are available as snelled hooks, as described below.

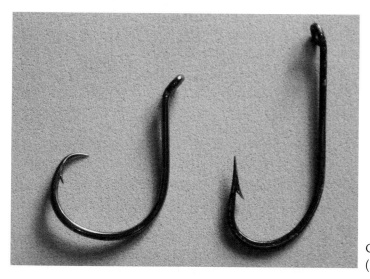

Circle hook (left) and J hook (right).

J hooks, which range in size from number 8 to a huge 8/0 for saltwater species, have been used with natural bait for hundreds of years. They work well for most species of fish and are preferred by recreational saltwater anglers. The J hook requires a solid pull of the rod to set it in a fish's mouth.

Circle hooks, sometimes referred to as C hooks, are basically round, but the point is bent about 90 degrees from the shank. Unlike the situation with a J hook, a fish tends to hook itself when it bites onto a circle hook and is much less likely to "throw" the hook and escape. Circle hooks grab the corner of a fish's mouth and hold firmly until the fish is landed, and thus have an excellent hook-up ratio (the number of fish securely hooked relative to the number of bites). This self-setting performance has made this the hook of choice for commercial longline fishermen for years. Circle hooks are becoming quite popular with saltwater hook-and-release anglers because they are easily removed with little if any injury to the fish. Circle hooks are not available in small sizes. They start at number 4 and go up to 15/0 and larger.

If you're accustomed to J hooks, using circle hooks involves some adjustment. Instead of setting the hook by sharply pulling back on the rod, apply steady pressure on the line, bringing it in evenly and slowly. Avoid jerking the rod to prevent pulling the hook from the fish's mouth.

Packaged snelled hooks have monofilament or wire leader attached. The strength of the leader can range from 30- to 80-pound test and above, and leader length varies considerably. The leader has a loop at the end opposite the hook, making tying on quick and easy. Snelled hooks are available in J and C designs.

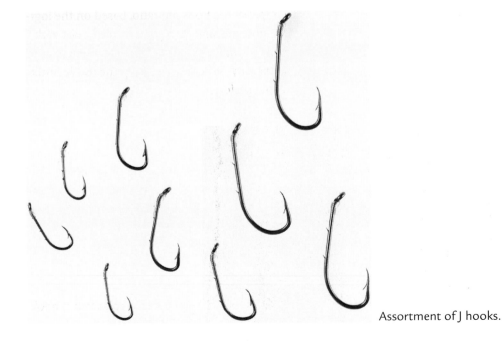

Assortment of J hooks.

Lure with treble hooks.

Some anglers snell their own hooks, buying their hooks in bulk and the leader material separately. Although snelling a hook takes a little time, it's not difficult. See Chapter 12 for instructions.

Most fishing lures have one or more sets of treble, or three-pointed, hooks. These range in size from number 6 through 8/0. Treble hooks are strong and can withstand abuse, but they require much care in handling, especially when you attempt to remove a lure from a hooked fish.

Manufacturers put treble hooks on lures to improve the hook-up ratio, based on the logical theory that three points are better than one. But some anglers replace treble hooks with J hooks for safety and convenience. Switching them is simple because the hooks are held onto the lure with split rings, which can be pried open easily. Whether you keep the treble hooks or replace them with J hooks is a matter of personal preference.

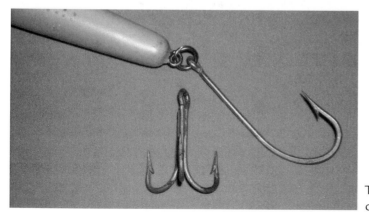

Treble hook replaced by J hook on a lure.

CHAPTER 8

SINKERS

Assortment of sinkers.

Sinkers, also called weights, are fastened to the end of the main fishing line to pull down a baited hook or lure and, often, to hold it on or near the bottom. Most lures are manufactured at the ideal weight for proper presentation and usually don't require additional weight, but for some fishing methods, sinkers are a necessity.

Sinkers are used primarily for stationary bottom fishing from boats, piers, docks, and jetties, and from drifting boats. The sinker keeps the hooks within range of bottom-dwelling species that roam in and around structure and forage for food on or close to the bottom. Sinkers are also used in surf fishing, to provide the extra weight needed for long casts, and occasionally for trolling, to run a lure at a specific depth.

LEAD SINKERS

Lead sinkers are available in various shapes and weights for different forms of presentation. Some state laws prohibit the use of lead sinkers for freshwater fishing to reduce lead poisoning of fish and other aquatic species. As a result, sinkers are now manufactured from tin, steel, tungsten, brass, or bismuth. Although these are available to saltwater anglers, lead sinkers are preferred because of the material's greater density.

Lead sinkers are not cheap, ranging in price from 10 to 25 cents per ounce at tackle shops. So minimizing loss is an important consideration in sinker selection.

SINKER SELECTION

Sinker selection depends on many factors, including the fishing method, the targeted species, the composition of the sea bottom (the "substrate"), the presence and nature of structure, the speed of the current, the depth of the water, and the strength of the fishing line. Use a nautical chart, or take a word-of-mouth survey, to find out the type of substrate and structure and the depth of the water where you intend to fish.

Most large sinkers are stamped or embossed with their weight in ounces; for example, the number 5 stamped on a sinker indicates 5 ounces. When bottom fishing or drifting, use the minimum amount of weight needed to "hold bottom." If the sinker is too heavy, fish can detect it easily, you waste energy when jigging and retrieving, and you put extra strain on your fishing line. If the sinker is too light, it won't keep your bait or lure on the bottom where you want it. You should be able to feel the weight hit the bottom by moving your rod tip up and down. If you can't feel it, your sinker is probably moving along the bottom with the current flow.

Sinkers are available in different styles for different fishing methods. After you select the appropriate style for whatever method you plan to pursue, keep a variety of weights on hand appropriate to different conditions of current, water depth, size of fish, etc., and to replace the inevitable losses. This may mean carrying around a few pounds of lead, which can make for a heavy tackle box. Some anglers haul their sinkers separately in a burlap bag to keep their tackle boxes more manageable.

COMMON SINKERS

Bank Sinkers

Bank sinkers are the most common type. With a partially rounded edge, which is a compromise between a fully rounded and a sharp-edged design, they are appropriate for most bottom fishing. Bank sinkers are available from ½ ounce to more than 15 ounces, the choice of weight being determined by the water current along the bottom. Bank sinkers are marginal for fishing over rough structure because they readily get hung up on obstructions. And they tend to roll in strong currents, making them a last resort for surf fishing.

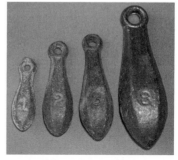

Bank sinkers.

Diamond Sinkers

Diamond sinkers are used for deepwater offshore fishing. They are not good for fishing over structure such as wrecks, oyster beds, and rocky areas because of their bulk, but they are acceptable for all other methods. Because of their broad, flat surfaces, diamond sinkers do not roll along the bottom. They range from 1 ounce to more than 20 ounces.

Diamond sinker.

Pyramid Sinkers

Pyramid sinkers are used on sandy or muddy bottom, where their sharp edges dig in readily to resist rolling in heavy currents. Weighing from 1 ounce to more than 10 ounces, they are good for surf fishing, but they're poor for use over structure.

Pyramid sinkers.

Ball Sinkers

Ball sinkers are sometimes called cannonballs. These sinkers are good for drifting, where they roll smoothly along the bottom, and for fishing over rough structure, where they resist fouling on rocks and debris. Because of their poor holding power, they are not recommended when you want the bait to remain stationary on the bottom. They range in weight from 1/64 ounce (as split shot) to more than 6 ounces.

Ball sinkers.

Egg Line Sinkers

Egg line sinkers (or simply egg sinkers) have a hole through the center axis to allow the main line to slide through easily. These sinkers are useful to minimize the amount of hardware on the bottom when surf fishing. The baited hook is free to move with the current, pulling the main line through the sinker, which keeps the hook close to the bottom. A variation of this, in which the egg sinker is also useful, is the "fish-finder" rig, in which the baited hook is allowed to float several inches above the bottom. This prevents the fish from feeling the weight of the sinker as it pulls on the baited hook, while at the same time keeping crabs from hitting the bait.

Egg line sinkers.

In-Line Sinkers

In-line sinkers are attached to the main line just above the hook leader or lure. One type of in-line sinker, the trolling drall, is used for deepwater trolling. Most trolling drall sinkers have a chain swivel, which allows them to rotate to minimize main line twist.

Trolling drall sinker.

Grooved in-line sinkers fit right over the main line. One design has two bendable tabs that clinch onto the line. Another design has a rubber core or insert: the line is placed in the groove, then the rubber ears are turned in opposite directions to secure the sinker to the line. These types of sinkers are usually positioned about 6 inches above the hook leader.

Grooved in-line sinkers, which are attached directly to the main line just above the hook leader.

SPECIALTY SINKERS AND LOCKS

Surf Sinkers

Also known as Sputnik sinkers, for their resemblance to those early Soviet satellites, surf sinkers are the only type of "mechanical" sinker readily available to recreational anglers. They offer excellent bottom-holding power on sandy and muddy bottom. The four wire arms, which you extend manually before casting, dig firmly into the bottom, and will spring closed when you begin the retrieve. These sinkers cast well and are considered the best type of sinker for surf, offering better holding power for their weight than any other sinker. They should not be used over rough structure, where they will get hung up. Surf sinkers cost $2 or more, but they are well worth the expense.

Surf sinker (left) and walking sinker (right).

Walking Sinkers

Walking sinkers, also called skid sinkers, are used for drifting. They slide or walk over the bottom, causing few hang-ups on mild debris. Their performance is not as good over rough structure, however.

Storm Sinkers

Storm sinkers are heavyweights, similar to pyramid sinkers and, like them, used for surf fishing. They cast well, dig readily into soft sand or mud, resist rolling, and generally hold the bottom well in most surf conditions. They are not recommended for methods other than surf fishing.

Storm sinkers.

Worm Weights

Worm weights are used with rubber or plastic ("jelly") worms. The cavity on the bottom of the weight fits over the eye of the hook to which the worm is attached.

Sinker Locks

Sinker locks are used to mechanically secure a sinker to the terminal end of the main line, which makes changing sinkers fast and easy. Most designs have a built-in swivel, which helps reduce line twist. Sinker locks should not be used over rough structure where hang-ups are a hazard, but I find them convenient when fishing over a known, sandy bottom.

Worm weights.

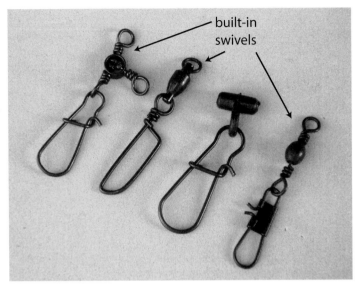

built-in swivels

Sinker locks.

MAKING YOUR OWN SINKERS

Because of the high cost of sinkers, some anglers choose to manufacture their own. Aluminum casting molds are available for most styles of sinkers; most of them have five cavities to cast an assortment of different weights. The molds can be purchased at most well-stocked tackle shops. Lead ingots are available in most hardware stores. Lead tire weights can be used instead, providing they are clean and free of oil and debris.

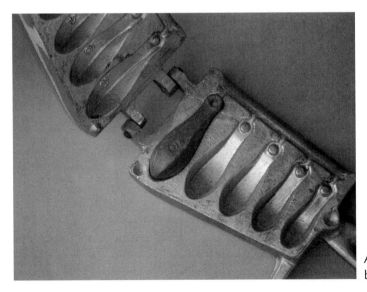

Aluminum mold used to cast bank sinkers.

Lead is extremely hazardous to work with. Do so in a well-ventilated area, preferably outdoors, and away from combustibles. Heavy-duty, heat-resistant gloves and a leather apron are necessary, as is a full-face shield.

Lead is easily melted in a cast-iron pot, after which it is gently poured into the mold with a special ladle. Relative to most metals, lead has a low melting point—"only" 621.5°F—but that's still plenty hot! Never work near water; just a drop of it will vaporize so quickly that it can splash molten lead throughout the area.

Casting your own sinkers can be fun and economical, but this isn't the place for a full description of the process. If you're intrigued, read up thoroughly on the process elsewhere before getting started. Remember, it's dangerous!

CHAPTER 9

NATURAL BAIT

Using natural bait is the most effective and productive way to catch fish. Natural bait is available in tackle shops live, dead, frozen, or even freeze-dried. Some anglers enjoy collecting their own natural bait before venturing out to the fishing grounds. This can be time consuming, however, and many anglers feel that it is not worth the effort.

The attractiveness of natural bait to most predator fish is an advantage and a liability: undesirable fish such as skates and dogfish find it just as tasty as targeted species do. That is why some anglers prefer artificial baits, which are carefully designed to resemble the baitfish that are attractive to specific, targeted species and attract few undesirables.

Nevertheless, natural bait remains more effective for most methods of fishing. The most frequent question asked by anglers when purchasing bait for the day is, "What are the fish biting on?" This is a good question, because fish change their diet from time to time during the fishing season, responding to seasonal changes of available food sources. You want your bait to duplicate, or closely approximate, the kind of food the fish are seeking instinctively at that time of year.

Typical tackle shop front window.

Fish are opportunistic feeders and will usually feed on whatever type of food is available if they're hungry enough. This is beneficial for the angler, but only to a limited extent, because fish are also somewhat single-minded: when they're thinking squid, it can be hard to get them to recognize a sand eel unless you virtually shove it in front of them.

Some bait must be presented as naturally as possible. For example, if you're using dead sand eels, you have to keep the bait moving by drifting the boat or playing the bait with the rod. On the other hand, no fish is going to view a piece of shucked clam as live prey no matter how you play it—it's simply a tasty tidbit that's worth eating. Allowing the clam to drift with the current may attract certain targeted species simply through its movement; otherwise, it can remain fairly stationary and its aroma will provide much of the attraction.

Refer to the table below for the most productive baits for various species.

NATURAL BAIT PREFERENCES OF POPULAR SALTWATER FISH

Bait	Targeted Species
Anchovy (large or small)	Almaco jack, bass (kelp, white sea), bocaccio rockfish, bonito (Pacific), California sheephead, cod (Pacific), croaker (white, yellowtail), halibut (California), jack crevalle (Pacific), petrale sole, roosterfish, snapper (cubera, red), tomcod (Pacific), yellowtail
Ballyhoo (whole)	Dolphinfish, wahoo
Bloodworm (whole or cut)	Bass (black sea, striped), bluefish, California sheephead, cod (Atlantic), corbina, croaker (all), flounder (starry, summer, winter), lingcod, mackerel (all), opaleye, pompano, sanddab (longfin, Pacific), scup, sea trout (spotted), sheepshead, snapper (cubera), snapper bluefish, spot, sturgeon (white), tautog, tomcod (Atlantic, Pacific), weakfish, whiting
Bunker (whole or cut)	Bass (striped), bluefish, drum (black), grouper, weakfish
Butterfish (whole or cut)	Bass (striped), bluefish, drum (black), tuna (albacore)
Clam (whole or cut)	Bass (black sea, striped), bluefish, cod (Atlantic), corbina, croaker (all), drum (black, red), flounder (starry, winter), grouper (all), haddock, halibut (Atlantic, California, Pacific), pollock, pompano, scup, sea trout (spotted), sheepshead, snapper (cubera, red), spot, sturgeon (white), tautog, tilefish, tomcod (Atlantic)
Crab (fiddler and green)	Bass (black sea), drum (black, red), sheepshead, tautog
Eel (live)	Bass (striped), bluefish, cobia
Killifish (live)	Bass (black sea), bluefish, flounder (summer), sea trout (spotted)
Mackerel (whole or cut)	Bass (striped, white sea), bonito (Atlantic), cobia, cod (Atlantic), bluefish, drum (black), halibut (Atlantic, California, Pacific), sheepshead, snapper (red), tarpon, tilefish, tomcod (Atlantic), tuna (albacore), wahoo, yellowtail
Mussel	California sheephead, corbina, croaker (all), flounder (starry, winter), opaleye, scup, sheepshead, tautog
Sand eel (large or small)	Bass (striped), bonito (Atlantic), cod (Pacific), flounder (summer), mackerel (all), pollock, sheepshead, snapper (red), tuna (albacore, blackfin), weakfish, whiting
Sand lance (whole)	Bocaccio rockfish, halibut (California, Pacific), petrale sole, salmon (chinook, chum, coho, sockeye)
Sandworm (whole or cut)	Bass (black sea, striped), bluefish, croaker (all), flounder (summer, winter), halibut (Pacific), mackerel (all), pompano, scup, sea trout (spotted), sheepshead, spot, tautog, tomcod (Atlantic), weakfish, whiting
Sardine (whole)	Almaco jack, bass (kelp, white sea), bonito (Pacific), cod (Pacific), flounder (starry), grouper, roosterfish
Shiner (whole)	Bluefish (snapper), flounder (summer), whiting
Shrimp (whole or cut)	Bass (black sea), bonito (Pacific), California sheephead, corbina, drum (black, red), mackerel (all), petrale sole, pompano, sanddab (longfin), sea trout (spotted), sheepshead, spot, spotfin, sturgeon (white), weakfish, whiting
Smelt (whole)	Bonito, bluefish, cod (Atlantic), flounder (summer), salmon (Atlantic), tuna (albacore), wahoo
Spearing (whole)	Bluefish (snapper), bonito (Atlantic), flounder (summer), mackerel (Spanish), snapper, tuna (albacore), weakfish, whiting
Squid (whole or cut)	Amberjack, bass (kelp, striped, white sea), bluefish, bocaccio rockfish, bonito (Atlantic, Pacific), California sheephead, cobia, croaker (all), dolphinfish, drum (black, red), flounder (summer), grouper (most), halibut (Atlantic, California, Pacific), lingcod, mackerel (all), marlin (blue, striped, white), sanddab (longfin, Pacific), spot, sailfish, salmon (chinook, coho, pink, sockeye), snapper (cubera), snapper bluefish, sturgeon (white), swordfish, tilefish, tomcod (Atlantic), wahoo, yellowtail, tuna (albacore, blackfin, little tunny, skipjack, yellowfin)

NATURAL BAIT TYPES

Sandworms and Bloodworms

Most fish will consume a worm if it is offered. Sandworms and bloodworms are the most common types of worms sold for saltwater fishing, and both work well.

Sandworms are the less expensive and more popular of the two. They have a slightly flattened body with tentacle-like appendages along their length. Usually 9 to 10 inches long or a bit more, they are used whole or cut, and are attractive to flounder, codfish, pollock, haddock, and several other species.

Bloodworms, which closely resemble night crawlers or earthworms, are usually 6 to 7 inches long. Their skin is tougher but smoother than that of sandworms. They survive longer on the hook when used whole; when cut, they bleed profusely and can make a mess, so bring along a cutting board that can be rinsed off throughout the day.

Sandworms and bloodworms are dug from sand flats at low tide by commercial diggers. They are sold by the dozen, packed in seaweed, and should be alive, plump, and brightly colored, without an odor. They must be kept moist and cool, so keep them out of direct sunlight. If you put them in your cooler, keep them out of melted ice water—the fresh water will kill them. Don't place bloodworms and sandworms in the same container: they are natural enemies and will kill one another. And keep your fingers away from the sharp, needle-like forceps at their mouth; their bite can be painful.

Both kinds of worms can be used whole on a hook as bait for larger species, or they can be cut into pieces for smaller fish and placed on the hook with the point and barb protruding through the flesh for security.

Fresh, lively sandworms stored in seaweed.

Whole bloodworm on a hook.

To hook a worm, grab it as close to the mouth end as possible and push the point of the hook into the worm. Continue pushing, leading the worm around the bend of the hook. When the worm's head reaches the hook's eyelet, you've gone far enough; push the point of the hook through the worm's side at that point. The worm will fight you all the way; you just have to persevere.

Because of their high mortality rate in storage, sandworms and bloodworms are stocked in only limited quantities by bait shops. Call in advance to see if they're available. If you're a good customer, the shop may be willing to put some aside for you.

If you have some worms left at the end of a day of fishing, simply put them back in the water, unless you plan to go fishing again in the next day or two. If you keep them in a refrigerator, slightly damp with seawater, bloodworms will survive for about a week, sandworms a bit less. It's iffy, though, and some people don't like to share their yogurt space with worms.

Squid

After sandworms and bloodworms, squid is one of the most productive and popular baits. Whole frozen squid can be purchased from bait shops and supermarkets. Whole squid can also be found fresh in supermarkets; when on sale, it's a good deal. Cut squid is available in plastic containers from tackle shops.

Squid cut into pennant-shaped strips can be placed, one strip at a time, on a hook by itself, or it can accompany a dead or live baitfish on the hook. A squid strip can also be placed on a bucktail jig (see Chapter 11) to make it more attractive. The fluttering action of the pennant-shaped strip is a good attention-getter.

Dead Baitfish

Common dead baitfish include sand eels, sand lance, anchovies, ballyhoo, sardines, shiners, bunker, butterfish, herring, smelt, and mackerel. They are sold fresh or frozen, and their popularity and availability vary by region.

When purchasing frozen baitfish, check for freezer burn, any sign of which indicates excessive time in storage. Freezer-burned baitfish get mushy when thawed and will not last a day out fishing.

Smaller dead baitfish, such as sand eels, sand lance, anchovies, sardines, ballyhoo, smelt, and shiners, are used whole on the hook. Larger dead baitfish, including bunker, mackerel, butterfish, and herring, can be used whole or cut into vertical chunks ¾ to 1 inch wide (see photos page 75). Bunker, mackerel, butterfish, and herring are oily fish whose odor is particularly attractive to predator fish.

Shiners that were packaged frozen and then thawed.

CLEANING SQUID

Whole squid must be cleaned and cut; long, pennant-shaped strips are the preferred shape. Begin by removing the head and tentacles (1). Hold the squid's pouch, or body, in one hand and the tentacles in the other. Pull the tentacles until the viscera separates from the inside of the pouch. Set the tentacles aside, with the head and viscera still attached.

Feel the inside upper portion of the pouch with your fingers to locate the quill, which runs the length of the pouch (2). Pull out the quill and discard it. Reach in and pull out any remaining viscera with your fingers.

Starting at the open end of the pouch, pull the purplish skin away from the flesh (3). Remove all the skin and discard it.

Cut the pouch lengthwise along one side to fully open it up (4). Trim the opened pouch into long, pennant-shaped strips.

Sever the tentacles from the head below the eyes (5); the tentacles and head should remain joined together by a narrow band of flesh. Cut the tentacles into smaller pieces for chunking. You can discard the head and viscera or save them for chunking too.

To store 2 to 3 pounds of cleaned squid, make a brine solution of 1 cup table salt and 2 cups fresh water. (Squid stored in fresh water will get soft and mushy.) Mix thoroughly, place the squid strips in brine, and place the container in the refrigerator to keep the squid firm and relatively fresh. Squid in brine will stay fresh for several days in the refrigerator; in a cooler when you're out fishing, it will last a day.

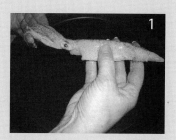

Remove tentacles and head from body of squid.

Locate the quill with your fingers, then pull it out and discard.

Cut the pouch lengthwise.

Remove tentacles from head for chunking.

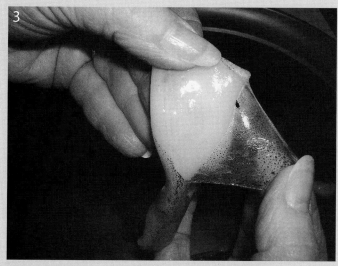

Remove skin from squid body.

Shiners on hooks.

Sand eel hooked and ready for presentation.

Whole bunker; it can be placed on a hook whole or cut into strips.

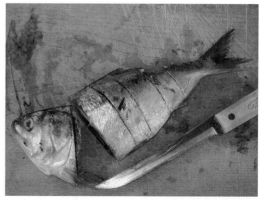

Cut larger baitfish, such as bunker (shown here), into 1-inch vertical chunks.

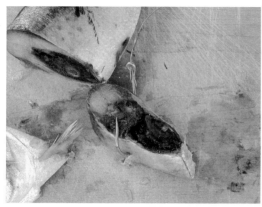

A cut chunk hooked through the skin for strength.

If using the head, hook it through the eyes.

Live Baitfish

Predator fish find injured fish almost irresistible. When you're fishing with live bait (also known as live lining), allow the bait to swim while they're fastened to the hook to attract attention. Live baitfish can be hooked in different ways: through the lips from the bottom up, through the back just below the dorsal fin, through the tail, or through the mouth and out one gill.

You can catch your own baitfish using conventional hook-and-line methods for larger types such as bunker, anchovies, scup, spot, and eels. Keep only those of legal size. These larger baitfish are also available at some tackle shops if you prefer not to fish for bait, but they can be expensive.

Smaller baitfish, such as killifish, shiners, pigfish, sand perch, peanut bunker, and eels, can also be purchased live from bait shops, or they can be trapped, or caught with a casting net

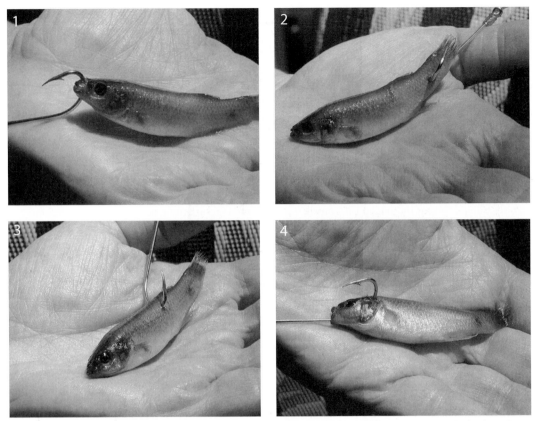

You can hook live baitfish, such as killifish (shown here), in the following ways: through the lips from the bottom up (1); through the tail (2); through the back (3); or through the mouth and out one of the gills (4).

(also known as a seine net). Smaller baitfish tend to swim along the shoreline and docks for food and protection. Such areas that have little or no wave action are ideal places for trapping smaller baitfish.

Bait traps are made from galvanized steel and have a maze-like interior arrangement so that the fish that enter can't find their way out. Bait the trap with chum or almost any other kind of food; tie the trap to a line, and tie it off on a dock, pier, tree, or other solid object. Set the trap into calm, shallow water that won't be exposed at low tide, and leave it there for several hours or a day. If it hasn't been tampered with by passersby in the meantime, it should collect some baitfish by the time you retrieve it.

Casting a net is a more active approach, which you may think is a lot of fun, or a lot of work. You have to find an area where you can actually see the fish swimming—docks and piers are generally better than shoreline. It takes some practice and skill to fling out the net so it flies like a Frisbee and falls flat on the water over the fish. Then pull the draw line to close the trap around the fish, and pull it in.

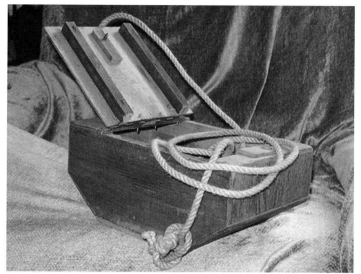

Portable bait pot that is floated to keep the baitfish inside it alive.

Of course, you can also buy live bait at a bait shop. Some bait is sold in plastic bags, and some species will stay alive for a reasonably long time that way—long enough to get them into the live bait well on your boat. Or you can bring a bucket—preferably a covered bait bucket to avoid spills—to the bait shop; they will fill the bucket with salt water along with the baitfish.

Unless you're fishing from a boat with a live bait well, you'll need a portable bait pot to keep the baitfish alive while you're fishing. A live bait well circulates water to keep it cool and aerated, and many have a lockable cover. Portable bait pots can be used from boats as well as from piers and docks. Simply tie the pot to a cleat and place it in the water. When you need a live baitfish, pull the pot up by the rope, open the trapdoor, remove the fish, resecure the door, and return the pot quickly to the water.

Here are descriptions of a few of the more popular types of live bait.

Eels

Live eels can be trapped in low grassy areas, using special eel traps, but most anglers prefer the convenience of buying them at a tackle shop.

When using live eels for fishing, it's best to grab hold of them with a rag because they are slippery. A humane way to put a live eel on a hook is to feed the hook through the mouth and out one gill, or through the lips.

Live eel with a hook through its mouth and out one of its gills.

Like all live fish, eels will suffocate if left too long in a bucket of still water. If their gills are kept moist, they can survive in air for several hours. To keep them alive for longer periods, place them on ice in a cooler, put more ice in a lidded Styrofoam coffee cup and place the cup right in their midst. Then cover them with a wet towel.

Sharp-toothed predator fish often bite a live-lined eel in half, taking the tail end and leaving the head and a portion of the body on the hook. If you're trying to fish with a live eel, you'll have to replace it.

Crabs

Crabs are the predominant bait for tautog, sheepshead, and other crustacean feeders. Green crabs and fiddler crabs can be used with success. Preparation for the hook depends on the size of the crab.

Most green crabs are too large to be used whole. Cut them in half with utility shears or a pair of large, sharp scissors, then place the hook through the meaty portion of the crab and pass it out through the bottom of the shell. Some anglers remove the legs and claws for ease of hooking. Live green crabs are supplied by party boats and charter boats; otherwise, you must buy them live at a tackle shop. Bring your own container.

For smaller species such as fiddler crabs, break off one claw and insert the hook through the socket and out the bottom of the shell, as shown.

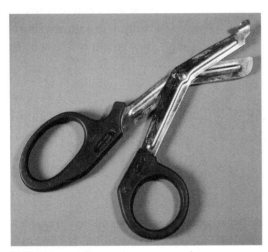

Utility shears for cutting green crabs.

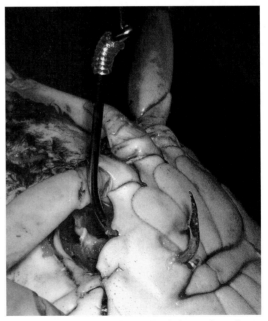

A fiddler crab properly hooked through a claw socket.

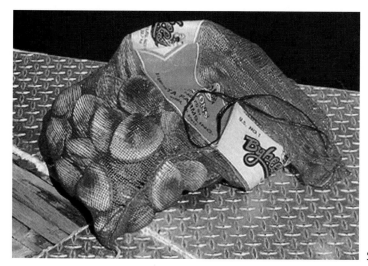

Sack of skimmer clams.

Clams

Most fish like clams—they're a soft, tasty morsel. For the most part, recreational anglers can use large "chowder" clams as bait and nothing smaller. Large skimmer clams, the meat of which is big enough to be cut into chunks, can be bought fresh in their shells or shucked (shells removed) and frozen in packages at bait shops, where they are called clam bellies. Fresh clams are usually more attractive to fish than frozen, but after they are shucked they spoil quickly. Keep fresh clams in their shells on ice, and don't shuck them until you're ready to use them. Be careful when shucking clams—it's easy to cut yourself badly. Use a sturdy, short-bladed knife that's especially made for the job, and have someone show you how to use it. To hook a clam, pass the hook through the thickest part of the foot.

Mussels

Mussels are excellent bait for most bottom feeders. They are sold fresh or shucked into packages in bait shops or can be found fresh at the supermarket in the seafood department. If they are large enough, they may be hooked securely through the foot. Smaller mussels, which are delicate and harder to hook securely, can be steamed first; this toughens them up and helps prevent the foot from breaking.

Mussels make excellent chum when bottom fishing. Their shells can be cracked, and the entire mussel, shell and all, can be placed in a chum pot.

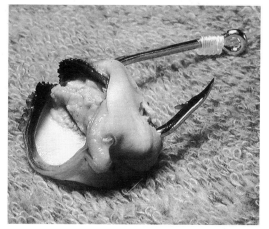

Hook baited with a shucked cooked mussel.

CHAPTER 10

ARTIFICIAL BAIT AND LURES

Artificial bait and lures are manufactured in every imaginable shape, style, size, and color. Although many artificial baits closely imitate a natural prey of one or more species of predator fish, other baits don't even remotely resemble fish or any other prey. Some predators are attracted to artificial bait and lures, and others are not, so it's important to know your quarry's preferences.

When retrieved through the water and worked properly, artificial bait and lures manage to catch their fair share of fish. Fish can hear extremely well and often hear their food before seeing it. As a result, many types of lures are designed to create noise along with imitating the motion of an injured or fleeing baitfish. Some expensive lures contain small balls or beads inside that rattle when jigged or while being retrieved. Others make gurgling or popping noises simply by passing through the water. In contrast, it is primarily the scent of dead natural bait that draws attention.

Except when trolling, almost all artificial baits and lures must be jigged or worked on the retrieve to provide action and noise. To jig, or create action, flick the tip of the rod up and down at various intervals as you retrieve the lure. If you're fishing from shore, this can mean constantly casting and retrieving, which can be tiring after a while. To compensate for this disadvantage compared to natural bait, artificial baits are cleaner, don't smell, and don't die.

Here are some of the most useful types of artificial baits and lures. Bucktail jigs, which are among the best, are addressed separately in Chapter 11.

Assortment of lures.

Rubber or plastic worms of different colors.

ARTIFICIAL BAIT TYPES

Rubber or Plastic Worms

Rubber and plastic worms (also known as jelly worms) are among the most effective inexpensive lures for attracting predator fish. However, rubber worms are not durable and, because they are so easily cut, are not suitable for sharp-toothed fish.

Rubber worms come in a variety of colors. Floating and sinking varieties are available, for use near the surface, at midwater depths, or near the bottom. Both types create noise by displacing water when being jigged during retrieval.

Plugs

Plugs, sometimes called hardbait lures, are shaped and painted to resemble a variety of baitfish, and designed to simulate the motion of a fleeing or injured baitfish when you apply action on the retrieve. Many game fish find this motion very convincing.

All plugs fall into one of three categories: surface, or topwater; diving, or crankbaits; and sinking. To be effective, all of them must be moved through the water, by trolling or by frequent casting and jigging or twitching the rod during the retrieve to create noise and motion. Plugs with noise-making beads inside cost more but are often worth the expense.

Popping plug filled with beads to make additional noise.

TEXAS-RIGGING A RUBBER WORM

The most popular worm rig is called the Texas rig, which works well for attracting fish.

1. Insert the hook point straight into the front of the worm until it's buried just past the barb.

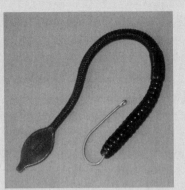

2. Rotate the hook out of the bottom of the worm, making sure it remains centered.

3. Continue to push the hook through the worm so the front of the worm is against the eye of the hook.

4. Rotate the hook so the point comes back into contact with the worm.

5. Push the hook through the worm, making sure it remains centered. Keep pushing until the barb is completely through.

6. This is what the finished rig looks like.

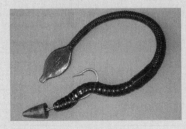

7. If you want the worm to sink, slip a worm weight through the leader snelled to the hook.

Most tackle shops stock a huge selection of tempting plugs. Plugs are expensive, however, so exhibit some restraint, and select only those that are best suited to your needs. To avoid losing them, exercise caution when fishing in surf, in and around structure, or from jetties or piers.

Surface Plugs

Surface, or topwater, plugs are floating lures that make a popping sound when you work them along the surface. Their action is a direct result of how you manipulate the rod tip during the retrieve.

The Knuckle-Head, made by Creek Chub, is a jointed topwater popper that provides excellent results at the surf. While it's being worked, the jointed feature exposes red gill-like surfaces to convincingly mimic a baitfish.

Two types of floating plugs.

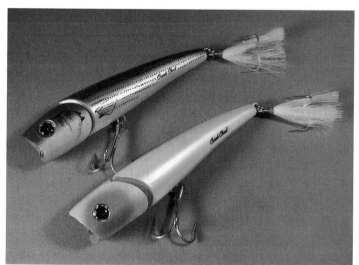

Knuckle-Head lures; the head and tail wobble.

Diving Plugs

Diving plugs, often referred to as crankbaits, usually float when at rest and dive just beneath the surface when being retrieved. A wooden, plastic, or metal bill at the front causes the lure to wobble and dive, the depths being determined by the length of the bill and the speed of retrieval. Shorter bills allow the lure to stay closer to the surface; longer bills tend to dive the deepest, in most cases allowing the lure to bump along the bottom if the speed of the retrieve is fast enough. (Longer bills are also more likely to get hung up on structure.) Metal bills can

resemble a fish or some other sort of prey. As shown in the photo, the body is placed along the hook in a manner similar to that of a Texas-rigged rubber worm. Notice the snap swivel in the eyelet, to prevent line twist during retrieval.

The leadhead jig is used to attract many predator fish, including bluefish, weakfish, and striped bass. Like any jig, it must be worked with a jigging action to attract attention.

Leadhead jig with a rubber body placed along the shank of the hook.

Parachute Jigs

The parachute jig is an ideal jig for trolling and jigging at the same time to entice midwater to surface-swimming predator species, including bluefish and striped bass. To entice a strike, the jig needs a great deal of action so the jig hairs repeatedly blossom and fold back.

Lure Storage

If carelessly stored in a tackle box, fishing lures can become a safety hazard as well as a nuisance. The treble hooks become tangled with one another, making it almost impossible to safely extract an individual lure. Artificial lures must be

Parachute jig in its natural position. The hairs will feather out as the jig is worked.

stowed properly, with one lure per compartment, to avoid tangling. I recommend using inexpensive clear plastic containers. They have hinged lids, click closed securely, and come in various sizes.

After fishing, rinse your lures with fresh water and allow them to dry completely before storing them to avoid rust.

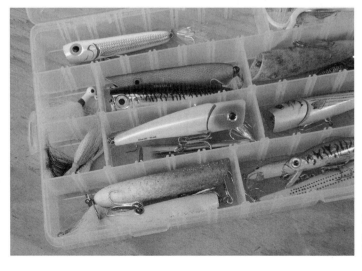

Inexpensive clear plastic container for safely storing lures of various sizes.

CHAPTER 11

BUCKTAIL JIGS

These bucktail jigs from SPRO have bulging eyes and a holographic finish and come in a variety of bright colors. (Courtesy SPRO Corporation)

The bucktail jig is an artificial lure that deserves special attention because of its versatility and productivity. Comprising just a few hairs tied to a leadhead jig, which can be painted any number of colors, the bucktail jig is basic, but it will catch almost any game fish if properly presented. Considered a universal lure, it can be used from a boat, at the surf, or from a jetty or dock.

The bucktail jig is among the oldest types of lures still in use. Its name comes from the days when anglers used hairs from deer tails to make the lure. Although the hairs are now usually synthetic, and the head design has undergone some changes, the basic concept goes back more than a century.

The bucktail jig has no built-in action. It drags across the bottom or runs in a straight line at any depth during retrieval. When fished this way, it may catch fish, but you can greatly improve its success by adding some sort of action. Fishing with a bucktail is not for the laid-back angler; it requires know-how along with some work.

SELECTING BUCKTAILS

The bucktail is available in an assortment of colors, each one intended to attract a specific species of predator fish in a given area. Selecting colors is usually a matter of trial and error,

Simple white bucktail.

or you can ask fellow anglers or your friendly tackle shop proprietor which colors work best. Buy one bucktail of each recommended; pay attention to what works, and stick with those colors in that area. In the absence of good advice, use white; it works in most areas.

Three other factors should be taken into account when choosing and using a bucktail: the species sought (so you can determine the hook size), the speed of the current (so you can choose the correct-weight jig), and the depth of the water (so you can determine how fast to jig the bucktail on the retrieve).

Bucktails can be effective at any depth of water, from bottom to topwater fishing. With deeper water and a swifter current, heavier versions must be used. This becomes a limiting factor if the targeted species is small, because hook size is proportional to the weight of the bucktail. Because the hook is molded into the body, it cannot be changed. Weights start at as little as $\frac{1}{16}$ ounce and go up to several ounces; $\frac{1}{4}$ ounce to $2\frac{1}{2}$ ounces are the most common.

Head shape varies greatly; the choice is a matter of preference and opinion. There is usually no difference in productivity between ball, bullet, flat, and tapered heads, although the tapered design moves better in a strong current.

USING BUCKTAILS

Presentation

Because bucktails have no built-in action, it's up to you to make the bucktail perform during the retrieve. Your objective is to create enough disturbance in the water to attract the fish's attention, and to make the motion convincing enough that the fish believes it's looking at an easy meal.

For bottom fishing, the best method is to bounce the jig off the bottom by lifting the rod tip with a flick of your wrist, then let the jig drop back to the bottom. If there is good current, simply working the rod is sufficient. If the current is slow or absent, retrieve a bit of line by taking a couple of cranks on the reel between lifts. Vary the speed and height of the lift and the amount of time that the lure remains stationary on the bottom. In general, the most productive retrieve is a fast, short jig followed by a slow, controlled drop-back with less than a second of rest on the bottom.

For surface fishing, allow the bucktail to settle a bit, then retrieve it with a jigging motion by repeatedly flicking the tip of the rod with wrist action. Keep the bucktail generally between midwater and the surface, or bounce it off the bottom and jig it to the surface, but don't allow it to remain stagnant on the bottom. Experiment to find the most tempting action, then try to duplicate that action with every cast and retrieve. A hit usually comes as the jig is settling between uniform jerks of the rod tip.

Most fish will recognize and drop an artificial lure of any type as soon as the lure is in its mouth, so you must be ready to set the hook with a sharp lift of the rod as soon as you feel the hit. A slow, controlled drop-back without line slack is most productive because it allows you to keep the feel of the lure.

More Bucktail Tips

Bucktail jigs tend to spin when they're being retrieved. The resulting twist in the main line will eventually cause problems. To prevent line twist, use a snap swivel between the bucktail and the main line, or a barrel swivel between the main line and the leader to which the bucktail is attached. Monofilament leader is acceptable for most fish; use wire for sharp-toothed species. Avoid shiny wire; black works best because it is the least visible.

Commercially manufactured bucktails are usually good quality. However, carefully inspect the jig before buying it to make sure the length of the hair doesn't interfere with the hook. (You may want to trim the hair from around the hook.) Keep the hook very sharp to ensure deep penetration. Use a sharpening stone or hook hone, passing it along the edges of the point and the barb of the hook.

Bucktail jigs can be enhanced by putting a pennant-shaped piece of squid or a length of pork rind on the hook. Pork rind should be in every tackle box. It's tough, and a single piece will last most of the fishing day, whereas squid require more frequent replacement. You may have to trim the rind to match the size of the bucktail, and slice the tail of the rind lengthwise for greater fluttering action.

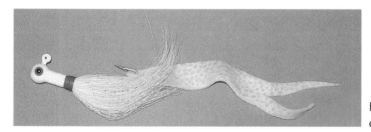

Bucktail with pork rind enhancement.

CHAPTER 12

TYING EFFECTIVE KNOTS

The average angler is almost always tying knots so it's important to tie each knot accurately and carefully. Learn this skill well; the quality of your knots can make the difference between landing fish and losing them.

Under ideal conditions, most fishing line loses 20 percent of its strength at the knot. To reduce friction that could cause the knot to lose as much as 50 percent of its strength, moisten the line with water or saliva before drawing the knot tightly together. It's also important to gather all loops smoothly and evenly, so the entire knot absorbs the forces imposed on it.

Each knot described in this chapter has a special purpose, and none is suitable for all applications.

> ## KNOT-TYING TERMS
>
> **Standing line:** The portion of line that heads back toward the reel or leader.
> **Tag end:** The loose end of the line; also, the short piece of line remaining after the knot is tied. Trim it off with a nail clipper or scissors.
> **Working line:** The length of line needed to tie the knot.

TYING PROPER KNOTS

1. Select the right knot for the job.

2. Tie the knot carefully and according to the instructions. If in doubt about the knot's quality, cut it off and tie another. Don't bet on a bad knot.

3. Always use the recommended number of turns in a knot, but more turns are better than fewer.

4. Avoid knives, teeth, or cigarette lighters for cutting line. Use sharp scissors, a fingernail clipper, or a line clipper.

5. Check knots frequently, especially if the line has been heavily used. Inspect each knot as the line is reeled in, and replace any damaged sections.

6. Avoid pulling monofilament line knots tight without first wetting the knot.

7. Draw the knot together slowly. Jerking it tight can distort and weaken the line.

8. Inspect and test each knot after tying it. Your goal should be perfectly tied knots every time.

9. Study and practice tying a few of the most useful knots. It's better to be proficient with a few knots than to tie a large number poorly.

KNOT TYPES

Sling Knot

The sling knot is used to create a loop in the line or leader, which provides increased action to a lure. This knot requires a good length of line to tie properly.

1. Thread the line through the eye of the lure and double it back 7 to 9 inches.

2. Form a loop with the doubled line and twist it around six times.

3. Thread the lure through the loop.

4. Tighten the knot by pulling the line and lure toward the eyelet of the lure to draw the knot tight. Trim any excess line from the tag end with a fingernail clipper or line clipper.

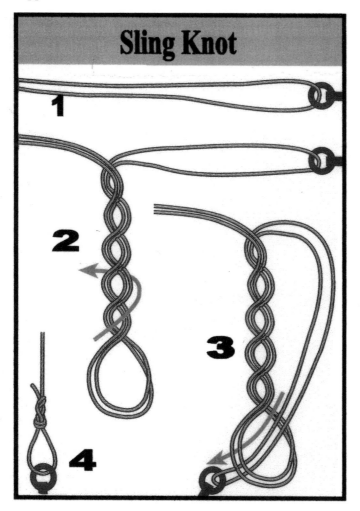

Tackle Uni-Knot

The tackle uni-knot is used to snell a hook or attach a swivel or terminal tackle to the main line.

1. Run the line through the eye and double it back, forming a circle or loop.

2. Twist the tag end around the double line six or seven turns, then through the loop.

3. Pull the tag end to tighten.

4. Pull the main line to tighten the knot.

5. Keep pulling the main line and pushing down on the knot until the knot slides tightly against the eye. Trim the tag end of the line with a fingernail clipper or line clipper.

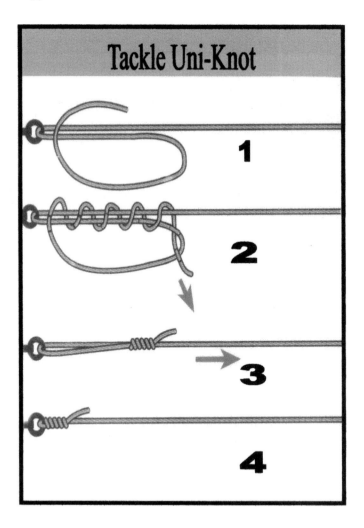

Double Improved Clinch Knot

The doubled improved clinch knot is used by most anglers to attach tackle to line, from as little as 2- to 60-pound-test line or greater.

1. Start with 4 to 7 inches of line. Double the line, and pass the doubled end through the eye of the swivel or lure.

2. With the doubled end, make six or seven wraps back around the two lead lines. Then thread the doubled end through the double loops just above the eye of the swivel or lure.

3. Hold the doubled end and lead lines while pulling the coils tight. Slide the knot tightly against the eye of the swivel or lure. Trim the tag end of the line with a fingernail clipper or line clipper.

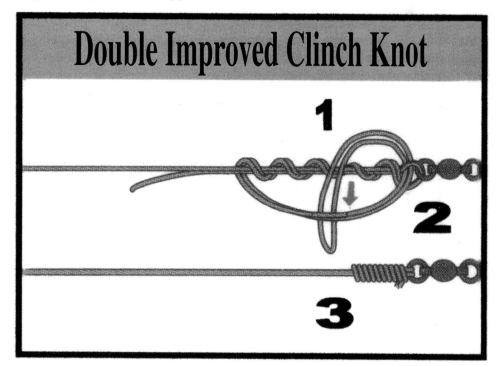

Offshore Swivel Knot

The offshore swivel knot is used to absorb shock caused by strikes from large offshore game fish.

1. Insert about 4 to 5 inches of doubled line through the eye of the swivel.

2. Flip the doubled end over the top of the doubled main line and hold it there.

Simplified Blood Knot

The simplified blood knot is used to join two sections of similar-diameter line.

1. Place the ends of the lines next to each other, facing the same direction, and tie a simple overhand knot. (This knot is temporary.)

2. Form a loop of the standing ends, then turn the knotted end around the line. Leave the twists loose.

3. Make five to seven turns, then pull the knotted loop through the center opening.

4. Hold the knotted loop loosely with your teeth and pull the ends apart to draw the knot tight.

5. Clip off the overhand knot made in step 1 to about ⅟₁₆ inch with a fingernail clipper or line clipper.

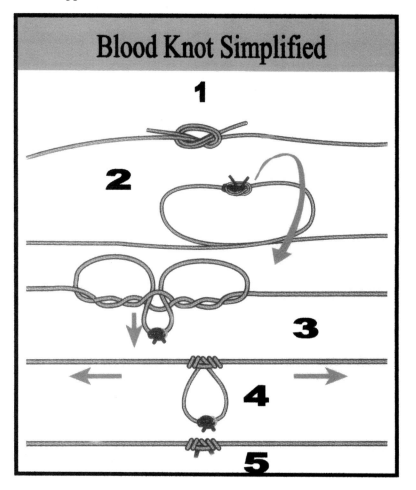

Blood Knot Simplified

Improved Blood Knot

The improved blood knot is used to join a smaller-diameter line to a larger-diameter line.

1. Double the small-diameter line and place it alongside the larger-diameter line.

2. Wrap each line three or four times around the other in opposite directions. Bring both of the ends back through the loop in the center.

3. Holding the tag ends with your teeth, carefully pull both ends of the lines and tighten the knot. Don't bite down too hard, or you may cut the line. Hold it just tightly enough to keep it steady. Trim the excess tag ends of line with a fingernail clipper or line clipper.

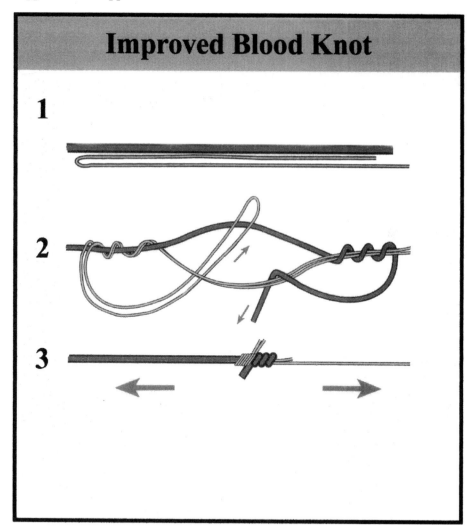

Improved Blood Knot

1

2

3

Dropper Loop

The dropper loop is used to attach a sinker or snelled hooks along the main line.

1. Form a loop in the line.

2. Take hold of one side of the loop, and turn the loop four to six times around the line itself.

3. This is the tricky part: keep an opening in the center—where the turns are being made.

4. Take hold of the other side of the loop and pull it through the center opening.

5. Holding this loop between your teeth, pull the ends apart and gather the turns.

6. Draw up the knot by pulling the lines as tight as possible. The turns will make a loop that stands at right angles to the main line.

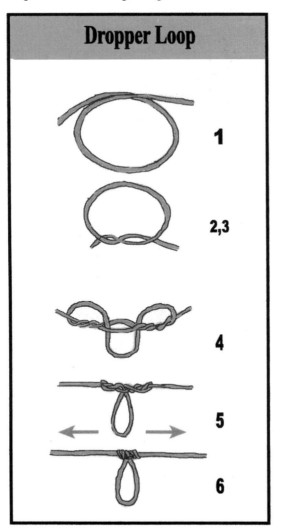

Dropper Loop

1

2,3

4

5

6

Arbor Knot

The arbor knot is used to tie line to a reel spool.

1. Run the line around the reel spool or arbor. Tie an overhand knot near the tip of the line.

2. Take the end of the line and tie an overhand knot over the main line.

3. Tighten the knot at the end of the line, then pull the line tightly around the spool.

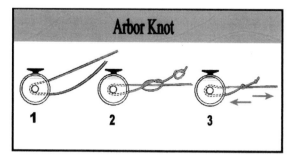

Double Surgeon's Loop

The double surgeon's loop is used to tie a loop at the end of monofilament leader.

1. Double the tag end of the line. Make a single overhand knot in the doubled line.

2. Holding the tag end and the standing part of the line in your left hand, bring the loop around and insert it through the previously made overhand knot.

3. Hold the loop in your left hand while holding the tag end and standing line in your right hand and pull tight.

4. Trim any excess from the tag end to about ⅛ inch with a fingernail clipper or line clipper.

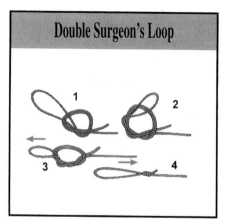

Crawford Knot

The versatile Crawford knot is not used as often as it should be by most experienced anglers. It can be used to tie a hook, swivel, or lure to leader or directly to the main line. This knot, which has excellent breaking strength, looks more difficult to tie than it really is.

1. Insert the tag end of the line through the eyelet, leaving about 8 inches to tie the knot. Bring the tag end back around the standing part of the line to form a loop.

2. Bring the tag end of the line under the standing part of the line and over the two parallel lines.

3. Bring the tag end of the line under the two parallel strands then back over all three lines, making an X.

4. Complete the knot by tucking the tag end between the standing line and the front portion, then back through just above the eye of the hook. Pull the knot tight, slide it down, and jam it against the eyelet. Trim the excess tag end with a fingernail clipper or line clipper.

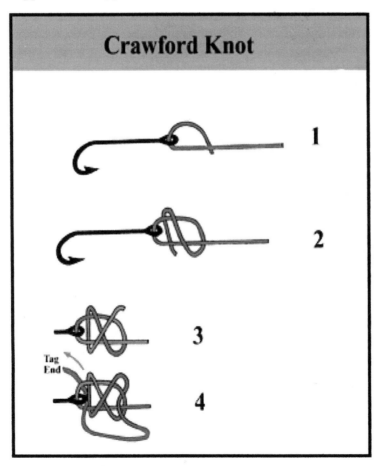

Crawford Knot

1

2

Tag End

3

4

Palomar Knot

The palomar knot is used to easily join line to a hook, swivel, or lure.

1. Double about 4 inches of line and pass the loop through the eyelet of the hook.

2. Letting the hook hang, tie an overhand knot in the doubled line. Avoid twisting the line, and do not tighten the knot.

3. Pull the loop end of the line far enough to pass it over the hook, swivel, or lure. Make sure the loop passes completely over the device.

4. Pull the tag end and the standing line until the knot is tight. Clip off the tag end of the fishing line using a fingernail clipper or line clipper.

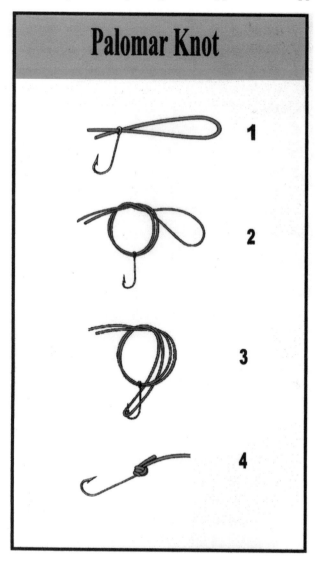

Palomar Knot

1

2

3

4

Shock Leader

The shock leader is used to tie heavier leader to thinner main line.

1. Double the ends of the leader and the main line back about 6 inches. Slip the loop of the main line through the loop of the leader far enough to permit tying a uni-knot around both strands of leader.

2. With the double line, tie a uni-knot around the two strands of leader. Use only four turns.

3. Put your finger through the loop of main line, then grasp the tag end and the standing end of the main line and pull the knot snug around the loop of the leader.

4. With one hand, pull only the standing end of the leader, *not both strands*. With the other hand, pull both strands of the main line. Pull slowly until the knot slides to the end of the leader loop and no slippage remains.

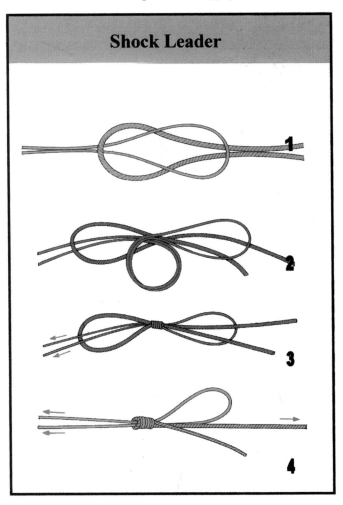

Shock Leader

CHAPTER 13

BOATS

Some of the best shallow-water fishing occurs in bays and inlets farther from shore than you can cast, and many of the most prized species of game fish are found only in deep water, miles offshore. To access these fishing opportunities, you need a boat.

You don't, however, have to *buy* a boat. Boats are the most expensive type of fishing "equipment," and there are several alternatives to ownership, including renting, chartering, and party boat fishing. No beginning angler should jump into the sport by buying a boat; it's something to consider after you've been fishing for a while, find that you love the sport, and are ready to make a commitment to a method of fishing that requires a boat. On the other hand, if you already own a boat intended for other recreational purposes, you may find that fishing offers new ways to enjoy it and the incentive to use it more often.

Not all boats are convenient for fishing. And depending on where you fish, not all boats are safe. A boat must be strong enough to withstand a considerable amount of abuse from rough conditions caused by wind, current, and tide, and stable enough to avoid rolling over or swamping. If you want to fish in shallow water, the boat must have a shallow draft. If you want to fish on the open ocean, a more powerful engine and a very different, more seaworthy hull shape may be required. This chapter provides a brief introduction to the types of boats commonly used for saltwater fishing.

Note that this book does not provide guidance on seamanship, navigation, safety, or other aspects of boat operation. These are large, complex, important subjects that require a great deal of care and study. Anyone who takes control of a powerboat or, for that matter, a boat of any kind should obtain that information elsewhere. I recommend the beginning boating and safety courses offered by the U.S. Coast Guard Auxiliary and the U.S. Power Squadrons, and books such as the third edition of *Getting Started in Powerboating* by Bob Armstrong (International Marine, 2005).

BOAT TYPES

Skiffs

Sometimes (improperly) called a dinghy, a fishing skiff resembles a small rowboat with a V-bottom. Usually 14 to 16 feet in length, these boats are often rented from fishing stations, which also serve as tackle shops in many coastal areas. Wooden fishing skiffs are less common these days; most are now made of aluminum or fiberglass. Skiffs are used exclusively in protected bays and inlets; with their small size, low freeboard, and lack of a deck, they are not sufficiently seaworthy for open water.

Fishing skiff.

A skiff can be rowed (if it has oarlocks), but most have a small (5 to 15 horsepower) outboard motor attached to the transom, allowing you to travel quickly between fishing locations in a bay.

A skiff provides the basic essentials for saltwater bay fishing and can handle up to three anglers and their equipment, as long as they pack judiciously. Although sufficiently stable under most conditions, a skiff can throw up a lot of spray when the water is choppy, so it's a good idea to pack foul-weather gear even if no rain is predicted.

To enter the boat, don't step on the gunwales (pronounced "GUN • uls")—the upper edge of the boat's sides—or anywhere near the outside edge of the seats. Step directly from the dock into the middle of the bottom of the boat; keep your weight low, and sit down promptly near the boat's centerline. Once you're seated, stay there. Small skiffs can be tippy. If you need to be a bit higher, don't stand; you may, however, kneel on a seat (carefully).

Aluminum boats are noisy, so when you're on your fishing grounds, avoid banging gear around inside the hull. The noise will scare away the fish.

Runabouts

Runabouts suitable for saltwater fishing are usually larger than skiffs, ranging from 15 to 20 feet or longer. They have higher freeboard and a wider beam (width) than skiffs and a larger engine(s), ranging from 40 to 200 horsepower and up. Most are powered by outboard motors, although sterndrive inboard engines are not uncommon on larger models. Fiberglass is the most popular hull material, but aluminum boats are also common.

Runabout heading out for a day of fishing.

Runabouts are much faster than skiffs, and they are capacious enough to accommodate a lot of fixed and movable fishing equipment, such as rod holders, a bait well, coolers, a rod storage rack, and a depth-finder. Typically drier and more seaworthy than skiffs, they are still not appropriate for offshore waters, and should generally be confined to bays, inlets, and other protected areas.

Some runabouts are good "do-everything" designs that work well for saltwater fishing as well as freshwater family fun; others are more purpose built, and don't cross over happily. For example, a deeper-V hull handles rough water better than a shallower-V or a flat-bottom hull. Also, plush carpeting and upholstery don't hold up well to repeated contact with hooks and fish guts, although a rugged, washable outdoor-type carpet makes for good, solid footing and can be a desirable safety feature.

Runabouts are usually kept in a slip or on a mooring, or kept on a trailer and launched at any launching ramp close to a good fishing location. Trailering is generally a lot cheaper, but a mooring or a slip is more convenient (if you plan to fish mostly in the same area). Whether you find trailering convenient or difficult will depend on the particular boat, your car, your skill at handling a trailer, and, to some extent, your physical cabilities.

Center Console Boats

Center console boats are runabouts on steroids, designed especially for fishing. With the controls, gauges, and instruments consolidated on a narrow pedestal, they provide unrestricted fishing on

Center console fishing boats.

all sides of the boat. They range in length from 16 to 20 feet or more. The smaller ones should be considered inshore boats, but many center consoles around 22 feet or so are capable of handling fairly rough waters offshore. The larger boats often have twin outboard engines with a combined horsepower of 300 or more.

You won't find plush, tufted vinyl upholstery, but you will likely find a high-quality depth-finder and navigation equipment. Other common equipment includes a built-in bait well, a fish well, rod holders, and cooler storage. For the most part, center console boats are not equipped for creature comfort because of their open design, although some of the biggest models do have a little enclosed space tucked into the console to house a portable chemical toilet. Failing that, a canvas-tent-like cover can be erected in the bow for the comfort facility.

It stands to reason that the larger the boat, the more anglers and equipment can be accomodated. Although many center console boats can *legally* carry more than six passengers, six is really the upper practical limit for even the larger models. More passengers than that, and you'll inevitably get in one another's way. But for minimum compliance, always observe the manufacturer's capacity guidelines.

Smaller center consoles are as readily trailered as small runabouts. Larger models push the limits of what you can pull even with a large SUV or pickup, and launching and retrieving the larger models at boat ramps can be quite difficult. Consequently, most larger center console boats are kept in the water throughout the boating season and trailered only for winter storage.

DEPTH-FINDERS

Anglers can readily see fish concentrations with the aid of a depth-finder, eliminating much of the guesswork. A depth-finder is used on most fishing boats to determine the depth of the water in a given area. In addition to being a virtually essential safety device, it's particularly useful to spot structure or holes along the bottom where fish tend to congregate. Some of the more expensive units also indicate the water temperature, which is another important consideration for locating fish.

Depth-finder. (Courtesy Lowrance Electronics, Inc.)

Flats-Fishing Boats

Flats-fishing boats (or simply flats boats) are large, open skiffs with extremely shallow draft to access the expansive, shallow waters—flats—common along much of the Florida and Gulf coasts and elsewhere. Immediately recognizable for the tall, stern-mounted poling platform over the outboard engine, they are designed to approach fish stealthily in waters as shallow as 8 to 10 inches.

Flats boats range in length from 16 to 21 feet and have a relatively high-powered engine with a short shaft to move the boat quickly to and from the flats. Most of these boats are fiberglass, and readily trailerable. Many have a built-in bait well and rod storage in below-deck compartments to keep the deck unobstructed when fishing. Freeboard is usually very low, putting the angler close to the water surface. Many older models threw a lot of spray in rough water, but newer ones are relatively dry. Some are equipped with an electric trolling motor to get the boat in position in shallow water.

Sportfishing Boats

Sportfishing boats (also known as sportfishermen) vary in length from 25 feet to more than 75 feet and have a large, open cockpit aft of a large, enclosed cabin. These boats are sturdy and seaworthy, and designed for offshore use. To reach distant fishing grounds quickly, they have one or two large inboard gasoline or diesel engines, either conventional or sterndrive. High freeboard up front enables them to handle heavy seas; low freeboard around the cockpit puts the angler close to the water. The helm (steering station) on the flying bridge puts the driver in a perfect position to watch the fishing action and maneuver the boat to assist the angler.

Although they are designed primarily for fishing, sportfishermen make good cruising boats as well, with plenty of interior space and comfortable accommodations. Most newer boats are made of fiberglass, but a few builders still specialize in wood construction, and there

These sportfishing boats are roomy enough for four or five anglers.

are plenty of older wooden boats on the used market. Although wooden boats can be plenty rugged, they do require more maintenance than their fiberglass counterparts.

Most sportfishing boats have an abundance of built-in rod and tackle storage compartments, and live bait and fish wells (not to mention a full galley, an enclosed head, multiple berths, flat-panel color television, etc.). They are usually equipped with full suites of electronics, including a depth-finder and radar, and many have one or two fighting chairs in the cockpit (for more on fighting chairs, see the Charter Boats section). A 25-foot sportfishing boat can comfortably handle four anglers or more.

Party Boats

Also known as open boats or head boats (as in "how many paying heads can it carry?"), party boats are seaworthy commercial vessels ranging in length from 65 feet to more than 125 feet and carrying fifty or more anglers at a time. Some party boats stay within the confines of a bay, but many venture out for deepwater offshore fishing. The number of anglers aboard the boat is based on the length of the boat and Coast Guard regulations. Party boats are rigorously inspected and licensed and are usually very safe.

Several party boats dockside.

Boarding a party boat.

Party boats usually fish for just one or two species on a trip, and the species change with the season. During warmer months, the boats operate seven days a week and nearly 24 hours a day; winter schedules are often weekends only, and some boats suspend operations altogether to catch up on maintenance.

Most trips are either half-day or full-day affairs, but some party boats offer overnight deep-sea trips, which usually run about 36 hours from dock to dock. Day-trip seats are usually available on a first-come, first-served basis; extended offshore trips often require reservations. Large groups should also call for reservations, even for shorter trips.

Some party boats provide free use of rods and reels; others charge a minimal rental fee. Natural bait and terminal tackle are usually included in the fare.

The captains of party boats are licensed by the U.S. Coast Guard and are exceptionally experienced anglers themselves. It's their job to know where the fish are on any given day, and they make every effort to put their customers over them. The captains also have to know which baits and fishing techniques suit the fish and the circumstances.

The mates are the backbone of the operation. They assist the captain with handling the boat, and they collect the fares, help anglers on board with their gear, organize the fish pool (for more on this, see the How to Fish (and Behave) on a Party Boat sidebar), provide instruction, rig rods with hooks and sinkers, and distribute bait. They'll net or gaff a fish, remove the hook from the fish, and, if you ask, clean your catch on the return trip (although some states prohibit this). Depending on the species sought, mates may ladle chum over the sides and, in shallow bays, stir the bottom with long poles to bring the fish closer to the boat.

The cabin provides a sheltered place out of the weather, as well as seating, tables, and heads (bathrooms). Boats that offer overnight trips usually have basic sleeping accommodations, but you have to bring your own sleeping bag and pillow. Some boats offer free coffee (be aware that caffeine can exacerbate motion sickness) and a snack bar where you can purchase food and soft drinks at a reasonable cost; on other boats you must bring your own food and beverages. Find out before you go. You should bring an ice-filled cooler to store any perishable items and the fish you catch.

To avoid motion sickness, don't drink alcoholic beverages while on board. Most party boat captains discourage or prohibit alcohol, as a safety measure and to ensure a wholesome atmosphere.

Party boat fares vary with the length of the trip and the type of species targeted. Most half-day trips average about $35 per adult, less for children and senior citizens. But there is a lot of variability, depending upon the locale, the boat, the season, the length of the trip, and maybe the whim of the owner. It's best to call in advance.

Many anglers first experience boat fishing aboard party boats. The fishing is usually productive, and the atmosphere is almost always friendly. And, overall, party boats are a real bargain.

HOW TO FISH (AND BEHAVE) ON A PARTY BOAT

Since party boats usually have a lot of people on board, proper etiquette is a must.

Rule number one is to stay out of the way of the crew and allow them to do their jobs efficiently and safely.

Rule number two is to always show respect for your fellow anglers.

There are usually bench seats surrounding the outside of the boat's cabin, and plenty of room below the benches to store your tackle box and cooler. Most experienced anglers arrive an hour or two early with their own rod and reel and take a favorite position as soon as they're on board.

Most boats have evenly spaced rod holders along the rail where you should stow your rod. Don't take more than one rod holder, and don't switch locations. The rod holder identifies "your" place; once you've staked it out, stay there. Don't bring more than one rod, and stay in your place when traveling to and from the fishing locations. If you want to make room for your group to sit together, you may ask another angler to move, but never move someone's rod without permission.

Most of the anglers on board will be friendly, and many will be helpful when asked for advice. Some will be well-seasoned party boat anglers; others will be new to the sport. To avoid conflict, try to stay out of the way of anglers who appear to have a chip on their shoulder. Fortunately there are very few of these characters.

While traveling to the fishing location, a mate will collect the fare and ask if you want to be in the *fish pool*. This is basically a simple fishing derby in which anglers wager a fixed amount; the angler who catches the heaviest fish of a given species wins the pool. The mate will explain the finer points of the contest, if any. If you enter, the mate will list your name on a sheet or provide you with a ticket stub.

Once at the fishing location, the captain will signal the start of fishing with one blast of the boat's horn or an announcement.

Because of the confined space on a party boat, you should never cast a line. Instead, drop the terminal rig straight down and try to keep the line tight with a suitable amount of weight. Don't allow the line to travel too far under the boat or wander too far to either side, which could create tangles with those fishing on either side of you.

Bench-type seating on a party boat.

Mates will be walking around the boat, providing help and advice.

Never discard trash over the side of the boat. Numerous trash receptacles should be provided on board. Most anglers are in tune with the environment and will not appreciate the improper discarding of debris.

When the captain determines that the time is right to move to another fishing location, he or she will signal with a single blast of the horn and/or an announcement. Quickly reel in your line and stow the rod in the rod holder, with the hook placed securely in the base of a rod guide support or on a hook keeper. Stay seated while the boat is underway. If you need help with any major adjustments to your rig, now is a good time to ask a mate.

At the end of the scheduled fishing period, the captain will signal with three short blasts of the boat horn or another announcement.

The captain always has the final word in all aspects of the boat's operation. He or she will determine pool winners and will settle any discrepancies that may occur.

Mates are usually very friendly and helpful. Tips are their main source of income, and they earn it, so compensate the mates who provide you with assistance and instruction.

Properly stowed rods on a party boat.

Charter Boats

Charter boats are privately owned offshore sportfishing boats ranging in length from 35 to 65 feet and more. Charter boats are usually chartered or rented for a full day of fishing (or longer). Most are limited to six or fewer anglers in addition to the captain and sometimes a mate or two.

Charter boats are rigged strictly for fishing. They are inspected by the U.S. Coast Guard, are very clean, and are kept in excellent operating condition. The captain is also licensed by the Coast Guard and is a master angler who knows the waters well. The captain and crew provide personal attention and "almost" guarantee fishing action.

Most charter boats target "big game" fish, although the species varies by season, and most captains will pursue whatever species the client desires, within reason. The species of fish sought must be determined in advance so the captain can properly plan and equip for the trip and determine a realistic fee.

Hiring a charter boat and its crew can be expensive, although costs vary with the species sought, the distance to be run, and the duration of the trip. Chartering a boat for a full day of inshore fishing may cost about $850, which will be shared by all the anglers on board. A charter includes rods, reels, tackle, and bait. You need to bring only your lunch, beverages, and a cooler full of ice. There are usually no galley provisions available.

Charter boats at dock.

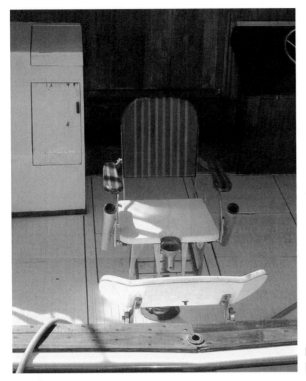

Fighting chair with rod holder on a charter boat.

Most larger charter boats are equipped with one or two fighting chairs bolted to the deck in the cockpit. The purpose of these pedestal-mounted swiveling chairs is to make the angler as stable and comfortable as possible and to bear much of the strain of fighting and reeling in a fish. A fighting chair is equipped with a gimbal (a tube-like device attached to the fighting chair that helps support the fishing rod) at the front of the seat to support the butt end of the rod, and most have a sturdy belt or strap to keep you in place. Some lock the reel in place as well. (This often requires a specially fitted reel.) The mate will show you how to get yourself set up and strapped in. When you're fighting a big one, the mate will also help rotate the chair to keep you aligned with the fish. It is customary to tip the mate at least 20 percent of the total fare for his or her efforts.

The mate and captain will provide instruction and all the assistance you need while fishing. In return, the captain expects anglers to demonstrate proper behavior while on board the boat (which usually belongs to the captain). Rowdy activity is not tolerated.

The captain has the final word on all matters pertaining to the operation of the boat. He or she determines if weather conditions will compromise the safety of the vessel and its passengers, and it's the captain's call to suspend, cancel, or postpone a trip. In such an event, anglers usually have the option of rescheduling or receiving a refund.

PART 3

FISHING TECHNIQUES AND METHODS

CHAPTER 14

HOOKING, PLAYING, CHUMMING, AND OTHER TECHNIQUES

There are many methods of fishing, among them bottom fishing, trolling, and fly fishing. We'll look at these in detail in the chapters that follow. All methods have certain techniques in common; other techniques are shared by two or more methods. Learn these basic techniques, and you'll be able to apply them in a variety of situations.

HOW LONG DO YOU GIVE THE FISH TO FIND YOU?

In Chapter 1 you saw how the sequence of the tides affects the presence of fish. The following chapters examine other ways to find fish. But once you've found them, what if they're not biting?

Fish can be very finicky at times, and you should be prepared to try all the available options. If you've exhausted your different bait options—switching from bait to lures or vice versa, changing your method of presentation, and chumming (see below)—it just may be that the fish aren't where you thought they were. Maybe it's time to move on.

Assuming that the stage of the tide is right, most anglers give a particular spot up to an hour before moving to the next spot. It's rarely worthwhile to spend more than 2 hours in a spot that's not productive. If you're on a boat, you have a great deal of flexibility in moving to alternate locations; if the fish aren't biting over one piece of structure, you can simply move to the next. If you're on a dock, pier, or jetty, your options may be more limited, although you can move from one end or one side to the other. If you're fishing at the surf, you may be limited only by how far you're willing to carry your gear. Many anglers who use natural bait in the surf will give an area up to an hour; those who use artificial bait usually move after a half hour or so because fishing with lures requires more work.

HOOKING AND PLAYING THE FISH

Fish can often tell that something's wrong as soon as they get the hook or lure in their mouth—it just doesn't feel like food to them—and many times they are able to spit it out. That's why you should be ready to set the hook as soon as a fish takes it. If you're fishing from a boat, a dock, or a pier, or surf fishing with lures, you'll have the rod in your hands at all times and, when you get a bite, you may feel a sudden and unexpected jerk, or a steady tug. If you're surf fishing with natural bait, a sand spike may be holding your rod for you, and you'll see the rod tip bend. In any case, depending on the size and species of the fish, the pull may be gradual and subtle, or it may be an unmistakable forceful yank. If you're not certain, pull the rod back gently to feel whether a fish is indeed there. If it is, take immediate action.

If you're using a conventional J hook, set the hook with a forceful pull-back of the rod. (Your reel's drag must be properly adjusted. If it's too loose, it will allow more line to pay out rather than forcing the hook into the fish's mouth.) In contrast, a circle, or C, hook does not need to be set—it is self-setting. (Refer back to Chapter 7 for more on hooks.)

Once properly hooked, the fish must be played differently depending on the species. You must determine the strength of the fish to get it landed. If the fish is large and strong, you can allow the reel's drag system to work on your behalf. Always keep the line tight to prevent the fish from throwing the hook. Keep the rod tip high, and crank in the line at the first sign of easing tension. Don't allow the line to go slack, and don't let the reel free-spool. If the fish makes a run for it, let it pull line off the reel against the force of the drag; this will tire out the fish.

Don't play with the drag setting when you're fighting a fish; too many things can go wrong. Trying to adjust it when you're playing a fish can result in lost fish and lines. The drag should be properly adjusted beforehand. If it isn't, just do the best you can.

In the case of especially strong, hard-fighting predator fish, you may need to *pump* the rod to gain any ground. Pull the rod up and back forcefully, then reel in *quickly* as you lower the tip again. Do this repeatedly. Each time you pump, you are hoping to gain a few yards of line, bringing the fish closer. Make sure you reel in fast enough to prevent slack from developing. A fish that's strong enough to require pumping will take immediate advantage of the least bit of slack to break your line or throw the hook.

CHUMMING

Chum is ground-up fish or fish entrails and other delightful morsels that are deposited into the water to release a scent that attracts most fish. Chum is the consistency of chunky soup and moves easily with the current. It can be used when fishing with live or dead natural bait, flies, or artificial lures at almost any depth. It's most often used when fishing from a stationary location, such as an anchored boat or a pier, but you can chum from a drifting boat. For certain species of fish, chumming is essential to success.

Chum is placed in a chum pot or a mesh bag (like an onion bag), which is lowered over the side of the boat to any depth or directly on the bottom. The chum particles seep through the holes in the pot or the bag and are dispersed by the current, creating an oily, smelly slick that attracts fish to the vicinity. Loose chum can also be ladled over the side of a drifting or an anchored boat to create a slick nearer to the surface for top-feeding species.

Chum is available from bait and tackle shops fresh or frozen in a large variety of flavors (so to speak), depending on the targeted species. Fresh chum is more effective and generally more convenient to use than frozen chum. Commercial chum is made from ground-up fish entrails, crustaceans, mollusks, and worms, with the addition of grain, bread, and dry pet food. You can also make your own, or use skimmer clams or mussels, which can be cracked and placed in a chum pot, shells and all.

Whenever I think of chumming, I think of the scene in the movie *Jaws* where Roy Scheider is ladling chum over the side of the boat when he sees the great white shark surface. Not wanting to be there, Scheider suggests that they head back in to get a bigger boat. Before seeing the shark, Scheider isn't happy with chumming and clearly indicates his dissatisfaction with the process. A point well taken. Chumming is not one of the more pleasant aspects of fishing, but it is important nonetheless.

How to Chum

Chum pots are available in many sizes. Most have lead ends so the pot will sink quickly and large-mesh screened sides to allow the chum to pass through easily. After chum is placed in the pot, strong but lightweight line is attached to the eyelet, the pot is lowered to the desired depth, and the line is secured to a cleat on the boat or a piling on a pier. Mesh bags are messier to use but work just as effectively. Some anglers place several sinkers in the bottom of the bag to keep it upright when it's hanging in the water column or resting on the bottom. To keep fish within a close radius of a boat, some anglers use two pots or bags—one at the stern and one at the bow.

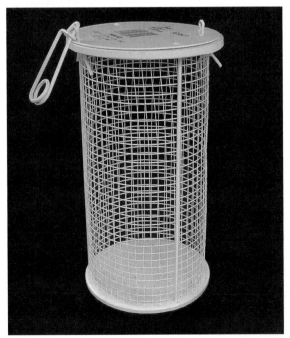

Commercially made chum pot.

Shake the chum pot at intervals, or bounce it on the bottom to loosen the contents and allow them to flow freely. Maintain a constant slick to keep the fish within hook distance. Once you've started chumming, don't slack off and allow the slick to disperse. If you're fishing with a buddy, share the work. Periodically, you'll have to refill the container.

With practice and experience, you'll know how much chum to use. Too little will not release enough scent to attract a good number of fish; too much will essentially provide them with a meal and reduce their desire to take a hook or lure.

The choice of chum mixture depends on the targeted species. Tuna, for example, respond best to ground and chunked herring or mackerel. Chum made from these oily fish spreads a wide-ranging slick whose smell attracts predator fish from far distances. Red snapper and grouper, on the other hand, aren't wide-ranging predators, so a ground-up mixture of forage fish such as scup or spot, although not as odiferous, is perfectly suited to their common tastes. Ask fellow anglers or a local bait shop owner what works.

Loose chum can also be hand-ladled over the side (rather than using a pot or bag) and left to move along the surface and settle toward the bottom. This method, although it uses a lot of chum quickly, can be very effective at attracting surface-feeding fish.

Some anglers prefer to grind their own chum. This is a good way to reduce costs, and it's a good use of fish that you catch but don't intend to eat. Place scrap fish parts, small chunks of cut fish, squid, shucked clams or mussels—almost any form of sea life—and old dry pet food into a blender and mix until you achieve the desired consistency. To preserve domestic harmony, don't use the family blender; invest in one that you reserve only for chum. You may wish to use a dedicated meat grinder to reduce larger pieces and fish heads before blending.

After preparing the chum, place it in plastic freezer bags and freeze it for later use. If you can't reserve a freezer exclusively for these packages, you may wish to double- or even triple-bag them. When you're ready to use them, empty the frozen chunks directly into the chum pot. They'll disperse bits of chum as they thaw in the seawater. It's best to take the bags out of the freezer a few hours in advance to give them a chance to soften but not thaw entirely.

This frozen chum will fit in a chum pot when removed from the plastic bag.

Chunking

Chunking is an "enhanced" method of chumming, using baitfish cut into small (½ inch or less) chunks or cubes rather than ground-up mush. It is usually done in combination with conventional chumming to attract relatively large surface-feeding predator species. Chunks are tossed alongside the boat into a chum slick and allowed to drift and settle. In essence, you're feeding the fish to keep them nearby. Chunking is pretty straightforward and requires no skill. However, use the chunk deposits in moderation. You want to attract the fish and keep them within range, not feed them so much that they lose interest in your line.

CHAPTER 15

BOTTOM AND PIER FISHING, TROLLING, AND OTHER METHODS

This chapter examines several basic methods of fishing: bottom fishing, drifting, trolling, jetty fishing, dock and pier fishing, and flats fishing. Although there is some overlap in these methods, it's still useful to consider them as distinct. Because surf fishing and fly fishing warrant somewhat lengthier treatment, they're discussed in separate chapters.

Most anglers concentrate on just one or two methods of fishing and rarely try any others. I encourage you to become familiar with the whole range of fishing methods. You'll learn which methods you enjoy the most, and you'll increase your opportunities to catch different species throughout the year.

BOTTOM FISHING

Bottom fishing places lures or hooks directly on or near the bottom of the bay or ocean. It can be done from a dock, pier, or jetty, in the surf, or from a boat. Because of its ease and relative simplicity, it is the most popular method of saltwater fishing. Bottom fishing can be done with live or dead natural bait or artificial bait.

When bottom fishing at a dock, pier, or jetty, or at the surf, you are restricted to where and how far you can cast your baited hook or lure. Boats give you the freedom to bottom fish over a larger area. Bottom fishing may be done from a boat at anchor or drifting over some form of structure, such as a reef, mussel bed, or shipwreck, over a sandy or muddy bottom, or over deep holes where fish tend to gather.

Even if you plan to do your bottom fishing from a pier, dock, or jetty, or in the surf, I recommend that you read the next section on bottom fishing from boats. Many of the techniques and considerations are identical.

Bottom Fishing from Boats

Bottom fishing from a party or charter boat is straightforward because the captain does most of the work to put you over the fish. The captain also advises you on what to do. You just have to follow instructions and try to avoid tangling lines with your fellow anglers.

If you're on your own, the local grapevine is your best guide to known fish locations. It sure beats random guesswork. An electronic fish-finder is also helpful in finding structure and determining whether any fish are down there.

There are three main factors to take into account before anchoring the boat: water temperature, water current, and wind direction. Current and wind will affect your anchoring position and technique; water temperature has a strong influence on what fish (if any) you will find. See Appendix B for information on the temperature preferences of various species.

One anchor is usually sufficient, but on windy days or in strong current two may be needed to prevent the boat from swinging off location. One anchor placed at the bow and one at the stern will keep the boat directly in line with or parallel to the structure. Sometimes just being a few feet away from the edge of a structure can mean the difference between lots of action and none at all.

Once you're over a good location, set up a chum slick using chum that's appropriate for the targeted species. Fill a chum pot or other suitable container and lower it overboard on a line that is tied securely to a cleat. If you're after bottom feeders, lower the chum container right to the bottom. Jostle it occasionally, and it will gradually release food particles, creating a scent that will attract fish to the vicinity of your hooks or lures. The chum slick will cause many types of fish to gather, including some undesirable species. Chumming can also be useful when fishing from jetties and docks, to bring the fish closer to you. Everyone fishing near you will benefit from your chum slick, but that's probably a good thing.

If you're using live or dead natural bait, place it on the hook and allow it to descend with the weight of the sinker to the bottom. Most terminal tackle for bottom fishing is designed to allow the bait to float freely a few inches off the bottom—just what many predators think looks like a good, easy meal—and out of the reach of crabs. A sinker is needed to keep the baited hook on or near the bottom and prevent it from drifting out of the fish's reach. Too much weight will interfere with your ability to feel the fish, so use weights that are just heavy enough to hold a position against the force of the current.

As long as there are no rocks or other debris on the bottom, you can use a swivel and a second hook without worrying about them getting hung up. But when fishing over structure, terminal rigs should be kept simple to prevent hang-ups. Remember to replace your bait at least every 15 to 20 minutes because it loses its scent in the water.

Select live bait based on the kind of baitfish found in the vicinity, although anchovies, killifish, and eel will work in most places. Check live bait every so often to see that it's still alive, and replace it if it's not.

Fishing with a lure is a different game. After casting it a distance from the boat, you must jig it with the motion of the rod along the bottom and up the water column to the surface. Jigging makes the lure behave like a live baitfish in distress. Raise the lure about a foot off the bottom at various speeds and let it fall back. Make sure the lure passes through the chum slick during the retrieval process. You can experiment with the speed of retrieval until you get satisfactory results.

Most bottom-dwelling fish try to stay on the bottom when hooked. This usually makes it easy to keep tension on the line. But once you begin to raise the fish off the bottom, you must prevent it from heading back down, where it may tangle the line around structure. If the fish heads toward you, reel in the line quickly to maintain tension. Don't allow the line to go slack.

At times, a fish may travel beneath the boat or run along its side. If this happens aboard a party boat, it can be difficult to maintain tension on the line while following the fish around the boat and avoiding other anglers. A mate can be helpful in clearing a path. Most party boat anglers are accustomed to this and will try to stay out of your way, although the process is bound to become confusing and can be almost comical to watch.

Bottom Fishing in Surf

Bottom fishing in the surf with natural bait requires a few technique changes. Most of the targeted fish here are roaming predators who respond well to a *fish-finder rig*, which consists of a sinker and a free-moving baited hook. The sinker holds the baited hook near but not on the bottom, allowing the hook to drift above the reach of crabs and preventing the fish from feeling the weight of the sinker when the fish takes the bait.

Bucktail lures are also useful when seeking bottom-feeding predator fish in the surf, as long as pork rind or a squid strip is added to the hook for additional action. Also consider using sinking or popper plugs. Work or jig these toward the beach during retrieval to generate plenty of action and noise.

See Chapter 16 for more on surf fishing.

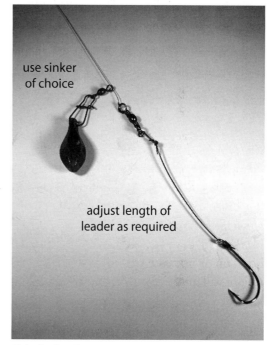

use sinker of choice

adjust length of leader as required

Fish-finder rig.

JETTY FISHING

Jetties, or breakwaters, are man-made structures, usually consisting of large but loosely fitted rocks or concrete slabs. Their numerous nooks and crannies below the surface harbor abundant plant growth that attracts small baitfish. Currents in, around, and through all the little spaces force the baitfish into the open, and this attracts various predator fish looking for an easy meal. Jetties also house crabs, mussels, and barnacles, which attract crustacean feeders such as tautog and sheepshead. And because jetties disturb the normal flow of alongshore currents, sandbars and sloughs often form in their immediate vicinity. (A slough, pronounced "sloo," is a gully along the sea bottom.) Like other forms of shelter, sandbars and sloughs also attract fish. Because jetties can be so productive, some anglers prefer jetty fishing above all other types.

Rock jetty.

Jetty fishing can be hazardous, however. Because of a jetty's rough construction, the walking surface is usually uneven, and it's easy to step into a deep gap between stones or slabs if you aren't paying attention to where you're walking. Jetties can also be quite slippery, so it's advisable to wear cleats or Korkers. And storm conditions—even storms that are hundreds of miles away—produce waves that can knock you down or sweep you into the water. When the waves are washing near or over the top of a jetty, it's best to stay away.

An 8- to 10-foot spinning rod with a matching spinning reel will give you sufficient power to cast beyond the rocks at the base of a jetty. Avoid using snap swivels, two-hook rigs, and complex rigs, such as the fish-finder rig, which can get hung up easily on structure and on the rock and mussel beds often located on the bottom nearby. If you must use a swivel to prevent twist in the main line, use a barrel swivel, which is less prone to hang-ups. Sometimes, however, hang-ups are unavoidable, so don't risk your most expensive sinking or deep-diving lures when you're jetty fishing.

When reeling in, keep the tip of the rod high, and reel in the rig as fast as possible to prevent the hook and sinker from snagging on rocks below the surface. This applies to artificial lures too. If you're using dead natural bait, reel it in at least every 15 to 20 minutes to replace it. If you're using live bait, check periodically to make sure it's still alive.

Jetties are also a good place for fly fishing; see Chapter 17 for details.

There is rarely any satisfactory place to set down your fishing rod on a jetty. As long as your hook is in the water, you'll have to keep the rod in your hands. The moment you set it down is probably the moment when a fish will take your bait—and your rod and reel along with it.

There are some big, powerful predator fish that frequent jetties, and some pretty strong smaller ones, too. Be ready to set the hook as soon as the fish takes it. You will feel a sudden jerk or a steady tug, and you may see some bouncing at the end of the line depending on the size and type of fish. Pull the rod back over your head and begin to reel in, keeping slack out of the line. If the fish is a strong fighter, you may feel a lot of resistance. Avoid the temptation to adjust the reel's drag during a fight. Hopefully, you've set it correctly beforehand. If not, live with it and fight the fish as best you can.

Once hooked, most fish try to head away from the structure and into open water. Actually this is helpful, because it makes it easier to keep tension on the line. Bad things happen if the fish heads toward the jetty: the line can go slack, get tangled on the structure, or be cut by a sharp-edged rock. Keep the tip of the rod as high as possible to prevent the line from tangling in the structure, and reel in quickly to prevent any slack from developing. The fish will eventually tire out, and you'll be able to reel it all the way in.

DOCK AND PIER FISHING

Dock or pier fishing is similar to jetty fishing but with fewer hazards. Although some docks and piers are on exposed ocean shoreline, most are in protected areas such as bays, and the walking surface tends to be safe, level, and regular. Some piers are intended specifically for fishing; others offer boat docking space, rod and reel rentals, bait and tackle shops, gift shops, restaurants, and rest rooms. Some of the latter prohibit fishing (or, indeed, any use by unauthorized personnel), whereas others welcome it.

Designated fishing piers can be several hundred feet long, providing access to deeper water than is possible when fishing directly from the shore. As such, they are a good option if you are "boatless." Some of these designated fishing piers are public facilities; others are privately owned and charge a fee for access. Fees are usually low and in most cases worth the cost.

The wooden stilts or concrete pillars that support a pier create alternating, frequently shifting areas of calm and turbulent or swirling

Pier fishing.

Dock fishing. Notice that the angler is at a safe distance from the edge.

water. Currents moving by piers carry plankton past the pilings, attracting small baitfish to seek shelter and food within the calm areas. Meanwhile, alert predator fish keep position nearby, feeding on any baitfish that stray too far from shelter or are injured while foraging and are carried out by current flow or wave action.

Remember that tides influence the feeding habits of fish (ebb and flood tides are the best times to catch fish), and plan your fishing accordingly. Of course, good anglers know this, so some piers can get very crowded. The far ends of piers, usually located over deeper water, fill up first. Get to the pier as early as possible to secure a good spot. When on a pier, look for sandbars and sloughs, and fish these areas for predator fish as you would in the surf. Be careful when casting to avoid hooking fellow anglers and passersby.

Only a modest amount of gear is required for pier fishing, and there is no "typical" equipment. A wide variety of fish is found along piers, including bottom and surface feeders, so decide what kind of fish you're after, and choose your equipment accordingly. A spinning reel and a medium-action rod from 6½ to 8 feet long will suffice for most outings. Use monofilament line between 15- and 30-pound test, depending on the species. Cut natural bait is the most popular, but artificial lures such as bucktail jigs can also be productive. If there is a bait and tackle shop on or near the pier, stop and ask about the best spots on the pier, the prevalent species, and the most successful baits, rigs, and techniques.

Docks or piers that are closer to the water lend themselves to landing the fish with a net or gaff; on high piers, land the fish by simply reeling it in. With its weight supported entirely by the hook and line, the fish must be well hooked. In spite of precautions, though, fish often manage to free themselves as soon as they're lifted out of the water.

Pier fishing is not physically taxing, but piers can be long. This should discourage you from bringing excess tackle, although some anglers bring carriages or carts of various types to haul large loads. Coolers with wheels are ideal for pier fishing. In addition to keeping your catch (and lunch and beverages) cold, they provide a good place to sit. Some anglers even bolt a rod holder to their cooler to provide a good place to set the rod.

As with jetty fishing, most fish that are hooked from piers try to head away from the structure and toward open water. Of course, not every fish is so accommodating, and some will do the opposite. Maintain tension on the line, and keep the fish from swimming beneath the pier, where the line can easily become tangled or cut. But don't hang over the edge of the dock or pier. No fish is worth a swim—much less a headfirst meeting with the sea bottom.

DRIFTING

Drifting is a fishing method in which the boat is allowed to move freely with the wind or current over likely fish concentrations. Drifting can be considered another form of bottom fishing, differing only in that the baited hook or lure is constantly moving along the bottom.

Most of the time, you play or jig a baited hook or lure directly off the bottom, where most fish dwell. Drifting is therefore often referred to as sinker bouncing. But you can actually present the bait or lure at any depth, depending on where the fish are swimming in the water column. The terminal rig usually consists of a three-way swivel, which allows the sinker leader, hook leader, and main line to be attached at a single location. The height of the hook is

Drifting for fluke.

determined by the length of the sinker leader on the terminal rig, and the hook is allowed to trail 36 to 48 inches behind.

Chumming and chunking are both highly productive when you're drifting. Before you begin, it's important to know—through observation, word of mouth, or fishing reports—that fish are likely to be in the vicinity. Place a marker buoy, tethered by a long line to a heavy sinker, where you intend to start your drift. Then distribute your chum. After drifting for 100 feet or so, return to the starting point and drift again through the slick.

As with other forms of bottom fishing, most hooked fish want to head back down toward the bottom. Don't let them. Keep the line tight, keep the rod pointing in the direction of the fish, and continually try to reel it in. Don't let the line run along the side of the boat; the line is bound to get snagged and break.

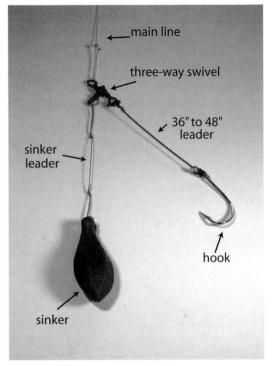

Typical drifting rig.

TROLLING

Trolling is superficially similar to drifting in that it involves a boat moving over the bottom. But whereas a drifted boat moves slowly with the wind and current, a trolled boat is under power—although its movement is still a slow 2½ to 3½ miles per hour (mph). And whereas drifting is a form of bottom fishing, trolling places the bait or lure anywhere from mid-depths to the water's surface.

From the lure or bait's motion through the water, predatory fish are fooled into the impression that it is live prey. Trolling is therefore a common and productive big-game fishing technique, although it also works well for many smaller inshore predators. Most types of boats can be used for trolling, but those with rod holders or outriggers make the work easier (for more on outriggers, see below). It can be tiring to hold a rod that's dragging a heavy lure for mile after mile.

The objective is to have the lure appear as natural as possible when it's moving through the water. It should move like a swimming or injured fish, not skip along the water surface or wallow around unnaturally. Because lure performance is affected by boat speed, current, waves, and wind, this can require nearly constant adjustments to the boat's throttle, the height of the rod tip, and the amount of line you let out.

You can observe the action of lures at various speeds by dragging them in the water next to the boat. After you see what speed works well for a particular lure, let out the appropriate amount of line. You will learn through experience which lures perform best at what speeds.

Boat speed should be influenced by the type of bait or lure you're using—which, of course, is determined by your target species. Most modern trolling lures, including parachute jigs, tuna feathers, umbrella rigs, and cedar plugs, are designed to function at higher trolling speeds; trolling too slowly reduces their effectiveness. Dead natural bait or cone-shaped lures work better with lower trolling speeds. Lures that have a concave front surface should be trolled slowly to make the desired popping noises; weighted lures require faster speeds to keep from sinking too deep. Because surgical tubes are slender and hard for the fish to see, they should be trolled at relatively slow speeds. If you're trolling multiple lures, the boat's speed should be appropriate to all of them, so choose lures that are compatible with one another.

Your choice of bait or lure, boat speed, and trolling pattern (that is, whether the boat moves in a circle, a straight line, or wide or shallow S-curves) should be influenced by your target species. Know your species' preferences before you begin; if you take random guesses, you probably won't catch anything.

For example, when pursuing a fast-swimming species such as albacore or bonito, which are accustomed to chasing relatively fast prey, the trolling speed should be about 5 to 7 mph; slower species, such as striped bass, cobia, and salmon, should be trolled at about 2 to 3½ mph.

While trolling in known fish locations, allow the baited hook or lure to travel 150 to 200 feet or more behind the boat. If you have a hard time estimating distance, you may be able to correlate speed with the distance between the waves in your boat's wake. For example, you may find that four wake waves equal 125 feet at 15 knots, and eight wake waves equal 250 feet at 22 knots. In rough water, increasing the distance of the hook or lure from the boat will usually put it in calmer water.

Whether you place the lure in the turbulent water of the wake or outside it depends on the species and the type of lure you're using. Rough water will give a hook more action, but it might not be realistic action, and it might make the lure harder for the game fish to see. Similar considerations come into play when deciding whether to troll directly off the stern or off to the side of the boat.

Remember, the farther away from the boat a baited hook or lure is being worked, the longer it will take to boat the fish. It's more difficult to constantly maintain line tension with longer distances, and anytime the line is allowed to go slack, there is a good chance that the fish will throw the hook.

Outriggers, which are often found on larger sportfishing boats, are long poles that put the lure or hook well out to the side of the boat. A suitable fishing rod is set into a rod holder beneath the outrigger. Line from the rod runs up to a line clip at the tip of the outrigger, and from there it goes into the water. When a fish is hooked, you take the rod from its holder, pull the line from the clip, and fight the fish in the usual manner.

Outriggers accomplish two things: they enable you to troll more lines, preventing interference with the lines that you're trolling directly behind the boat; and they place the lure into water that is undisturbed by the boat's wake. (Depending on the boat's design and speed and the prevailing water conditions, the water off to the side might be rougher or smoother than the water directly behind the boat.) While trolling, be ready to set the hook as soon as a fish is hooked. If you're holding the rod, you'll feel a sudden jerk or a steady tug. If the rod is in a rod holder, you'll see the rod tip take a sudden, deep bend that should look distinctly different from the slight, constant flex from resisting the baited hook or lure moving through the water. At this point, you should pull back on the rod so that the tip is over your head. Do this swiftly and firmly but smoothly—don't jerk it back. This will set the hook in the fish's mouth

Outriggers are the angled rods on each side of a boat.

and take in any slack that may exist. Then immediately begin to reel in the fish, and play it if necessary.

Most fish that are hooked by trolling try to head away from the resistance, which helps keep tension on the line. If a big fish is running away from the boat, the boat's speed should be reduced to avoid putting too much tension on the line. If the fish heads toward the boat, you must react quickly by reeling in the line to maintain tension, and the speed of the boat should be increased accordingly. The boat's operator should observe what's taking place to aid the angler. Many anglers and boat operators work out a series of quick, easy-to-use hand signals or voice commands as an aid to communication.

Sometimes a hooked fish will swim beneath the boat. Keeping the rod tip pointed in the direction of the fish, crank in on the reel, keep your line tight, and don't allow the line to rub against the boat's hull.

Trolling Lures

There is little hard evidence that lures of particular colors work better in certain situations, although anecdotal information, "common knowledge," and word of mouth among fellow

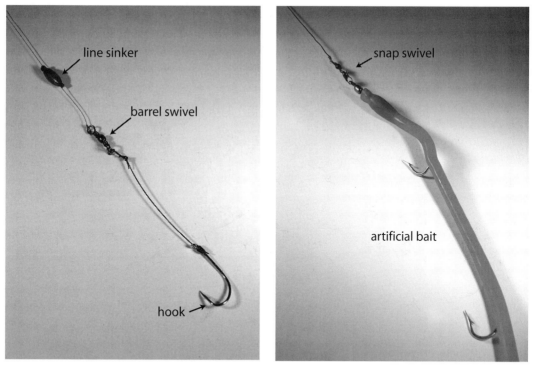

Typical natural bait trolling rig.

Typical artificial lure rig.

anglers and tackle shop owners may say otherwise. On the other hand, dark-colored lures (usually the blues, greens, and darker reds) and brightly colored ones (chartreuse, hot pink, hot red, and yellow) seem to work better than light-colored lures.

One effective lure is an umbrella rig, which resembles an opened umbrella frame without the fabric. It is designed to hold four or five hooks with surge tubes attached to the frame by approximately 8 inches of leader. To a predator fish, this looks like a small group of baitfish swimming together.

Another productive trolling lure is the parachute jig, which attracts predator fish with sound and motion. The jig hairs are designed to streamline in as the jig moves forward quickly, then blossom or flare out as the lure's speed decreases while it is allowed to settle briefly (see photos next page). The speed of the boat is critical to allow the hairs to move properly.

To use a parachute jig, stand near the stern of the boat with the rod over the side. Let out 100 to 250 feet of line, hold the tip of the rod down toward the water, and work the rod by moving it toward you and away from you, as if you're raking leaves. Make sure the line doesn't come into contact with any part of the boat. If the boat speed is right, every time you move the rod tip away from you, the jig will begin to settle and its hairs will flare out; whenever you pull it toward you, the hairs will streamline in.

Hairs on the parachute jig close when you move the jig toward you and open as you move the jig away from you. Predator fish are attracted to the noise and moving hairs as the parachute jig is being worked.

SALTWATER FLATS FISHING

Flats fishing has little in common with other forms of saltwater fishing from boats. The required equipment is a specially designed flats-fishing boat, which enables the angler to enter water as shallow as 8 to 10 inches, and very light spinning rods and reels or saltwater fly fishing gear. The common targets of saltwater flats fishing are bonefish, permit, red drum, barracuda, lemon sharks, jack crevalle, and tarpon.

Flats fishing is basically a two-person operation: one person fishes from the bow of the boat, facing forward, while the other propels the boat slowly across the flats by pushing against the sea bottom with a long push-pole. (A few types of flats boats can accommodate a second angler.) The pole operator is usually a paid fishing guide because few anglers find poling a fun alternative to actually fishing. Regardless, the poler directs the action. He or she sees the fish, maneuvers the boat toward them as close and as stealthily as possible, and tells the angler where to cast using the "clock" system (that is, twelve o'clock is straight ahead of the boat; three o'clock is to the right, etc.) and gives the angler an estimate of the distance.

CHAPTER 16

SURF FISHING

Surf fishing is possible on almost any coast, because there are always plenty of baitfish following the contours of the shoreline, and plenty of predator fish right behind them. The predators can be caught by standing on the shore and casting artificial lures or baited hooks.

Surf fishing is primarily done from sandy or pebbly beaches. Surf anglers almost have to be bird-watchers: lots of diving gulls and terns are a sure indicator of baitfish swimming close to the surface to avoid predator fish attacking from below.

Surf fishing is not as straightforward as it appears. Simply walking to the water's edge and tossing a baited hook or lure into the

Lone surf angler playing a lure.

water is not a likely scenario for success. For starters, specialized tackle is required. The surf rod and heavy-duty spinning reel must be capable of slinging 6 to 8 ounces of lead weight or fishing lure up to 75 to 100 yards, to get beyond the breaking surf (also called suds).

A multitude of specialized lures, bait, and terminal tackle is needed to make up the rigs. And some of the techniques for using these rigs are unique to surf fishing.

SURF FISHING EQUIPMENT

Here's a look at some equipment that is highly specific to surf fishing. See Part 2 for more information on basic equipment, such as rods, reels, bait, and tackle.

The surf fishing environment is an exposed one, offering little protection from sun, wind, and spray. You will need suitable apparel. For your top half, bring along a waterproof parka (I prefer the pullover type). A pair of waders will keep your feet and legs dry and warm in cold water. These watertight pants, which are worn over your regular pants, are usually chest high and supported by suspenders. It's a good idea to wear a belt snug around your waist outside of the waders. If you fall in the surf, the belt will prevent water from rapidly filling the inside of the relatively loose-fitting waders. The extra weight of that water can make it difficult or impossible to move around, or even stand up, and has been the cause of more than one drowning. One more bit of "apparel": use a finger cot to protect your finger from cuts and chafing from repeated casts.

Typical waders used for surf fishing. The design shown requires separate wading boots. On other models, the boots are attached to the bottom of the legs. (Courtesy Patagonia, Inc.)

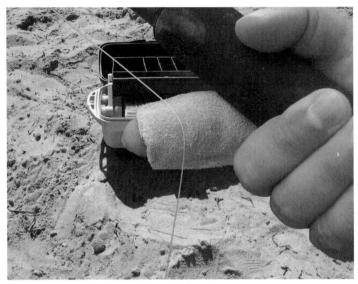

A finger cot protects against cuts and chafing.

Sand Spikes

A sand spike holds the rod and reel in a vertical position, keeping it off the sand while you change terminal tackle or bait your hooks. You will need a sand spike for every rod you bring. Never place the rod and reel on sand, which will play havoc with the internal workings of your reel. Don't use the sand spike to support a hooked fish—it may fall over with that much weight and thrashing.

Longer sand spikes are more effective for holding the line above the waves in higher surf, which is useful when you're bottom fishing with natural bait and want the rig to remain stationary on the bottom—not to mention that you don't have to hold the rod for extended periods.

Shorter sand spikes are better when you're fishing with lures, since you'll be casting and retrieving constantly to impart the desired movement to the lure. In this instance, the only time you'll use the sand spike is when you're changing tackle.

Two surf rods supported by sand spikes.

Sand spikes can be homemade from PVC pipe with an inside diameter large enough to accept the butt end of the rod. Cutting one end of the pipe at a sharp angle makes it easier to pound it into the sand (with a block of wood, a rubber mallet, or a handy rock or piece of driftwood) when you reach your destination.

Tackle

Two rods can be helpful when surf fishing with bait—to double the chances for a strike and to test different baits. Most surf anglers use no more than two rods at a time. Longer rods can throw the terminal tackle farther, making it easier to cast past higher surf and keep the line from being tossed about by the surf following the cast. A 9- to 10-foot rod with medium action is satisfactory for most low surf conditions. Higher surf may require a rod in the 12- to 14-foot range.

If the bottom is rocky, taller rods also help keep the fishing line clear of the bottom to minimize abrasion on the retrieve. Nevertheless, a rocky bottom calls for abrasion-resistant line.

The surf reel should be a large spinning type with a line capacity of at least 150 yards. It must have a high retrieval ratio, 4.5:1 or higher, to handle fast-swimming species, and be strong enough to handle the stresses of fighting heavy, powerful fish.

In calm conditions, pyramid or storm sinkers of about 4 to 6 ounces are usually sufficient to hold bottom. When the surf is strong, heavier sinkers are needed to keep the baited hook from moving with the surf. It can take a lot of muscle and a two-handed cast to fling that much sinker—plus the weight of the bait and rig—100 yards or farther into the surf.

Surf Bait

As always, you should choose natural bait that is native to the area you're fishing and that is sought by your targeted species. Because of the rugged surf environment and the powerful casts required, select bait that is durable and will stay on the hook. This includes whole or cut squid, crabs, bloodworms or sandworms, clams, eels, smelt, anchovies, sardines, sand fleas, shrimp, and whole or cut fish, such as bunker, herring, and mackerel. Use a fish-finder rig to keep the bait off the bottom and away from crabs. Change the bait at least every 15 to 20 minutes to keep the scent fresh.

Artificial baits, including bucktail jigs and a great variety of lures, are also effective in the surf if used with some sort of jigging action. But surface-swimming lures are recommended in rocky areas, where baited hooks could hang up and rigs could be lost.

There are deep and abiding arguments among surf fishing aficionados concerning the use of baited hooks versus lures. Some consider the use of natural bait to be a laid-back way of surf fishing, because after you've made your cast, you can allow the rig to remain on the bottom, waiting for a bite. Regardless of your feelings about being laid-back, many game fish find natural bait more appealing than lures. Then there are anglers who feel that throwing and retrieving lures is a more active method, necessitating greater skill and keeping the angler more involved in the process. The counterargument is that lures require more work, make you expend energy uselessly, and are not any more effective than natural bait—and maybe less so. Even its proponents concede that throwing a lure into the surf for hours at a time can be fatiguing.

The bottom line is that although natural baits have a higher catch ratio, both methods can be productive, and the choice is a matter of personal preference. You can have fun either way.

Beach Buggies

Four-wheel-drive vehicles have become popular with surf anglers to carry tackle and their catch. Most coastal states allow these vehicles on beaches with special permits, which are usually purchased from state park or environmental departments. Four-wheel-drive pickup trucks, SUVs, and even motor homes can be used as "beach buggies" and can be equipped with a plethora of special equipment to make fishing more convenient.

In fact, most states impose equipment requirements, most of them related to safety or environmental protection. These vary by state but may include approved tires, a spare tire, a portable air pump or properly charged air tanks for inflating the tires, a tire pressure gauge, a suitable jack and jack board, a shovel, a tow chain or rope, and a self-contained portable toilet. As with fishing licenses, a current beach vehicle permit must be available for viewing by law enforcement personnel upon request.

Other useful equipment and supplies include a cell phone, a CB radio, a fire extinguisher, a tool kit, a flashlight, a first-aid kit, garbage bags, at least a gallon of fresh water, and—especially—rod racks. A large cooler can be carried on the front bumper on a special platform commonly referred to as the front porch (but be aware that this can interfere with the flow of cooling air to the radiator).

"Front porch" containing cooler and rod rack.

ROD RACKS FOR YOUR BEACH BUGGY

Because surf rods are so long, special attention must be given to transporting them conveniently and safely. Commercially made roof-mounted rod racks are readily available; ski racks also work well.

With a little ingenuity, you can make your own rod racks. Some pickup owners install a wooden frame over the bed that is high enough to clear the cab roof, and add PVC tubing and/or household broom or utility clips to hold the rods in place. PVC tubing can also be mounted vertically on the front or rear bumper or the front porch, although, depending on the length of your rods, this can make for very high clearance. Be aware of the chances of theft, and don't leave your rods and reels unlocked on the rack.

Rod roof rack on a four-wheel-drive SUV.

To protect the vehicle against the effects of sand and salt, rinse the vehicle (including the undercarriage) with fresh water after your beach excursion. Use a hose, take the vehicle to a car wash, or place a lawn sprinkler beneath the vehicle and let it run for several minutes. Consider having an aftermarket anticorrosion coating applied to the undercarriage and body of the vehicle.

READING THE SURF

Most surf looks the same at first glance, but fishing success depends on finding places at the surf that look a little different. It's up to you to "read" the surf—to locate variations in the shape of the bottom; the presence of sandbars, sloughs, and rocks; the effects of jetties on wave action; and the state of the tide. All of these factors influence the presence of fish.

Even after you've found the good spots, you still have to be a student of the surf. Currents and tides constantly change the shape of the coastline, altering sandbars and sloughs, and causing bottom conditions to change on a daily basis. Experience—knowing how past tides and storms have influenced the surf—makes the task easier, but direct observation of prevailing conditions is required every time you go surf fishing.

Sandbars

A sandbar is a raised area on the bottom of the sea consisting of sand, shells, and other natural debris. Sandbars can be just a foot or two high, or rise 12 feet or more off the bottom; they can remain submerged or be exposed at low or high tide. They can be just a few yards long or extend for miles parallel to shore. Although usually gradually sloped, they can have sharp drop-offs on one side, or they can be an exposed extension of the beach or isolated from it by an expanse of water. Sandbars are constantly changing, creating difficulties as well as opportunities for anglers.

An angler can easily locate sandbars by observing the surf, seeking places where the waves crest and break offshore. These waves will not run up directly onto the beach but instead will subside in the deeper water between the sandbar and the beach. The waves will break a second time on the beach itself. Arriving at the beach at dead low tide is another way to identify sandbars, many of which are exposed at low water.

Although sandbars often run parallel to the beach, jetties or other structures alter the direction of alongshore currents and can cause them to deposit sand in other places.

Now that you know how to find a sandbar, you also know how to find a slough—and that's where you'll find fish.

Notice the breaking waves on the left side of the jetty, indicating the presence of a sandbar.

Sloughs

Sloughs are depressions in the sea bottom that surround sandbars, jetties, and other structures. Sloughs are created by the accelerated speed of the current running past these obstructions. Because sloughs provides shelter for small baitfish, they serve as a magnet for predator fish.

Action in sloughs is influenced by the state of the tide. When tidal currents are strong, the baitfish take shelter there, which attracts predator fish. During slack tide, when currents are weak or absent, baitfish come out to forage, becoming dispersed over a larger area and reducing the concentration of game fish. Consequently, for about an hour on either side of full high and full low tide, fishing will be slow or even futile. The duration of slack tide varies considerably by region.

When the tide changes, the action picks up. If it's an ebb tide, baitfish will seek shelter from the current in the slough on the "outside" of the sandbar—that is, the side farthest from the beach. That's also where you'll find the predators, and that's where you should place your rig. On a flood tide, work the "inside" slough—the one on the beach side of the sandbar.

In addition to observable sandbars and sloughs, birds are an excellent indicator of good surf fishing potential. Predator fish frequently force baitfish to the surface, where they become prime targets for feeding seabirds, including gulls, terns, and pelicans. Thick clusters of birds may give the sky the appearance of an impending storm. The birds will be flying and diving in a seemingly haphazard manner above the baitfish. Don't concern yourself with a passing bird or two; but if a feeding frenzy is going on, try to duplicate the baitfish that the birds are pursuing, and cast your lure or baited hook into the general vicinity. The action can be fast and furious.

HOW TO FISH THE SURF

Before setting out for your first surf fishing experience, review the surf fishing safety tips outlined on pages 14–15.

There is a tendency to wade into the water to achieve longer-distance casts. Be careful. Avoid strong waves and currents, which can undermine your footing and pull you down, and stay out of deep water. If you must wade in the surf, wear a PFD.

Always be ready to set the hook. Many targeted surf species are strong enough to pull down a poorly set sand spike and drag your rod right into the water. If you're using a baited hook and the rod is supported by a properly hammered sand spike, you'll see the tip of the rod bend with a quick, erratic motion. Alert bells (see pages 23, 24) will help draw your attention should you be momentarily distracted. If you're fishing with lures, you'll feel a sudden jerk of the rod or a steady tug on the line.

As soon as you think there's a fish on the line, pull back gently on the rod to confirm the strike and set the hook. (If necessary, remove the rod from the sand spike first.) Then begin to reel in the line.

When hooked, most fish try to head out to sea, which will help you keep tension on the line. If the fish instead heads toward the beach, you must crank in line quickly to prevent slack from developing. The moment slack enters the line, the fish can turn around and gather enough speed to snap the line—if it doesn't simply throw the hook before that.

Although the fish may be strong and put up a battle, the reel's drag system should be working properly, paying out line when necessary to avoid breakage. When the fish eventually tires, it will be easier for you to reel it in. When you've gotten the fish near the beach, place a hand into its gill to lift and carry it from the water. Avoid the temptation to wade in too far—you could lose your footing and lose the fish you've worked so hard to land.

"Good" fishing areas can be ephemeral, and sometimes fish won't bite even in a perfect-looking slough. Water salinity might also play a role, as can water temperature or adverse currents. Or maybe there are simply no fish in the area.

Most surf fishing anglers who use natural bait spend a good deal of time (about an hour) at one location, because the targeted species are roaming predators who may come along at any point. Anglers who use lures usually give it 30 to 60 minutes before moving to another location.

Crowded Beaches

Anglers tend to congregate in areas of known productivity or in areas with sandbars or other structure. At times, beaches may be crowded with surf anglers fishing nearly elbow to elbow.

Crowds increase the chance of tangling lines or being hooked by another angler's stray cast so try to avoid them. By arriving at the beach early in the morning, you may get in a few good hours of uncongested fishing (choose a day when the tides are cooperative). If you must fish in a crowd, stay even with or in line with the other anglers on the beach, and make your casts parallel to the casts of others to avoid tangles. Check around you before casting, and always make overhead casts in crowded situations. By following these few simple guidelines, you and your fellow anglers can fish together pleasantly and safely, even in close proximity.

CHAPTER 17

SALTWATER FLY FISHING

Saltwater fly fishing, almost unknown a few years ago, has recently become extremely popular. It offers new challenges to experienced anglers and, like freshwater fly fishing, has the reputation of being the "thinking man's" method of fishing. I'm not sure that saltwater fly anglers are really any more intelligent, creative, or reflective than their spin-fishing colleagues, but one thing is certain: it's a totally different sport, requiring different equipment and techniques.

Saltwater flies are extremely lightweight lures that imitate baitfish, insects, or crustaceans. Many of them are so light that they float on the water's surface; others are lightly weighted or are designed to become waterlogged so that they sink slowly. Flies are made from materials such as animal fur (natural or synthetic), feathers, and foam rubber cunningly tied to hooks. The whole rationale of fly fishing—the reason for the lightweight "lures"—is that they can be placed gently in the water; so gently, in fact, that there is no splash to frighten away the fish.

But because of their light weight, flies cannot be cast by the usual methods on conventional monofilament fishing line. Instead, they require a special heavyweight fly line to carry them out to their desired destination, and this special line requires a special rod and reel to cast it. Even so, casts are typically only 30 to 40 feet. Compare that to the 100-yard casts that are common in surf fishing, and you'll get the idea that saltwater fly fishing is more about refined

This fly successfully attacted several bluefish.

technique and less about power or strength—at least until you get a bite. For in spite of the lightweight equipment and the highly refined techniques required to use the equipment properly, it is possible to take fish as large and aggressive as any you'd pursue with conventional equipment—including sharks, tarpon, and tuna—in addition to smaller surface-feeding species such as red drum, striped bass, bluefish, spotted sea trout, mackerel, albacore, and bonito. And you can fly-fish almost anywhere you can use other methods: from boats on the open ocean, at the surf, or in shallow water in bays and estuaries. Another nice feature is that there's no natural bait to mess with.

Fly fishing requires greater concentration and attention to technique than most other methods, including careful control of the cast and constant work to manipulate the fly properly to convincingly imitate a live baitfish or other prey on the retrieve. Finding the fish that respond to flies also requires more work; it's not a reliable way to bring home supper. Unlike a good bottom-fishing spot, good fly fishing locations tend to be ephemeral, because surface-feeding species move around a lot more in their search for food. Once you've located two or three promising areas through word of mouth, fishing reports in the newspaper, various Internet sites (such as www.noreast.com), or the local tackle shop proprietor, give them a try, but realize that any area's productivity will vary with the time of day, the state of the tide, and the weather.

Nevertheless, you'll undoubtedly have to accept some unproductive days with fly equipment.

So maybe it really is the thinking person's method of saltwater fishing. There must be something there that makes fly aficionados among the most committed and enthusiastic anglers, in the face of having to constantly search for fish, work more while you're fishing, and put up with a higher proportion of catch-less days. What is certain is that few anglers who take up the sport go back to other methods of saltwater fishing.

EQUIPMENT

To get started in saltwater fly fishing, you need a correctly matched rod, reel, and fly-line outfit, suitable fly line, and flies—all of which are determined by the type of fly fishing you intend to do.

Fly Rods

Fly rods have come a long way since they were invented back in the 1700s. They were originally made from Calcutta cane, later from ash and other hardwoods. Nowadays a few purists insist on Tonkin bamboo rods, and pay dearly for the pleasure, but most anglers consider these to be works of art and not practical gear for serious fishing. Most modern fly rods are made from fiberglass and carbon fiber (graphite).

Saltwater fly rods range in length from 8½ to 12 feet and are designed to cast a number 7- to 15-weight line; rods using line in the 10- to 15-weight range are intended for larger species of fish. (Fly line weights are explained below.) All saltwater rod manufacturers list the weight of line that the rod is designed to cast. Good rods cost anywhere from $100 to upward of $500; the more expensive ones usually are lighter in weight and have a better strength-to-weight ratio and more generous warranties. If you're just starting out, you should invest no more than $100 for a decent 8½- to 10-foot rod until you decide whether saltwater fly fishing is for you.

Different rod weights and actions are available. Weight issues are about the same as with conventional spinning equipment (basically, use heavier, stiffer rods for bigger fish). If you have no experience with any form of fly fishing, you may want to take some lessons from a competent fly caster who can coach you in each of the casting strokes and help you select the proper action for your casting style. Go to a well-stocked fly tackle shop and test-cast the various rods that meet your requirements in length, line type, weight, and price. You should always test-cast any fly rod before buying it.

When you complete a cast, there should be very little bounce at the rod tip. Bounce introduces waves into the line that you've so carefully cast out, reducing the distance of the cast. Better rod blanks dampen this vibration more effectively.

Fly rods are available in two, three, or four pieces. Two-piece rods are the most common and least expensive; three- and four-piece rods are convenient if you travel frequently.

Most modern fly rods have an adequate number of line guides spaced at good intervals along the rod blank. (One guide per foot of rod length is a good rule of thumb.) The guides are located closer to the blank than on spinning rods to guide the line in a straight line as it shoots out during the forward cast. The common snake guide design, which is like a small section of a helix rather than a full circle, is lightweight and rugged. The two guides closest to the reel seat, however, should be large ceramic rings to avoid excessive line resistance.

Shorter rods allow for faster casts; longer ones let you cast for longer distances. Of course, light weight is always a benefit. A good choice for a beginner is a 9- to 10-foot medium-action graphite fly rod. This will allow you to pursue spotted sea trout, red drum, bluefish, dolphin, albacore, bonito, mackerel, and many other species.

Fly Reels

Most saltwater fly reels cost between $35 and $500; $100 will buy you one of good quality, with a good drag system and sufficient line capacity for most uses. Good-quality reels are made from stainless steel, titanium, anodized aluminum, and/or fiber-resin composites; they have brass or bronze components, and ball bearings as opposed to bushings.

Two basic designs are available. A single-action reel turns the spool one revolution for each turn of the handle; a multiplying reel multiplies each turn of the handle by a factor of two or three at the spool. Although a single-action reel is more durable and significantly lighter, a multiplying reel makes it easier to maintain a tight line when fighting larger fish that make long runs. Thus, for saltwater fly fishing, the multiplying type is the better choice.

Another distinction is between direct-drive versus anti-reverse models. In a direct-drive reel, the handle turns "backward" as a fish takes out line. In an anti-reverse reel, the handle remains stationary. Most anglers who go after large, fast-running fish prefer the anti-reverse reel

Fly reels. (Courtesy Pure Fishing America)

to avoid hand injuries from the fast-spinning reel handle. Anglers who pursue smaller fish often value the ability to manually let out line in a highly controlled fashion with the direct drive. In some reels, the rim of the spool extends above the frame, allowing the angler to palm the rim for a kind of manual assist to the reel's mechanical drag system.

None of these distinctions is mutually exclusive. Single-action and multiplying-action models are available in direct- and anti-reverse drives, and all are available with (and many without) rim control in addition to or in lieu of a drag system.

The reel's capacity is determined by the diameter and the width of the spool. Select a reel that is capable of holding the amount and type of line plus backing (see below) that you intend to use.

Fly Line

Between the fly and the reel is the line. But wait—it's not that simple. There are actually four lengths of line—each with distinct characteristics and purposes—tied end to end. Starting at the fly, they are the leader, the tippet, the fly line proper, and the backing. Henceforth in this discussion, any reference to "fly line" means the third component—the fly line proper. That's pretty complicated all by itself. Now pay attention, because this discussion proceeds in order of importance, not the order on the rod mentioned above. First, the fly line proper.

Fly line is usually sold in 90- to 115-foot lengths. The immense variability in fly line design and performance is designated by a series of three groups of letters and numbers, such as WF-8-F. The first letter or pair of letters indicates the line's taper; the number in the middle indicates its weight; and the final letter or pair of letters describes its density (how it sinks or floats).

Taper

Taper primarily determines how a fly line casts. Four types of taper are available: level taper, double taper, weight forward, and shooting taper.

Level (L) taper line has a constant diameter along its entire length.

Double taper (DT) line is thin at the ends and thicker in the middle. Neither L or DT line casts well and neither is recommended for saltwater fly fishing.

Weight-forward (WF) taper line allows you to cast greater distances. This line is tapered at both ends, but not symmetrically as with DT line. It tapers up to its maximum diameter close to the fly end, then about 30 feet back it quickly tapers down to a thin shooting line. WF line is good for saltwater fly fishing.

Shooting taper (ST) line is similar to weight-forward line, but the taper back to the shooting line is more gradual. Designed for distance casting, this is also a good saltwater fly fishing line.

Weight or Strength

Fly line strength is not measured in pound test as conventional fishing line is. Instead, a scale of 1 to 15 is used, with the higher numbers indicating larger diameter and, presumably, greater strength. Line suitable for saltwater fishing ranges from 8 to 15 weight.

Density

Density refers to the line's flotation characteristics. Five types are available: floating, sink tip, intermediate, sinking, and fast sinking.

Floating (F) line floats along its entire length. It cannot be cast great distances, but it makes lifting the fly off the water relatively easy. Floating line is easy to cast, and it works well even for subsurface fishing; the weight of the leader pulls the fly down, and the line's flotation makes retrieval easy.

Sink-tip (ST) line allows the first 10 to 30 feet of the line to sink while the remainder floats. This carries the fly below the surface but still allows for an easy retrieve.

Intermediate (I) line sinks uniformly along its entire length at a slow rate. This type of line is ideal for submerging the fly just below the surface and keeping it at a fairly constant depth. Beginners often find this line more difficult to handle, however.

Sinking (S) line sinks at a moderately fast and uniform rate; it is used for fishing at somewhat deeper, but still controlled, depths. Rates for individual lines range from 2 to 10 inches per second and are listed on the packaging. Sinking line is more difficult to lift from the water than intermediate line.

Fast-sinking (FS) line sinks like a rock and is used for fishing in deep water, making this the line of choice for many saltwater species. As with sinking line, the rate of sinking is listed on the package. Fast-sinking line is the most difficult to lift from the water and should be avoided by beginners.

Sinking and fast-sinking lines have a smaller diameter than floating line, making them less affected by wind and easier to cast on windy days.

Leader

Between the fly and the tippet is the leader, whose purpose is the same as in conventional spin fishing: to guard against bite-offs and to visually isolate the lure (in this case, the fly) from the more visible tippet and fly line. The longer the leader, the farther away the fly will be from the bulky, easily seen fly line and therefore the less likely the fish are to see it and become spooked.

Leader strength is measured like conventional fishing line, with 10- to 20-pound test being the most useful choices for saltwater fishing. Leader tapers in diameter, starting thicker at the fly line end and becoming thin at the tippet end. Longer leaders (8 to 10 feet) are recommended for use with floating or intermediate (slow sinking) lines; shorter leaders (3 to 4 feet) are preferred for use with sinking or sink-tip lines. Some anglers use a simple rule of thumb instead, choosing leaders that are one and a half

FLY LINE COLORS

Fly line is manufactured in a variety of colors ranging from somber brown to bright yellow, fluorescent green, and orange. Fish do not distinguish color as humans do. Because the ability of fish to see the line in the water is often critical for fly fishing, brightly colored lines may be preferred.

Yet some anglers prefer dark colors for sinking lines on the assumption that fish are less likely to see them. This is debatable, because in most cases the fish approach the fly from below, and darker line may show up better than light-colored line against the sky. No good answers here: you pays your money and takes your chances.

times longer than their fly rod. For example, if they have an 8-foot rod, they use a 12-foot leader.

Most fish are not especially line shy, and monofilament leader is suitable for most uses. However, for sharp-toothed fish, it's important to use a wire leader.

Tippet

Fly line cannot be spliced, and because of its complicated taper, any breakage means complete replacement—at a cost of $20 or more. So the tippet, which is 18 to 24 inches long, is tied between the leader and the fly line and serves as a bit of sacrificial line to protect the valuable fly line. Should the fish break or bite through the leader, it's easy to retie a new fly to the tippet.

Most tippets are monofilament or fluorocarbon line; special wire that can take a knot is used for sharp-toothed fish. Tippets are identified by a numeral plus an X, with lower numbers indicating thicker tippets. Because of the large flies used in the saltwater environment, saltwater anglers tend to use thick tippets with low numbers—2X, 1X, or 0X. But the numbers are not entirely standardized among manufacturers, so it's often more practical to look carefully at the package to learn the tippet's actual pound-test strength. For a 6-weight rod, use a 6-pound-test tippet; for a 10-weight rod, use a 9- to 11-pound-test tippet; for a 14-weight rod, use a 12- to 15-pound-test tippet.

Backing

Backing is used on all fly fishing reels to provide the additional length of line needed if the fish takes a run. A minimum of 150 yards of backing is typical. Backing is tied to the reel spool with an arbor knot, and the fly line is tied to the backing with an improved blood knot. See Chapter 12 for how to tie these knots.

Most backing is made of Dacron, which stretches about 5 to 10 percent. Gel-spun line has a better strength-to-weight ratio than Dacron, permitting the use of thinner line and allowing greater lengths to be packed onto the reel spool. Dacron line in the 20- to 30-pound-test range is sufficient for small and most moderately sized saltwater fish. Large species, such as tuna, tarpon, and shark, may require a gel-spun line as heavy as 80-pound test.

Knots

The expense of saltwater fly fishing demands that each and every knot be strong and slip resistant. The weakest links in fly tackle are the leader and the points at which the diameter of the fly line and leader are at a minimum. Because fly line cannot be spliced, as conventional monofilament can, you should replace the entire length of line if you see any signs of wear.

Here are the knots most often used for saltwater fly fishing. They are detailed in Chapter 12.

- **Arbor knot:** used to attach the backing to the reel spool
- **Double surgeon's knot:** used to connect the leader to the much heavier tippet

- **Improved clinch knot:** also used to attach the leader to the tippet, and to attach the fly to the tippet
- **Simplified blood knot:** used to attach a like-diameter leader and tippet

Flies

There are well over a thousand fly patterns used for saltwater fly fishing, and no one can say with confidence which fly works best for a particular species of fish. Furthermore, what works well today may not work tomorrow, for fish are constantly responding to changes in their food supply. Start by studying your target species and understanding their feeding habits; browse through other books on fly fishing; and pursue word-of-mouth knowledge in your area. Collect many different ideas and opinions, then buy a variety of flies, and try each one until you find what works.

Flies can be expensive, however. To help keep costs down, many serious fly anglers learn to tie the fly patterns that they find successful. Fly tying is also a way to stay involved in fly fishing during the off-season. Some anglers find it as fascinating and engrossing a hobby as fishing itself. Of course, special fly-tying equipment and materials are needed, so it may take you a while to realize any savings from tying your own flies. The gear can be purchased at many well-stocked tackle shops and online, and many books are available on the subject.

Stripping Basket

One more piece of equipment bears mention here: the stripping basket. It is strapped to your waist, and line is stripped from the reel directly into the basket in a neat coil. The basket holds the line loosely while you repeatedly whip your rod backward and forward, allowing you to get the line airborne. The basket is not essential—many anglers simply drop the stripped line on the beach or in the water—but most find it helpful in preventing the line from getting tangled on rocks, weeds, or their own feet.

Small, inexpensive laundry basket used as a stripping basket.

FLY CASTING

The technique for throwing a fly is entirely unlike that of casting conventional lures or bait, because in fly fishing the weight of the line must carry the fly to its destination, not vice versa.

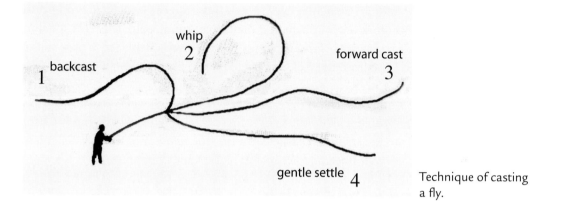

Technique of casting a fly.

A series of backcasts and forward casts is necessary to free enough line from the reel to get the fly where you want it. Just before beginning the first backcast, pull 5 to 10 feet of line from the reel, straight out and down, letting it rest on the water or beach or in a stripping basket.

To begin the backcast, quickly lift the tip of the rod in back of your shoulder. Stop the tip of the rod abruptly at about the eleven o'clock position; the momentum of the whip should pull the line from the stripping basket up into the air. Then cast forward, bringing the rod tip to about the two o'clock position.

While the line is still airborne and just before the forward cast, peel additional line from the reel with the line hand (that is, the hand not holding the rod). Repeat backcasts and forward casts until a sufficient length of line has been placed in the air, then take one more forward cast and allow the line and fly to settle gently onto the water.

Needless to say, with all this line whipping around in the air, accidents can happen. Always check around you before beginning a cast to make sure that no one is in the danger zone.

Attracting and Fighting the Fish

Always cast a fly well past where fish are suspected to be. Let the fly settle a bit, perhaps moving with the wind and current, or wait until it sinks to the depth desired, then begin the retrieve with your line hand by pulling in line from near the line guide closest to the reel. As you pull in the line, allow it to fall into the stripping basket. Keep the fly in motion, varying the pulls from about an inch to a foot long in quick intervals, along with a few subtle pauses. This irregular motion is the most tantalizing and effective way to attract a fish, regardless of depth. Retrieve the fly past the area where you suspect the fish are located.

Maintain a low rod tip angle and a relatively tight, straight line. Work the line with your line hand rather than the reel.

When the fish strikes the fly, set the hook by jerking sharply on the line with your line hand. If there is excess line in the basket, allow the fish to run, limiting its speed by applying resistance with your line hand until the basket is empty. Release the line in short bursts to avoid line burn on your hand. When all the line has run out from the basket, you can begin to allow the rod and reel to work on your behalf. If the fish is strong, palm the reel's spool in free spool mode to provide resistance before engaging the reel's drag system. Try to prevent the fish from taking too much line from the reel, and try to control its direction with the action of the rod.

Allow the fish to take additional line if necessary; retrieve the line when possible, always keeping a tight line. Some anglers elect not to use the reel at all when retrieving the fish, instead pulling the line into the stripping basket with the line hand until the fish is landed. Whether you use the reel or your line hand is a matter of personal preference.

Sight Casting and Blind Casting

One of the most popular methods of saltwater fly fishing is sight casting—casting the fly into waters where you can actually see the feeding fish. Sight casting can be done at the shoreline or in a boat. Polarized sunglasses are virtually a necessity, as is calm, clear water.

When baitfish are pushed shoreward by a rising tide, predator fish are sure to follow. Look for the telltale signs, such as swirling ripples, and fish tails and dorsal fins protruding from shallow water. Cast your fly toward these areas, and be prepared for a lengthy fight if you happen to hook a large predator.

The fly must be presented in front of the fish where it will see the fly float on the surface or settle slowly into the water. Accurate casting is therefore important, as is the ability to anticipate the fish's movements.

Blind casting is done when the fish cannot be seen readily, due to turbulence or sediment in the water. As you would expect, the success rate for blind casting is not as high as for sight casting because you're never entirely sure that a fish is there at all. Nonetheless, you can still look for the telltale signs that fish are present, and pay attention to other factors such as the presence of sloughs and other structure, and areas of past, known productivity.

Night Fly Fishing

Most fish avoid the shoreline during the day. The shallow water is too warm, and the environment too noisy, spooking the fish and preventing them from feeding on or near the surface. At dusk, the winds tend to calm down, the surface water begins to cool, and there is little noise. The fish head for the shallows, taking their ease after the pressures of the daylight hours. The calmness of this magic hour is soothing and comforting—for the fish and for anglers as well. When the wind dies, you will be better able to cast lightweight flies accurately, and work the fly more precisely in the water. On the other hand, sight fishing is difficult or impossible unless you happen to be fishing near streetlights. Although you should definitely have a flashlight with you, you should not shine it toward the water. The sudden appearance of light will spook the fish, and they'll vacate the premises immediately.

If you fish at night, wear some sort of waterproof footgear; waders are highly recommended. So is fishing with a buddy or two.

CHAPTER 18

56 QUICK SALTWATER FISHING TIPS

ROD AND REEL TIPS

1. When purchasing a rod, look for one with a lot of line guides. The more guides, the better the rod will perform.

2. Never purchase a fishing rod that is not comfortable to hold. Check the feel with a suitable reel in place.

3. Conventional small-diameter line guides are good for bottom fishing or trolling with up to 40- or 50-pound-test line. For heavier trolling, the entire rod should be equipped with roller guides.

4. Conventional bait-casting reels are best suited for bottom fishing, for drifting natural bait in the current, or for trolling.

5. Lubricate new fishing reels to ensure that no critical areas were overlooked at the factory. Use lightweight fishing reel grease sparingly at least once a year.

6. When you are finished fishing for the day, remember to loosen the drag on your reel.

7. After each use, rinse your rod and reel with a gentle spray of fresh water to remove salt deposits and prevent corrosion.

8. Before storing a reel for an extended period, soak it in fresh water for a couple of hours to remove salt deposits, then allow it to dry thoroughly.

9. Never place a reel directly on the sand while surf fishing. Always use a sand spike to support a surf rod and its reel to prevent the sand from damaging the reel.

10. Fishing rods can break if they're placed in a car carelessly. Never leave a rod sticking out from a car door or window, or from under a trunk lid. The rod tip is the most frequently broken part. Use a rod holder on the roof of the vehicle.

11. Never keep a fully spooled fishing reel in the trunk or glove compartment of a car for extended periods. The heat buildup will weaken the fishing line and may damage the reel.

TACKLE TIPS

12. Always use tackle and line that are in good condition to avoid failure. Discard or repair worn gear.

13. Use circle hooks whenever possible for ease of hook-up and removal. Fish seldom get these types of hooks caught in their throat.

14. Keep a hook honing stone in your tackle box to dress up the point of the hook, and a piece of oiled emery cloth to remove rust deposits from equipment.

15. Choose the lightest leader practical for the method of fishing. A heavy leader is visible to fish (and might spook them) and will affect the action of the lure or baited hook.

16. Use wire leader when fishing for sharp-toothed species.

17. Use light leader to tie your sinker to the rig when bottom fishing. If the sinker gets hung up, the leader will break and you won't lose the entire rig.

18. Always use some type of swivel to prevent the main line from twisting during the retrieve.

19. Use a barrel swivel when fishing over heavy structure.

20. Choose ball bearing swivels; they're a better investment than their cheaper counterparts.

21. Choose bucktails if you're fishing in fast current; they can also be allowed to sink for bottom fishing.

22. Improve your fishing success with diamond and bucktail jigs by placing a piece of squid, pork rind, or worm on the hook.

23. Try using silver, white, and yellow lures; these colors are productive because they mimic natural baitfish when being retrieved.

24. When fishing for bluefish in the surf, use heavy spoons or surface plugs. Use fresh bunker or butterfish baits near the bottom.

BAIT AND CHUM

25. Use ground-up bunker for chum; it also makes excellent bait if sliced. You can cut it or use it whole for striped bass, bluefish, or other predator fish.

26. Keep live saltwater baitfish away from fresh water to keep them alive.

27. When fishing for large predator fish, don't overlook whole live natural sandworms or bloodworms. They are productive throughout the fishing season.

28. To find the predators that chase baitfish, check the protected areas of inlets and jetties where baitfish seek shelter from storms and wait until the surf calms down.

29. Use whole squid or squid cut into small strips; squid is among the best baits to use for predator fish.

30. Use chum whenever you're fishing for bottom-dwelling species.

31. When fishing with natural bait, if you feel a fish but fail to hook it, reel in and rebait the hook if necessary. Chances are good that the fish managed to clean the bait from your hook.

32. Use only name-brand fishing line. Bargain-priced line and unknown brands often fail at the worst possible moment.

33. When monofilament line starts to feel rough or look dull, change it; it's no longer strong. Cut off the worn section and splice on a new section using the simple blood knot (see Chapter 12).

34. Use the improved blood knot (see Chapter 12) to splice dissimilar-diameter fishing line.

WHEN FISHING . . .

35. Always wait an extra second, or until you feel a lot of pressure, before reeling in.

36. When trying to free a line that is hung up on the bottom, don't attempt to pull the line with your hand. Instead, wrap the line around the outside of the reel or around the reel seat of the rod at least three times, then yank. You will either pull the line free from the bottom or break the line, but at least you'll prevent injuring your fingers or hand.

37. To prevent slack line above the water from developing into "belly" under windy conditions, keep the tip of the rod low and pointed toward the water. This will let you feel a strike more readily.

38. If a fish manages to foul the line on structure, slacken the line and wait until the fish swims out again, possibly freeing the line. Attempting to force the fish out by reeling in will likely result in a broken line, a lost terminal rig, and a lost fish—which may remain hooked to the structure by the fouled line.

39. When fishing in the surf, set the reel drag according to the lure being used. Use a lighter drag for surface plugs than for metal spoons, jigs, and sinking plugs. To make setting the hook easier when you're baitfishing with a sinker, set the drag tighter than you would when fishing with lures.

40. When fishing for bottom-dwelling species with natural bait, drop the tip of the rod a few inches as soon as you feel a bite. Doing this will give the fish a chance to take the hook more completely into its mouth.

41. When drifting, allow the sinker to bounce along the bottom 3 to 6 inches below a snelled hook.

42. When fishing with bait, select a sinker appropriate to the bottom composition to hold bottom effectively and avoid hang-ups.

43. When bottom fishing, use the lightest sinker possible that will still hold bottom.

44. When using jigs to fish from a boat for bottom-dwelling predator fish, lower the jig under the boat and begin to jig the lure up and down, or cast the jig away from the boat and slowly retrieve it while providing lots of action.

45. When fish are feeding on the surface, never run your boat through them. It will frighten the fish and incite them to dive. Instead, slowly run the boat about 75 feet from the edge of the feeding school, then turn off the engine and drift toward the school.

46. Never attempt to stand while fishing from a 16-foot skiff.

47. Take motion-sickness remedies before heading offshore.

48. Be courteous to your fellow anglers when fishing aboard a party boat. It will make the experience much more pleasant and productive for everyone.

49. Follow the advice of the crew on board a party boat or charter boat. The crew has a great deal of knowledge of local fish and conditions.

50. When surf fishing, always look behind and to each side of you to make sure the area is clear before you cast.

WHERE TO FISH

51. Use marine charts to locate potential fishing locations in your area. You will clearly see the dead-low-water depths, depressions along the bottom such as deep holes, inlet mouths, estuaries, and structure locations.

52. Sandbars in most inlets are good places to locate predator fish on the ebb tide.

53. Predator fish are often found in white-water areas at the surf. Work your lure or baited hook in these areas.

54. When fishing at the surf, walk along the beach and work the surf by casting several times into one area, then move to the next spot and cast again until a fish hits your line.

55. A flock of gulls or terns hovering and diving over one spot is a sign that baitfish are being chased to the surface by predator fish. Cast your lure or baited hook into the area.

56. If the birds are not landing on the water, the feeding fish are probably a sharp-toothed species such as bluefish.

PART 4

THE PAYOFF

89 POPULAR SPECIES AND HOW TO CATCH THEM

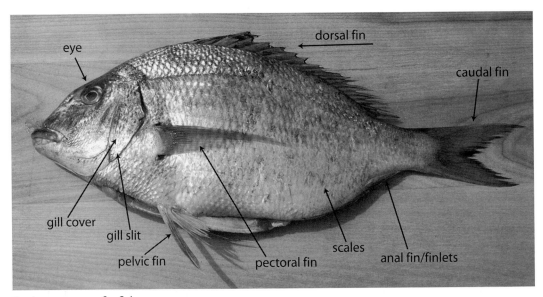

Basic anatomy of a fish.

Following are 89 species of popular game fish that may be found on one, two, or all three of America's coasts plus parts of Canada and Mexico. These species were selected by various criteria. Most of them are common enough that you'll have a good chance of finding and catching them no matter where you fish, and the majority are inshore or nearshore species that don't require large offshore sportfishing boats and special equipment to pursue. Many of them are good eating; others are just plain fun to catch.

Pay careful attention to the physical descriptions that follow, and to the appearance of the fish you catch. Little details, such as the number of spines in the dorsal fin, or the presence of certain spots or stripes on the skin, may be all that readily distinguish specific related species. Although the difference may not seem important to you, law enforcement personnel find that it can make a big difference in whether a fish is a legal catch or not.

Pay attention also to a species' spawning season. Many species come together in large numbers only to mate, so their spawning season is the only practical time to pursue them. It seems that humans aren't the only ones who get into trouble when they're on the lookout for the opposite sex.

ALMACO JACK

Almaco jack ranges from Southern California to south of Peru; it is also found in the Gulf of Mexico and the Atlantic Ocean. It has a uniform body that is amber to brown in color, lighter

Latin name
Seriola rivoliana

Best time to catch
Early spring through late fall

Also known as
Amberjack, greater amberjack, longfin, Pacific amberjack, yellowtail

toward the belly. It has a long snout, a long dorsal fin, a long anal fin, and a distinctive dark stripe running diagonally through the eyes that diminishes with age. Its caudal fin is deeply forked and ranges from dark brown to nearly black in color.

Older almaco have no stripes or bars on their head or body. Almaco are more oceanic than other amberjack species and are frequently found in open ocean rather than inshore waters. Almaco are sometimes confused with greater amberjack, lesser amberjack, and banded rudderfish, although the almaco jack has a more flattened body and a larger, more pointed compressed head.

It is believed that spawning takes place offshore at various times throughout the spring, summer, and fall, depending on the fish's location. The almaco jack found in the Atlantic reaches 1 to 2 feet in length and weighs less than 20 pounds. In the Pacific Ocean it reaches about 5 feet in length and weighs 50 to 65 pounds. In the Gulf of Mexico, almaco jack ranges from 10 to 20 feet and can reach 75 pounds.

It is a warm-water species and prefers the deep, open ocean. It inhabits deep ocean reefs and frequents offshore rocks, wrecks, and oil and gas platforms; it is not found over inshore reefs. Younger almaco jack are often found near offshore floating objects. The adults are largely nomadic while in search of food. Almaco jack feeds primarily during the daylight or evening hours on sardines, anchovies, and squid at or near the surface.

The almaco jack has excellent fighting abilities and will not give up easily when hooked. The species is not often targeted by anglers because of its small size compared to that of the greater amberjack.

As with all species of jack, almaco can be infested with tapeworms near the tail, although the affected areas can be cut away and discarded before cooking.

Fishing Tips

Almaco jack are surface swimmers and can be caught while trolling tuna feathers, shiny spoons, or live bait. Anglers should focus their attention on deep edges of offshore reefs. However, open water near reefs can also be productive. The lure should be trolled at or near the surface at moderate speeds.

Bait

Artificial lures or jigs are primarily used for almaco jack while drifting. The preferred natural baits are pieces of squid, herring strips, whole sardines, or whole anchovies.

Lures

Almaco can be jigged with shiny spoons, bucktails, or diamond jigs.

Equipment

I recommend a 6- to 7-foot moderate-action trolling rod with a matching conventional bait-casting reel filled with 30- to 40-pound-test monofilament line. For jigging, you can use a 7- to 8-foot moderate-action spinning rod with a matching spinning reel filled with 20- to 30-pound-test monofilament line.

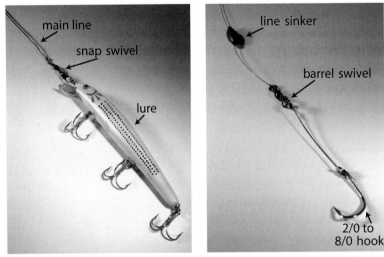

Rig used for surface jigging.   Rig used for trolling natural bait.

GREATER AMBERJACK

There are four species of amberjack, which are known as greater amberjack, lesser amberjack, almaco jack, and the branded rudderfish. The greater amberjack is the largest and most abundant of the four, and is the most sought after by anglers.

Latin name
Seriola dumerili

Best time to catch
Most of the year

Also known as
AJ, horse-eye bonito, horse-eye jack, jack amber, jack hammer

The greater amberjack can be caught off the coast of Florida in the Atlantic Ocean or in the Gulf of Mexico. The largest concentrations of fish are found in the Atlantic Ocean from North Carolina south to Florida and in the Gulf of Mexico. It has a bluish to olive color body with a silver or white belly, and a longitudinal olive band that extends from the front of the eye to the base of the caudal fin. The pectoral and pelvic fins have a light yellow cast. A short forward dorsal fin is followed by a larger dorsal fin that is pointed at the top and tapers to just before the caudal fin. The anal fin begins about midway below the rear dorsal fin; it closely resembles the rear dorsal fin but is about half its size.

Both sexes grow at the same rate and spawn at about 2 or 3 years of age. They usually spawn offshore throughout most of the year at about 34 to 40 inches in length and 25 to 50 pounds in weight. The amberjack has a bluntly pointed head and averages about 40 pounds; it can exceed 170 pounds in weight, but this is rare.

Larger greater amberjack do not school. They often gather together over reefs and wrecks while searching for food but are solitary while hunting. Smaller greater amberjack (less than 8 pounds) tend to congregate in tight schools. Middle-aged fish generally form looser schools. All greater amberjack are structure-loving fish and are frequently found around wrecks, reefs, buoys, and oil and gas rigs. Note that the lesser amberjack (Seriola fasciata) weighs less than 10 pounds and is found in deeper water than the greater amberjack.

Greater amberjack is migratory. It occasionally travels to inshore waters or bays over structure. It is occasionally infested with tapeworms in the muscles ahead of the caudal fin. These worms are harmless to humans and can be cut away and discarded.

It is an aggressive predator that hunts primarily offshore near various types of structure from the surface to the bottom looking for prey. It spends most of its time at the bottom feeding on herring, smaller fish, and squid.

Be aware that it is high on the list of fish that can cause ciguatera poisoning.

Fishing Tips

The fighting ability of the greater amberjack matches that of most tuna. You won't soon forget a fight with a greater amberjack. It hits a baited hook or lure aggressively. When hooked it swims fast and dives deep.

It can be found in great numbers over deep structure at almost any depth in late February and March. Larger fish are found in April. Look for reefs, wrecks, and other structure to find large numbers of fish.

The most popular method of fishing is jigging with live or cut bait. Jigging with bucktails or spoons can be effective as well. It's best to keep the baited hook or lure moving to attract attention.

Bait

Natural cut bait such as herring, menhaden, mullet, or large squid strips or whole squid work well. Live natural bait such as blue runners, goggle eyes, pinfish, croaker, or most any small fish common to the area fished will get a strike.

Lures

Use bucktails or spoons.

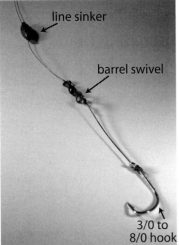
Typical baitfishing rig for amberjack.

line sinker

barrel swivel

3/0 to
8/0 hook

Equipment

I recommend a 7- to 8-foot fast- to extra-fast-action rod with a matching conventional bait-casting reel filled with 30- to 60-pound-test monofilament line.

Hook size will range from 3/0 to 8/0 depending on the size of fish you're after.

YELLOWTAIL

The yellowtail is often referred to as yellowtail kingfish or yellowtail amberjack. Yellowtail ranges from Chile to the Gulf of California and can occasionally be found as far north as Washington State. The adult yellowtail is dark blue along the back fading to silvery white along the belly, with a yellow band that runs longitudinally from the snout to the base of the yellow caudal fin. It has a long body and a slender head.

It matures sexually between 2 and 3 years of age. A female weighing about 10 pounds will produce about 450,000 eggs. A female weighing 25 pounds will produce more than a million eggs. Yellowtail spawn from June through October. The eggs are free floating and hatch within two or three days. Yellowtail is a slow-growing species; individuals gain 3 to 4 pounds per year during most of their lives. However, larger fish may grow 1 to 2 pounds per year. A fish that is 20 inches long and weighs 3½ pounds is about a year old; one that is 28 inches and 10 pounds is

Latin name
Seriola lalandi

Best time to catch
Summer

Also known as
Amberjack, forktail, gold-striped amberjack, kingfish, kingie, king yellowtail, mossback, yellowtail amberjack, yellowtail kingfish

about 3 years old. The average weight of caught fish ranges from 4 to 12 pounds in northern California waters and about 12 to 18 pounds off Baja California. Yellowtail can weigh as much as 160 pounds and exceed 6 feet in length, but this is rare.

The yellowtail inhabits warm temperate water near the coastline, along offshore islands, and among reefs. The yellowtail is often associated with structure, such as reefs, oil rigs, kelp beds, and jetties. It often forms large schools inshore or along offshore reefs and can be found in deep water near jetties and over wrecks or artificial reefs. Yellowtail habitat ranges from the surface to as deep as 250 feet in inshore waters or over the continental shelf. Adults travel in loose schools of small groups and can be located near rocky shoreline. The young tend to travel in large schools offshore near the continental shelf in water that ranges from 65 to 75°F; however, they also frequent cooler water.

These fish are opportunistic and will feed during the day on anything that happens to be abundant. They consume small fish, squid, or crustaceans and often feed along the surface on anchovies or sardines. It is known to be a fast swimmer and strong fighter when hooked.

Fishing Tips

Yellowtail is an unpredictable species and a powerful fighter. It's best to hire a charter boat whose captain knows where to find larger yellowtail. Trolling or drifting are the most predominant techniques. The only time the boat anchors is when concentrations of yellowtail are located.

Yellowtail is usually located around some sort of structure, such as reefs, kelp beds, or oil and gas platforms, or over wrecks that have plenty of water current and a water temperature of 65°F or slightly higher. Yellowtail does not wander too far from structure, so you should be directly over it; otherwise, you won't catch fish regardless of how much chum is used. Yellowtail can also be found about 50 to 100 yards away from drifting kelp beds in large, open-ocean expanses far from any form of structure, aside from the kelp beds themselves. The fish can also be more than a hundred feet deep in the vicinity of structure, or they can be near the surface. Surface-feeding yellowtail are smaller; larger fish tend to be closer to the bottom. Look for feeding birds to locate schools of surface-feeding yellowtail.

When fishing structure, be aware that yellowtail tend to dive into structure when hooked, which will often cut lines. Always keep the line tight; when you feel a fish, set the hook and don't allow any slack to develop in the line.

When fishing on the surface, cast and work a jig or baited hook by slowly retrieving and working the offering. You can chum in moderation with live anchovies to draw fish closer to the boat. Although yellowtail is occasionally taken from the shoreline, it is most often taken from boats with live bait, such as anchovies, sardines, or cut mackerel or squid. Small-boat anglers can take inshore yellowtail with trolling jigs or feathers over structure in areas that yellowtail tend to inhabit. In the Baja California area, fishing is done in 90 to 300 feet of water with heavy sinkers directly on the bottom.

Bait

It's best to use live or dead anchovies, but cut squid or cut mackerel are also okay.

Lures

A surface plug can be used near where birds are diving. Any surface lure will work well if it provides side-to-side motion with an occasional jigging motion when being retrieved. For trolling, use swimming plugs at depths that range from the surface to as deep as 30 feet or more.

Equipment

For average-sized fish, use a 6- to 7-foot moderate-action boat rod with a matching conventional bait-casting reel filled with 20- to 30-pound-test monofilament line. For larger yellowtail when using baited hooks, use a 7- to 8-foot rod with a matching conventional bait-casting reel filled with 30- to 40-pound-test monofilament line. To deal with the rocky structure below when fishing deep, it's best to use a 7- to 8-foot fast- to extra-fast-action rod and matching conventional bait-casting reel filled with 40- to 60-pound-test line.

Seasoned yellowtail anglers carry an assortment of rods and reels filled with different test monofilament line because they never know what size fish they'll encounter, especially when bottom fishing.

three-way swivel

24" to 36" leader, 30 lb. test (the pound test will vary)

6"

1/0 to 6/0 hook

Typical drifting rig for yellowtail.

GREAT BARRACUDA

The great barracuda is an Atlantic Ocean species found mostly off Florida and the Florida Keys and is not readily found north of the Carolinas. It is more aggressive than the Pacific, or California, barracuda (see next entry). It is grayish brown or bluish gray along the back and has a green cast that turns silvery on its sides; it has a white belly. It may have eighteen to twenty-three vertical dark stripes along its back and sides without having any pattern. The young have dark crossbars on their back along with blotches on their sides. The great barracuda has a long, slender, streamlined body, which helps it swim fast.

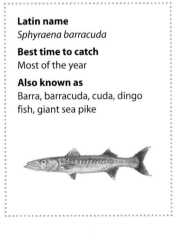

Latin name
Sphyraena barracuda

Best time to catch
Most of the year

Also known as
Barra, barracuda, cuda, dingo fish, giant sea pike

It has two widely separated dorsal fins. The second dorsal fin, anal fin, and caudal fin vary from violet to black with a white tip along the outside edges. The great barracuda has a pointed head with a flat portion between the eyes. The large mouth has long, razor-sharp teeth that fit in holes on the opposite jaw, allowing the fish to completely close its mouth. When it clamps down on its prey, the victims have little chance of escaping. The great barracuda has a protruding lower jaw, which aids in biting prey and makes it look intimidating, especially when it opens its mouth.

It reaches sexual maturity at about 2 years of age for males, 4 years of age for females, and about 4 pounds. Spawning takes place in spring offshore in deep water. The eggs are dispersed by the current. The young can change their color pattern to closely match their surroundings to hide from predators and prey. They also form schools and congregate among floating sea grass or areas that offer cover from predators. When the young reach adulthood, they move to deeper reefs and become solitary at night. The great barracuda can exceed 5 feet in length and weigh over 100 pounds. Individuals average between 5 and 25 pounds; larger fish are scarce. The great barracuda can live to more than 15 years of age.

The great barracuda resides along nearshore reefs, among sea grasses, or around coral reefs near the surface while feeding; it ventures to sandy bottom at depths of about 350 feet. The great barracuda stays well away from fresh water.

The great barracuda feeds on smaller jacks, grouper, snapper, tuna, killifish, herring, squid, and anchovies. It can feed on larger fish if they're chopped into bite-size pieces, and it will feed along the bottom to the surface. It usually locates its prey by sight, not by smell, and grabs hold of its prey quickly. It can reach speeds of 40 mph in short, quick bursts. It prefers water temperatures of 75 to 83°F, although it is frequently found in cooler water. It will destroy more than it eats with its sharp teeth and has been known to attack divers and cause severe wounds. These fish are surely the tough guys of the sea, lurking and waiting for a sign of weakness.

Although smaller great barracuda can be safely eaten, larger great barracuda can cause ciguatera poisoning, so it's best to release larger fish soon after you catch them.

Great barracuda is a curious species; it will follow bathers and is drawn to flashy objects that move through the water. So it's wise not to wear any bright objects while in the water to keep from being attacked.

Fishing Tips

Because of their sharp teeth, landed or boated great barracuda should be treated with a tremendous amount of respect. They can cause serious injury to arms, hands, or legs. Never attempt to remove a hook from a thrashing fish. If you intend to release the fish, firmly grab hold of the fish behind the head and remove the hook, or cut the leader at the eye of the hook and release the fish.

When you're fishing inshore or along the shoreline, spinning or bait-casting tackle will work well. Fly tackle can also be used. Of all the lures available, a surge tube works the best. The speed of trolling and retrieval should be rapid and accompanied by plenty of erratic action. Most fishing for great barracuda is done by trolling; however, sight casting will work as well.

Always work the baited hook or lure just below the surface. When hooked, a barracuda will hit hard, and its fight is energetic and strong as it shakes its head and makes hard turns. Barracuda can also be caught from saltwater fishing flats with lures, flies, or bait.

Bait

Recommended bait includes live sardines, live or dead herring, anchovies, ballyhoo, or needle-fish. An array of other types of baitfish will also work.

Lures

Lures are the predominant method used to catch these fish when trolling. I think the surge tube works best. The tube should be 18 inches long and contain wire through its center and a J hook on the end. Surge tubes can be trolled, as can spoons, feathered jigs, and bucktails.

Equipment

For trolling, I recommend a 6- to 7-foot moderate- to fast-action boat rod and matching conventional bait-casting reel filled with 30- to 60-pound-test monofilament line. Always use wire leader to prevent bite-offs because of the great barracuda's sharp teeth. Use a number 3/0 to 5/0 hook.

For surface fishing, use a 7- to 8-foot moderate- to fast-action rod and matching spinning reel filled with 25- to 40-pound-test monofilament line. Use wire leader to prevent bite-offs because of the great barracuda's sharp teeth. Use a number 3/0 to 5/0 hook.

For fly fishing, use whatever type of fly rod and fly line you prefer. Flies should closely resemble a thin needlefish, or they can be blue and white to resemble an anchovy or green and white to resemble a sardine. Tie the flies to a number 1/0 to 3/0 hook.

PACIFIC BARRACUDA

The Pacific, or California, barracuda ranges from Kodiak Island, Alaska, to southern Baja California; most concentrations are along the central California coast. It frequents kelp beds, where it stalks its prey. In Southern California it is found along the surface and in deep water offshore. The Pacific barracuda has an elongated, slender body that is slightly blue to brown along the back and silver below a straight lateral line. The caudal fin is yellow and deeply forked. Females have a black edge on the pelvic and anal fins; males' fins are edged with yellow. The fish has a long, pointed snout with large, sharp teeth, and the tip of the lower jaw extends beyond the upper jaw. The body can be slimy and difficult to hold, so be careful when removing a hook.

Latin name
Sphyraena argentea

Best time to catch
May through October

Also known as
Barracuda, barry, California barracuda, scoot, scooter, snake

The male Pacific barracuda matures sexually at about 2 years of age; the female matures at about 3 or 4 years of age. The fish spawns mainly between April and September, peaking in May and June. Females may produce from 40,000 to 500,000 eggs per spawn. The eggs float freely in the sea until they hatch. A 4- or 5-year-old is usually about 28 inches; an 11-year-old is about 40 inches long and weighs about 10 pounds. The average life span of this fish is about 10 or 11 years.

During the spring the Pacific barracuda moves from deepwater offshore areas to nearshore areas in search of prey, then returns to deeper water offshore toward the end of October. When in nearshore waters, it frequents the surface and the outer edges of kelp beds or reefs along the California coast during the warmer months and all year off Mexico. Although it is easily found in less than 50 feet of water when it's near the shore, some have been located as deep as 130 feet. Larger barracuda do not swim in schools and, unlike smaller barracuda, seem to prefer a solitary life. Although it does not grow as large as the great barracuda of the Atlantic, looks less menacing, and is harmless (to humans) in the water, it can still bite and can be aggressive when provoked. It often attacks fish that it can eat whole.

Larger Pacific barracuda can cause ciguatera food poisoning, which can cause serious illness.

Fishing Tips

Pacific barracuda is mostly taken from a boat in nearshore areas by casting or trolling, depending on the season. During the fall, Pacific barracuda is usually trolled for during its migration offshore. The Pacific barracuda prefers live bait that are worked near the surface, although dead bait will work also. It also takes various types of artificial lures. It feeds on anchovies and other small fish. Using light tackle can be extremely rewarding as well as exciting. When hooked, the Pacific barracuda puts up a reasonable fight. Using wire leader on the rig prevents any bite-offs due to the fish's sharp teeth. But some anglers use heavy monofilament leader, or tie their hooks directly to the main line for increased hook-ups.

Pacific barracuda will attack most artificial lures if baitfishing does not suit your needs. However, it's best to ask what type of lure to use in the area you intend to fish. Larger fish can be caught in inshore areas during the spring and summer months and offshore during the fall and winter. To help improve the stocks, it's best to release most of the fish you catch. Avoid using treble hooks on lures so you don't have to place your hand dangerously close to the mouth of the barracuda while fighting to remove the hook. Instead, replace all of the treble hooks on the lure with conventional J hooks. Never allow children to remove a hook from a barracuda.

Bait

Although the best bait is live, such as anchovies, sardines, or whole small squid, Pacific barracuda will take most any type of natural bait you present.

Lures

Try floating plugs, shallow-diving plugs, and any number of flies.

Equipment

For casting, use a 7- to 8-foot moderate- to fast-action spinning rod with a matching spinning reel filled with 20- to 25-pound-test monofilament line.

For trolling, use a 6- to 7-foot moderate- to fast-action boat rod with a matching conventional bait-casting reel filled with 25- to 30-pound-test monofilament line.

BLACK SEA BASS

Black sea bass inhabits areas from Cape Cod to Florida and into the Gulf of Mexico and is most common from Long Island to South Carolina. Its overall color is iridescent black-green for the larger of the species and dark brown for smaller fish. It has a fatty hump in front of the dorsal fin, which consists of sharp spines; they will cause injury if the fish is not handled carefully.

Latin name
Centropristis striata

Best time to catch
May through December

Also known as
Black bass, blackfish, black will, common sea bass, humpback, pin bass, rock bass, sea bass

All black sea bass are initially females; some larger fish between 2 and 5 years old change their sex and become males, which occurs between February and May in southern waters and from June to October in northern waters. It reaches sexual maturity between 2 and 4 years of age, and weighs 1 to 2 pounds. It spawns from January through March. It is a slow-growing fish. A 1-year-old is about 5 inches long; a 5-year-old is about 12 inches long. It can live more than 10 years and can grow to a maximum of 24 inches. Its average length is about 6 to 18 inches, and it may reach 5 pounds. Individuals longer than 15 inches are approximately 8 years old and are uncommon in bays; they're usually found offshore over structure.

Black sea bass is considered a temperate reef fish. Most younger fish migrate offshore in December, although some remain in bays throughout the winter months. Most adults prefer offshore reefs and water from 20 feet to several hundred feet deep in fast-moving currents. It doesn't usually travel in schools but can be found in large groups over clam or oyster beds, around breakwaters, piers, and jetties, and over structure, such as wrecks, reefs, and rocky bottom. It feeds during the daylight hours and relies on swift currents to capture its prey, eating whatever is available, although their usual diet consists of crabs, shrimp, sandworms or bloodworms, clams, and smaller fish.

Fishing Tips

To fish for black sea bass, the boat must be anchored precisely over wrecks, reefs, or rocky structure. A few feet off the structure can mean the difference between a boatload of fish or no fish at all. Expect to lose terminal fishing rigs because of the structure. Larger black sea bass are taken by bottom fishing from a boat with bait or jigs; smaller ones are taken from the shoreline. While you're fishing for black sea bass, you'll probably also encounter cod and tautog (blackfish), giving you a mixed bag of fish. The time of year, water temperature, tides, and current all play a large role in catching fish. Flood or ebb tides are the best; slack tide usually produces no fish. The fishing season is usually from May through October and can last into December.

The best bait is skimmer clams cut in 3-inch strips, with a small portion of the clam hanging off the hook. Be ready to set the hook the moment the bait hits the bottom; don't leave any slack in the line, so you can feel the fish's subtle tapping on the baited hook. This fish will steal the bait if given a chance. And use caution when removing the hook because of the fish's needle-sharp dorsal fins.

Bait
Recommended bait includes clams (the most common), cut squid, sandworms, bloodworms, shrimp, live killifish, and fiddler or green crabs.

Lures
Try plastic worms or bucktail jigs.

Equipment
Use a 7- to 8-foot fast- to moderate-action rod and a matching conventional bait-casting reel or a spinning reel filled with 20- to 30-pound-test monofilament line. Depending on the current, use a 4- to 10-ounce sinker.

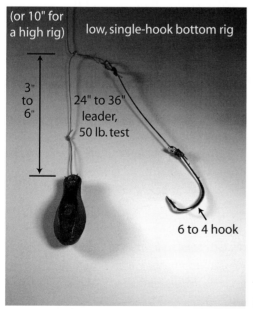

(or 10" for a high rig)

low, single-hook bottom rig

3" to 6"

24" to 36" leader, 50 lb. test

6 to 4 hook

Typical black sea bass rig. Using the least amount of terminal tackle without swivels is best.

GIANT SEA BASS

The giant sea bass is found along the California coast and is the largest marine bony fish in California; actually it is the largest of the nearshore sport species. It is a heavy, full-bodied fish, and is widest near its head. It is dark gray with large black spots along the sides. The dorsal fin has many spines; soft rays (that is, soft to the touch rather than spiny) protrude farther back, and the caudal fin is slightly indented.

Latin name
Stereolepis gigas

Best time to catch
May through September (currently under moratorium)

Also known as
Black, black sea bass, California black sea bass, California jewfish, giant bass

Giant sea bass mature sexually at about 11 to 14 years of age and about 50 to 60 pounds. Spawning usually takes place from June to September; females can produce more than 60 million eggs during a single spawn. Younger giant sea bass feed on anchovies, sardines, and squid. It is a slow-growing, late-maturing species. It can grow to 7½ feet in length, weigh up to 570 pounds (although this is rare), and live to nearly 100 years of age.

The giant sea bass feeds on almost anything it can capture, including large Pacific mackerel, ocean whitefish, stingrays, white croaker, small sharks, crabs, lobster, sea worms, squid, and bonito.

Fishing Tips

There is presently a moratorium on catching and keeping giant sea bass in California waters because of the species' near extinction.

KELP BASS

Kelp bass is one of the most sought-after sport fish in Southern California. It ranges from the mouth of the Columbia River, in Oregon, to Bahia Magdalena, in Baja California. It has a greenish brown body with a white belly and white blotches between its dorsal fin and its faint lateral line. The dorsal fin has ten or eleven spines (the third spine is about the same length as the fourth and fifth spines) and twelve to fourteen soft rays toward the rear of the dorsal fin; the anal fin has three sharp spines at its forward edge.

Latin name
Paralabrax clathratus

Best time to catch
Spring to fall

Also known as
Bull bass, calico bass, California kelp bass, kelp salmon, rockfish, rock sea bass, sand bass

It is slow growing, taking 5 or 6 years to reach 12 inches in length and about 5 pounds, at which size it is capable of spawning. The spawning season for kelp bass is from May through September, peaking in July. Fish that weigh 8 to 10 pounds can be 12 to 15 years old and about 18 inches long. A 24-inch fish might be 20 years old.

This fish is a member of a large group of sea bass that inhabit the eastern Pacific. It puts up a powerful fight and requires skill to hook and land consistently. (It can be caught year-round in its southern ranges.) The kelp bass can be easily confused with the spotted sand bass, which has twelve or thirteen spines on its dorsal fin (the third spine is much longer than the fourth and fifth spines) followed by fifteen to seventeen soft rays toward the rear of the dorsal fin. These subtle aspects distinguish the two fish from each other.

Kelp bass is territorial and does not migrate. It is usually found in or near kelp beds, around rock jetties, or over structure such as reefs and wrecks in shallow water (no deeper than about 150 feet), although the larger of the species are found in deeper water. It is considered an ambush feeder; unlike most surface-feeding fish, which run down their prey, kelp bass sits in cover within kelp or structure and waits for its prey to pass by. It is a voracious feeder and prefers crustaceans, squid, shrimp, octopus, worms, and smaller fish.

Fishing Tips

Most half- or full-day party boats target kelp bass during the summer months. These boats know where the fish are on any given day. Also, private boats can be used along or above any form of structure where kelp bass tends to congregate. It will take an assortment of different lures if they are presented properly.

Bait

Kelp bass will take live anchovies or sardines, or cut squid strips.

Lures

Any type of swimming plug is ideal for kelp bass. Present these lures in suspected areas and play the line while reeling in the lure; provide plenty of action to attract attention.

When fly fishing for kelp bass, it's important to try and imitate a nervous but unsuspecting type of prey by slowly retrieving the fly, moving the rod tip, and playing the fly line (your choice of line).

Equipment

If you're trolling, use a 6- to 7-foot moderate-action boat rod with a matching conventional bait-casting reel filled with 10- to 15-pound-test monofilament line.

If you're casting lures, use a 6- to 8-foot moderate-action spinning rod with a matching spinning reel filled with 10- to 15-pound-test monofilament line.

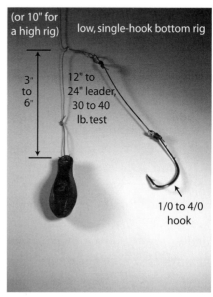

(or 10" for a high rig)   low, single-hook bottom rig

3" to 6"

12" to 24" leader, 30 to 40 lb. test

1/0 to 4/0 hook

Typical bottom rig for kelp bass.

STRIPED BASS

Striped bass is the largest, most widely distributed, and most prized game fish along the East and West coasts. It is found from Nova Scotia to northern Florida in the Atlantic Ocean and in the Gulf of Mexico. About 100 years ago, striped bass was introduced to the Pacific coast, where it now ranges from mid-California to southern British Columbia. It is also the most regulated species along all coasts of the United States. Nearly made extinct because of overfishing along the East Coast, striped bass has made an excellent comeback due to size and catch limits and is once again found in great numbers.

Latin name
Morone saxatilis

Best time to catch
April through November

Also known as
Greenhead, linesider, rock, rockfish, squid hound, striped sea bass, striper, striper bass

It is identified by seven or eight prominent black stripes that run longitudinally along the sides of its long, sleek silver-colored body. The two dorsal fins are completely separated. The first dorsal fin has eight to ten spines; the second has ten to thirteen soft rays. The anal fin has three spines followed by seven to thirteen soft rays.

Striped bass is considered *anadromous*, meaning it lives in the ocean but returns to freshwater rivers (and areas of brackish water) to spawn. The Hudson River and Chesapeake Bay are the most prominent spawning grounds. Between 5 and 8 years of age, the female (called a cow) reaches sexual maturity. Spawning occurs from late spring to early summer at water temperatures of about 65°F. The eggs hatch three days after being fertilized; the fry are vulnerable to predators for about eight weeks after hatching. Its life expectancy is at least 20 years, and it can grow to more than 4 feet in length; females grow larger than males.

Striped bass appears in southern waters about mid-April and in northern waters around June. In its northern range during the winter months, striped bass are in near hibernation and don't feed as readily as those that reside farther south. Those in the south actively feed primarily during the morning and evening hours. It tolerates the most diverse water conditions. It inhabits inshore bays, preferring rocky shoals and moving currents, and is very active in areas with tidal and current change as well as in the wash of breaking waves at the surf.

It is a mainly top- to midwater feeder but can also be found on the bottom. It feeds in turbulent waters and will flow with an incoming wave right up to the beach while chasing bait. Peak feeding water temperature ranges are from 55 to 65°F. It becomes nocturnal during the midsummer months and feeds mostly from dusk to dawn. The diet of the striped bass consists mainly of smelt, eels, and smaller fish such as bunker, snapper bluefish, small weakfish, and squid, although it consumes most types of fish. It also consumes clams, mussels, sandworms, bloodworms, and sea worms.

Because excessive splashing causes bonefish to run, avoid sinkers of any type. Cast sideways with a lure or baited hook to prevent splashing. As you retrieve the baited hook or lure, whether you cast from a boat or the shallows while wading, start jigging almost immediately. When hooked, they are capable of a long, sustained run and can unload a reel in no time, so you need a reel that can hold at least 250 yards of 8- to 10-pound-test monofilament line.

Once netted, a bonefish is usually released because it has little food value to most anglers.

Bait
The best natural bait is small lengths of conch or sandworm. Small crabs or strips of clam also work well.

Lures
When fly fishing, use fast-sinking flies.

Equipment
For fly equipment, use a 9- or 10-weight fly rod, depending on wind conditions and the weight of the fly. The reel should hold at least 200 yards of backing material. Most anglers prefer a floating line, although the choice of line is yours. The leader varies from 40- to 20-pound test, depending on the length of the rod and the fly line used. Generally, a 9-weight line requires a 30-pound-test leader. A fluorocarbon tippet of 15-pound test is adequate.

Although numerous fly patterns can be used for bonefish, flies that sink fast are best; they allow the fly to sink ahead of where the bonefish is likely to be heading.

As for a spinning rod, use a 6- to 8-foot medium-action rod with a matching reel filled with 300 yards of 6- to 10-pound-test monofilament line. Hooks should be number 4 to number 2, depending on where you're fishing.

COBIA

Cobia is a highly rated and hard-hitting game fish prone to long, powerful runs along with an occasional leap. It ranges from Nova Scotia to Argentina, and is most abundant from Chesapeake Bay south and throughout the Gulf of Mexico. It has a long, slim, torpedo-shaped body and a narrow, compressed head, with a broad snout and a lower jaw that extends beyond the upper jaw and has no teeth. The body is dark brown with a yellow-white underside. A long lateral line extends from just behind the eyes to the base of the tail. The first dorsal fin is composed of seven to nine short, strong, isolated spines not connected by a membrane. The second dorsal fin is long, with its front portion elevated. The

Latin name
Rachycentron canadum

Best time to catch
Early spring to fall

Also known as
Black kingfish, black salmon, cabio, crab eater, flathead, lemonfish, ling, runner, sergeant fish

anal fin originates beneath the apex of the second dorsal fin. The pectoral fin is pointed. The cobia lacks a swim bladder.

Cobia spawn during daylight hours between June and August in the Atlantic Ocean off Chesapeake Bay, between May and June off North Carolina, and in the Gulf of Mexico from April through September. Females reach sexual maturity at 3 years of age, males at 2 years. They range in weight from less than 50 pounds to more than 80 pounds, occasionally to 130 pounds, but the average is 20 to 45 pounds.

They prefer tropical waters during the winter months, then move to temperate waters, between 68 and 85°F, inshore or offshore from spring to fall. They are frequently found swimming along with large rays and respond to live bait or a lure when presented near a ray. Anglers often see the wing tip of a ray near the surface, which indicates that cobia may be present. They are not normally a schooling fish but travel in small groups. They are often seen in packs of three to a hundred fish hunting for food during migrations in shallow water along the shore.

Cobia are structure-loving fish and spend a lot of time around buoys, wrecks, reefs, pilings, anchored boats, and, in the Gulf of Mexico, near oil and gas rigs. When they migrate north along the Atlantic coast, they inhabit the surface water over the continental shelf. They also seek shelter in bays, inlets, and mangroves. They are frequently attracted to areas with current and wave action.

Cobia are unpredictable; they often chase food from the surface to the bottom and can be found in either place. While offshore, they can be difficult to locate. They feed primarily on crabs, shrimp, and other crustaceans, but also on eels, mackerel and other small fish, and squid. They often follow turtles, rays, and sharks, and feed on whatever these leave behind.

Fishing Tips

Cobia can be caught year-round but are most easily caught during the summer south of Chesapeake Bay. They stay close to the surface during the summer months. Cobia are found in small groups around structure such as buoys and bridge pilings and around the accumulations of grass that form near them. They frequently investigate boats that are idling or at anchor—an ideal opportunity for sight casting. Use a bucktail or large spoon; cast ahead of the fish, and retrieve the lure (or baited hook) back toward them. At times they are aggressive and will strike at anything that is cast their way; at other times they can be picky, taking only live bait. Frequently, anglers employ buoy hopping—moving from buoy to buoy in search of cobia and sight casting artificial or live bait to fish visible near the surface. Structure fishing is most productive from late July through September. It's best to fish for cobia during a moving tide.

Although some fish are caught by drifting or trolling, bottom to surface fishing at anchor in known cobia vicinities with cut bait can be the most productive method. Live bait is better for larger fish. The combination of cut and live bait will increase your chances of success. It's best to use chumming and chunking techniques to attract and keep fish near the boat. Locate the edge of a shoal, drop anchor, and set up a menhaden chum slick (fresh chum is best) behind the boat, and pair this with chunking techniques. Some anglers also use a steady drip of menhaden oil, allowing it to flow into the chum slick to help create an additional scent enticement.

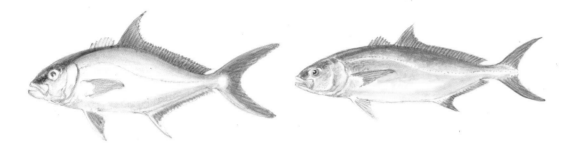

Almaco Jack *(Seriola rivoliana)*

Greater Amberjack *(Seriola dumerili)*

Yellowtail *(Seriola lalandi)*

Great Barracuda *(Sphyraena barracuda)*

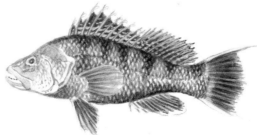

Pacific Barracuda *(Sphyraena argentea)*

Black Sea Bass *(Centropristis striata)*

Giant Sea Bass *(Stereolepis gigas)*

Kelp (Calico) Bass *(Paralabrax clathratus)*

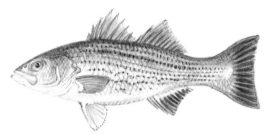

Striped Bass *(Morone saxatilis)*

White Sea Bass *(Atractoscion nobilis)*

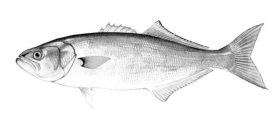

Bluefish *(Pomatomus saltatrix)*

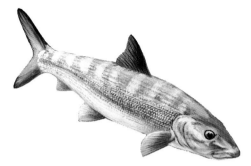

Bonefish *(Albula vulpes)*

Cobia *(Rachycentron canadum)*

Atlantic Cod *(Gadus morhua)*

Pacific Cod *(Gadus macrocephalus)*

California Corbina *(Menticirrhus undulatus)*

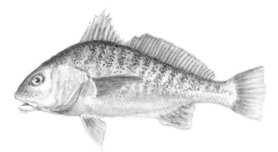

Atlantic Croaker *(Micropogonias undulatus)*

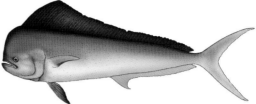

Dolphin *(Coryphaena hippurus)*

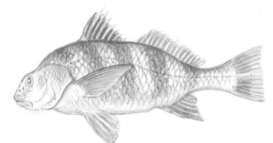

Black Drum *(Pogonias cromis)*

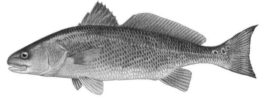

Red Drum *(Sciaenops ocellatus)*

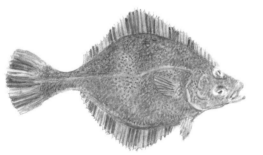

Starry Flounder *(Platichthys stellatus)*

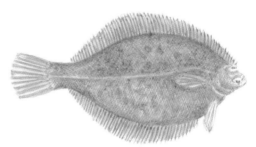

Winter Flounder *(Pseudopleuronectes americanus)*

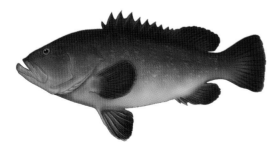

Dusky Grouper *(Epinephelus marginatus)*
found in the eastern Atlantic and western Indian oceans, and in the
western Atlantic Ocean from southern Brazil to Argentina

Haddock *(Melanogrammus aeglefinus)*

Atlantic Halibut *(Hippoglossus hippoglossus)*

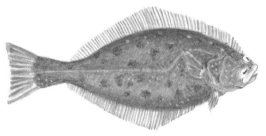

Pacific Halibut *(Hippoglossus stenolepis)*

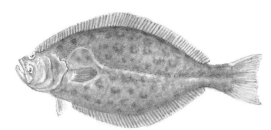

California Halibut *(Paralichthys californicus)*

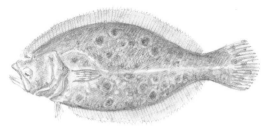

Summer Flounder *(Paralichthys dentatus)*

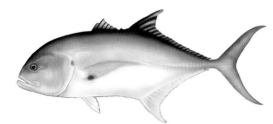

Jack Crevalle *(Caranx hippos)*

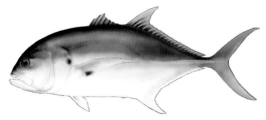

Pacific Jack Crevalle *(Caranx caninus)*

Lingcod *(Ophiodon elongatus)*

Atlantic Mackerel *(Scomber scombrus)*

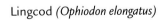

Spanish Mackerel *(Scomberomorus maculatus)*   Pollock *(Pollachius virens)*

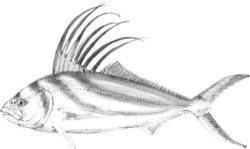

Florida Pompano *(Trachinotus carolinus)*   Roosterfish *(Nematistius pectoralis)*

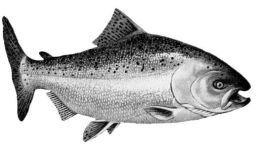

Salmon, Atlantic *(Salmo salar)*   Salmon, Chinook *(Oncorhynchus tshawytscha)*

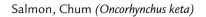

Salmon, Chum *(Oncorhynchus keta)*   Salmon, Coho *(Oncorhynchus kisutch)*

Salmon, Pink *(Oncorhynchus gorbuscha)* Salmon, Sockeye *(Oncorhynchus nerka)*

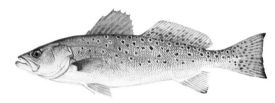

Spotted Sea Trout *(Cynoscion nebulosus)* Weakfish *(Cynoscion regalis)*

Sheepshead *(Archosargus probatocephalus)* Pacific Cubera Snapper *(Lutjanus novemfasciatus)*

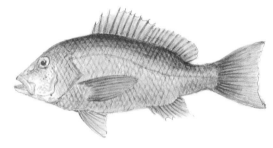

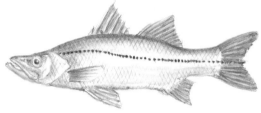

Red Snapper *(Lutjanus campechanus)* Common Snook *(Centropomus undecimalis)*

Spot *(Leiostomus xanthurus)*

White Sturgeon *(Acipenser transmontanus)*

Swordfish *(Xiphias gladius)*

Black Marlin *(Makaira indica)*

Blue Marlin *(Makaira nigricans)*

Striped Marlin *(Tetrapturus audax)*

White Marlin *(Tetrapturus albidus)*

Sailfish *(Istiophorus platypterus)*

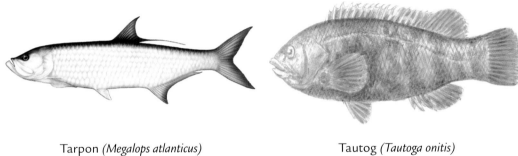

Tarpon *(Megalops atlanticus)*

Tautog *(Tautoga onitis)*

Atlantic Bonito *(Sarda sarda)*

Pacific Bonito *(Sarda chiliensis)*

Albacore *(Thunnus alalunga)*

Bluefin Tuna *(Thunnus thynnus)*

Wahoo *(Acanthocybium solandri)*

Whiting *(Merlangius merlangus)*

When you feel a strike while using live bait, don't set the hook immediately. The fish needs some time to turn the bait around in its mouth, and even start moving away.

Once hooked, a cobia that's bottom fishing becomes a fierce fighter and instinctively makes an initial run toward the closest structure. Try to turn the fish around to keep it from reaching the structure, which will surely cut your line. When a hooked fish reaches the surface, it will sometimes jump.

Cobia can sometimes be brought close to the boat without much of a fight, but large cobia can fight hard and are known for their strength and ability to do considerable damage to boats, and to cause injury if brought into the boat before they're tired out. If your fish doesn't want to give up the battle even after being boated, club it to keep it from thrashing about. Use caution when handling cobia to avoid their sharp dorsal fin spines.

Bait
Cobia will take crabs, squid, mullet, eels, and cut bait.

Lures
A large jig with a large piece of squid or a length of pork rind is the most successful type of artificial lure. Or try a bucktail or large spoon. Cobia frequently take poppers and streamers of just about any pattern, providing they closely resemble baitfish. The size and action of the artificial lure is important. Streamers should be 4 to 6 inches long and extensively played.

Equipment
Use a 6- to 8-foot medium-action boat or spinning rod with a matching conventional bait-casting or spinning reel filled with 15- to 30-pound-test monofilament line. Cobia can also be caught with fly equipment.

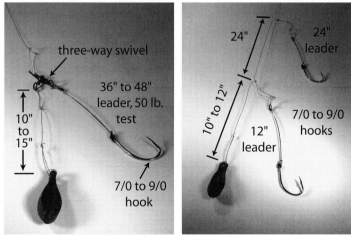

Typical single-hook bottom rig for cobia.

Typical double-hook rig for cobia.

ATLANTIC COD

Atlantic cod is a popular offshore fish that ranges from the Arctic Ocean to Virginia and is most abundant from the coast of northern Labrador to just off Massachusetts. Cod can be readily distinguished from other species by its three separate dorsal fins and two separate anal fins, which resemble the two top rear dorsal fins. Cod has a *barbel*, a whiskerlike feeler, just below its lower jaw.

Latin name
Gadus morhua

Best time to catch
Year-round

Also known as
Cod, codfish, codling, scrod

Cod spawn at about 5 years of age in about 200 feet of water. They can reach 5 to 6 feet in length but are usually about 40 to 45 inches long and weigh about 25 pounds. Cod found inshore are smaller—usually 26 to 35 inches long and weighing about 6 to 15 pounds.

Atlantic cod prefers deep (200 to 250 feet), cold water over a rough bottom composed of sand, rock, mussel beds, and shells or over structure such as shipwrecks. It prefers a water temperature of about 35 to 45°F during the summer months. During the winter cod can be found at depths of 285 to 435 feet over some form of structure at temperatures of 30 to 40°F.

Cod do not school but travel in small groups when seeking food. They eat anything that fits into their mouth, including shrimp, clams, mussels, crabs, herring, mackerel, and other smaller fish.

Fishing Tips

Cod are fished from private, party, or charter boats that can travel long distances offshore and withstand rough water conditions. Cod can be found over offshore wrecks or reef structures while at anchor in deep water. Because the current below the surface can be swift in deep water, heavy sinkers are needed to get the baited hook to the bottom and keep it there. Cod do not wander too far off the bottom.

The best bait is a large piece of skimmer clam securely placed on the hook(s). When the sinker hits the bottom, reel up any slack in the line, then gently move the rod up and down, feeling the bottom with the sinker. The sinker must hold the bottom or the bait will be out of reach of the cod below. When hooked, cod don't put up much of a fight. They are primarily dead weight.

Decent-size tautog can be expected when you're cod fishing. Blackfish also reside in and around codfish territory and are often caught along with cod, producing a mixed bag of fish.

Cod are primarily fished during late fall and into the winter when it's cold in North Atlantic waters, so it's important to wear layers of clothes to keep warm. You can always remove a layer or two if you get too warm. Wear rubber boots to keep your feet dry and rubber gloves to keep your fingertips from freezing. A hooded jacket will keep the cold air from hitting your neck as well as protect your ears.

Large cod can also be caught offshore during the summer months. Regardless of the season, the techniques for fishing are the same.

Bait

A fresh large skimmer clam works best. Shrimp, mussels, whole bloodworms or sandworms, large pieces of squid, crab, or cut bait will also work.

Equipment

Use a 7- to 8-foot fast- to extra-fast-action rod with a matching conventional bait-casting reel filled with 200 to 300 yards of 30- to 45-pound-test monofilament line. Because of the strong currents near the bottom, use a 10- to 18-ounce or heavier bank sinker. Use a number 5/0 to 8/0 hook (either a single- or double-hook rig).

Because of its weight, the fish needs to be gaffed to bring it on board the boat once it's on the surface. Don't try to horse the fish over the rail.

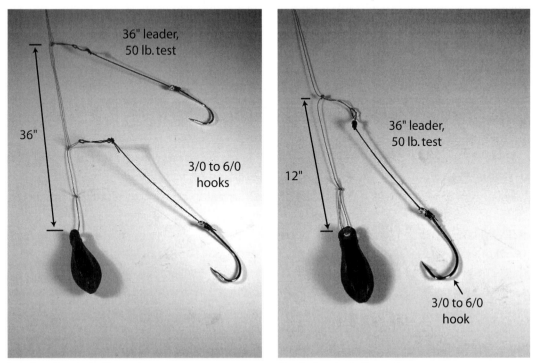

Tandem-hook rig for cod.

Single-hook rig for cod.

PACIFIC COD

Pacific cod is related to the Atlantic cod but is smaller in size. It ranges from Santa Monica, California, to northwestern Alaska. It is a soft-finned fish with a gray to brown back and lighter shades along the sides. Its back and sides are generally speckled with numerous brown spots. The body is moderately slender. It has three distinct dorsal fins; the last two mirror the two anal fins. It has a barbel at the end of the lower jaw.

Latin name
Gadus macrocephalus

Best time to catch
Year-round

Also known as
Cod, gray cod, true cod

In central California Pacific cod matures sexually at 3 years of age, and in northern regions of Alaska at 5 years. The female spawns from January to April, producing free-floating eggs in waters from 130 to 395 feet. Females can produce 225,000 to 6.4 million eggs per year depending on location. Females spawn only once each season (which ranges from winter to early spring). The young are hatched with a yolk sac—the remains of the egg yolk on which the fry will feed until it's completely gone, usually within ten days. The fry, which grow rapidly, inhabit sandy bottom, kelp beds, or eelgrass vegetation. As the fry grow, they move into deeper water. The adults and larger juveniles prefer the soft bottom associated with clay, sand, or mud. Adult Pacific cod commonly weigh from 6 to 8 pounds and can reach 30 inches, depending on their location. Adults inhabit depths ranging from 32 to 2,870 feet, although most are found from 164 to 984 feet. Its life span is usually 8 or 9 nine years, although it can live up to 12 years in the western Pacific.

Pacific cod have a closed swim bladder, which makes them susceptible to internal injuries when brought to the surface from deep water. The injuries result from gas building up and expanding within the swim bladder, with the resulting pressure damaging vital organs. Most Pacific cod succumb when being brought up from deep water.

The Pacific cod is a schooling species. Unlike their eastern cousins, which reside over structure, Pacific cod can be found over soft, sandy bottom. Pacific cod feed on smaller fish, octopus, smelt, shrimp, anchovies, herring, salmon, sardines, sea worms, and crustaceans.

Fishing Tips

Pacific cod are primarily bottom feeders, requiring that the baited hooks be directly on or near the bottom. They will take most any natural bait; however, octopus pieces or cut herring seem to be the best. Anglers can drift, providing that the drift is slow, or can anchor over known Pacific cod areas. The fish tend to congregate in deep water, so the sinker weight should be appropriate for the current below.

Bait

Try octopus, herring, salmon, sardine, anchovy, worms, or smelt.

Equipment

I recommend a 7- to 8-foot fast-action, medium-weight rod with a matching conventional bait-casting reel filled with 25- to 40-pound-test monofilament line, depending on the weight of the fish you're after. Use hooks ranging from 1/0 to 5/0, depending on the fishing location.

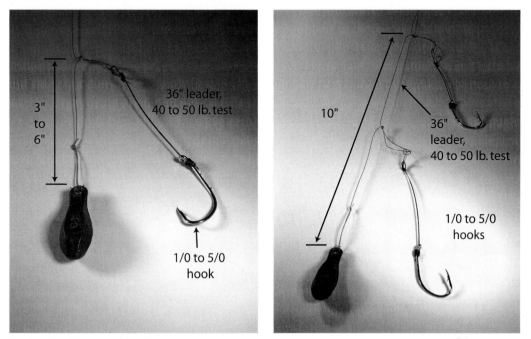

3"
to
6"

36" leader,
40 to 50 lb. test

1/0 to 5/0
hook

10"

36"
leader,
40 to 50 lb. test

1/0 to 5/0
hooks

Typical Pacific cod baitfishing rigs.

CALIFORNIA CORBINA

Corbina range from the Gulf of California to Point Conception, California, and Magdalena Bay in Baja California. It has a long, slender, cylindrical body that's gray with iridescent reflections on the back. The gray fades to white on the belly. It has a small mouth with a single barbel on its lower jaw. The forward dorsal fin is small and high; the second dorsal fin is long and low. There is only one soft spine at the front of the anal fin. The pectoral fins range from dark brown to black. California corbina is related to the Atlantic coast black drum, red drum, and weakfish.

Latin name
Menticirrhus undulatus

Best time to catch
Early summer through early fall

Also known as
California king croaker, California whiting, surf fish

Females grow faster than males and reach a larger size. A 3-year-old female is about 15 inches long, compared to 13 inches long for a male of the same age. Corbina that inhabit bays grow much faster than those along the open coast. Female corbina mature sexually at 3 years of age, males at

2 years of age. The spawning season is from May through September, peaking from June to August. Although corbina don't migrate, they spawn offshore, where females deposit their eggs.

Although larger corbina are solitary, smaller corbina travel in small schools within the surf from shallow water to as deep as 50 feet. Most are caught in about 6 feet of water. Corbina inhabit shallow depths over sandy bottom along the surf where they often feed, as well as within shallow bays. At times, they are seen feeding in the surf, then they isolate the food by pumping the sand out through their gills. Fry feed on small crustaceans. As they grow, they eat sand crabs.

Fishing Tips

Corbina is considered one of the most difficult fish to catch in Southern California when it is feeding along the bottom in small schools and only rarely takes a baited hook. However, it will take bait on occasion if it looks natural and it's directly on the bottom.

Corbina can be caught from the surf, from piers, docks, and jetties, or from a boat over a sandy bottom. However, the most action is found at the surf. Corbina like to feed in shallow water, so you can fish within 50 feet of the shoreline and not have to throw your baited hook very far. The best action occurs about 2 hours after high and low tide begin. The fish tend to linger in sandy or muddy holes. Consider fishing for corbina at night, when they seem to bite better.

Your hook, along with a length of small-diameter leader, should be totally covered with bait. Corbina are frightened by the sight of heavy-diameter leader and shiny hooks and will avoid such a presentation altogether.

Bait

Use sand crabs, bloodworms, clams, fresh mussels, or small pieces of shrimp.

Equipment

I recommend a 6- to 7-foot moderate-action spinning rod with a matching spinning reel filled with 10- to 15-pound-test monofilament line.

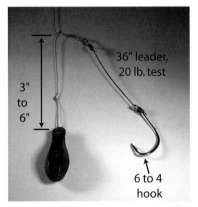

Typical single-hook bottom rig for corbina.

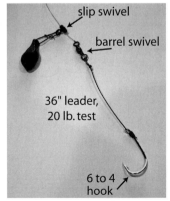

Typical corbina surf fishing rig.

ATLANTIC CROAKER

Atlantic croaker, a common bottom-dwelling fish south of New Jersey, is one of the most abundant inshore southeastern Atlantic and northern Gulf of Mexico species. It belongs to the

Latin name
Micropogonias undulatus

Best time to catch
March through September

Also known as
Croaker, crocus, golden croaker, hardhead, King Billy

same fish family as spot, black drum, and red drum. It is named for the croaking sound that emanates from its swim bladder. The Atlantic croaker's peak abundance is from May to September and sometimes into October.

Atlantic croaker appears pink when first removed from the water and is highly iridescent. It has a slightly pointed tail and subtle stripes across the back that are usually less visible on larger adult fish. Six to ten barbels on the underside of the lower jaw are used to locate food along the bottom.

Depending on where they reside, Atlantic croaker reach sexual maturity at about 2 or 3 years of age; females can produce more than a million eggs at a time and usually spawn over the continental shelf from September to early December. Croaker that inhabit northern areas spawn at sea during the winter, where the water is warmer than over the continental shelf. The average size for Atlantic croaker is about 12 inches and 3½ to 4 pounds (although most weigh less than a pound). Larger Atlantic croaker are often incorrectly identified as red drum. Atlantic croaker can live up to 8 years, but most don't live beyond 5.

Young croaker prefer brackish to fresh water, and in fall move into deeper areas of tidal rivers, where they stay during the winter. Larger fish are not normally found at temperatures below 50°F, however. Juveniles frequent areas of lower temperatures. The juveniles travel south with adults during the following fall into deeper southern offshore waters along the Atlantic coast. Croaker migrates into bays in spring and randomly moves throughout these bays during the summer months. They eat sandworms, bloodworms, squid, clams, and mussels.

Large numbers of small croaker fall prey to predators such as striped bass, weakfish, summer flounder, spotted sea trout, bluefish, and adult croaker.

Fishing Tips
Atlantic croaker can be found over all types of bottom at depths from 20 to 350 feet and in water ranging from 50 to 90°F. The baited hook must be directly on the bottom to hook these bottom feeders. They are feisty, and hooking two at a time on tandem rigs is not uncommon. They have sharp, prickly gills, so handle them with a rag or gloves when removing the hook. Small Atlantic croaker have been used as live bait for larger predator fish.

Bait
Because of the fish's small mouth, use small pieces of bloodworm, sandworm, squid, clam, or mussel.

Equipment

I recommend a 6- to 7-foot fast- to extra-fast-action rod with a matching conventional bait-casting reel filled with 10- to 15-pound-test line or a spinning rod with a matching spinning reel filled with 10- to 15-pound-test monofilament line. Atlantic croaker has a small mouth requiring hooks from 1/0 or smaller. The sinker must be heavy enough to keep the baited hook(s) directly on the bottom.

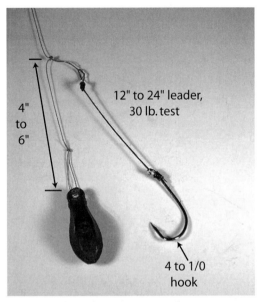

Single-hook rig for Atlantic croaker.

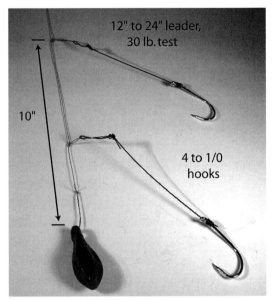

Typical tandem-hook bottom rig for Atlantic croaker.

SPOTFIN CROAKER

Spotfin croaker is the most abundant species south of Los Angeles. It has a metallic blue-gray back and brassy-colored sides that become silver, then white toward the lower body. It also has a characteristic black spot on the base of the pectoral fin. This medium-bodied fish has a steeply profiled head and a blunt nose. The mouth terminates at the rear of the eye; there is no barbel beneath the lower jaw. The first dorsal fin has ten spines; the second dorsal fin has a long base consisting of twenty-four to twenty-six rays. The teeth, which are in the throat, crush the heavy shells that are part of their diet.

Male spotfin croaker mature sexually at 2 years of age and about 9 inches long, females at 3 years and about 13 inches. All spotfin croaker are sexually mature at 14½ inches. They can reach 28 inches, but the average length of caught

Latin name
Roncador stearnsii

Best time to catch
Late summer through early fall

Also known as
Golden croaker, spot, spotties

fish is 16 to 18 inches. During the breeding season, females develop blackish streaks on their belly; larger males have golden pectoral fins and are referred to as golden croaker. Spawning occurs offshore from June to September. The fish form small schools of usually fifty individuals, although schools of several hundred fish have been occasionally encountered.

Spotfin croaker ranges from Mazatlán, Mexico, to Point Conception, California, and resides over sandy to muddy bottom in the shallow water of bays and along the coast, and prefers deep holes close to shore.

Spotfin croaker is a bottom dweller and feeds mostly on clams, worms, and small crustaceans.

Fishing Tips

Spotfin croaker can be caught throughout the year, but fishing is best in late summer. Most fishing is from piers and jetties, along beaches, and in bays. This fish is primarily caught from the surf using a fish-finder rig. It stays fairly close to shore, so present the fishing rig about 50 feet from the shore in deep sandy or muddy croaker holes, which typically surround sandbars at the surf. Spotfin croaker is occasionally taken by private boat but rarely by commercial fishing boats. You can use conventional or spinning tackle to catch these fish; they follow the tide, requiring you to do likewise. It's best to fish 2 hours before and after high tide, especially during late afternoon or evening tides. Early evening and nighttime is the best time to catch spotfin croaker.

Bait

I recommend clams, ghost shrimp (also called glass or grass shrimp), fresh mussels, and bloodworms.

Equipment

Use a 6- to 7-foot moderate-action spinning rod with a matching spinning reel filled with 10- to 15-pound-test monofilament line.

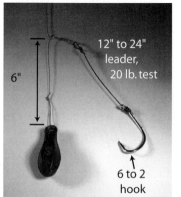

Typical single-hook bottom rig for spotfin croaker.

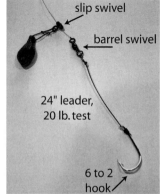

Typical spotfin croaker surf fishing rig.

WHITE CROAKER

The white croaker, similar to the yellowfin croaker, is one of five croaker species that reside along the Pacific coast from Magdalena Bay, Baja California, to Vancouver Island, British Columbia, although it is rare north of San Francisco. It has an extended body with a long head, a blunt nose, and tiny barbels beneath the lower jaw. It ranges in color from metallic gray to light black, with amber to yellow on the fins.

Latin name
Genyonemus lineatus

Best time to catch
Year-round

Also known as
King croaker, kingfish, Pasadena trout, shiner, tommy croaker, whiting

Adult white croaker spawns near shore in shallow water from November through May. Females produce up to 40,000 eggs, which drift into shallow areas of bays and estuaries. The eggs hatch a week after spawning, and the fry travel to the bottom. With age the fry head for deeper water, where they reach maturity at about 1 year of age. The smallest member of the drum family, white croaker weighs from ½ pound to 3 pounds.

White croaker is a schooling species and can be found in shallow water in the ocean and bays. It frequents the sandy or muddy bottom of bays and estuaries and areas just outside the surf zone of the ocean. Fish in schools feed along the bottom. White croaker feeds on almost anything, primarily at night. It prefers water no deeper than 100 feet. Fish living in bays accumulate contaminants because of ground runoff that enters the water. Those caught in the ocean have less contaminant buildup.

Fishing Tips

White croaker tend to be a nuisance because they're so easy to catch. They hit on almost any type of bait, and will steal bait intended for more desirable species. It is caught from piers, bridges, the surf, or boats. They often hit a baited hook while it's descending or as soon as it reaches the bottom, so don't allow the main line to go slack; you want to feel the fish. They can be caught almost anywhere.

Bait

Use anchovies, clams, cut squid, or bloodworms.

Equipment

I recommend a 6- to 7-foot moderate-action spinning rod with a matching spinning reel filled with 10- to 15-pound-test monofilament line, or a 6- to 7-foot moderate-action conventional boat rod with a matching conventional bait-casting reel filled with 10- to 15-pound-test monofilament line.

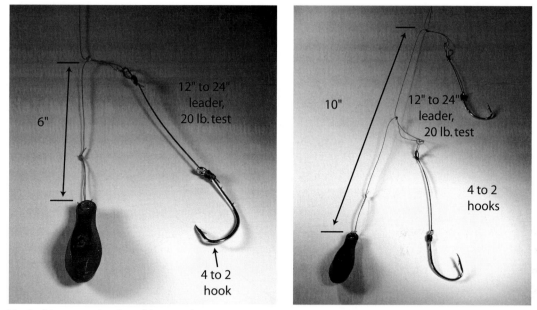

Typical bottom rigs for white croaker.

YELLOWFIN CROAKER

The yellowfin croaker, similar to the white croaker, is one of five croaker that reside along the Pacific coast from Mexico to Point Conception, California. It has an attractive elliptical body with an arched back in tones of gray. The back has a series of yellow-brown stripes, and the fins are mostly yellow. It has a pronounced chin barbel.

Yellowfin croaker matures sexually at about 9 inches in length. Spawning takes place in about 30 feet of water from late June to late August. Females produce from 60,000 to 100,000 eggs. The eggs hatch a week after spawning, and the fry travel to the bottom, becoming bottom dwellers. Yellowfin croaker can grow to 20 inches, but this is rare. Fish in most areas weigh about 2 pounds or less.

Yellowfin croaker frequents shallow sandy bottom in inlets, bays, channels, harbors, and other nearshore waters. It is more abundant during the summer months along the beaches, then moves to deeper water for the winter. It prefers warm water that is no deeper than 100 feet, and is mostly found in water less than 30 feet deep.

It travels in loose schools and feeds along the bottom on smaller fish, crustaceans, and worms during the day or early evening.

Latin name
Umbrina roncador

Best time to catch
May to October

Also known as
Catalina croaker, golden croaker, yellowfin drum, yellowtailed croaker

Fishing Tips

Yellowfin croaker is a scrappy little fish that is often taken at the surf by anglers while using natural bait. It can be caught during the summer months at piers, docks, and jetties, in harbors and bays, or from a boat.

These fish often hit a baited hook while it's descending or as soon as it reaches the bottom, so don't allow the main line to go slack; you want to feel the fish.

Bait

Use live or dead anchovies, clams, mussels, cut squid or herring, or bloodworms.

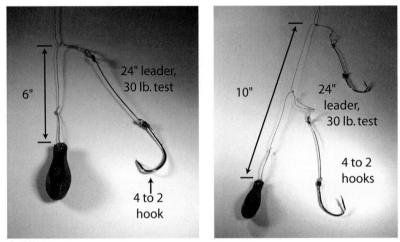

Typical bottom-fishing rigs for yellowfin croaker.

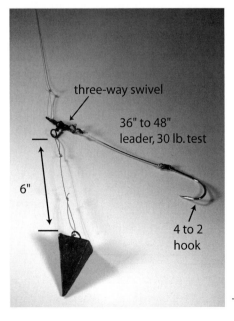

Typical surf rig for yellowfin croaker.

Equipment

Yellowfin croaker are typically caught with light spinning tackle. I recommend a 9- to 10-foot moderate-action surf rod with a matching spinning reel filled with 10- to 15-pound-test monofilament line.

DOLPHIN

Dolphin (the fish, not the mammal) is one of the most sought after offshore fish during late spring and into late fall and is considered one of the most exciting offshore game fish. It is found in tropical water in the Atlantic Ocean and from Oregon south in the Pacific Ocean. It is generally bright greenish blue along the back and yellow along the sides, although the color can vary, including purple, chartreuse, and an irregular pattern of blue or golden blotches on their sides. When hooked, it displays an almost neon color—yellow to metallic green, green-gold to dark blue with silver markings—and puts up an exciting, high-jumping, tail-walking display during the fight. It is slender with a deeply forked tail and a long, dark-colored dorsal fin that extends from just above the eyes to the caudal fin. It has needle-like teeth. Males (called bulls) have a high, nearly flat, vertical forehead. The forehead of a female (called a cow) has a gracefully sloping forehead as high as that of the male. Dolphin can be found in 100 to 400 feet of water along the southeast coast of Florida and the Florida Keys, which are the best dolphin-fishing waters.

Latin name
Coryphaena hippurus

Best time to catch
Spring to late summer

Also known as
Dolphinfish, dorado, goldmakrele, mahimahi, mahi mahi, shiira

Dolphin spawn continually throughout their life in the warm, open waters of the Gulf Stream, where females release their eggs to be fertilized. A female begins to spawn at about 21 inches in length during its first year of life. It produces up to 550,000 eggs per spawn, and spawns repeatedly during the season. (Because of the spawning regularity, dolphin fishing is not regulated.) The fry mature in three months and at about 14 inches in length. The dolphin is considered a fast-growing species; it can grow 1½ to 2½ inches per week. (In the Gulf of Mexico, it grows about 5 inches per month.) Males grow faster than females and can exceed 80 pounds; females seldom exceed 45 pounds. Dolphin that live in the Atlantic Ocean have a life expectancy of about 5 years; those in the Gulf of Mexico live about 2 years.

The dolphin is a schooling and migratory species that inhabits tropical and warm temperate seas, preferring water temperatures between 78 and 85°F. Although basically a deep-water species, it can be found swimming among floating debris, including large masses of sargassum weed, in its search smaller dolphin, flying fish, squid, shrimp, and sea horses, which seek shelter in such debris.

Smaller dolphin travel in schools of several dozen; adult fish take on a relatively solitary, nomadic life and travel alone or in pairs. Off South Carolina, dolphin are present virtually year-round in the warm waters of the Gulf Stream, which is about 55 to 75 miles offshore. Dolphin move to within 10 miles of the shore as the waters warm. They are extremely fast swimmers and feed primarily on flying fish, squid, and other smaller fish.

Most dolphin that are caught are females, because females and young dolphin of both sexes spend most of their time on the surface among floating debris and seaweed, making them easy to locate. Larger males frequent open water, traveling between patches of seaweed where the females are located.

Fishing Tips

Dolphin are very structure oriented and are often found along the surface among seaweed and floating debris. Keep a lookout for birds feeding on baitfish near the surface; the fish could have been driven there by feeding dolphin. When hooked, dolphin may leap or tail-walk, darting first in one direction, then another.

Trolling with natural bait such as ballyhoo is about the most productive method for catching dolphin. Ballyhoo averages about 10 to 12 inches in length and is considered excellent bait for dolphin.

To rig a ballyhoo, simply pass the hook through its mouth and out its anal opening. Rig about two dozen baits and keep them on ice, so you're prepared if the fishing becomes heavy.

It's best to fish with a single hook, so you won't accidentally get hooked when you're removing another one. Dolphin thrash about violently and can injure anglers. It's best to gaff the fish, then swing it immediately into an open ice chest, close the lid, and sit on it until the fish calms down. Only then (when the fish is almost dead) can you safely remove the gaff and hook.

Dolphin are inquisitive and will follow a hooked member of the school up to the side of a boat. Leaving a hooked dolphin in the water near the boat will draw the rest of the school. Don't pull the hooked dolphin into the boat until someone else gets a hook-up; then continue the cycle for the duration.

Bait

The dolphin is not very choosy and will jump at most bait presented, including flying fish, mullet, and squid. Live bait such as pinfish is often used. Dead ballyhoo works well when rigged for trolling (it can be trolled naked or with a skirted lure over its head).

Lures

Try feathers, spoons, and yellow or white bucktail jigs.

Equipment

For trolling, use a 6- to 8-foot medium-action trolling rod with a matching conventional bait-casting reel filled with 30- to 40-pound-test monofilament or Dacron line.

For spinning tackle, use a 6- to 7-foot medium-action spinning rod with a matching spinning reel filled with 30- to 40-pound-test monofilament line. Remove all treble hooks from the artificial lure and replace them with a single hook for safety.

Hook size varies from 2/0 to 8/0, depending on what size fish you're after.

Sturdy fly tackle can also be used for dolphin.

Fishing for dolphin is considered offshore deepwater fishing and can be dangerous for those who are not familiar with it. Hiring a charter boat ensures an exciting and safe day of fishing.

POMPANO DOLPHIN

The dolphin *(Coryphaena hippurus)* and the pompano dolphin *(Coryphaena equiselis)* are the two species of dolphinfish. The pompano dolphin is more of an oceanic species than the dolphin. The pompano dolphin frequents the coast off North Carolina, Florida, and Bermuda, and the Gulf of Mexico and the Caribbean Sea. In the Pacific it ranges from Peru to Oregon. Unlike the dolphin, the pompano dolphin is rarely caught in coastal waters and is rarely found in water colder than 75°F at the surface.

Latin name
Coryphaena equiselis

Best time to catch
Spring to late summer

Also known as
Blue dolphin, dolphinfish, little dolphin, mahimahi, pompano dolphinfish, small dolphin

The pompano dolphin has a more streamlined snout than the dolphin; the body color is almost identical. The dorsal fin on the pompano dolphin is long and extends along the length of the body to the deeply forked caudal fin.

Females mature sexually at 9 to 12 inches in length and spawn throughout the spring and summer months. They can grow to 20 to 30 inches and weigh up to 5 pounds.

The pompano dolphin schools under floating seaweed or debris and under boats. It's not uncommon for pompano dolphin schools to follow drifting debris or boats for many days. It feeds along the surface on small fish and squid.

Fishing Tips

As with the common dolphin, pompano dolphin are structure oriented and can be found near the surface among seaweed and floating debris. Trolling with natural bait is very productive.

Bait

Pompano dolphin will jump at most bait presented, like the common dolphin.

Lures

Try feathers, spoons, and yellow or white bucktail jigs.

Equipment

For trolling, use a 6- to 8-foot medium-action trolling rod with a matching conventional bait-casting reel filled with 30- to 40-pound-test monofilament or Dacron line.

For spinning tackle, use a 6- to 7-foot medium-action spinning rod with a matching spinning reel filled with 30- to 40-pound-test monofilament line. Remove all treble hooks from the artificial lure and replace them with a single hook for safety.

Hook size varies from 2/0 to 8/0, depending on what size fish you're after.

Sturdy fly tackle can also be used for dolphin.

BLACK DRUM

Black drum gets its name from the drumming sound made with its swim bladder. The sound is supposedly associated with spawning behavior to locate members of the opposite sex. Males make a loud drumming sound, females a softer sound. Black drum resides in the Atlantic Ocean from southern New England to the Gulf of Mexico, with large concentrations in the Chesapeake Bay area and in tidal waters off Georgia, Florida, Louisiana, and Texas. Larger drum can be found in Delaware Bay during the spring.

Latin name
Pogonias cromis

Best time to catch
April to early June

Also known as
Banded drum, butterfly drum, common drum, drum, gray drum, oyster drum, sea drum, striped drum

The black drum is chunky, with a high back, and numerous barbels under the lower jaw used to find food by feel and smell. Young black drum have four or five dark vertical bars on their sides that disappear with age. The belly of older fish is white. The color of the back and sides varies with location; for example, fish from the Gulf of Mexico are light gray to silver. Fish living in muddy water are dark gray or bronze on the back and sides. Some drum are solid silver gray or jet black. Black drum has no canine teeth but does have large cobblestone-like teeth in its throat, allowing it to easily crush the oysters and barnacles it consumes.

Black drum reaches sexual maturity at about 4 or 5 years of age and 14 inches in length. Adults form schools and migrate into bays to spawn. The female produces up to 6 million eggs at a time depending on her size. In the Gulf of Mexico, spawning occurs from February to May; along the East Coast it's from January to April. Spawning usually occurs during early evening. The fry remain in shallow muddy water until they're 4 to 5 inches in length, then move closer to shore. Black drum can reach 47 inches in length and live for more than 30 years. Their average weight is 20 to 40 pounds.

Drum cannot survive in temperatures below 37°F and prefer temperatures from 53°F to more than 85°F. Adults adapt to varying levels of salinity; the young prefer fresh to brackish water. Under 3 years of age, black drum do not migrate and generally reside in estuaries.

Primarily a bottom-dwelling species, drum often feeds with its head lowered, allowing its barbels to search for food along the bottom. Then it stops swimming and inhales the food. It eats marine worms, shrimp, small crabs, and small fish. Larger black drum feed on crustaceans and mollusks and prefer blue claw crabs, shedder crabs, oysters, mussels, and squid. The teeth in their throat crush the shells, then small residual deposits pass out through the gills; larger pieces are discharged through the mouth. Black drum feeds mainly during the daylight and evening hours, although less so in the early morning. Black drum is sluggish and does not strike quickly or with force, but when hooked it puts up a tough fight.

Fishing Tips

Black drum usually feeds in estuaries on the flood tide and leaves as the tide ebbs. The best time to catch drum is on the ebb tide when it's about half to three-quarters out. Black drum is a schooling species that can be found in brackish or salt water near breakwaters, jetties, bridge and pier pilings, over clam and oyster beds, in bays, channels, estuaries, and marshes, and along the shore over a sandy bottom. Younger fish are common over muddy bottom in estuaries; larger drum are found over shoals and in channels.

Black drum is best caught with live natural bait that is directly on the bottom, although it can be caught with lures, spoons, or bucktails. Larger black drum can be fished from piers, the surf, from an anchored boat, or through slow trolling. Black drum tend to mouth natural bait, so you should wait several seconds before setting the hook with a sharp jerk of the rod. Hooking a drum is like hooking a large locomotive. The fish tends to make short powerful runs when it sees the boat. The fight of an 80-pound black drum rivals that of a 50-pound tuna. You could fight a black drum weighing 30 to 40 pounds for more than an hour. So adults should be ready to take over the fight or provide support when a child manages to hook a large black drum.

Smaller black drum (10 to 15 pounds) are often infested with parasites, but the area of infestation can be readily seen and cut away and discarded. Nevertheless, black drum should be thoroughly cooked before consumption.

Bait

Use squid, clams, crabs, cut fish or herring, or shrimp.

Lures

Use metal jigs or bucktails.

Equipment

For boat fishing, use a 6½- to 7-foot fast- to extra-fast-action rod with a matching conventional reel filled with 30- to 45-pound-test monofilament line.

When fishing from a jetty or pier or at the surf, use an 8- to 9-foot fast- to extra-fast-action spinning rod with a matching spinning reel filled with 30- to 45-pound-test monofilament line.

Choose a sinker heavy enough to keep the bait on the bottom.

Black drum will take a sinking fly if it's presented well.

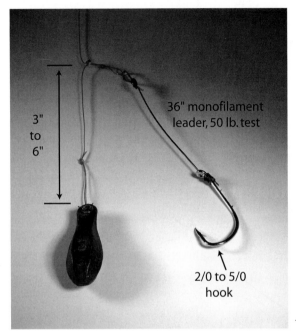

3" to 6"

36" monofilament leader, 50 lb. test

2/0 to 5/0 hook

Typical bottom rig for black drum.

RED DRUM

Red drum, often called redfish, ranges from Maine to the Florida Keys and throughout the Gulf of Mexico. It is most abundant in the Chesapeake Bay area and is rare north of Maryland.

Latin name
Sciaenops ocellatus

Best time to catch
Late winter to early fall

Also known as
Bull red, channel bass, drum, puppy drum, rat red, red bass, redfish, red horse, school drum, spot tail bass

A member of the croaker family, it has a reddish to bronze upper body and a blunt nose. The tail is square with at least one round black spot toward the top forward portion.

Male red drum mature sexually at 4 years of age and about 15 pounds and 30 inches in length. Females mature sexually by 6 years of age at 18 pounds and 35 inches in length. Red drum do not generally migrate and tend to stay in the same area where they were spawned. Spawning occurs along beaches and inlets at dusk from late summer to fall. The eggs hatch from August to September depending on the spawning date. The fry are carried by the current toward fresh shallow water in estuaries, where they feed on zooplankton, small crabs, shrimp, and marine worms.

Red drum has a very energetic courtship ritual. Males follow females for hours at a time while drumming loudly and butting the females with their nose. Often, several males pursue a single female. The color of the male intensifies during courtship; the back and flanks turn bronze against the bright white belly. Females produce an average of 1 million eggs or more and may spawn every three to five days. Although tens of millions of eggs are produced in a spawning season, many fry are consumed by predators so only a few reach adulthood.

Red drum is a schooling species that resides over sandy, rocky, or muddy bottoms along inshore waters such as estuaries. It has been found over oyster reefs and in rivers over a muddy bottom with submerged vegetation. Adult fish travel in schools in inshore waters during the spring and migrate offshore during the winter months. Red drum can live for 20 years or longer. Adults average about 28 inches in length and weigh about 15 pounds; size varies with location. A 30-pound red drum is rare south of the Carolinas, but red drum weighing more than 60 pounds can be caught offshore, although this is very rare.

Red drum are aggressive and opportunistic bottom feeders. In shallow areas, they can often be seen head down with their tail out of the water, called tailing. They locate food by sight and by touch; adults eat crabs, shrimp, mullet, pigfish and other small fish, spot, and marine worms.

Fishing Tips

Although the fishing season is year-round, fall is the best time of year to catch large red drum in the surf. Younger red drum remain in bays year-round, often over oyster beds or rocky structure and near piers. Red drum can be fished from the shore, from an anchored or drifting boat, or by trolling. It consumes crabs, shrimp, clams, or squid. It can also be taken with jigs, spoons, plugs, or streamer flies. Red drum can be caught from saltwater fishing flats with lures, flies, or bait. It is a strong, hard fighter when hooked.

The best method is to use cut bait with fish-finder rigs (also called slip-sinker rigs) directly on the bottom. Red drum will take natural and artificial baits. Live shrimp are fished with a popping cork. With the float in the water, rapidly move the rod from the two o'clock position in an arch to the eleven o'clock position. The fast whipping action of the rod causes the float or cork to make a popping sound, attracting the fish.

Bait

Use crabs, live shrimp, live fish, cut mullet, clams, or squid.

Lures

Use spoons, jigs, bucktails, or flies.

Equipment

For smaller fish, I recommend a 6- to 7-foot moderate- to fast-action spinning rod with a matching reel filled with 20- to 25-pound-test monofilament line.

If you're fishing over oyster beds or rocks or near pilings, use a moderate- or fast-action boat rod with a matching conventional bait-casting reel filled with 25- to 30-pound-test monofilament line. If you're fishing the grass flats, it's best to use spinning equipment with 8- to 15-pound-test monofilament line.

For surf fishing, use a 10- to 12-foot fast- to extra-fast-action surf rod with a matching spinning reel filled with 20- to 25-pound-test monofilament line.

Fly tackle can also be used for surface-swimming red drum.

For fishing with conventional tackle, feed the main line through the upper eyelet of a barrel swivel. Attach a snap to the barrel swivel where the sinker is attached. Once on the bottom, the sinker will hold fast while the baited hook is allowed to drift along with the current. Or use a metal or nylon sleeved swivel instead of a barrel swivel; it has an attached snap to hold the sinker. It works on the same principle as the barrel swivel rig. Both of these rigs work well for keeping crabs from attacking the baited hook. The rigs allow the hook to seek its own level just off the bottom. They also prevent the fish from feeling the weight of the sinker as it runs, allowing you to feel the fish. The rigs are excellent for surf fishing with dead or live natural bait.

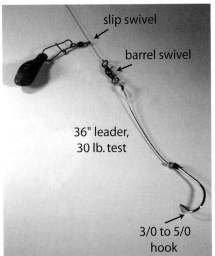

slip swivel

barrel swivel

36" leader, 30 lb. test

3/0 to 5/0 hook

Typical rig for red drum live lining.

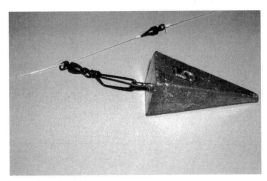

Barrel swivel rig.

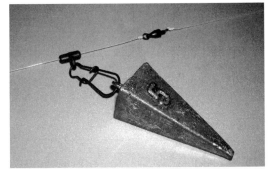

Slip swivel rig.

STARRY FLOUNDER

Starry flounder ranges from Santa Barbara, California, to the Bering Sea, Alaska, along the Arctic coast to Coronation Gulf in the Northwest Territories, and from the Bering Strait to Korea and southern Japan. It is common in central and northern California and is heavily fished in the San Francisco Bay area. Starry flounder is known for its unique appearance. With both eyes on the left or right side of the head, it is either a left-eyed or a right-eyed species, respectively. Although about 60 percent of the fish have their eyes on the left side, starry flounder is still considered a member of the right-eyed flounder family.

Latin name
Platichthys stellatus

Best time to catch
December through March, depending on location

Also known as
California flounder, diamond back, emery flounder, emery wheel, great flounder, grindstone, leatherjacket, rough jacket, sandpaper flounder

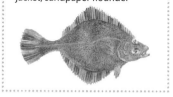

Starry flounder is easily distinguished by the alternating white to orange and black stripes on the dorsal, anal, and caudal fins. There are areas of rough starlike scales throughout the pigmented side of the body—hence the name "starry." The head is pointed, and the mouth is small. The anal spine is strong; the caudal fin is square or slightly rounded. This fish can change color to blend with the surroundings.

Females mature sexually at 4 to 6 years of age, males at about 2 to 4 years. Females grow faster and larger than males. The maximum age for starry flounder is about 15 to 20 years. Females produce between 900,000 and 2.5 million eggs. The eggs hatch in from two to fourteen days, depending on water temperature. Starry flounder can grow up to 3 feet in length and weigh as much as 20 pounds, although most caught off piers are less than 18 inches long.

Starry flounder is not considered migratory, although adults move inshore in winter and early spring to spawn and to deeper waters offshore during the summer and fall. Spawning occurs annually in a short time frame during the winter and spring, depending on location. In California, starry flounder spawn from November to February, peaking in December. In Puget Sound, spawning occurs from February to April, peaking in March. In British Columbia and the Gulf of Alaska, spawning occurs from February to May, peaking in early April.

Starry flounder has a high tolerance for a wide range of salinity and is found in brackish and fresh water. Adults and juveniles are known to swim great distances up major coastal rivers; the adults to spawn, and the juveniles for food.

Starry flounder is a bottom-dwelling species found in shallow water with sand, gravel, mud, or eelgrass. It is not particularly targeted, but it's taken quite often by anglers fishing from boats or from steep rocky shoreline. It feeds on crabs, shrimp, clams, worms, sardines, and anchovies.

Fishing Tips

Starry flounder can be taken throughout the year but is caught more frequently between December and March. It can be caught from public fishing piers, private docks, or boats (while drifting or at anchor, also using chumming techniques) in protected bays and river mouths. The fishing rig and bait must be directly on the bottom. It can be caught on a wide range of baits or lures, although natural bait attracts more fish. It is a strong fighter when hooked.

Bait
I recommend clams, ghost shrimp, fresh mussels, and bloodworms. Larger starry flounder can also be taken with sardines or anchovies.

Equipment
Use a 6- to 7-foot moderate-action boat rod with a matching conventional bait-casting reel filled with 10- to 15-pound-test monofilament line.

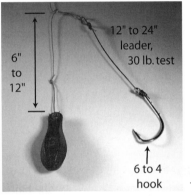

Typical bottom-fishing rig for starry flounder.

WINTER FLOUNDER

Winter flounder is a member of the flatfish family; with both eyes on the right side of the head, it is considered a right-eyed (or right-handed) fish. It is easily distinguished from summer flounder (fluke; see entry on page 216) because of the eye position, smaller size, and small, toothless mouth. The color varies on the top and sides to match the immediate surroundings.

Winter flounder populations have dwindled in recent years because of overfishing, and most states have strict laws protecting the species in an effort to bring it back to its former abundance. For anglers from Labrador to Georgia, the appearance of winter flounder usually marks the start of the fishing season (generally around St. Patrick's Day in northern waters, and sooner down south).

Males and females reach sexual maturity at 3 years of age and can live about 12 to 15 years. A 12-inch flounder is about 2 or 3 years old; a 20-inch flounder is about 9 or 10 years

Latin name
Pseudopleuronectes americanus

Best time to catch
As per state law

Also known as
Blackback, black flounder, dab, flatfish, flounder, lemon sole, mud dab, snowshoe flounder, sole

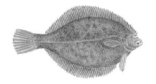

old. The female produces about 500,000 to 1.5 million eggs per year, depending on her size, between January and May, peaking in February, when the water temperature is the coldest (32 to 39°F) in northern waters. The eggs clump together on clean, sandy bottom and hatch fifteen to eighteen days later. Female winter flounder grow faster than males.

Winter flounder displays limited seasonal migration. It stays in inshore areas during the winter and hibernates during December and January. It becomes active in spring when the water warms, when it rises from the mud in search of food; the larger of the species usually move to deeper water, although they're usually not found in water deeper than 175 to 180 feet.

A bottom-dwelling species, it buries itself in the soft bottom and waits for its quarry, then attacks with surprising speed. It feeds during the daylight hours on sandworms, bloodworms, clams, shrimp, and small fish.

Fishing Tips

Winter flounder prefer inshore areas such as bays, harbors, or river mouths. Larger winter flounder favor the deeper holes in these areas. The best places to locate winter flounder are in areas where the tide changes. The flood and ebb tides usually produce the best action. Winter flounder can be caught along the shore within bays, and from docks or party or private boats.

Most boats anchor over deep, soft, muddy holes, which attract large concentrations of fish. It's best to chum with a chum pot or two filled with ground clams or mussels that's placed directly on the bottom.

Various types of terminal tackle are used to catch winter flounder, and it's rare that they break a line or throw a hook. They have a small mouth, requiring small, long-shank hooks. The baited hook must be absolutely on the bottom to catch fish. Raise the rod from time to time to bounce the sinker on the bottom. When the sinker hits the bottom, it disturbs it enough to dislodge surrounding organisms, which attract fish to the hook. To help attract fish, some anglers use yellow or hot pink painted sinkers and/or yellow beads on the leader just above the hook.

For their size, winter flounder put up a decent fight on light tackle. If two hooks are used at the end of the line, it's not uncommon to hook two fish at a time.

Bait

The best bait is sandworms or bloodworms cut into inch-long pieces and slid onto the hook. Winter flounder also take clams, mussels, or squid cut into small pieces. Use clams or mussels in a chum pot to attract and hold fish in the vicinity of the hook. Remember that winter flounder has a very small mouth, so the bait should be small, long, and thin so the fish can inhale it with ease.

Equipment

If you're fishing from a boat, use a 5½- to 7-foot moderate-action boat rod with a matching conventional bait-casting reel filled with 10- to 15-pound-test monofilament line.

If you're fishing from shore off a pier or dock, use a 6- to 7-foot moderate-action spinning rod with a matching spinning reel filled with 10- to 15-pound-test monofilament line.

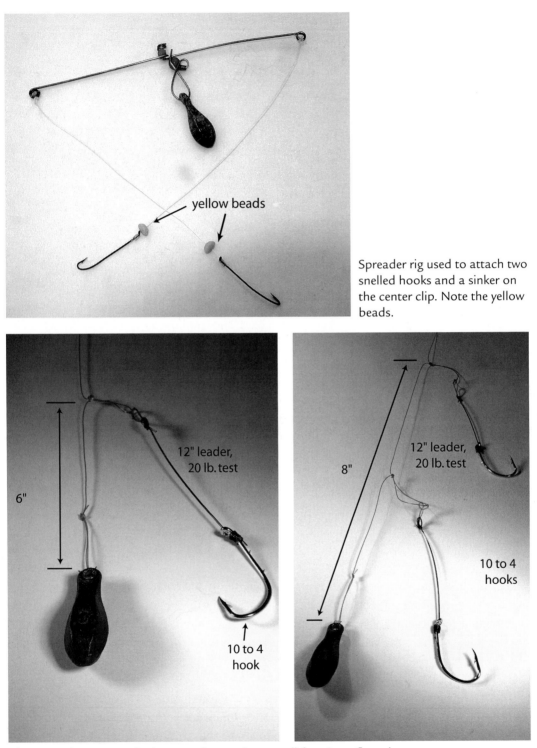

yellow beads

Spreader rig used to attach two snelled hooks and a sinker on the center clip. Note the yellow beads.

6"

12" leader, 20 lb. test

10 to 4 hook

8"

12" leader, 20 lb. test

10 to 4 hooks

These two rigs are popular because they work very well for winter flounder.

GROUPER

There are many different species of grouper, all members of the sea bass family. Grouper are found in almost all temperate waters, ranging from North Carolina to Florida, and are predominantly found in the Gulf of Mexico. Mature grouper reside in holes at depths of 60 to 250 feet and inhabit hard bottom, such as rocks, reefs, and wrecks. Some species prefer shallow water; others inhabit deep, dark regions far offshore. Young grouper are often found close to shore. Some grouper lead solitary lives, hiding in reef crevices and caves. All are large, chunky, oblong fish having small scales with sawtooth-like edges. An overhanging lower jaw is characteristic. Many species have two strong canine teeth at the front of the upper and lower jaws. All species have a coarse, spiny, one-piece dorsal fin and three spines at the front edge of the anal fin.

Latin name
Various

Best time to catch
January through December, depending on location

Also known as
Black grouper, gag grouper, Nassau grouper, red grouper, snowy grouper, yellowedge grouper, yellowfin grouper, yellowmouth grouper, to name a few

Grouper begin life as females; some later change to males as they grow. They spawn between January and late spring, depending on the species and location. Depending on the species, grouper can grow in excess of 50 inches and weigh more than 65 pounds. The goliath grouper, formally known as the jewfish, is the largest of the grouper species; it can weigh more than 800 pounds. It spawns during the summer months and can live more than 40 years. Because of dwindling stocks, it is protected from harvest in most places.

Although grouper are considered rough and tough, they are not active fighters (although they do pull strongly when hooked). They do not seem afraid of fishing rigs, and will investigate.

Fishing Tips

Grouper are bottom dwellers and feed no higher than 6 to 8 feet above a reef or wreck. They hide in a lair to ambush their prey (squid, crustaceans, and smaller fish), then dart with surprising speed and power (given their usually sluggish nature) to grab an unsuspecting morsel and head back to their hole to devour the meal.

Depending on the species, grouper can be fished during the daylight hours or the evening, when it usually feeds actively.

Grouper can be fished from an anchored or a drifting boat. The baited hook must be on or close to the bottom. Because of the bottom conditions where grouper reside, expect to lose hooks and sinkers and have an ample supply of terminal tackle on hand. Keep the fishing rigs as simple as possible, with little or no hardware, to prevent losses. Because of the spiny dorsal fin, use caution when removing the hook.

Bait

Use greenies, silver mullet, blue runners, minnows, sardines, or large pieces of pennant-shaped squid.

Lures

You might try a bucktail.

Equipment

I recommend a 6- to 8-foot fast- to extra-fast-action rod with a matching conventional bait-casting reel filled with 40- to 100-pound-test monofilament line, depending on the species.

The weight of the sinker varies from 6 to 12 ounces or more, depending on the depth of the water and the water current.

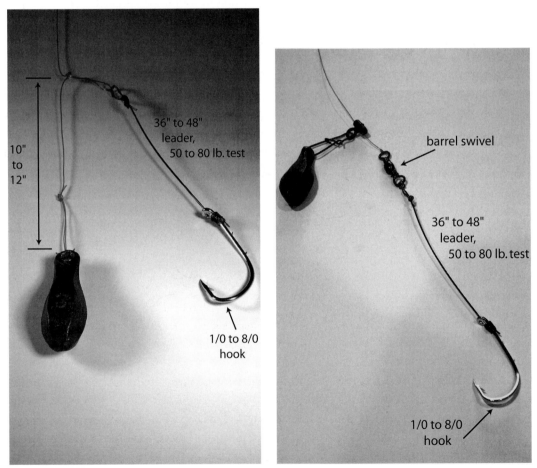

Typical bottom rig for grouper.

Typical grouper rig.

HADDOCK

Haddock inhabits the Atlantic Ocean along the coasts of North America and Europe. It is a member of the cod and pollock family. The dorsal and anal fin arrangement is similar

Latin name
Melanogrammus aeglefinus

Best time to catch
May through November

Also known as
Haddie, scrod

to that of the Atlantic cod, except that the front dorsal fin is taller, and triangular in shape. It has a lateral black line the length of the body and a large spot just above the pectoral fin.

Males and females mature sexually at about 2 to 3 years of age. They reproduce on rocky, sandy, or muddy bottom during March and April off the Massachusetts coast. Spawning occurs at depths from 100 to 600 feet at water temperatures of about 36 to 46°F. Large females produce about 3 million eggs in a single spawn. Haddock average 1 to 2 feet in length and weigh from 1 to 5 pounds. They live to about 15 years of age. Young fry and adults feed on small crabs, clams, sea worms, sea urchins, and squid found along the bottom.

Haddock inhabits deep water and rarely frequents inshore estuaries and river mouths. It can be found at depths of about 145 to 400 feet; it avoids shallows of 30 feet or less. It swims in large schools and prefers a water temperature of 35 to 55°F. During the winter months, it inhabits deep water, where the temperature remains consistently warmer compared with that of shallow areas. In early spring, the fish move to shallow northern waters off New England and on Georges Bank, where they remain all summer.

Fishing Tips

These deepwater fish are sought by private, party, and charter boats that can travel long distances offshore and withstand rough conditions. Haddock can be found at the bottom over gravel, smooth rock, shell, or sand. Baitfishing rigs for haddock are similar to rigs for Atlantic cod, consisting of one or two hooks holding skimmer clam or a strip of squid. You can use a swivel just above a 3½-foot 40- to 50-pound-test leader to prevent the main line from twisting. Tie a 10- to 18-ounce or heavier bank sinker (the weight depends on the current below) to the bottom of the leader to allow the hook(s) to remain on the bottom One or two 3/0 to 6/0 snelled hooks complete the terminal tackle rig.

Haddock lightly tap at the baited hook; they do not give a sharp tug, as do cod. It's best to place a forefinger under the line at the reel so you can feel the subtle taps of the fish below. Unlike Atlantic cod, haddock must be played after being hooked because of their soft mouth. In addition, the hook must be set with a steady pull rather than being jerked. Haddock provides some action, unlike the dead weight of the cod, until it gets the bends when being brought up from very deep water.

Bait

A fresh skimmer clam works best, or you can use a strip of squid. If you like, you can use a bucktail jig with a clam as an additional offering. Make sure to jig the arrangement up and down, so the jig travels between the bottom and a few feet off the bottom.

Equipment

Use a 7- to 8-foot fast- to extra-fast-action rod with a matching conventional reel filled with 30- to 45-pound-test monofilament line. Because of strong currents near the bottom, use a 10- to 18-ounce or heavier bank sinker to hold bottom.

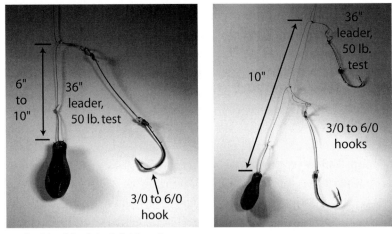

Typical haddock baitfishing rigs.

ATLANTIC HALIBUT

Atlantic halibut occurs in the Atlantic Ocean along the coasts of North America and Europe; in the western Atlantic, it ranges from Labrador to Virginia. It is the largest in the flatfish family; it averages 20 to 50 pounds, although it can grow to 450 pounds or larger, and fish weighing 100 pounds are common. Any fish weighing more than 300 pounds is considered exceptionally large and is called a "barn door." Females outlive males and grow larger than males, which rarely exceed 45 to 50 pounds. Halibut is highly migratory; adult fish will travel more than 1,500 miles.

Atlantic halibut has an elongated body shape compared with that of other members of the flatfish family. It is dark to dirty brown with blotches on the top; the belly is bright or dirty white depending on where the fish resides on the bottom. The mouth has a large gape that extends to the midline of the eyes, and the teeth are sharp, curved, and well devel-

Latin name
Hippoglossus hippoglossus

Best time to catch
Late March to November

Also known as
Chicken halibut, common halibut, giant halibut, right-eyed flounder

oped. The eyes are on the right top side of the head. Like winter and summer flounder and other flatfish, halibut buries itself in the bottom and waits for its prey.

A slow-growing species, halibut do not reach maturity until about 8 years of age; they spawn between February and May at depths that range from 1,000 to 2,000 feet or greater. The female may lay more than 2 million eggs; they drift with the ocean current and prevailing winds, usually toward shallow water. The eggs hatch about sixteen days after spawning. Young fry have one eye on each side of the head, but the left eye soon begins to move over the top of the head toward the right side. This process continues until the eye is completely relocated on the right side of the head (at this point the fry are about 1½ inches long). When the fry reach about 2 inches in length, they move to the bottom and begin swimming with their blind side (which is white) toward the bottom as they slowly migrate to deeper water off the continental shelf.

Halibut is a smooth-bottom dweller and resides over sand, gravel, or muddy bottom in cold water. It can be found offshore as far south as Virginia. It also inhabits ledges and rocky outcrops. It is an aggressive sight feeder. It eats small cod, pollock, haddock, herring, crabs, lobster, squid, and shrimp on the bottom or at midwater depths.

Fishing Tips

Some states have restrictions on catching Atlantic halibut because of its scarce numbers. It is usually caught from party or charter boats that are fishing for cod, often off the coast of Maine.

Atlantic halibut is not considered a fierce fighter. Hooking a fish feels as though you've snagged something on the bottom, although sometimes it puts up a struggle and tries to head back toward the bottom after being pulled up a bit.

The bait must be on the bottom while drift fishing. This requires heavy weights because of strong currents near the bottom. Using 6 pounds of weight is not uncommon in extremely deep water.

Bait

The best bait is 8- to 10-inch herring (strips or whole). Pieces of cut-up fish, clam, or crab, or whole squid will work too.

Equipment

Use a 6- to 7-foot fast-action rod with roller line guides at the tip and a roller guide next to the reel, and a large-capacity conventional bait-casting reel. For this type of fishing, 75- to 125-pound-test Dacron line has proven to be better than monofilament line.

Large halibut are strong and can injure people and cause extensive damage if brought on board alive, so you'll need a way to kill a large fish (30 pounds or more) before bringing it on board. If you're on a charter boat, the captain or mate will kill the fish for you.

The photo on the next page shows what the basic terminal rig looks like. Most seasoned anglers use barrel and snap swivels (not shown) on the rig. Some place surgical tubing along the length of the hook leader to keep it from tangling during the rig's descent. A large snap swivel (not shown) is attached to the end of the leader so that sinkers of various weights (the weight is determined by the current below) can be easily changed.

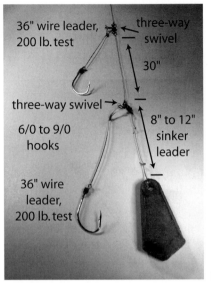

36" wire leader, 200 lb. test
three-way swivel
30"
three-way swivel →
6/0 to 9/0 hooks
8" to 12" sinker leader
36" wire leader, 200 lb. test

Basic tandem bottom rig for halibut.

Conventional J hooks can be used, but C hooks are usually used for easy hook-ups. There is little chance that crabs and the like will reach the top baited hook because of its location.

PACIFIC HALIBUT

Pacific halibut is largest of all the flatfish in the Pacific Ocean. It is found from Santa Rosa, California, to Nome, Alaska. It has a small head and a large mouth, and a long body with comparatively small scales for its size. The upper jaw has a double row of numerous sharp teeth. The eyes are on the left side of the head. The eye side is dark brown (although the color can vary with location) with numerous irregular blotches that extend to the caudal fin; the blind side is white. The fish can change color to avoid detection by prey or predators. It has a lateral line with a heavily pronounced arch above the pectoral fin. The caudal fin is curved and longer at the tips than in the middle. Except for its size, they can be confused with petrale sole because of the similar colors and large mouth.

Latin name
Hippoglossus stenolepis

Best time to catch
Spring, summer, or early fall, depending on location

Also known as
Giant halibut, northern halibut

Male Pacific halibut reach sexual maturity at about 6 to 8 years of age, females at about 8 to 12 years. Females spawn in the north Pacific Ocean during the winter months; depending on their size, they deposit from 2 to 3 million eggs each year. The free-floating fertilized eggs hatch about thirteen to fifteen days later. The larvae float for about six months and are carried up to several hundred miles offshore by the currents of the north Pacific. The larvae are then carried to shallow waters and the fry travel to the bottom and inhabit soft bottom for about 4 to 6 years. Until they reach 10 years of age, they migrate to the Gulf of Alaska in the summer; older Pacific halibut do not migrate. Adults range from 28 to 50 inches long and weigh from 10 to 65 pounds.

Pacific halibut can reside at water depths of 3,600 feet but more often between 75 and 750 feet. During the winter and spring, they inhabit deep water, at times to 900 feet or more. They prefer cool water temperatures, from 35 to 47°F. They are most commonly found over gravel, sand, cobble, or mud bottom. As summer approaches halibut up to 10 years old migrate toward shallow banks in search of food, often positioning themselves alongside sharp drop-offs, edges, holes, gullies, or depressions while on the bottom, and wait for baitfish and the like to wash past. They feed on small fish, such as herring, sand lance, and Pacific cod, as well as sea worms, squid, and octopus.

Fishing Tips

Since Pacific halibut like deep water, use a quality depth-finder to determine where the fish are.

It's best to use a charter boat for offshore fishing. The captain will have all the necessary gear. The best Pacific halibut fishing is off Alaska, where the fish tend to be large.

Use caution when fishing for Pacific halibut weighing 30 pounds or more. If mishandled, they can damage the boat and injure or even kill an unsuspecting angler.

Smaller Pacific halibut can be caught closer to shore by drifting or anchoring over suspected locations. Most anglers elect to drift and use bottom rigs designed for that.

In any case, use circle hooks, which have a history of outperforming the conventional J hook. Allow 15 to 20 seconds to allow the fish to hook itself. Circle hooks are easily removed and do less harm to a fish if you intend to release it.

In many areas dogfish or other scavengers play havoc with baited hooks, so some anglers use artificial bait to avoid catching these pests.

Bait

Herring, Pacific cod, squid, sand lance, crabs, octopus parts, sandworms, or clams will work fine. Rigs that contain combination baits, such as herring and halibut skins or herring and small pieces of octopus, on a single hook also work well.

Lures

Try leadhead jigs, fluorescent red tail jigs, and bucktail jigs; shiny spoons of all types work well if they're jigged to attract attention. The weight of the jigs will vary (probably between 5 and 16 ounces), depending on the strength of the current below.

Adding a Texas-rigged plastic or rubber worm to the jig will increase the effectiveness of the lure. You can use pork rind or a piece of herring or halibut skin, although any type of natural bait attached to a jig may attract a scavenger fish.

Equipment

I recommend a fast- to extra-fast-action, heavy or extra-heavy boat rod. These rods should be equipped with a conventional bait-casting reel that contains 25- to 40-pound-test monofilament or Dacron line for inshore fishing or 60- to 120-pound-test monofilament or Dacron line for offshore fishing. Hook size will vary depending on location. If you're fishing inshore, use hooks ranging from 5/0 to 8/0. Use larger hooks if you're fishing offshore.

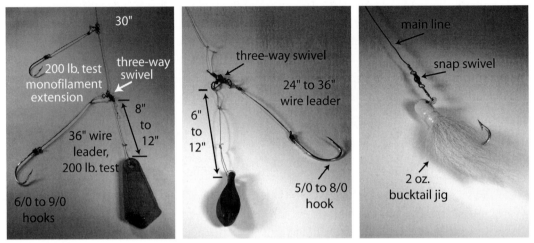

Terminal rig for fishing in very deep water.

Typical drifting bottom rig for Pacific halibut.

Typical artificial rig with a bucktail jig.

CALIFORNIA HALIBUT

California halibut ranges from Magdalena Bay, Baja California, to British Columbia. The California halibut has a deeply compressed body. The eyes are usually on the left side but can be on the right. The top side of the body can be dark brown to nearly black with light to dark blotches; the blind side is white. The mouth is large and has sharp teeth, which are highly visible. The dorsal fin originates just in front of the eyes; the caudal fin is slightly outward in the middle. The lateral line is exceptionally arched over the pectoral fin.

Males mature sexually at about 2 or 3 years of age, females at about 4 or 5 years. (A fish that measures 11 to 17 inches in length may be 5 years old.) They spawn in shallow water twice a year, depending on their location; most spawn during March and April and again in September and October. Depending on their size, females can produce up to 1.5 million eggs in a single spawn. Spawning fish are active feeders. California halibut can live for about 30 years.

Latin name
Paralichthys californicus

Best time to catch
Year-round

Also known as
Alabato, barn door, bastard halibut, California flounder, chicken halibut, flattie, flatty, fly swatter, Monterey halibut, portsider, southern halibut

Considered a bottom-dwelling species, it resides over soft, sandy bottom, away from the surf line, in bays and estuaries. It can change color to match the surroundings to avoid detection by predators or prey. It can also bury itself beneath the sandy bottom—as can most bottom-dwelling flatfish—with only its eyes protruding from the sea floor.

California halibut primarily feeds during the daylight hours primarily on anchovies, sardines, and other small fish. It is very active and is frequently chasing baitfish. At times it can be seen jumping out of the water while chasing anchovies near the surface. It also eats crab, sea worms, crustaceans, and squid.

Fishing Tips

California halibut can be caught year-round in bays and estuaries or at the surf. The most productive locations are where sandy bottom meets some form of structure, although fishing over deep structure can also be productive. Decent-sized fish will usually lurk around structure in search of food. Most fishing is done by drifting baited hooks over suspected locations. Trolling with lures or bait is another good technique. Make sure the baited hook is close to the bottom.

When fishing with artificial lures or spoons, set the hook as soon as you feel a fish. Because the lure will not taste natural or be lively, the fish will recognize that something is wrong and drop it. When using natural bait, you can wait to set the hook to give the fish enough time to grab it.

Never attempt to pull a halibut out of the water with the rod; you risk breaking the line or the fish dislodging itself from the hook. Instead, keep the fish flat in the water and gaff it aboard the boat. Smaller fish can be netted safely aboard.

Bait

The best bait is live anchovies, although mackerel, small queenfish, small white croaker, California butterfish, squid, small herring, or herring strips cut lengthwise will also work.

Lures

Try bucktails, shiny spoons, or Texas-rigged plastic or jelly worms. Retrieve the artificial bait slowly, and make sure to provide plenty of action. Be prepared for a halibut to strike a lure almost near the surface.

Equipment

Use a 7- to 8-foot fast-action, medium-weight rod with a matching conventional bait-casting reel filled with 25- to 40-pound-test monofilament line, depending on the weight of the fish.

Hook size varies with location. If you're fishing inshore, use hooks that range from 5/0 to 8/0.

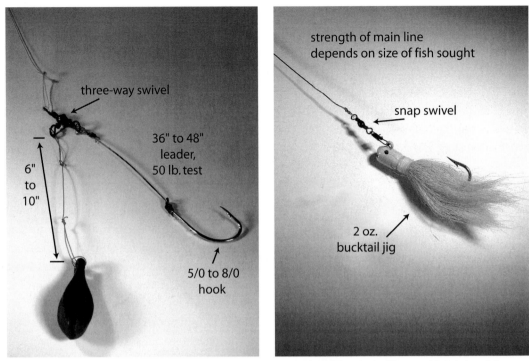

three-way swivel

36" to 48" leader, 50 lb. test

6" to 10"

5/0 to 8/0 hook

strength of main line depends on size of fish sought

snap swivel

2 oz. bucktail jig

Typical California halibut drifting baitfishing rig.

Typical California halibut artificial rig with a bucktail jig.

SUMMER FLOUNDER

The summer flounder ranges from Maine to northern Florida. Commonly referred to as fluke or doormat, it is a member of the flatfish family. Like other fish in this family, summer flounder has both of its eyes on one side of the head, in this case the darker-colored left side (so it's known as a left-eyed fish). It rests on the bottom (on its right, or blind, side, which is white), often digging itself in the sand or mud. It can change color to match the color of the bottom to hide from unsuspecting prey and predators alike.

Latin name
Paralichthys dentatus

Best time to catch
May through September

Also known as
Doormat, flounder, fluke, northern fluke

Summer flounder matures sexually at 3 years of age. It spawns in the late fall through early winter. Adult fish average about 16 to 20 inches in length and weigh from 4 to 6 pounds.

It migrates to inshore shallow areas such as inlets, harbors, bays, estuaries, canals, and creeks, and along the shore, often near piers and bridges, in early spring when the water warms and remains until fall, when it migrates back into deeper water (200 to 500 feet) to spend the colder winter months.

It prefers sandy or muddy bottom. Young fish often swim among eelgrass or dock pilings in search of food and for protection from predators. They bury themselves with only their eyes protruding from the bottom.

Summer flounder are fierce and very active when in pursuit of prey. They often chase schools of small fish right up to the surface. They feed by ambush or by pursuit during daylight hours on moving tides, feeding on squid, shrimp, sandworms, bloodworms, sea worms, and crabs. They also consume smaller fish such as killifish, sand eels, weakfish, winter flounder, smelt, small snapper bluefish, and squid. They have excellent eyesight, so all fishing baits should look as natural as possible.

Summer flounder have a mouth full of sharp, needle-like teeth. Exercise caution when removing hooks or you may sustain a few puncture wounds in your arm or hand.

Fishing Tips

Summer flounder have been known to chase their quarry to the surface and will strike at most baits presented. The most effective method is from a boat while drifting, to cover large areas of water. They can be taken by chumming from an anchored boat, by trolling, or by casting from the shore or a pier. When fishing with bait while drifting, use a fluke rig consisting of a three-way swivel tied to the end of the line coming off the reel. Tie a sinker to a 6-inch length of leader on the second eyelet of the swivel, then tie a 36- to 48-inch snelled hook to the remaining eyelet of the swivel. The sinker should be heavy enough to hold bottom; the object is to keep the snelled hook about 6 inches off the bottom. You should feel the sinker bouncing along the bottom as the boat drifts. It's best to fish during an ebbing or flooding tide or just after a storm, when the fish tend to feed more heavily.

Because summer flounder inhabit rocky (as well as sandy or muddy) bottom, expect to lose some fishing rigs. Use natural bait (about 6 inches long) whenever possible.

Bait

The most productive bait for summer flounder are live killifish, pennant-shaped squid strips, large fresh or frozen sand eels, spearing, whole smelt, whole sandworms or bloodworms, or artificial lures such as bucktails. Most anglers tandem a pennant-shaped squid strip or a length of pork rind with a live killifish on a single hook, which works well. A bucktail with a 3- to 6-inch piece of pennant-shaped squid or a length of pork rind will also work well. The fluttering action of the squid or pork rind tends to attract fish.

Lures

Try small spoons, spinners, teasers, or feathers.

Equipment

Use a 6- to 8-foot fast- to extra-fast-action rod with a conventional bait-casting reel for drifting, or a spinning reel filled with 15- to 25-pound-test monofilament line for jigging. Make sure that the drag works well on whichever reel you use.

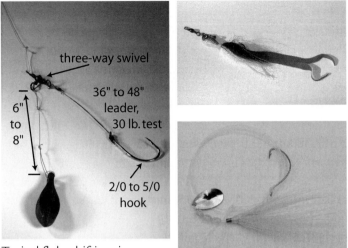

three-way swivel

36" to 48"
leader,
30 lb. test

6"
to
8"

2/0 to 5/0
hook

Typical fluke drifting rig.

Bucktail jig with a pork rind added.

Summer flounder teaser.

You will also need a large-mouth fishing net to bring the fish aboard the boat. Don't try to horse the fish aboard; chances are it will free itself from the hook before you land it.

JACK CREVALLE

The jack crevalle is a relative to permit, pompano, amberjack, and bluefish. It is considered a game fish and not often taken for consumption. The Atlantic species is a deep-bodied, rounded-profile fish with long pectoral fins, a large head with a large mouth, and silver gray to amber coloring. The back ranges from bluish green to greenish gold; it has a silver or yellow belly. The tail and anal fin may be yellow or light amber in color. It has a predominant black spot on the gill cover and another at the base of each pectoral fin. The dorsal and anal fins are almost equal in size.

Latin name
Atlantic species: *Caranx hippos*
Pacific species: *Caranx caninus*

Best time to catch
Year-round

Also known as
Atlantic species: common jack, crevally, horse crevalle, toro, trevally
Pacific species: cavalla, crevally, toro

The Pacific species is nearly identical, except for being slightly smaller and having differently shaped dorsal fins and anal fin.

Jack crevalle never stop moving; their mouth and gill structure requires them to keep moving to ensure that clean water flows over their gills.

In the Pacific Ocean, jack crevalle ranges from San Diego, California, to Peru. It often travels in large schools and plays havoc on schools of baitfish. It feeds primarily on smaller fish, such as anchovies and sardines, as well as shrimp and other invertebrates, and debris deposited from boats. The Atlantic species is found from Nova Scotia to the northern reaches of the Gulf of Mexico.

Jack crevalle spawns offshore from March through September. It averages from 3 to 20 pounds and can exceed 40 pounds, although this is rare. It is common in inshore and offshore waters. It can tolerate a wide range of salinity and is often found in brackish rivers. It frequents shore reefs, harbors, and shallow bays while searching for food over sandy and muddy bottom. It can be found at depths of 135 feet and often travels into cooler water during the summer months.

Huge schools of young jack crevalle, averaging 5 to 10 pounds each, flood inshore waters during the cooler months of winter. Soon after their arrival, smaller schools of medium-sized fish (perhaps a hundred fish in a school averaging 10 to 20 pounds each) move in. Both groups remain in inshore waters until spring or summer, then begin to travel north.

Jack crevalle is a voracious predator. Although large jacks tend to be solitary, small jacks have been seen chasing small fish onto the beach, into seawalls, and at times into boats. They are known to rush in from all sides to herd prey into tight masses, choosing the prey while pursuing it. They seem to enjoy trapping their prey anyplace where the means of escape is restricted. Such a feeding frenzy produces excitement for young and old anglers alike.

Fishing Tips

It's best to hire a guide who knows where to locate jack crevalle at any given time. You can catch jack crevalle with live bait or lures. To hook large fish, use 9- to 12-inch lengths of mullet or pinfish, which will produce savage hits.

If you happen to see them work a school of mullet against a seawall, use it to your advantage. If you're in a boat, throw your lure or baited hook right up to the wall, then quickly begin to retrieve it. If you're on the wall itself, make sure that the retrieved lure travels right up to you. The faster the retrieve, the more frequent the catches. The fish frequently miss the hook on the first pass, so continue retrieving the lure. Just keep it moving until a fish hits it again.

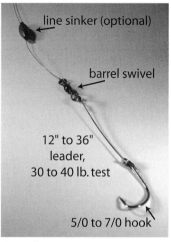

If you're fishing with yellow or white jigs in hot to cooler temperature conditions, slow the retrieve down a bit and exaggerate an up-and-down jigging motion during the retrieve to attract fish.

Jack crevalle can also be caught on saltwater fishing flats with lures, flies, or bait.

It is not good eating and should be released soon after being netted to fight another day.

Bait

Live, whole mullet or pinfish work well.

Lures

Topwater plugs of any design, bucktail jigs, plastic grubs, or spoons work fine.

Typical live bait rig for jack crevalle.

Equipment

Use a 7- to 8-foot moderate-action spinning rod with a matching reel filled with 15- to 20-pound-test monofilament line.

LINGCOD

Lingcod (not related to the codfish family) is found from Baja California to the Gulf of Alaska and is most abundant from Point Conception, California, to Alaska. It has a long, slender body that tapers toward the tail, a large head with bulging eyes, and a large, gaping mouth with eighteen to twenty sharp, long, pointed teeth. The dorsal fins, which occupy most of the back, consist of a row of spines followed by a section of soft rays. The caudal fin is almost squared off at the end; the pectoral fins are fairly large. Lingcod ranges from greenish blue to brownish red and is mottled with darker spots or blotches along the upper body.

Latin name
Ophiodon elongatus

Best time to catch
Most of the year

Also known as
Blue cod, bluefish, buffalo cod, cultus cod, green cod, ling, white cod

Lingcod matures sexually at about 2 or 3 years of age. It spawns from November to early March, supposedly during the evening hours. Depending on their size at the time of spawning, females produce 60,000 to 550,000 eggs. The eggs cluster into large formations—up to 30 pounds in a single mass—over rocky structure. The males maintain the egg mass during incubation, fanning the water to oxygenate it over the eggs. The eggs hatch in about six to seven weeks depending on the location. The fry live just below the surface of the open ocean for about three months, or until they are about 3 inches long, then settle along sandy bottom until they reach 13 inches in length at about 1 year of age. Then they move to rocky reef areas. When they are 3 years old they are about 22 inches long.

Lingcod can grow to about 5 feet in length, weigh as much as 60 pounds, and live to about 14 years of age. Most caught fish range from 15 to 35 pounds. Lingcod resides in cooler coastal waters, over kelp or eelgrass beds that have a strong current flow and plenty of food. It inhabits depths of up to 1,400 feet but prefers depths from 12 to 450 feet deep with rocky structure. Lingcod feeds on herring, flounder, small Pacific cod, hake, greenling, rockfish, squid, crustaceans, and smaller lingcod.

Fishing Tips

Lingcod is a bottom dweller and can be found over rocky structure. You can fish from an anchored or a drifting boat or from shore with natural bait or jigs. The fishing rig must be about 3 to 6 inches above the sinker or directly on the bottom. (Because of the rocky structure, expect to lose some terminal rigs.) Slack tide is the most productive time to fish.

Lingcod's long, sharp teeth can injure unsuspecting anglers, so use caution when removing the hook.

Bait
I recommend cut herring or squid, or bloodworms.

Lures
Try rubber worm jigs.

Equipment
Use a 7- to 8-foot fast- to extra-fast-action rod with a matching conventional bait-casting reel filled with 30- to 45-pound-test monofilament line.

If you're using a jig, I recommend a 7- to 8-foot fast- to extra-fast-action spinning rod with a matching spinning reel filled with 30-pound-test monofilament line.

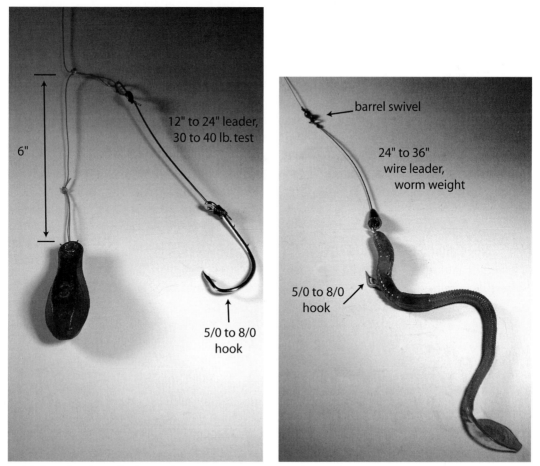

Baitfishing hook rig for lingcod.

Artificial rubber worm jig for lingcod.

ATLANTIC MACKEREL

There are several species of mackerel, each long bodied. They are considered top or surface feeders and spend most of their time near the water surface. They are members of the tuna family; they don't have the endurance of tuna but are faster and more agile.

Latin name
Scomber scombrus

Best time to catch
April through October

Also known as
Boston mackerel, common mackerel, mackerel

Of all the mackerel species, the Atlantic mackerel—often called Boston mackerel—is the most recognized. Atlantic mackerel has a bright green upper body with numerous dark stripes in an irregular pattern. It has a number of small finlets between the second dorsal fin and the tail, as well as finlets along the underside near the tail.

Atlantic mackerel spawns during April and May; the females deposit about 500,000 eggs, which float along the surface of the water due to an oil bubble in each egg. The fry hatch in about six or seven days, grow quickly, and reach sexual maturity at about 3 years of age. During this time the young mackerel school with others of their size and age (14 to 18 inches and about 1 to 3 pounds) and migrate together. Mackerel feeds primarily on young mackerel, small herring, smaller baitfish, squid, and shrimp.

Fishing Tips

Mackerel are found frantically feeding in large schools—by the thousands—along the surface of the water. Mackerel are top feeders and will feed on most live or dead natural baits presented. They will attack spoons, jigs, or other chrome-plated lures. Mackerel trees (fishing rigs that contain up to five hooks in short pieces of surgical tubes of different colors or the same color) are sold in most tackle shops. These rigs are dropped down 6 to 12 feet from a boat, then jigged up and down. Allow the rig to settle during the retrieve between jigs. Sometimes all of the hooks on the rig will contain fish, providing you with a lot of action. Also, small shiny jigs can be used to hook mackerel during a feeding frenzy.

Mackerel can be fished from the shore or in deep water, in bays, off jetties, from the surf, and from anchored, drifting, or trolling boats. The depth of a school of mackerel may vary widely, from right at the surface to the bottom in 50- to 80-foot depths.

It often helps to spread a light chum slick of groundfish. The slick will bring the mackerel swarming to the surface, where they readily hit most any lure tossed their way.

When hooked, mackerel put on a spectacular fight. If you're using a baited rig with a line sinker, they will strike hard, then release the bait. It's best to wait for the second strike before setting the hook. During a feeding frenzy, most mackerel will hook themselves. Mackerel have sharp teeth, so be careful when removing the hook.

Bait

Use sand eels, whole sandworms, or squid strips.

Lures

Use mackerel rigs and small diamond jigs.

Equipment

I recommend a 6- to 8-foot moderate- to extra-fast-action rod with a matching spinning reel filled with 15- to 20-pound-test monofilament line. A line sinker weighing up to 2 ounces will increase the speed of fishing. Hook size can be 1/0 to 3/0, depending on the size of the fish. Fly tackle can also be used.

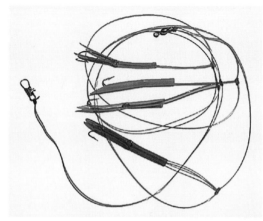

Four-hook mackerel tree.

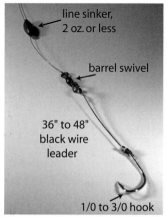

line sinker,
2 oz. or less

barrel swivel

36" to 48"
black wire
leader

1/0 to 3/0 hook

Baitfishing jigging rig for mackerel.

SPANISH MACKEREL

Spanish mackerel is a fast-swimming oceanic species that can be found from New York to Florida and in the Gulf of Mexico. It is most common from Chesapeake Bay to Florida. Its slender hydrodynamically shaped body enables it to swim at high speeds. The back ranges from iridescent steel blue to shades of green; the sides are silver blue with bronze-colored spots the length of the body. A lateral line curves downward just under the second dorsal fin, and the fins are rigid. Eight or nine finlets behind the second dorsal fin extend to the tail; there are also eight or nine finlets between the anal fin and the tail, and a distinctive black patch on the leading edge of the first dorsal fin. The Spanish and cero mackerel have scales on the pectoral fins, unlike other species of mackerel.

Latin name
Scomberomorus maculatus

Best time to catch
Late March through early fall

Also known as
Atlantic Spanish mackerel

Spanish mackerel is a fast-growing species and may reach 12 to 15 inches in the first year. It can reach 1½ to 3½ feet and weigh as much as 11 pounds, although 1 to 3 pounds is the average weight (which is about 3 years of age or younger). It can reach 8 years of age but more often only 5 years.

Males and females reach sexual maturity at about 2 years of age. The spawning season is from April through September off North Carolina and Virginia. Females produce between 550,000 and 1 million eggs per season.

Spanish mackerel school with others of the same size and age at or near the surface. They feed on smaller fish, herring, menhaden, mullet, shrimp, and squid.

Spanish mackerel prefers warm waters and is rarely found in water less than 68°F. Extremely migratory for the purposes of feeding, it hunts in large schools and migrates north in search of food in spring when the water warms. It can be found inshore or in offshore waters. When inshore, it is usually in shallow-water estuaries. It has excellent eyesight and can be considered line shy. It will head south when the water temperature drops to below 68°F in northern locations.

All mackerel are more or less fished in the same manner. Because of instinct, they act in the same manner regardless of their location. Following are brief descriptions of some other mackerel species.

Cero Mackerel

Cero mackerel weigh about 4 to 6 pounds. This species is found in tropical and subtropical waters in the western Atlantic Ocean.

Frigate Mackerel

Frigate mackerel generally weigh less than 2 pounds and can reach about 19 inches in length. This species is common in the Atlantic Ocean in warmer climates.

King Mackerel

King mackerel average less than 11 pounds (although they can grow up to about 100 pounds) and grow to about 2 to 4 feet in length (although they can reach up to 5½ feet). This species is common in the western Atlantic Ocean and the Gulf of Mexico.

Cero mackerel
Latin name
Scomberomorus regalis

Also known as
Black-spotted Spanish mackerel, cero, king mackerel, spotted

Frigate mackerel
Latin name
Auxis thazard

Also known as
bullet mackerel, frigate tuna, leadenall, mackerel tuna

King mackerel
Latin name
Scomberomorus cavalla

Also known as
giant mackerel, kingfish

Pacific Jack Mackerel

Pacific jack mackerel can weigh 4 to 6 pounds and range from 18 to 20 inches long. This species is common in the eastern Pacific Ocean.

Pacific Sierra Mackerel

This species closely resembles Spanish mackerel. It is common along the coasts of Mexico and Central America.

Fishing Tips

All mackerel are swift, strong fish. They roam in large schools, staying close to shore and around channel mouths and moving offshore later in the season. They are active in water that is 68°F or slightly warmer in nearshore areas. It's best to hire a charter boat for mackerel because the captain will know where to locate the schools.

These fish are spectacular fighters when hooked. They are considered an excellent game fish and can be taken with a wide variety of lures and bait. Lures should be retrieved rapidly with an occasional jerk of the rod tip to duplicate the darting motion of a baitfish. Feather lures or spoons are also used. Minnows and live shrimp are considered the best natural bait.

Mackerel force their prey to the surface in tight bundles, then attack them from below. During these feeding frenzies, the baitfish often jump out of the water, where seabirds prey upon them. One way to spot mackerel is to look for seabirds diving into the water to feed. Mackerel can be found anywhere offshore or in inshore waters. It's best to fish for them at early dawn and dusk on the flood tide. While they're feeding at the surface, mackerel are often joined in the frenzy by spotted sea trout, jacks, and bluefish.

Mackerel can be taken with spinning or trolling tackle using small spoons (2 ounces), mackerel trees, or small feather jigs. They often hit small, fast-moving lures and are attracted to shiny spoons or lures colored with chrome or gold.

Slow trolling is usually the best method for finding mackerel. Keep the lures or baited hooks about 18 to 24 inches below the surface. If you find surface action while trolling, maneuver the boat so it will not pass through the school but will pull the lures or bait into the vicinity of the school. Mackerel will strike at trolled lures or baited hooks hard enough to set the hook themselves. They are a hard-fighting fish and will make a strong run when hooked. They have sharp teeth and can easily cut through leader or fingers when you're trying to remove the hook.

Bait

Use shrimp, squid, or small fish.

Lures

Mackerel will take a variety of artificial lures. They prefer shiny metal spoons or mackerel trees, diamond jigs, or small lures. During early spring, small, shiny spoons are best. Use a black swivel to prevent the fish from attacking the shiny swivel instead of the lure. If you prefer trolling, a mackerel tree is a good choice.

Equipment

I recommend a 6- to 7-foot medium-action boat rod and a matching conventional bait-casting reel filled with 15- to 20-pound-test monofilament line.

If you want to cast lures, use a 6- to 8-foot medium-action spinning rod with a matching spinning reel filled with 15- to 20-pound-test monofilament line.

It's best to use a short length of wire leader to prevent the fish's sharp teeth from cutting through the line.

Fly tackle can also be used for mackerel.

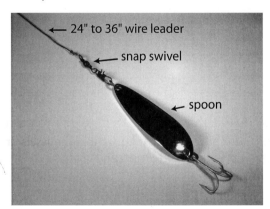

Casting spoon rig for mackerel.

Typical shiny spoon for mackerel.

OPALEYE

The opaleye ranges from San Francisco to Baja California. It is perch shaped but heavier bodied than perch. It is oval in shape, with prominent scales, a small mouth, and a rounded snout; it is dark olive green, with one or two light spots at the base of the dorsal fin. The eyes are blue and large. It has one long dorsal fin with twelve to fourteen spines and twelve to fifteen rays; the anal fin has three spines and seventeen to twenty-one rays. The rear profile is rounded and the caudal fin is slightly indented at the center.

Opaleye mature sexually and spawn when they're about 7 to 10 inches in length at about 2 or 3 years of age. Spawning

Latin name
Girella nigricans

Best time to catch
Most of the year, depending on location

Also known as
Black perch, blue-eyed perch, bluefish, button back, green perch, Jack Benny, opaleye perch

takes place in large schools in shallow water from April through June. The eggs are free floating and can be found several miles offshore. The young form schools of several dozen individuals. As the fry grow, they seek deeper water.

Opaleye reside in shallow reefs, rocky shorelines, and kelp beds from about 30 feet to about 100 feet in depth. The largest concentrations are at 65-foot depths. It can grow to 25 inches and 13 pounds in weight, but this is rare. It tolerates water temperatures as low as 45°F to as high as 95°F.

Opaleye primarily consume marine algae, which includes boa kelp, giant kelp, sea lettuce, and coralline algae. It also consumes small tube worms and red crabs.

Fishing Tips

Opaleye is considered one of the better sport fish on light tackle. It is generally found in shallow natural rocky or artificial reef areas and can be fished from the shore, piers, or docks. It is not often fished from boats because of the dangers of fishing within rocky formations. It can be caught during the winter months and early spring. It is difficult to hook and tends to put up a fight. Since it usually travels in schools while feeding on various forms of vegetation at any depth, present your fishing rig at various depths so it passes through the vegetation. Because you'll be fishing among rocks, be prepared to lose rigs.

Bait

Because of the opaleye's vegetarian diet, some anglers use moss or enough thawed frozen peas placed on the hook to completely cover the hook and shank. However, fresh mussels or pieces of bloodworm or small rock crab will attract opaleye as well.

Equipment

Use a 6- to 7-foot moderate-action spinning rod with a matching spinning reel filled with 10- to 15-pound-test monofilament line.

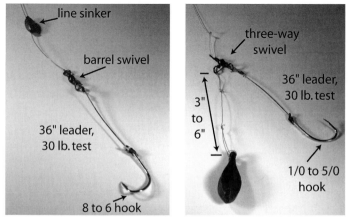

Acceptable terminal fishing rigs for opaleye.

POLLOCK

Pollock is considered the most active member of the codfish family. It can be found from Massachusetts to Virginia. Pollock has an olive green to brownish green back, ranging to yellow on its sides. The dorsal and anal fin arrangement is similar to that of the codfish.

Latin name
Pollachius virens

Best time to catch
May to October

Also known as
Blisterback, Boston bluefish, coalfish, coley, green cod, saithe

Males mature sexually at about 4 to 6 years of age, females at about 5 or 6 years. They spawn during the fall and early winter at depths of 80 to 300 feet when the water cools to about 45 to 60°F. Females produce about 4 million eggs per year. The fertilized eggs float near the surface until they hatch in about six to nine days. The fry remain near the surface for about three months before moving down to become bottom dwellers. Pollock grows about 5 inches per year and reaches 3½ feet, and can weigh from 5 to 15 pounds; it can live to about 20 years of age, but most live an average of about 15 years.

Like cod, pollock resides in deep water but, unlike cod, it is also found in shallow water. It prefers rocky bottom. It is predominantly a daytime sight feeder; unlike cod, it often chases its prey to the surface. It can tolerate temperatures as low as 34°F but is most abundant in water that is about 50 to 60°F. It migrates inshore in large schools during the spring, then moves offshore when the water cools and remains offshore during the colder months.

Adults feed on crustaceans, such as shrimp, and smaller fish, such as herring, sand lance, cod, smelt, haddock, and hake.

Fishing Tips

Pollock is an aggressive feeder and strong fighter; it will strike at fast-moving lures. Small pollock can be found close to shore from spring to late fall. The larger, older fish can be found in deeper waters offshore.

Pollock is pursued by private, party, or charter boats that can travel long distances and withstand rough water conditions. The fish can be found over wrecks or reef structure in deep water. The same tackle that is used for cod can also be used for pollock. Pollock can be fished at anchor or by trolling with 3/0 to 6/0 hooks with skimmer clams for bait, or with a jig. When hooked it makes short, powerful runs and occasionally leaps and shakes on the surface.

If you're on board a party boat and everyone is using bait, jigging is not advisable, unless the boat is nearly empty and using jigs is authorized by the captain. Chances are that everyone on board will be using bait rather than jigs.

Bait

For offshore fishing, skimmer clams are the primary bait.

Lures

For inshore fishing, try casting spoons, tube lures, spinners, or plugs.

Equipment

Use a 7- to 8-foot fast- to extra-fast-action rod with a conventional bait-casting reel filled with 30- to 50-pound-test monofilament line. Once on the surface, the fish needs to be gaffed or netted, depending on its size, to bring it on board.

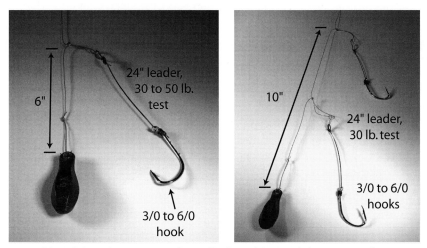

6"

24" leader, 30 to 50 lb. test

3/0 to 6/0 hook

10"

24" leader, 30 lb. test

3/0 to 6/0 hooks

Typical baitfishing bottom rigs for pollock. Fishing with bait is usually very productive and will not tire out the angler, unlike jigging.

FLORIDA POMPANO

Florida pompano ranges from Massachusetts to the Gulf of Mexico but is found mainly from Chesapeake Bay to Florida. It is abundant in tropical waters off Florida.

Latin name
Trachinotus carolinus

Best time to catch
Late summer to early fall off the Carolinas; Spring and fall off Florida

It has a deep, flattened, oval-shaped body with a small mouth, a short, blunt snout, and a deeply forked caudal fin. It ranges from greenish gray on the back shading to silver along the sides. The belly, throat, and pelvic and anal fins are gold toned. The first dorsal fin is short and hard to detect; the second dorsal fin is a single spine containing twenty-two to twenty-seven soft rays. The anal fin is slightly behind the second dorsal fin and consists of twenty to twenty-three soft rays.

Adult Florida pompano closely resemble permit except that permit has a deeper body and is much larger. (Adult Florida pompano usually average about 3 pounds, whereas permit can weigh 25 to 30 pounds.) Young Florida pompano and permit are the same size, look the same, and have nearly the same instincts.

Florida pompano reach sexual maturity at 1 year of age and spawn offshore between March and September, peaking between April and June. They live to 3 or 4 years of age and rarely exceed 6 pounds. A mature female of 16 inches long can produce more than 600,000 eggs. The young fish grow rapidly, attaining a length of 8 inches by the end of the first year.

Florida pompano inhabit inshore waters along sandy beaches and oyster bars; they can be found in the turbid waters of brackish bays and estuaries and in water up to about 130 feet deep. They form small schools and travel close to shore while migrating north and south along the Atlantic coast. They prefer water temperatures ranging from 81 to 90°F.

Most Florida pompano are caught by fishing on the bottom with natural bait. They feed on mollusks, crustaceans, and other invertebrates. They are difficult to catch with artificial bait that resemble fish because fish is not a staple of their diet.

Fishing Tips

Florida pompano can be fished off the bottom with a sinker. It should be small enough to hold down the baited hook but not so heavy as to hinder the movement of the hook with the current along the bottom. Recommended baits include sandworms, bloodworms, and crustaceans. Allow the bait to rest on the bottom for a couple of minutes, then slowly retrieve it. The fish will hit the bait hard and quickly hook itself. Florida pompano are always searching for food that was washed up against bridge pilings. It's best to fish on the landward side of pilings during a flood tide and on the seaward side on an ebb tide.

Chumming will increase your chances of catching fish. Chum can be barnacles or mussels tossed into the water in limited amounts not far from the bridge piling and around the boat about every 15 to 20 minutes. Barnacles can be carefully scraped from the pilings with a garden scraper and extras placed in a bucket for later use.

If you prefer jigs, you can use ¼- to ½-ounce yellow or white bucktail jigs with the hair trimmed to the bend of the hook. Florida pompano are notorious for being short strikers; trimming the hair will ensure that the fish is hooked.

Florida pompano is a schooling species, so where one is seen there are always a lot more. Cast the baited hook or lure into the area until one grabs the offering. The best fishing is in early morning or late afternoon on a flood tide. To fish for Florida pompano from the beach, look for a lot of sand fleas near the edge of the water. The fish wait for the sand fleas to be deposited by the receding waves. Have some insect repellent along with you to try and keep the sand fleas off you; their bite can draw blood. They hop along the high-water mark in warm climates

Sand fleas.

and are found in abundance during late dusk; they burrow in the sand during the day. Large sand fleas resemble small crabs and can be placed on a hook to attract Florida pompano.

Florida pompano can be caught in shallow water close to shore. You can also use surf-casting or fly fishing equipment from the shoreline.

Bait
Natural bait such as small crabs, clams, sand fleas, whole sandworms or bloodworms, or shrimp is best.

Lures
Try yellow or white bucktail jigs or Texas-rigged rubber worms.

Equipment
Use a 7-foot medium-action spinning rod with a matching spinning reel filled with 6- to 12-pound-test monofilament line.

For surf fishing, use a 9- to 14-foot medium-action surf rod and a matching spinning reel filled with 20- to 30-pound-test monofilament line. The rod should be capable of throwing 6- to 8-ounce sinker weights.

For fly fishing, use your preferred weight fly rod and matching reel filled with the desired type of line—floating or sinking depending on wave conditions. The backing should be 100 yards or more.

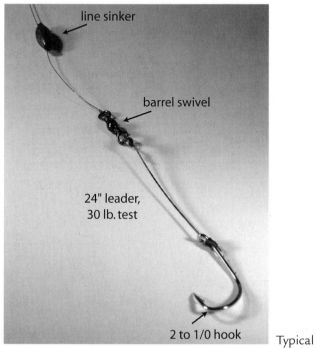

line sinker

barrel swivel

24" leader, 30 lb. test

2 to 1/0 hook

Typical Florida pompano rig.

BOCACCIO ROCKFISH

Bocaccio is one of the largest of about seventy species of rockfish that inhabit the Pacific coast from the Gulf of Alaska to Mexico. It is abundant off the central and southern coast of California.

Latin name
Sebastes paucispinis

Best time to catch
None, due to restrictions (see text)

Also known as
Pacific red snapper, red snapper, rock cod, salmon grouper

It has a fairly large mouth. The upper jaw is long and extends beyond the eyes; the lower jaw is considerably behind the upper jaw. The forward dorsal fin is notched and has sharp spines. The body color ranges from olive to burnt orange or brown on the back and from pink to red along the belly.

As with all rockfish, the eggs hatch in the female, and she gives birth to live young. Bocaccio mate in early fall; the young are released several months later. Depending on her size, each female produces from 20,000 to 2.3 million eggs. The fry move toward the surface of the water and remain there for several months. Later they settle as a group anywhere from nearshore areas to depths of 95 to 395 feet. They grow rapidly and can reach 9 inches in length by the time they are a year old. They feed on plankton at first, then on crustaceans. When large enough they feed on smaller rockfish. Bocaccio can live 30 years or more, weigh as much as 24 pounds, and reach 36 inches in length, although most range from 20 to 24 inches in length.

Adults prefer bottom to midlevel waters over gravel-littered rocky formations and kelp beds from 250 to 725 feet deep.

Bocaccio numbers have been severely depleted because of heavy fishing pressure over the past twenty years or so. Releasing any bocaccio you catch will help increase the stocks.

ROOSTERFISH

Roosterfish ranges from San Clemente, California, to Peru, although it is rare north of Baja California. A member of the jack family, it has a gray back and a silver body with a

Latin name
Nematistius pectoralis

Best time to catch
May through July

comb of seven distinct spines above the dorsal fin. The caudal fin is deeply forked—typical of all jacks. Two long, dark streaks extend from the dorsal fin and along the sides and end just before the caudal fin. Roosterfish does not have sharp teeth.

It can grow in excess of 100 pounds and reach more than 4 feet in length. The average fish caught ranges from 25 to 40 pounds and can be found 100 to 200 yards offshore.

It prefers 75°F water and frequents inshore sandy stretches, often lingering around nearshore reefs or rocky formations. It patrols the shoreline in search of baitfish schools and often herds sardines, anchovies, and mullet into tight circles, then slashes through the school in a feeding frenzy. While feeding in the surf, roosterfish put on a fantastic show. It prefers heavy surf, which disorients the baitfish and makes it easier for the roosterfish to feed. Dead giveaways to a feeding frenzy are diving birds and boiling water.

Fishing Tips

The type of leader you use depends on the clarity of the water. With crystal clear water it's best to use the lightest-weight leader—about 40-pound test; if the water is murky, use at least a 50-pound-test leader. Avoid using a swivel near the hook leader; instead place a 75- to 125-pound swivel about 12 inches above the leader. Larger roosterfish tend to be leery of additional hardware.

Surf fishing and trolling are the most popular methods for catching roosterfish. Natural bait is preferred for surf fishing, but crocodile or Hopkins lures—shiny spoonlike lures that attract roosterfish and most other types of predator species—can also be used. But be aware that roosterfish do not often hit artificial lures at the surf.

For trolling, the bait should be trolled 50 to 75 feet behind the boat. It's best to use live bait to hook a decent-sized roosterfish, although lures will work. When using live bait, use circle hooks for easier hook-ups. If using lures while trolling, use topwater lures, and try to keep the lure from becoming airborne. Always keep it near the surface of the water but never out of the water. Use a 3-ounce lure that's colored red and white. Roosterfish are attracted to this color lure more than any other color.

Roosterfish have a soft mouth, so you need only a firm pull-back of the rod to set the hook if you're using a conventional J hook.

Generally you'll encounter smaller fish in schools during the winter or spring months, and larger fish, who do not school, during the summer months.

Fly fishing for roosterfish is tremendously exciting. Popper-type flies equipped with at least 2/0 size hooks work best; elongated streamers up to 6 inches in length also work well. The preferred colors include blue, white, or green with plenty of silver to attract attention.

Regardless of technique, be prepared for a heavy fight. Roosterfish are furious fighters with unpredictable slashing moves, jumps, and long runs.

Bait

Live bait is best, specifically mullet, sardines, and anchovies.

Lures

For surf fishing, try crocodile or Hopkins lures.

For trolling, use a 3-ounce red and white topwater lure if it's worked or jigged well.

Equipment

For trolling, use a 6- to 7-foot medium-action boat rod with matching conventional bait-casting reel filled with 20- to 40-pound-test monofilament line. Use short-shank bait hooks that range from 1 to 5/0. You can also use Rapalas, tuna feathers, or wahoo types of lures.

For surf fishing, use a 10- to 12-foot medium-action surf rod with a matching fast-retrieve-ratio spinning reel filled with 20- to 30-pound-test monofilament line.

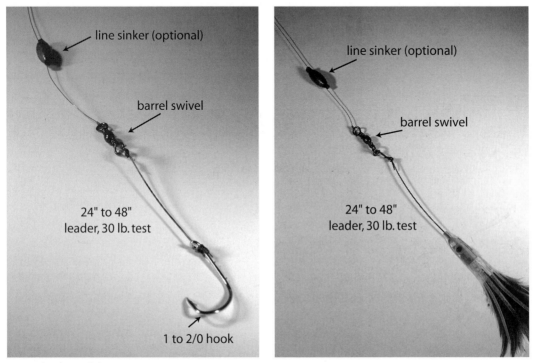

line sinker (optional)

barrel swivel

24" to 48"
leader, 30 lb. test

1 to 2/0 hook

line sinker (optional)

barrel swivel

24" to 48"
leader, 30 lb. test

Typical roosterfish rigs.

SALMON

Five species of salmon—chinook, sockeye, coho, chum, and pink—ply the Pacific coast; one species—Atlantic salmon—can be found along the Atlantic coast. Of the Pacific coast species, the chinook salmon is the largest and most popular for sportfishing.

Pacific and Atlantic salmon can find their way back to their natal stream, supposedly guided by the distinct odor of the stream. It's believed that the sun also plays a role in directing salmon toward their natal waters.

General Fishing Tips

Most salmon are caught by trolling baited hooks or lures. Frozen or fresh anchovies or herring are the most popular baits for saltwater salmon fishing. The bait must have some sort of action while being trolled to attract fish. However, you will also have success with a variety of spoons or other types of lures. Rigs that consist of dodgers or flashers catch the attention of salmon.

Dodgers or flashers are designed to make a commotion, imitating the lifelike erratic motion and sound of a natural baitfish, while trailing a baited hook or lure. They create powerful vibrations in the water. Salmon can sense these vibrations from as far as 30 to 40 yards away and will travel toward the source of the noise.

Place dodgers or flashers about 30 inches ahead of the baited hook or lure, along with ball bearing swivels at both ends of the dodger or flasher, to allow them freedom to move without causing main-line twist. When trolling, make sure to control the speed of the boat so the dodger sways from side to side and/or the flasher rotates 360 degrees. Flashers usually work better at speeds slightly faster than those used for dodgers. Most salmon lures perform well at trolling speeds of between 2 and 2½ mph. The lure should shake, wobble, or roll in an erratic manner. The action will attract more fish. If the lure is not reacting as it should, slow the trolling speed or change the lure. Dodgers or flashers can produce excellent results because you can cover large areas of water in a short period of time while trolling.

For trolling, use a 7- to 8-foot fast- to extra-fast-action trolling rod with a matching conventional bait-casting reel filled with 30- to 40-pound-test monofilament line. Downriggers are advisable if the fish are deep (as indicated on a depth-finder).

The baited hook or lure should have plenty of action. Erratic action, simulating a wounded or struggling fish, will get the salmon's attention.

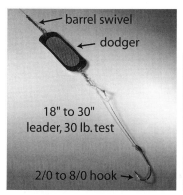
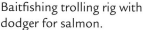

Baitfishing trolling rig with dodger for salmon.

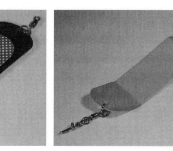

Dodger.   Flasher.

As with most predator fish, a salmon does not need to see or smell the baitfish, just detect their wiggling motion. The motion provides enough vibration in the water for a salmon to locate the baitfish.

Salmon usually attack a baitfish from the front in an effort to injure or kill it and swallow it head first. Because the salmon can't attack the bait with a leader attached at the front of a baited hook or lure, you have to entice the salmon to chase the offering, then grab hold of it by the tail. To do this, the trolling speed must be perfect. And absolutely sharp hooks are needed to prevent missed hook-ups if the salmon attacks the bait at the tail.

The most popular colors for artificial bait for salmon are red, dark green, chartreuse, blue, white, black and white, or chrome. However, the success of any color varies according to the particular day. One day one color will catch fish and the next day another color will do the job. Carry an assortment of each color in the tackle box when trolling for salmon. Try different colors until you get a response from a fish, then stay with that color for the rest of the day.

The most popular colors and/or surfaces for dodgers or flashers are chrome, hammered chrome, chartreuse, watermelon, red, blue, Kelly green, or white, depending on the area being fished. To fish deep water, use wire line, lead-core line, downriggers and dralls, or keel-type sinkers, along with reflective dodgers or flashers to attract attention.

Regardless of method, observe the type of baitfish in the area being fished, and try to match the size of the artificial lure or jig to it. The natural bait used most often in the ocean is anchovies or herring. Avoid lures that are too heavy; they hinder the action of the dodger or flasher, making them ineffective.

As with most types of fishing, feeding birds are an indicator of the whereabouts of the fish. Salmon attack their prey from underneath, pushing the baitfish to the surface, where the birds readily feed on them. Another indicator that salmon are present is other boats that have located feeding schools. Salmon feed on specific types of baitfish; it's best to match them. Salmon always follow the baitfish and stay in one area as long as the baitfish are around, sometimes for months. When the baitfish move, the salmon follow them.

For fly fishing, use a sinking line to get the fly to the level of the fish without hitting bottom. For saltwater fly fishing, use long casts if fishing from the shore. You'll need at least a 9-foot fly rod. Rods 10 feet or longer help you gain distance but necessitate heavier-weight line; the combined weight of rod and line can tire you out quickly.

Atlantic Salmon

The Atlantic salmon is the only salmon that resides along the East Coast in the Atlantic Ocean. It is considered a graceful fish, with a long, hydrodynamically shaped body and a slightly forked caudal fin. It is blue-green along the back tapering to silver along the sides, and has a white belly while living in the ocean. It has a few spots above the lateral line and no spots beneath it. During spawning the males change to greenish or reddish brown mottled with red or orange. The mouth extends to just below the rear of the eye; the teeth are well developed. Their finely tuned senses of hearing, smell, and taste help them to locate food and to sense danger by feeling the waves across their body. Other than during spawning, when they do not feed, they often strike aggressively at artificial lures. The Atlantic salmon, the sec-

Latin name
Salmo salar

Best time to catch
Late spring through early fall

Also known as
Fiddler, grilse, grilt, Kennebec salmon, king

ond largest of all the salmon species, is not to be confused with the chinook salmon, also known as "king."

Males and females reach sexual maturity at about 2 years of age. They spawn in October through November, peaking in late October. During the spawning period, the head of the male elongates, developing a hook-shaped lower jaw that is used in fighting. The females select a nesting place, called a *redd*, over a gravel bottom. The males drive away other males during courting. The female produces about 700 to 800 eggs per pound of her body weight; she buries the eggs in the gravel bottom at a series of redds she creates until she deposits all her eggs. Some Atlantic salmon die after spawning; some survive to spawn a second or third time. The survivors, called *kelts*, must be returned when caught by anglers. They are identified by their thin body, a longer than usual vent between the anus and the anal fin, and maggots on the gills or on the red gill filaments. Kelts may return to the sea after spawning or may remain in the river for the winter and return to sea the following spring, where they resume good health.

For the first 2 to 3 years of life, Atlantic salmon reside in fresh water over a gravel bottom. Then they migrate out to sea for about a year or two, traveling great distances in small groups in search of food, such as squid, shrimp, and small fish. Atlantic salmon can grow to 60 inches in length and weigh from 5 to 60 pounds. They generally don't live beyond 9 years of age. While in the ocean they reside at depths of 10 to 50 feet at water temperatures from 39 to 53°F; they avoid temperatures higher than 80°F and cannot survive at temperatures lower than 20°F.

Atlantic salmon are known for the fantastic leaps they take when returning to their birth stream. They can clear obstacles as high as 12 feet.

Fishing Tips

Atlantic salmon can be caught in the ocean by using drift fishing, fly fishing, or trolling techniques. Bait size varies from small to large depending on water visibility. When fishing in water with low visibility, use large bait so the fish can see it; as the clarity improves, use smaller bait. Because Atlantic salmon can be almost anywhere within their vast range, it's best to ask at a local tackle shop where to find them.

All rear treble hooks on lures should be replaced with a single conventional J hook to keep from foul-hooking the fish in the gills or face. When using lures of any kind, provide plenty of action when working the lure.

Bait

Atlantic salmon feed on herring, sand eels, small baitfish, squid, and surfacing-feeding crustaceans.

Lures

Try shiny spoons.

Equipment

For trolling from a boat, use a 6- to 7-foot medium-action rod and matching conventional bait-casting reel filled with 15- to 30-pound-test monofilament line.

For surf fishing from a beach, use a 10- to 12-foot medium-action surf rod and matching spinning reel filled with 15- to 30-pound-test monofilament line.

Chinook Salmon

The chinook salmon, the largest of all the salmon species, can exceed 90 pounds in weight around Alaska and up to about 40 pounds in other areas. It ranges from Southern California to Alaska, with the greatest concentration along the British Columbia coast.

Latin name
Oncorhynchus tshawytscha

Best time to catch
Spring to fall

Also known as
Blackmouth, Columbia River salmon, king salmon, quinnat, Sacramento River salmon, spring salmon, tule, tyee

The chinook salmon can be red, pink, orange, or white or a mixture of all these colors. There are numerous black spots on the back and along the upper sides, the top of the head, and the fins. It has a black mouth with white gums. During the spawning season, the color changes to scarlet, copper, or deep olive. Males are more strikingly colored than females. Males develop a hooked upper jaw during the spawning season.

Like all salmon, the chinook salmon spawns in its natal freshwater stream and spends a portion of its life in the ocean. In any spawning run, the size of the fish varies depending upon their age when sexually mature, which can occur between 4 and 6 years of age. In Alaskan streams, the spawning run lasts from May through July.

They do not feed during the spawning migration, but use stored body fat for energy. Females deposit from 3,000 to 15,000 eggs in constructed gravel nests called redds. All chinook salmon die after spawning. The eggs hatch from late winter to early spring, depending on the spawning period and the water temperature. The young stay in the gravel and live from their egg yolk sac, then emerge from the gravel and begin to feed on plankton, and later on insects.

The fry remain in their natal stream for 2 years, then migrate (at which point they are called smolts) to the Pacific. Chinook salmon feed on herring, sand lance, squid, and various forms of crustaceans at water temperatures from 53 to 59°F. They grow quickly and double their weight in a summer season. They average between 18 to 25 pounds, although you may catch fish that weigh between 25 and 35 pounds. They live from 3 to 7 years of age.

Fishing Tips

Salmon are predictable in their habits. They usually migrate at the same time before entering their natal stream. The migration period usually starts months before they enter the stream. It's best to know their migration period in advance before heading out.

The mostly widely used technique for catching salmon at sea is trolling at dawn or dusk. Other popular techniques are fly fishing and drifting.

Trolling with natural bait such as herring is probably the best method, although artificial lures can also be trolled to attract the salmon's attention. The baited hook or lure must have plenty of rolling and erratic action.

Most fishing techniques for chinook salmon use what is known as bar fishing, which is fishing sandbars at the mouth of the salmon's natal stream when they start their migration back up it. You can troll along these sandbars with baited hooks or with lures that have a flasher or a dodger attached to the main line. Or you can cast into these areas from a nearby shoreline with baited fish-finder rigs or with lures that are aggressively jigged.

Bait
Use small adult baitfish such as sand lance, or use long pieces of squid.

Lures
Lure colors that work well are red, dark green, chartreuse, blue, white, black and white, or chrome. However, the color that works one day may not work the next, so have on hand a variety of common salmon colors. There are many designs of lures used for salmon fishing; it's best to ask at the local tackle shop which lures work best for the area you intend to fish. Also ask at what depth the fish are being caught, so you can set up a strategy before you're on the water.

Equipment
If you're trolling from a boat, use a 6- to 7-foot medium-action rod with matching conventional bait-casting reel filled with 15- to 30-pound-test monofilament line. Use a number 5/0 to 8/0 hook.

If you're fishing from the beach, use a 10- to 12-foot medium-action surf rod and matching spinning reel filled with 15- to 30-pound-test monofilament line.

Chum Salmon

Chum salmon range from the Sacramento River in California to the Mackenzie River in the Northwest Territories, and inhabit fresh water and the Pacific Ocean. It is metallic greenish blue on its back, with no distinct black spots, and silver on the sides. Spawning males turn dark olive with red vertical bars along the sides—hence the name calico salmon. Spawning males also develop a typical hooked upper jaw and white tips on the anal and pelvic fins.

Chum salmon are often confused with sockeye and coho salmon. By looking deep into the gills, you'll see that chum salmon have fewer but larger gill rakers than other species

Latin name
Oncorhynchus keta

Best time to catch
Late spring through early fall

Also known as
Autumn salmon, calico salmon, chum, dog salmon, fall salmon

of salmon. Gill rakers are bony or cartilage-like projections that point forward and inward from the gill arches, just in front of the gill filaments. Basically a coarse filter, a gill raker prevents large debris from entering and damaging the gills. Gill rakers also help the fish with feeding.

They spawn when they reach about 4 years of age and can weigh from 3 to 20 pounds. Chum salmon are the last of the salmon species to make their spawning run; they enter freshwater streams sometime after mid-June, and reach their natal stream in November or December. Because of their late spawning run, there is little interest in fishing for them in streams, although they are fished when they're in salt water.

Male chum salmon average 10 to 15 pounds in weight (females are usually smaller) but can reach as much as 30 pounds. All chum salmon can live from 3 to 7 years.

While at sea, adult chum salmon feed on herring, sand lance, squid, and crustaceans; they do not feed during their spawning run in fresh water.

Fishing Tips

The tackle should match the size of the fish, which fight hard and are extremely fast. They can be fished with natural bait or lures (although natural bait is best) while trolling or drifting. Use a flasher or dodger when trolling to help attract fish.

Bait

Use small sand lance, anchovies, or squid.

Equipment

For trolling from a boat, use a 6- to 7-foot medium-action rod with matching conventional bait-casting reel filled with 15- to 30-pound-test monofilament line. Use a number 5/0 to 8/0 hook.

For sight casting, use a 7- to 8-foot medium-action spinning rod with matching spinning reel filled with 15- to 30-pound-test line.

Coho Salmon

Most coho salmon reside in the eastern Pacific and along the West Coast, moving to the Gulf of Alaska beginning sometime in June. They later migrate along the shore until they reach their natal stream. The coho salmon is a dark metallic blue or blue-green along the top and turning silver on the sides and belly. It has several black spots on the back and along the upper portion of the caudal fin. It can be distinguished from the chinook salmon by its lack of spots on the lower portion of the tail, and its light gray gums. The chinook salmon has small dark spots on its caudal fin and has

Latin name
Oncorhynchus kisutch

Best time to catch
Early spring through fall

Also known as
Blueback, hookbill, hooknose, sea trout, silver salmon, silversides

black gums. The coho salmon resides in the same waters as large chinook salmon and fights harder than the chinook.

As with all species of Pacific salmon, coho salmon spawn and hatch in freshwater streams, then spend a portion of their lives in the Pacific Ocean. They return to their natal stream when they are about 3 years of age. Unlike sockeye salmon, coho salmon spend only a year in their natal stream. They enter spawning streams at different times of the year depending on location. In California, they enter streams from September through March—most from November through January. In Alaska, they enter streams from July through November—most in August and September.

When spawning, adult coho salmon develop a darker back and head and maroon to scarlet sides. The male's head turns green along the top and bright scarlet on the side; the body is blackish below. The females turn pinkish red on the sides. When spawning, males develop a double hooked jaw that, combined with their large teeth, makes it almost impossible for them to close their mouth.

Coho salmon do not grow as large as chinook salmon; caught fish average between 4 and 10 pounds, although fish as heavy as 30 pounds have been caught around Alaska. Coho salmon range from 25 to 30 inches in length and live for 4 years.

When in the Pacific, coho salmon feed on herring, sand lance, squid, and various crustaceans. Like all salmon, coho do not feed once they enter their natal stream for spawning.

Fishing Tips
Coho salmon follow a southerly migration along the coast toward their natal stream. They may mill about in front of their natal stream for two weeks or so (a good time to catch them) before entering the stream to spawn.

Bait
Recommended natural bait includes herring, small baitfish, squid, and crustaceans.

Lures
The most effective lures are brass, silver, blue, or green. Bring along some of each.

Equipment
If you're trolling from a boat, use a 6- to 7-foot medium-action rod with matching conventional bait-casting reel filled with 15- to 30-pound-test monofilament line. Use a number 5/0 to 8/0 hook.

For sight casting, use a 7- to 8-foot medium-action spinning rod with a matching spinning reel filled with 15- to 30-pound-test line.

Pink Salmon

In the eastern Pacific pink salmon range from the Sacramento River in northern California to the Mackenzie River in the Northwest Territories. It is the smallest of all the Pacific salmon.

Latin name
Oncorhynchus gorbuscha

Best time to catch
Spring through fall

Also known as
Fall salmon, humpbacks, humpback salmon, humpy, pink humpback, pinks

Its average weight ranges from 3 to 6 pounds, although a 12-pound pink salmon can be caught. When young, pink salmon are silver in color and have no spots on their body. When in the Pacific Ocean, pink salmon have spots on their back and their entire caudal fin. Pink salmon has a distinct humped back that develops on males just before they enter their natal stream. The hump is just in front of the dorsal fin and behind the head. Spawning males also have a slightly hooked upper jaw.

Pink salmon is usually metallic blue with tiny scales and numerous black spots along the back. The caudal fin is heavily marked with large oval spots. During spawning, the males change to red along the sides and develop large olive spots. Females develop an olive green color along the back and dusky bars; they are pale below.

The young are hatched in streams, where they remain for several months before migrating to the Pacific Ocean. They remain in the Pacific for 2 years, then migrate back to their natal stream to spawn. They die after spawning.

Depending on the year, pink salmon can be found in the ocean in large numbers between July and September. They return to streams in southern British Columbia during odd-numbered years and to streams in northern British Columbia in even-numbered years.

Adult pink salmon feed on small fish, squid, crustaceans, and plankton.

Fishing Tips

Although pink salmon can be difficult to locate in the open ocean, once found they are easy to catch because they travel in large schools while searching for food. Look for diving and feeding birds, and fish leaping out of the water while they're chasing baitfish.

Live bait will catch more fish, but lures, jigs, and flies will work, too, if you choose the right color; pink and red are best.

From early summer to late fall, adult pink salmon migrate toward their natal river from the sea. They may hold themselves at the mouth of the river for several days or weeks before entering. This is a good chance to catch them, while they're still feeding and in salt water.

Bait

Adult pink salmon feed on squid, small fish, and small shrimp and other crustaceans.

Lures

Among artificial lures, small pink spoons are productive in salt water, as are small spinner baits that contain the color pink.

For fly fishing, use pink or red flies for the best results.

Equipment

Use light tackle and light spinner types of artificial baits that are pink or red in color. Use a 6- to 7-foot medium-action spinning rod with matching spinning reel filled with 8- to 12-pound-test monofilament line.

For fly fishing, use a number 5- or 6-weight rod depending on the water conditions.

Sockeye Salmon

Sockeye salmon ranges from northern California to southern Alaska. When at sea, it has a dark greenish blue back and silver sides. There are no distinctive spots on the back or dorsal or caudal fins. All adults return to their natal stream between July and October, depending on location. As males mature, they develop a pale green head, a humped back, hooked jaws, and an increasingly red body color. During the spawning season, their head turns dark green and their body turns scarlet red (hence the name "red salmon").

Latin name
Oncorhynchus nerka

Best time to catch
Spring through fall

Also known as
Big redfish, blueback salmon, red salmon, sockeye

When sockeye salmon are about to spawn, the females swell with mature eggs. Later the females construct nests (redds) in gravel depressions, then deposit 50 to 100 eggs, which are soon fertilized by a single male. The females continue the process until they have deposited about 2,000 to 5,000 eggs. The adults die a few weeks after spawning. The eggs hatch during April or May, and the young begin to feed on their yolk sac, then plankton. Shortly after, they become predators and feed on insects, invertebrates, and other small fish. A year or two later, the young salmon (smolts) begin to migrate to the Pacific. They reside there for 1 to 3 years before returning to their natal stream. They do not feed in the stream but live on their accumulated body fat. Adult sockeye salmon weigh between 4 and 10 pounds; sockeye salmon live from 3 to 5 years.

When at sea, sockeye salmon feed on plankton, crustacean larvae, and small fish, and take squid on occasion.

Fishing Tips

Sockeye salmon are stimulated by flashing light—more so than any other species of salmon. The more flashers in the water while trolling, the better. The flashing light and noise attract a sockeye to within range of the moving lure. Sockeye salmon are known to follow behind lures for great distances without biting. To help trigger a strike, change the action of the lure from time to time by slowing or stopping the boat and jigging the lure for a moment before you resume trolling. The more action applied to the lure, the better.

When in the Pacific Ocean, sockeye salmon travel deep. A depth-finder will help locate concentrations of fish. The trolling speed should be slow and the lure fished within 20 to 35 feet of the surface.

Bait
Use squid or small adult baitfish.

Lures
Use almost any spoon type of lure that is painted orange or red or variations thereof.

Equipment
For trolling, use a 6- to 7-foot medium-action rod with matching conventional bait-casting reel filled with 15- to 25-pound-test monofilament line.

LONGFIN SANDDAB

The longfin sanddab ranges from Costa Rica to Monterey, California. It has a flat, oblong body with a straight lateral line that runs the entire length of its eye side. It has fairly large scales and a large mouth. It is a left-eyed species. It is dark brown with small white spots and a black pectoral fin along the eye side. The blind side is off-white to tan. The pectoral fin is longer than the head. The caudal fin is slightly rounded and the same color as the body.

Latin name
Citharichthys xanthostigma

Best time to catch
Year-round

Also known as
Catalina sanddab, sanddab, soft flounder

Female longfin sanddabs are generally larger than males and sexually mature at about 3 years of age. They produce 25,000 to 50,000 eggs per spawn, and spawn more than once during the spawning season, which extends from July through September.

It frequents sandy or muddy bottom from 10 to 650 feet deep. It feeds along the bottom in deep holes seeking squid, octopus, and small fish. It also eats shrimp, fish eggs, crabs, sandworms, bloodworms, and sea worms. As with most flatfish, longfin sanddab buries itself in the sand or mud with only the eyes protruding from the bottom. It can change color to camouflage itself for protection from predators.

Fishing Tips
It's best to fish deep holes in deepwater sandy or muddy areas. Drift over suspected areas while keeping the baited hook directly on the bottom with a suitable weight sinker.

Bait

The longfin sanddab will leap on a baited hook. Terminal fishing rigs can vary from one to ten hooks or more per rig, although most anglers use from one to four hooks per rig because of simplicity. Use strips of cut squid, cut octopus, shrimp, crabs, sandworms, or bloodworms.

Equipment

If you're using ten hooks or more, the rod of choice will have roller guides to reduce the friction on the line. Use a 6- to 7-foot fast- to extra-fast-action boat rod with matching conventional bait-casting reel filled with 25- to 40-pound-test monofilament line. This setup should be sturdy enough to haul in several fish at a time.

With one to four hooks, use a 6- to 7-foot moderate- to fast-action boat rod with matching conventional bait-casting reel filled with 20- to 30-pound-test monofilament line.

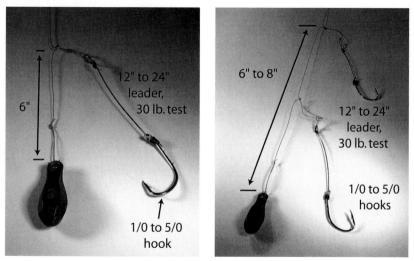

Single- and multiple-hook rigs for longfin sanddab.

PACIFIC SANDDAB

Pacific sanddab ranges from Cape San Lucas, Baja California, to the Bering Sea. It is a left-eyed species of flatfish that is easily identified by a nearly straight lateral line that runs the entire length of the eye side of the fish. Its oblong, flounder-like body is light brown mottled with yellow and orange on the eye side. The dorsal fin originates over the eyes; the anal fin is located below the pectoral fin. The anal and dorsal fins extend almost to the caudal fin.

Females are usually larger than males and are sexually mature at about 3 years of age. Spawning occurs from late

Latin name
Citharichthys sordidus

Best time to catch
Year-round

Also known as
Megrim, mottled sanddab, sanddab, soft flounder, sole

winter through the summer, depending on the location. Off California, spawning takes place from July through September, peaking in August. Females may spawn twice during a single season. The eggs settle to the bottom, where they hatch. Pacific sanddab can grow to 16 inches in length and weigh up to 2 pounds, although most caught fish are only up to 10 inches long and weigh about ½ to ¾ pound. It can live up to 10 years.

It is found along sandy or muddy bottom at depths from 30 to 1,800 feet, although it is most abundant from 115 to 295 feet deep. It seldom inhabits shallow water. Adults feed directly on the bottom on shrimp, crabs, sandworms, bloodworms, sea worms, squid, octopus, and smaller fish; they also eat an assortment of eggs. Their diet is determined by food availability.

As with most flatfish, Pacific sanddab can bury itself in the sand with only its eyes protruding to camouflage itself for protection from predators and to hide from unsuspecting prey.

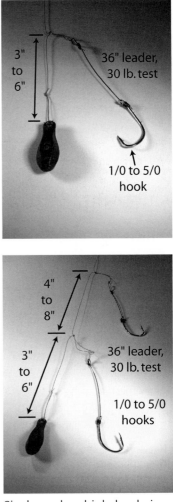

Fishing Tips

Fishing for Pacific sanddab usually requires drifting over suspected areas (sandy or muddy bottom in deep water) while keeping the baited hook directly on or slightly above the bottom with a suitable weight sinker.

Pacific sanddab will pounce on a baited hook. Terminal fishing rigs can vary from one to ten hooks or more per rig, although most anglers limit themselves to one to four hooks per rig for simplicity.

Bait

Use strips of cut squid, cut octopus, shrimp, crabs, sandworms, or bloodworms.

Equipment

If you're using ten or more hooks, use a rod with roller guides to reduce the friction on the line. Use a 6- to 7-foot fast- to extra-fast-action boat rod with matching conventional bait-casting reel filled with 25- to 40-pound-test monofilament line. This setup should be sturdy enough to haul in several fish at once.

For one to four hooks, use a 7- to 8-foot moderate- to fast-action boat rod with matching conventional bait-casting reel filled with 20- to 30-pound-test monofilament line.

Single- and multiple-hook rigs for Pacific sanddab.

SCUP

Scup, also known as porgy, is a scrappy little fish that ranges from Nova Scotia to Florida, although it is rare south of North Carolina. It has a steep, sloping nose and sharp, needle-like dorsal and anal fins for defense, which can cause injury if you're not careful. It is usually silver in color and has rather large scales for its size.

Latin name
Stenotomus chrysops

Best time to catch
June through October

Also known as
Bay porgy, humpback, porgy, sand porgy

Males and females mature sexually at about 2 years of age and about 6 inches in length. Scup usually doesn't reach more than 6 pounds. They are given different names by size to help identify them: the sand porgy weighs about ½ pound, the bay porgy about 1 pound, and the humpback about 1½ to 3 pounds. Because of their bony structure, scup are not filleted unless they weigh more than a pound.

Adult fish form large schools and prefer areas with a hard bottom or submerged structure, where they search for invertebrates. Scup are seasonal migrants, traveling northward and inshore during the spring and summer months and southward and offshore during the fall and winter. Offshore scup found from late September to late November tend to be larger and feistier. They are affected by changes of water temperature and many succumb to sudden temperature fluctuations.

Scup feed during daylight hours over gravel, sand, or rocky bottom and move to mid-depths at night. During the fishing season, they can be found from 10 to 80 feet deep.

Fishing Tips

Scup are located at the bottom over inshore or offshore banks, shellfish beds, artificial reefs, shipwrecks, or rocky or sandy bottom. You want to feel the sinker on the bottom because scup don't usually travel more than a foot off it. They can be found along bridge abutments, piers, and bulkheads, although larger schools prefer deeper water toward channels. Scup can be fished from shore or from an anchored boat. They will take most natural bait offered, although they prefer clams, cut squid, sandworms, and bloodworms.

The best fishing is from late spring into late fall, although June and early July are the best months to catch bay porgies. Catches remain good into September and late November offshore for humpback porgies, which weigh up to about 3 pounds or more before they head south to deeper water.

Catching scup is fun for the entire family, especially those new to saltwater bottom fishing. In spite of its small size, scup packs a lot of fight when hooked on light tackle. Party and charter boats frequently fish for them throughout the season, although they mainly target humpbacks offshore from mid-September through November in northern waters and later south of Long Island.

When fishing for scup, cut bait into small pieces (because of the fish's small mouth). Keep the baited hook close to the bottom. Move the rod tip slowly up and down, but don't let the baited hook rise higher than a foot off the bottom. Keep the line tight when you feel the bottom with the sinker.

Bait

Scup will hit most soft baits. Cut sandworms or bloodworms, squid, clams, or mussels are excellent bait.

Two nice humpback scup (out of fifteen) caught off Montauk Point, Long Island.

Equipment

Use a 6- to 7-foot moderate- to fast-action boat rod with a matching conventional bait-casting reel filled with 10- to 15-pound-test monofilament line. The weight of the sinker depends on the current below.

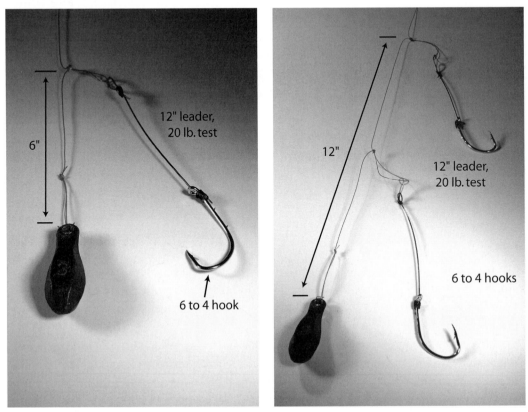

12" leader, 20 lb. test

6"

6 to 4 hook

12"

12" leader, 20 lb. test

6 to 4 hooks

Typical terminal rigs for scup.

SPOTTED SEA TROUT

Spotted sea trout, also called weakfish, is a member of the drum family. It is found in shallow areas of bays and estuaries along the Atlantic coast from Long Island, New York, to the Gulf of Mexico. It has a dark gray-green back, with numerous distinctive black spots extending from the first dorsal fin to the tail, and a white or silver belly. Its lower jaw protrudes; its upper jaw has one or two canine teeth.

Latin name
Cynoscion nebulosus

Best time to catch
January through October

Also known as
Black trout, gator trout, salmon trout, speck, speckled trout, spotted squeteague, spotted weakfish, trout, winter trout, yellow mouth

Males mature at a much smaller size than females. Regardless of when the males were spawned, they become sexually mature the following May at as small as 7 inches. Females become sexually mature once they reach about 10 inches in length. However, most spawning populations are composed of 2- to 4-year-olds. Spotted sea trout spawn in estuaries with swift-moving currents from April through early September, depending on location. During the spawning season, males make a drumming sound from their swim bladder; females are attracted to areas where large numbers of males have gathered. Spawning usually takes place at dusk and ends by midnight.

The eggs are transported by currents to shallow water, where they remain until they hatch. The fry prefer mud, oyster bars, or marshes, where they feed on crustaceans, ghost shrimp, and smaller fish. At about 6 inches in length, the fry move to deeper water in creeks and along the edges of channels and remain there from December through March. When the water warms in spring, the young form schools and travel throughout the estuary in flooded marshes, continuing to feed on ghost shrimp and smaller fish.

Females grow faster than males after the first year. Their age is determined by their size. One-year-olds are about 8 to 9 inches long, 2-year-olds range from 14 to 17 inches, and 6-year-olds are 19 to 25 inches or longer. Spotted sea trout typically weigh less than 5 pounds; they can weigh as much as 16 pounds, but this is rare. Most large fish caught are females. Spotted sea trout can live to about 10 years of age.

Spotted sea trout is an inshore schooling species that doesn't migrate, but does travel to deeper water during the fall when the water cools and return to the shallow water of bays during the spring as the water warms. Although it is a bottom-dwelling species, it feeds at any level of water on shrimp, baitfish, killifish, crustaceans, and sea worms.

Fishing Tips

During the warm months, it's best to fish shallow areas from early morning into the evening hours. During high-heat periods, the fish tend to move into deeper water, such as channels or near oyster reefs, where the water temperature ranges from 55 to 80°F. If you're fishing from a boat, look for birds feeding on shrimp and smaller fish. Perhaps they're being chased to the surface by schools of spotted sea trout. A sea trout will take almost any bait presented during a feeding frenzy.

During the colder months, it's best to fish the deeper portions of harbors, rivers, and channels. Spotted sea trout can be fished from a drifting or an anchored boat by trolling, jigging, surf casting, or fly fishing and can be caught in salt or brackish water.

Most proficient anglers use a small popping cork or float while fishing for spotted sea trout. With the float in the water, rapidly move the rod from the two o'clock position in an arch to the eleven o'clock position. The fast whipping action of the rod causes the float or cork to make a popping sound; it attracts fish because it mimics the sound of another spotted sea trout feeding. The fish will not bite if the float does not make a popping sound.

Spotted sea trout have a soft mouth that tears easily, so don't attempt to set the hook hard when you feel a fish. Instead, set the hook gently, and don't try to horse the fish in. If you're fishing from a boat, use a net to bring the fish over the gunwale.

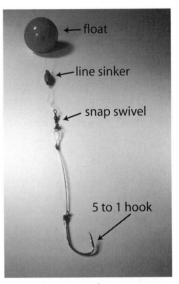

Popping cork rig for sea trout.

Bait

Live shrimp is the bait to use for most spotted sea trout. To catch larger fish, live baitfish such as small croaker or killifish are a better choice. Live baitfish are usually fished below a popping cork. Spotted sea trout are also drawn to bloodworms, sandworms, dead shrimp, small croaker, and mullet strips.

Lures

Silver or gold spoons, bucktail jigs, or plugs work well. Just remember to use plenty of action by working the lure to create a commotion.

Equipment

Use a 6- to 8-foot fast- to extra-fast-action boat or spinning rod with a matching bait-casting or spinning reel filled with 10- to 20-pound-test monofilament line. Use a hook ranging from 5 to 1 in size.

A popping cork rig is good for fishing depths from 2 to 10 feet using dead or live natural bait. Any deeper, the rig may get tangled while you're casting.

Fly fishing tackle can also be used for surface-swimming spotted sea trout.

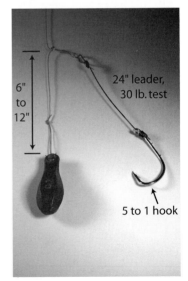

Rig to use when bottom fishing for sea trout.

WEAKFISH

Weakfish, also known as sea trout, ranges from Cape Cod to Florida. The best places to find it are Peconic Bay (southwest of Gardiners Bay on Long Island) and Chesapeake Bay. It can be found from North Carolina to Florida during the winter months and from New York to Delaware in summer. Weakfish is named for its fragile jaw muscles, which tear when the fish is hooked. Weakfish, which closely resembles spotted sea trout, is called gray trout, summer trout, or squeteague from Rhode Island north, and trout or gray trout from Delaware south. It has a trout-shaped body that is greenish on the back and blue to green on the sides. Its upper jaw has two canine teeth.

Latin name
Cynoscion regalis

Best time to catch
May through July

Also known as
Common sea trout, common weakfish, gray trout, northern sea trout, northern weakfish, squeteague, summer trout, tiderunner, weakie, yellowfin

Weakfish is a member of the drum family, which is known for the drumming noise it makes with its swim bladder. Only males make the sound, which increases during the spawning season. Males and females mature sexually at about 3 years of age and spawn in spring in nearshore locations, such as estuaries; this is when the best fishing occurs. Spring runs begin along the Northeast coast from late April to mid-May. The fish arrive in Chesapeake and Delaware bays at about the same time as in Peconic Bay. It begins its offshore winter migration in mid-September, continuing into October for southern offshore locations.

The average size of caught weakfish is from 1 to 3 pounds; some weigh up to 12 pounds, but this is rare. Large fish are called tiderunners because they run in and out with the tide.

Depending on the location, weakfish inhabits bays and prefers water temperatures of 60°F or higher. It does not frequent deep water during the spawning season but resides in shallow water close to shore. Weakfish is a schooling species and usually a selective feeder but strikes hard when feeding on baitfish.

Fishing Tips

Weakfish may be taken at any depth and from a drifting or an anchored boat. Other successful techniques include trolling, surf fishing, and fishing from bridges or jetties. When hooked, weakfish takes long runs that include unpredictable changes in direction.

It feeds during the day but is most active when the water has cooled down, usually between 5 and 9 p.m. The best places to fish at night are at bridges or from a drifting boat beneath a bridge (see next section). Weakfish can also be caught during the day in open bays.

It puts up a strong fight when hooked on light tackle. When bringing in a weakfish, be careful not to yank the hook from its mouth, which can tear. Keep the drag of the reel relatively loose.

Bridge Fishing

Locate a quiet spot near and below a bridge during the evening hours and look for streetlights on the bridge. Under them is where weakfish will gather in search of ghost shrimp attracted by the light. Cast a baited hook toward the light reflection and begin to reel the line in. Weights aren't needed, at least at first; the weight of the baited hook should be enough. Because weakfish swim near the top of the water in pursuit of food, use a fish-finder rig to keep the baited hook away from the crabs on the bottom. If you have no success after a couple of casts, add a small line weight to the line until you locate (with a strike) the fish.

Boat Fishing

During the day weakfish are usually fished from a drifting boat, although the boat can be anchored if ghost shrimp are used as chum in areas of weakfish concentrations. When chumming with ghost shrimp, don't be too generous or too skimpy with them. Releasing five to ten shrimp at 2- to 3-minute intervals should keep a constant chum slick to keep fish near the boat.

Bait

Use whole sandworms or bloodworms, squid strips, shrimp, bunker, or sand eels. If you're drifting in a boat, a whole live sandworm or bloodworm placed on the hook and allowed to drift 50 to 75 feet from the boat will usually draw attention. Don't use sinkers. The baited hook will drift just below the surface until it's spotted by a fish.

Bloodworm on hook without a line sinker for weakfish.

Lures

Try a Texas-rigged plastic (jelly) worm, or a bucktail jig or leadhead jig topped with a sandworm, a squid strip, ghost shrimp, or a pork rind trailer.

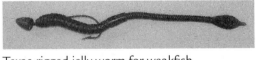

Texas-rigged jelly worm for weakfish.

Leadhead and rubber tail jig for weakfish.

Bucktail and pork rind trailer for weakfish.

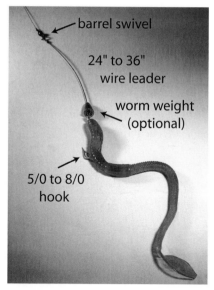

barrel swivel

24" to 36"
wire leader

worm weight
(optional)

5/0 to 8/0
hook

Typical weakfish Texas-rigged jelly worm. It can be used with or without the line sinker depending on the water current and the speed of drift. A whole natural bloodworm or sandworm can be placed on the hook.

Equipment

When fishing from a boat, use a 6- to 7-foot fast- to extra-fast-action rod with matching conventional bait-casting reel filled with 20- to 25-pound-test monofilament line. If you're casting jigs or rubber worms from a boat or the shore, use a 7- to 8-foot fast- to extra-fast-action rod with matching spinning reel filled with 20- to 25-pound-test monofilament line.

Bring a large-mouth net to retrieve the fish. Avoid horsing a weakfish over the gunwales of the boat. The weight of the fish could tear the hook from its jaw.

Fly tackle can also be used for surface-swimming weakfish.

CALIFORNIA SHEEPHEAD

California sheephead ranges from Monterey Bay to the tip of Baja California. Adults have a steeply sloping forehead and large doglike canine teeth, which are used to pry food from rocks. The single dorsal fin extends from the pectoral fin to the back of the anal fin. Males have a brick red mid body, a white chin, and a black caudal fin; females are reddish brown.

Latin name
Semicossyphus pulcher

Best time to catch
Most of the year

Also known as
Billygoat, fathead, goat, humpy, red fish, sheepie

All California sheephead are female until they reach 7 or 8 years of age, when some of them change permanently into males. It spawns from spring through early summer. The young live close to rocks, and when disturbed they seek shelter within rock formations. At about 2 years of age the fry are about 6 to 8 inches long and acquire typical female coloration: uniform pinkish red with a white lower jaw. The young are reddish on the sides with a single white stripe, white pectoral fins, and white dorsal and caudal fins with large black spots. California sheephead can grow to 3 feet long and weigh as much as 37 pounds, but this is rare. Most California sheephead caught range from 10 to 15 pounds. California sheephead can live for 35 to 40 years.

It is a bottom-dwelling species that resides over rocky kelp areas near shore, usually at depths from 20 to 100 feet, although it can be found as deep as 180 feet. It feeds on mollusks, urchins, crabs, mussels, squid, snails, and smaller fish.

Fishing Tips

The best fishing is along the bottom in any rocky formations and dense kelp beds or over mussel beds at depths from 20 to 100 feet. Place your rig directly on the bottom because California sheephead is primarily a bottom feeder. Expect to lose some rigs because of the kelp plants and rocky structure below. California sheephead can be caught from piers or from the shoreline providing that there is some form of structure. It can be taken with hooks from 3/0 to 5/0 in size that are baited with mussels, rock crabs, lobster, shrimp, clams, or cut fish strips. Be aware that California sheephead is an excellent bait stealer.

California sheephead usually puts up a strong tugging battle. During the battle, make every effort to prevent the fish from running within rock formations or around kelp beds, to avoid lost fishing rigs.

Bait

Use live or dead anchovies, shrimp, ghost shrimp, bloodworms, rock crabs, mussels, or cut squid.

Equipment

I recommend a 6- to 7-foot fast- to extra-fast-action rod with a matching conventional bait-casting reel filled with 25- to 40-pound-test monofilament line.

If you must cast to reach certain locations, use a 7- to 8-foot extra-fast-action spinning rod with a matching spinning reel filled with 25- to 40-pound-test monofilament line.

Avoid using any extra hardware on the fishing rig, regardless of the technique used, to prevent rig hang-ups.

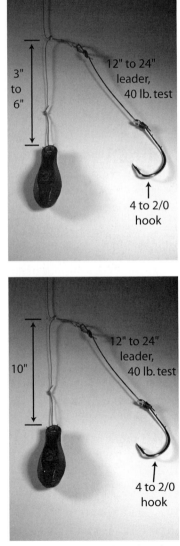

Typical California sheephead terminal fishing rigs.

SHEEPSHEAD

Sheepshead is a member of the scup (porgy) and sea bream family. It ranges along the Atlantic coast from southern New Jersey to Florida, with dense populations off southwest Florida. It

Latin name
Archosargus probatocephalus

Best time to catch
September through November

Also known as
Convict fish, sheepshead sea bream

has a greenish gray body with five or six vertical dark stripes along each side. The mouth is medium sized and contains large incisor teeth and molars, enabling the fish to crush mollusks, crabs, and barnacles. It has soft cheeks, but the hard roof of the mouth is difficult to penetrate with a hook. The dorsal and anal fins have short, sharp spines.

Males and females mature sexually at about 2 or 3 years of age. From February through April, they migrate to offshore or inshore waters, depending on the water temperature, to spawn. Females can deposit 14,000 to 250,000 eggs during each spawn (the average deposit is about 90,000 eggs), and they spawn several times each season. The eggs are buoyant and hatch about 28 hours after spawning. The fry live above muddy bottom in sea grass flats, where they feed on algae and zooplankton. When they reach about 2 inches in length, they leave the grass flats and mass inshore with the adults around pilings, piers, and jetties. It can reach a maximum weight of about 20 to 25 pounds and a length of 30 inches, which is considered a large porgy, although the average caught fish weighs 4 to 8 pounds. It lives about 15 to 20 years.

It resides in salt water but in the winter months it moves to the brackish water of coastal rivers. It frequents jetties, dock pilings, bridge abutments, shipwrecks, reefs, and other structure that support the mussels, barnacles, clams, and oysters it feeds on.

Fishing Tips

Sheepshead is located at the bottom along pilings, jetties, and oyster beds and over wrecks and reefs either inshore or offshore. It is a strong fighter and an excellent bait stealer. You should be prepared to set the hook as soon as the sinker hits the bottom, and allow no slack in the line. In warm climates you can fish sheepshead year-round.

Some anglers take barnacles from the sides of pilings and sprinkle them around the boat as chum to attract the fish to the vicinity of the hook.

If you think you've hooked a sheepshead, slowly lift the tip of the rod about 2 feet. If you feel any pressure, continue lifting the rod tip. If a fish has the bait in its mouth, it will begin to move away from the pressure. When that happens, reel in a bit faster to increase the pressure. The fish will move a little faster too and hook itself in the soft tissue on the side of its cheek. Without using too much pressure, play the fish to prevent it from pulling the hook from its cheek.

Set the drag very tight to prevent the fish from going around structure and tangling the line on it. Regardless of your precautions, however, you can expect to lose several terminal rigs.

Use care when removing a hook from a sheepshead to avoid the sharp spines of their dorsal fin.

Bait

Sheepshead prefers fiddler crabs but also takes shrimp, mussels, clams, sandworms, bloodworms, sand eels, cut mackerel, and squid.

Equipment

If you're fishing from a boat, use a 6- to 7-foot moderate- to extra-fast-action boat rod with a matching conventional bait-casting reel filled with 25- to 30-pound-test monofilament line.

If you're fishing at the shore, use a 7- to 8-foot spinning rod with a matching spinning reel filled with 30- to 40-pound-test monofilament line.

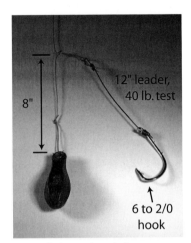

Typical sheepshead rig.

PACIFIC CUBERA SNAPPER

The Pacific cubera snapper is a solitary species that ranges from extreme Southern California to northern Peru. It is distinguished by its wide, stocky body and immense size. The color

Latin name
Lutjanus novemfasciatus

Best time to catch
Early spring to early fall

Also known as
Dog snapper, Pacific cubera, Pacific dog snapper, snapper

varies from deep brownish red to light red, with several stripes on the sides of the upper half of the body. The pectoral fin is just short of the anal fin and can appear translucent. It has a large mouth with thick lips and a projecting lower jaw. Both jaws are powerful. It has four large canine teeth that are visible even when its mouth is closed. The Pacific cubera snapper can grow to well over 5 feet in length and can reach 100 pounds in weight, although this is rare. It can be confused with the gray snapper, except that gray snapper ranges from 8 to 10 pounds; it can reach 36 inches long and weigh 26 pounds, although a fish weighing more than 15 pounds is unusual.

It spawns close to shore for a short time in July. During spawning the eggs are scattered in the open water and are fertilized externally.

The young are found in grass beds in shallow water close to shore.

Pacific cubera snapper is found in 80 to 125 feet of water or deeper. It is considered an aggressive bottom feeder. It feeds on medium-sized fish, crabs, sandworms, bloodworms, shrimp, squid, and lobster.

The Pacific cubera snapper is related to the more plentiful Atlantic cubera snapper, or Cuban snapper *(Lutjanus cyanopterus)*, which is found off the Florida Keys and seldom north of Florida, although it has been sighted in Delaware. Like the cubera, the Atlantic snapper can reach about 80 pounds in weight and can achieve a length of more than 4 feet. It spawns along the Florida Keys from late summer to early fall.

Both species are primarily solitary, and frequent underwater structure, such as shipwrecks, artificial or natural reefs, and oil rigs.

Fishing Tips

The Atlantic and Pacific species are fished in the same manner. They are usually caught along rocky bottom near structure such as reefs, shipwrecks, or oil rigs. They are excellent fighters and can pull extremely hard in an attempt to head back into structure. Keep your terminal tackle along the bottom when using natural bait. Jigs also can be effective when tipped with a piece of cut squid or cut herring. When fishing over heavy structure, have an ample supply of terminal fishing rigs, because you're sure to lose some.

They are usually fished from an anchored boat, but can be fished from a rocky shoreline in less than 15 feet of water using artificial lures or live bait. Fish for these fighters during the evening hours, when they usually feed.

You can also fly cast for cubera snapper. They often chase smaller fish in shallow inshore areas such as bays and estuaries where you can sight cast to them.

Bait

Use live or dead anchovies, clams, cut squid, cut herring, or bloodworms.

Lures

Try jigs, spoons, feathers, or plugs.

Equipment

If you're fishing from shore, use a 9- to 10-foot fast- to extra-fast-action surf rod with a matching spinning reel filled with 30- to 40-pound-test monofilament line.

If you're fishing from a boat, use a 6- to 7-foot fast- to extra-fast-action boat rod with a matching conventional bait-casting reel filled with 30- to 40-pound-test monofilament line.

If you're fly fishing, you can use the length of rod you're most comfortable with. Use 10- to 12-weight line and big flies.

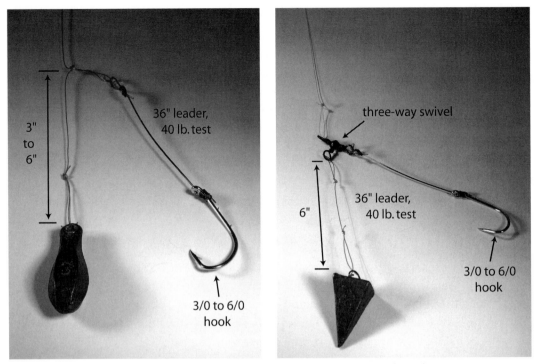

Boat bottom rig for cubera snapper.

Shoreline bottom rig for cubera snapper.

RED SNAPPER

Red snapper ranges from Massachusetts to Florida, although it is most abundant in the Gulf of Mexico and is seldom found north of the Carolinas. Red snapper is full bodied, with a continuous dorsal fin, a sharply pointed anal fin, and a slightly concave caudal fin. It has rose-colored skin and a white belly. It has a large mouth, a long rectangular snout, and brilliant red eyes. The protractile mouth has many teeth, including some large canine teeth.

Latin name
Lutjanus campechanus

Best time to catch
As per state law

Also known as
American red snapper, genuine red snapper, mutton snapper, northern red snapper

Red snapper matures sexually at about 3 or 4 years of age and spawns between late May and early October. A 5-year-old female can produce as many as 13,000 eggs per spawn; a 10-year-old female weighing 20 pounds and measuring 30 inches long can produce as many as 920,000 eggs per spawn. The eggs are buoyant after spawning and float to the surface; they hatch in about 24 hours. The fry grow quickly; after about twenty days they begin to settle to the bottom, perhaps on old broken shell beds rather than open sand or muddy bottom. Later the fry move onto reef structures; by this time they are strong and robust enough to hold their own against predators. After growing about 4 inches a year for the first 6 years, its growth slows. Its average size is about 20 pounds and 1 to 2 feet; it can reach a maximum of 50 pounds and 3½ feet, but this is rare. Red snapper that weigh more than 10 pounds can be found along suitably structured types of bottoms. It can live more than 20 years, although the average age is about 15 years.

Red snapper is a schooling fish that does not migrate, although it often seeks cooler water around shallow reefs (75 to 120 feet deep) during the winter and early spring and moves to deeper water (up to 300 feet). It prefers irregular hard bottom formations at depths of 50 to 300 feet that consist of sponges, and rock and limestone covered with coral; it is also found around offshore oil and gas rigs. It can live for a long time on the same structure, which provides protection from predators and is a prime hunting area. Red snapper feeds on crustaceans, sea worms, and smaller fish as well as eels, anchovies, pigfish, squid, and sea lice.

Fishing Tips

Red snapper can be found between 50 and 300 feet deep about 6 to 12 inches above the bottom. Bigger red snapper are usually suspended above the smaller red snapper. It's important to keep your boat directly above the edge of the structure or reef, and to fish during early morning for increased catches. It is considered to be line shy and avoids excessive noise and visible fishing line, so use the smallest-diameter leader possible—no more than 50-pound test if you're going for large snapper offshore, and 30- to 40-pound test if you're going for small fish closer inshore. A leader length of about 4 feet will keep the sinker and baited hook well apart from each another, allowing the baited hook to flow freely with the current below.

The red snapper has a big mouth, which requires large bait, and it it prefers still to slow-moving bait. It also is a nibbler and a picker and a notorious bait stealer, so a soft touch is needed to feel it on the line. Take all the slack out of the line in an effort to feel the fish below. Drop the baited hook until it hits bottom, then bring it up a few feet and return the hook to the bottom. Repeat the process until you suspect that the bait was taken. It won't be down too long before you feel a bite. When you feel even a slight twitch, consider that your bait may be gone and you might as well reel up your terminal rig to rebait your hook. It's best to use a circle hook instead of a conventional J hook, because C hooks are self-hooking, so you won't need to set the hook when you feel a fish. When hooked, these fish put up a tremendous fight, all the while shaking their heads to free themselves from the hook.

Red snapper caught in deep water are often found with their stomachs protruding from their mouth—a result of expanding gases in their swim bladder when they're brought to the surface. Most fish survive when released with this condition if you're careful not to puncture their stomach.

Bait

Use squid and large pieces of medium-sized cut or strip fish bait. The bait can be smaller whole fish or large fillets of fish, depending on the size of the red snapper you're after.

Equipment

Use a 7- to 8-foot fast- to extra-fast-action boat rod with a matching conventional bait-casting reel filled with 25- to 40-pound-test abrasion-resistant fluorocarbon line.

The hook can be a 5/0 to 7/0 J hook or a 5/0 to 7/0 circle hook.

Always keep your terminal tackle as simple as possible to prevent hang-ups on the structure below. With the rigs shown, there is less possibility for hang-ups or fouled bait.

If you want to use fly tackle, use chum to entice red snapper up to the surface.

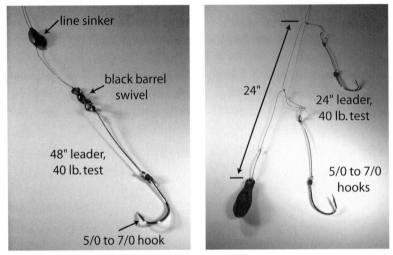

Typical baitfishing jigging rig for red snapper.

Double-hook bottom rig without a three-way swivel for red snapper.

COMMON SNOOK

Common snook is found in the western Atlantic, primarily in southern Florida, and off the southeastern coast of the Gulf of Mexico. It has a sloping forehead, a protruding lower jaw, and a prominent lateral line from the top of the gill plate to the caudal fin. The body is elongated, with a concave snout just in front of the eyes and a large mouth that has bristle brush–like teeth. The two dorsal fins are bright yellow; the pelvic fin, which is pale colored and has a flattened tip, is just in front of the caudal fin. It can grow to 49 inches and weigh as much as 39 pounds, making it the most highly preferred game fish of all the snook species. It is very popular with anglers because of its strong fighting ability and good flavor.

There are three other inshore species of snook native to the Florida coast, but they don't grow large enough to warrant more than a brief mention here. The fat snook *(Centropomus*

Latin name
Centropomus undecimalis

Best time to catch
Depends on when fish leave their wintering locations

Also known as
Linesider, robalo, saltwater pike, sergeant fish, soap fish

parallelus) a averages about 18 inches and 5 to 8 pounds and is found among mangroves. The swordspine snook *(Centropomus ensiferus)* resides in estuaries and averages about 12 inches and about a pound. The tarpon snook *(Centropomus pectinatus)* usually weighs less than a pound and is 12 inches long. The swordspine and tarpon are rare on the west coast of Florida.

All common snook are born male. Some males change to females in fall just after the start of the spawning season. The sex change occurs between 1 and 7 years of age. Males reach sexual maturity at 18 inches and 5 pounds, at about 2 years of age, females at 30 inches at about 3 to 4 years of age. Spawning, which occurs off Florida from May through October, depends on the climate and air temperature. Snook normally spawn at the mouths of coastal rivers and inlets in the Atlantic Ocean and the Gulf of Mexico. They usually return to the same locations to spawn each year. Female snook release their eggs during the late afternoon and early evening; the timing is not restricted to a particular tide. Females may spawn every two days and release about 1,275,000 eggs per spawn. The eggs hatch in the estuaries, where the fry remain until they mature. Females live for about 20 years and can exceed 48 inches in length and 45 to 50 pounds. Males live about 15 years and can exceed 39 inches in length and 30 to 35 pounds. No external differences distinguish males from females.

Common snook usually inhabit areas with good water quality, sloped-bottom banks, minimal water current, and areas of vegetation that provide shade and a place to hide, such as structure, mangroves, rocks, or pilings, from where they can attack their prey.

Snook is not known to migrate long distances; those that reside in the Gulf of Mexico don't travel far at all. The common snook winters in areas of low salinity (although it can tolerate a wide range of water salinity) and later travels to the spawning locations, remaining there throughout the summer. It requires water temperatures no lower than 60°F; it will succumb to shock or even die if it encounters lower temperatures.

Snook feed in large groups about 2 hours before sunrise, and again about 2 to 3 hours after sunset. They are opportunistic feeders and eat smaller fish, shrimp, sandworms, sea worms, and crustaceans.

Fishing Tips

Fishing for snook is always challenging and can be frustrating at times. It is often fished with artificial lures during the winter months and live bait during the spring and summer months.

The best place to find snook is where they spawn, such as around passes and inlets during a full moon or new moon. They are most often fished for in channels throughout inshore flats; they normally pack themselves into channels and cuts between islands, points adjacent to sandbars, and areas close to beaches, where the tide is able to support their eggs for hatching. They can also be found around mangroves.

It's best to fish the first 2 to 3 hours of the ebb tide or the flood tide, when they increase their feeding behavior. A good place to fish is around bridges and pilings. Cast the baited hook or lure to the base of the structure, then slowly reel it in while providing some action. Remember that deeper holes at river mouths and in channels always contain larger fish, which are encouraged to grab a baited hook when the offering is on an outgoing tide and contains a live sardine.

Snook are fished for in the same manner regardless of the location. However, it's important to know the water temperature wherever you pursue them. On average, smaller snook are most often found over the flats; larger fish can also be found on the flats. Regardless of where they're being fished, always cast ahead of and never at the fish, then begin to retrieve the baited hook or lure. Remember that snook are ambush predators and will not follow their prey any great distance.

Bait
Use anchovies, pinfish, whole sandworms, live shrimp, ladyfish grunt, sardine, killifish, or a small blue crabs. For fly bait, use flies that resemble shrimp, anchovies, or some other small baitfish.

Lures
Try using a chartreuse or red lure.

Equipment
Use a 7- to 8-foot medium-action spinning rod with matching spinning reel filled with 15- to 20-pound-test monofilament line.

For fly fishing, use a 9- to 10-foot fly rod with your choice of line.

PETRALE SOLE

The petrale sole is considered a right-eyed member of the flatfish family. It ranges from the Bering Sea to northern Baja California. It is found throughout the Gulf of Alaska. It is sometimes confused with the California halibut because of the similar color patterns and large mouth. The petrale sole has a slender, oval body and a fairly large mouth for its size, with two rows of small teeth along the upper jaw and a single row along the lower jaw. The eyes are medium sized and on the same side of the body, which is light to dark brown and blotched along the dorsal and anal fins. The blind (white) side sometimes has traces of pink. The caudal fin is longest at the center and is slightly indented near the edges. The lateral line is curved above the pectoral fin.

Latin name
Eopsetta jordani

Best time to catch
Year-round

Also known as
Brill, California sole, Jordan's flounder, roundnosed sole, sole

Petrale sole spawns from November through March, varying with the spawning grounds. Males sexually mature at about 3 or 4 years of age, females at about 4 or 5 years. Females spawn once a year. A large female can produce 400,000 to 1.3 million eggs, which are buoyant when hatched. The fry spend the first five to seven months near the water surface before they travel to the bottom. Male petrale sole reach about 20 to 25 inches in length; females are about 7 inches longer than the males. It can live for up to 15 to 20 years of age, although most caught fish range from 5 to 7 years of age.

It resides in 60 to 420 feet of water from April through October and 900 to 1,500 feet of water during the winter months. It lives over rocky structure or along a soft, sandy bottom and feeds on herring, crabs, sand lance, shrimp, sandworms, bloodworms, sea worms, and smaller fish such as anchovies and other flatfish. As with most flatfish, petrale sole can bury itself in the sand or mud with only its eyes protruding for protection from predators and to hide from its prey.

Fishing Tips

It's best to fish deep sandy or muddy areas for petrale sole. Fishing usually requires drifting with a drifting rig over suspected areas while keeping the baited hook no higher than 3 inches off the bottom with a suitably weighted sinker.

Bait

Use cut strips of herring, anchovies, shrimp, crabs, or sandworms.

Equipment

Choose a rod that will accommodate the weight of the sinker, which will vary depending on the depth and water current conditions along the bottom. For shallow depths, use a 6- to 7-foot moderate- to fast-action boat rod with a matching conventional bait-casting reel filled with 15- to 25-pound-test monofilament line.

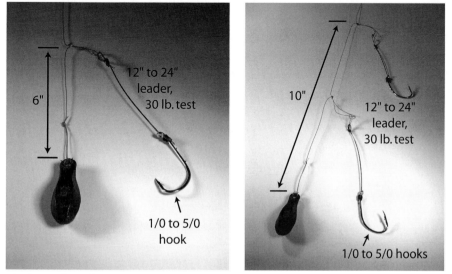

Single- and tandem-hook rigs for petrale sole.

SPOT

Spot is a close relative of the Atlantic croaker and is most abundant along the mid-Atlantic coast from Delaware to Georgia, and in the Gulf of Mexico. It has a humpback body that is grayish silver with narrow golden stripes on the upper sides. It has a predominant black spot about the size of its eye behind the upper portion of the gill cover.

Latin name
Leiostomus xanthurus

Best time to catch
Late June through October

Also known as
Flat croaker, Norfolk spot, sand digger, spotted croaker

Spot reaches sexual maturity at about 2 years of age. Adult spot move offshore to spawn in water that ranges from about 60 to 70°F. The spawning season varies with location: off Chesapeake Bay, spot spawns between September and November, off North Carolina from October through February, and off Florida from December through March. The eggs are carried inshore by winds and currents. The fry move toward brackish or freshwater estuaries, where they winter. Spot rarely reaches 2 pounds and averages about ½ to ¾ pound. It lives for about 5 years.

Spot is found in water temperatures ranging from 35 to 90°F; it prefers shallow water during the summer months, and moves offshore for the winter to depths of 200 feet. A bottom-feeding species, it travels in schools of a hundred or more in search of food, including clams and other mollusks, crustaceans, sandworms, bloodworms, small fish, and detritus. Spot is prey to striped bass, bluefish, weakfish, and summer flounder and can be used for live lining.

Fishing Tips
Spot can be caught around piers, bridge abutments, and jetties; along the surf; or from a boat. It provides lots of action with light tackle. Because of its small mouth, small amounts of bait are all you need to use on a hook. Keep the baited hook directly off the bottom where the fish are feeding. Fishing is best before or just after the flood tide. It's not uncommon to hook two spot on a double-hook rig.

Bait
Use small pieces of shrimp, clams, sandworms, bloodworms, or squid.

Equipment
I recommend a 6- to 7-foot moderate- to fast-action rod with a matching conventional bait-casting reel filled with 6- to 10-pound-test monofilament line. The weight of the sinker used is determined by the current below.

You can also use a 6- to 8-foot moderate- to fast-action spinning rod with a matching spinning reel filled with 6- to 10-pound-test monofilament line.

Hook size will vary depending on the size of the fish you're after. To start, use a number 6 hook; if needed, work up to a hook no larger than a number 1. You can use a tandem hook rig, with one hook on the bottom and the other hook about 12 inches above the sinker, or you can fish with just one hook directly on the bottom.

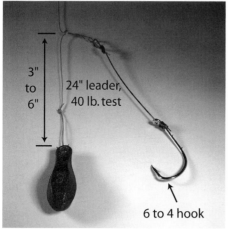

3" to 6"

24" leader, 40 lb. test

6 to 4 hook

Single-hook rig for spot.

WHITE STURGEON

White sturgeon is the largest freshwater species in North America that is also caught in salt water. Its range is from Alaska to Mexico. It has a long, cylindrical body with five rows of bony plates along the back. It has a bluntly rounded snout, which is depressed just below the forehead. Its toothless mouth requires that it suck in food while feeding. Four barbels extend from the underside of its snout.

Latin name
Acipenser transmontanus

Best time to catch
Winter to early summer

Also known as
Columbia sturgeon, Oregon sturgeon, Pacific sturgeon, Sacramento sturgeon, sturgeon

Females sexually mature at 18 years of age, males at 14 years. Spawning usually takes place every 5 to 10 years from early April to early July in turbulent freshwater streams with water temperatures of 50 to 64°F. Eggs are laid in locations ranging from shallow, pebbly or sandy bottom to deeper main channels containing boulders or cobble. Females release from 300,000 to 3 million eggs. Not all the eggs become fertilized; those that do become attached to the bottom will hatch about eight to fifteen days later. Younger white sturgeon prefer slower-moving water for obtaining food. It grows slowly; the average growth rate is about 1 to 1½ inches per year. It can grow to about 20 feet in length and weigh as much as 1,300 pounds. White sturgeon has a relatively long life span; some are known to be more than 100 years old.

Although it spawns in freshwater streams, it spends most of its time in the Pacific Ocean or in the brackish water of estuaries. White sturgeon feed along the bottom and since white sturgeon have poor eyesight, they use their sensitive barbels to locate prey along the bottom. They feed primarily at night on a wide variety of foods, including crustaceans, fish eggs, shrimp, clams, crabs, worms, mussels, snails, frogs, and smaller fish.

The Atlantic sturgeon *(Acipenser oxyrinchus)*, similar to the white sturgeon, is a protected species and is not discussed here because of its decline due to overfishing.

Fishing Tips

White sturgeon can be caught anywhere along the Pacific coast but is mainly fished for at the mouths of larger streams or rivers. Deep holes are usually the best places to fish for white sturgeon.

There are three size classifications of white sturgeon: shakers, keepers, and peelers. A *shaker* is less than 46 inches in length and weighs about 10 to 12 pounds. The fish vigorously shakes the rod when it's hooked on the line. Usually the faster the rod shakes, the smaller the fish.

A *keeper* is between 46 and 72 inches in length and weighs about 15 to 20 pounds. It is easily identified because it shakes the rod at a slow rate and runs hard as it takes line off the reel for a few seconds after being hooked.

A *peeler* averages 6 to 10 feet long and weighs 110 to 540 pounds. It will spool (or "peel") a reel and is difficult—if not impossible—to stop. You have to cut the line or try to fight the fish. These fish tend to put up a long, hard fight and are not for the timid or inexperienced angler. Rely on the reel drag to tire the fish.

When fishing in saltwater bays, it's best to fish from an anchored boat on an incoming or outgoing tide. The best fishing is during the last half of the outgoing tide. The baited hook must be directly on the bottom, which requires a sinker suitably weighted for the current below, regardless of which type of water you're fishing.

Bait

White sturgeon are not fussy feeders. Use any natural bait, including ghost shrimp, smaller dead fish, worms, and pieces of cubed cheese.

Equipment

If you're fishing for shakers, use a 7- to 8-foot moderate-action rod with a matching conventional bait-casting reel filled with 20- to 40-pound-test monofilament line. For keepers, use an 8- to 9-foot fast- to extra-fast-action rod with a conventional bait-casting reel filled with 30- to 50-pound-test monofilament line. For peelers, use a 7- to 8-foot extra-fast-action, heavy to extra-heavy rod equipped with a conventional bait-casting reel filled with 50- to 60-pound-test monofilament line or stronger.

You can use a conventional bottom rig with a single hook. However, because white sturgeon are bottom feeders a fish-finder rig may be best. Toss out the fish-finder rig and let it settle to the bottom. The sinker should hold the bottom while allowing the baited hook to drift along. When a fish picks up the baited hook, it will not feel the weight of the sinker.

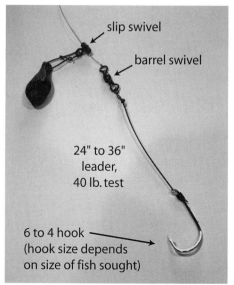

slip swivel

barrel swivel

24" to 36"
leader,
40 lb. test

6 to 4 hook
(hook size depends
on size of fish sought)

Typical bottom rig for white sturgeon.

SWORDFISH

The swordfish is found in the Atlantic, Pacific, and Indian oceans and in the Mediterranean Sea. It has a cylindrical body that is blackish brown along the top of the back fading to lighter brown below. It lacks scales and teeth, and is distinguished from other billfish by the shape of the flattened, oval-shaped bill, or sword, which extends far beyond their lower lip. It has two dorsal fins—one high and rigid, the second just in front of the caudal fin—and two anal fins—the rear is one considerably smaller than the forward one. It does not have pelvic fins but has a high, crescent-shaped caudal fin, which provides speed and the ability to turn quickly. The fins are light to dark brown.

Latin name
Xiphias gladius

Best time to catch
Depends on location

Also known as
Broadbill, broadbill swordfish

Swordfish reach sexual maturity between 3 and 4 years of age. Swordfish spawn in water less than 250 feet deep. Spawning occurs year-round off the Florida coast and other temperate locations. In cooler water, spawning occurs during the spring and summer, when the water temperature increases. The males chase the females during the spawning season. Females can carry 1 million to 30 million eggs. The eggs are buoyant and begin to hatch about two and a half days after fertilization. Fry swordfish consume zooplankton, fish larvae, small fish, squid, and other life forms that live near the surface. Swordfish reach a maximum length of 180 inches and weigh as much as 1,500 pounds, but rarely reach that size because of overharvesting. Adult females grow faster, become larger, and live longer than males. Females usually weigh more than 300 pounds, whereas adult males seldom exceed 200 pounds. Adult females living in the Atlantic

Ocean can weigh up to 700 pounds; Pacific Ocean adult females weigh more. They can live longer than 20 years.

It is a migratory species, moving to tropical, temperate waters in winter and cooler waters in the summer. Swordfish visit New England waters in the summer, entering far offshore from the Gulf Stream sometime around June and departing for warmer waters in late October.

Swordfish are not a schooling species, but travel in very loose formations, as much as 40 feet apart from one another. Primarily a mid- to upper-water species, it can also be found searching for food at depths from 650 to 1,980 feet, where the water temperature is between 65 to 75°F. When searching for food in colder water (even at 20 to 25°F), specialized tissue keeps its brain warm.

Swordfish often feed near the surface, eating squid, bluefish, mackerel, butterfish, bonito, herring, and whiting at night or during the day. Considered opportunistic predators, they also feed on the bottom at a depth of about 2,000 feet, where they eat octopus and other species that inhabit the near bottom. They use their sword for defense and to attack larger prey by slashing, maiming, or killing them before consuming them at their leisure.

Adult swordfish are prey to killer and sperm whales; young swordfish are prey to sharks, blue marlin, black marlin, sailfish, yellowfin tuna, and dolphin.

Fishing Tips

Fishing for swordfish is a specialized form of fishing and requires exceptional skill. The equipment needed to catch swordfish can run well over a thousand dollars for just the rod and reel. I recommend hiring a charter boat and its crew, who have the experience and necessary equipment to safely catch swordfish. It can be dangerous for those who lack the required knowledge. The following tips also apply to the other billfish described below.

Fishing for swordfish is considered deep-sea fishing and occurs from 45 to 65 miles offshore, usually in temperate to tropical waters. Swordfish are regarded as the toughest of all the billfish because of their deep, quick dives when hooked. The drag setting on the reel should be set to a minimum to prevent stressing and breaking the line.

Swordfish are often seen basking at the surface of the water (when the water temperature is about 70 to 80°F), with their dorsal fin and the upper portion of their caudal fin exposed.

Trolling is the preferred method for fishing for swordfish. They can also be taken by drifting, although it's not often done. When trolling, the baited hook must be quietly placed into the water once a fish is spotted basking on the surface. The fish may not take the bait if it becomes alarmed or frightened by an oncoming boat or an unusual commotion.

The bait must be presented carefully and repeatedly before the swordfish will take the hook. Their soft mouth makes hook-ups uncertain, and their slashing bill can destroy the line or the leader in no time.

Hooking a swordfish is a coordinated effort among the mates, the captain, and the angler alike. Fighting a swordfish is an experience you will never forget. You will swear that your arms stretched an additional 2 feet after battling a fish weighing 200 pounds or more.

Because of the depleted stocks of swordfish, hook and release has become normal practice. Most charter boats will tag and release the fish for research purposes; very few swordfish are kept.

You should be secured in a fighting chair with the butt of your rod in the rod gimbal on the seat. Have your rod and reel ready. When a fish is spotted, pick up the rod, toss the baited hook overboard, and allow it to extend about 200 feet behind the boat, which should be moving very slowly. The baited hook should be about 2 feet below the surface; it must never be allowed to surface; otherwise, the fish may dive, requiring the entire procedure to be started over again. The boat should be maneuvered so the baited hook is about 20 to 25 feet away from the fish.

The biggest thrill is when the fish spots the baited hook, dives under, and comes up on the hook. The boat should be placed in neutral until the fish takes the hook. After it takes the hook, place the reel in free spool mode. At this point, you or the mate should signal the captain to move ahead at no more than 3 knots. Once the boat is in motion, quickly engage the reel and strike hard several times with the rod to set the hook, in an attempt to turn the fish toward the boat. Keep the line tight. There will be a spectacular fight when the fish realizes it has been hooked. It will jump out of the water, twisting and turning while trying to dislodge the hook from its mouth. Try to maintain control of the rod, reel, and fish. The captain should maintain the necessary boat speed to help you keep the line tight until you bring the fish near the boat. The fish must be gaffed to bring it on board. The line is cut just above the hook, which eventually works itself out.

During the summer season, deepwater rigs are needed for day fishing because swordfish are seldom near the surface. They prefer water temperatures of no more than 80°F and will swim deeper to reach cooler temperatures.

Bait

The bait is usually whole squid, whole bonito, or whole small mackerel, rigged with double hooks. The forward hook is placed below the gill of the bait and the second hook at the tail to prevent the swordfish from being foul hooked, meaning that the hook is not in the fish's mouth properly.

Lures

Try feathered lures or skirted trolling lures.

Equipment

Use a fast-action heavy to extra-heavy trolling rod with a roller guide to help place less force against the line. Because you never know what size fish you'll hook, use 30 feet of leader with a test strength of 400 to 900 pounds. The reel should have a smoothly operating drag system and a line capacity of no less than 400 yards. Use at least 500-pound-test braided Dacron line. Monofilament line of the same strength can be used, but it will not set the hook as well as braided Dacron line, which can stretch. The hook size ranges from 14/0 to 16/0.

OTHER BILLFISH

Billfish are considered offshore game fish. Because they are frequently found along the continental shelf, fishing for them requires a charter boat with a knowledgeable crew.

Depending on the species, each fish can weigh more than 200 pounds and be tremendously strong, requiring extensive knowledge and experienced handling of the fish once hooked. Billfish fishing is not for the casual angler.

Black Marlin

Black marlin is found in tropical and subtropical waters in the Indian and Pacific oceans. Individuals that have migrated around the Cape of Good Hope are occasionally found in the

Latin name
Makaira indica

Best time to catch
Most of the year

Also known as
Giant black marlin, Pacific black marlin

Atlantic Ocean. Black marlin has an elongated body with a long, pointed, stout bill. It has a dark blue to black back with occasional vertical bars with a silvery white belly. The first dorsal fin is low, rounded, and retractable; the second dorsal fin begins just in front of the second anal fin. It has a relatively high forehead, unlike all other billfish. It has rigid pectoral fins that cannot be compressed against their body without the joints breaking. It is often confused with blue marlin, but the pectoral fins of blue marlin can be compressed against the body, and blue and striped marlin have blotches along the body. The fins tend to turn black when dead—hence their name.

Black marlin can grow to 16 feet and weigh as much as 1,600 pounds. It is a strong, powerful fish that swims exceptionally fast. Black marlin migrates, and will inhabit any depth. It feeds on other fast-swimming fish, such as tuna, mackerel, trevally, and swordfish, as well as smaller fish, squid, and large crustaceans. It uses its bill or sword to slash its prey before swallowing it.

When hooked, black marlin usually mixes jumping with fast runs and high fighting characteristics. It can jump at anytime and often does so alongside a boat when it's about to be landed.

Blue Marlin

Blue marlin is found in tropical and temperate waters in the Atlantic, Pacific, and Indian oceans. It has a cobalt blue back, and the belly and sides are silvery white. Its high, pointed dorsal fin is black or cobalt blue with no spots. The second dorsal fin is considerably smaller. The pectoral fin is flexible and can be folded flat against the sides. The anal fin is also large and pointed. The lateral line is a series of loops along the sides. The upper jaw extends into a spear-like sword.

Latin name
Makaira nigricans

Best time to catch
Most of the year

Also known as
Atlantic blue marlin, Cuban blue marlin, Pacific blue marlin

Not much information is available about their spawning. The blue marlin is the largest of the Atlantic marlins; it can reach 11 feet in length and weigh as much as 2,000 pounds. However, most blue marlin caught weigh between 150 to 450 pounds. The larger ones tend to be females; males may weigh only about 300 pounds. Fish older than 15 years of age are uncommon; most live about 10 years.

They are not selective eaters; they feed on squid, smaller fish, and almost anything they can catch. They are prevalent in areas with large quantities of food and are scarce where food sources are sparse.

They are strong and fast and, unlike sailfish, usually fight at depth; hooking and landing a blue marlin is a team effort. A large blue marlin may spool the reel on its first run. It fights deeper than black or striped marlin and jumps repeatedly, often spinning or reversing direction while fighting on the surface (which can result in a damaged or cut line). The fight could last well over an hour with a large fish.

Striped Marlin

The striped marlin, found in tropical and warm temperate waters of the Pacific Ocean, has an elongated, compressed body. The upper jaw is more extended than that of the blue marlin. It has a dark blue back with dark cobalt blue stripes that fade to a silvery white belly. It is distinguished from other billfish in California waters by its rounded spear and higher first dorsal fin, which is 75 to about 100 percent of its body depth. The pectoral fins are pointed and generally straight with a slight curve toward the bottom; they can easily be folded back against the body.

Striped marlin spawns in the northwest Pacific Ocean. Females reach sexual maturity at about 55 to 85 pounds. Striped marlin feed on smaller fish, squid, crabs, and shrimp. They sometimes use their spear as a weapon for defense and for capturing food. When hooked it is extremely acrobatic, making numerous surface runs and jumps. It does not fight as deep as the blue marlin.

Latin name
Tetrapturus audax

Best time to catch
Most of the year

Also known as
Barred marlin, marlin, Pacific marlin, Pacific striped marlin, spearfish, spikefish, striper

White Marlin

White marlin has a high, rounded dorsal fin. The pectoral and first anal fins have rounded tips. The pectoral fins can easily be folded against the sides.

It spawns in spring. It matures at about 55 inches in length. While not as large as the Atlantic blue marlin, it can reach 10 feet in length and weigh as much as 200 pounds.

It is a migrating species and favors deep temperate waters, although it will frequent depths of 50 feet if there are

Latin name
Tetrapturus albidus

Best time to catch
Most of the year

Also known as
Atlantic white marlin, spikefish

warm currents and baitfish. It sometimes travels in small groups and does not school, as do most marlin. It is found along the continental shelf, frequently following baitfish and feeding primarily on squid, herring, mackerel, and mullet.

Sailfish

The sailfish is found in the Atlantic and Pacific oceans in warm offshore waters. In the eastern Pacific it ranges from Baja California to Peru; and in the western Atlantic it ranges from Massachusetts to Brazil. Sailfish has a large slate or cobalt blue dorsal fin with many dark spots. The second dorsal fin is considerably smaller and has six to eight rays.

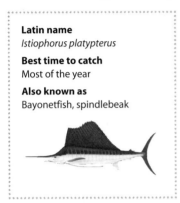

Latin name
Istiophorus platypterus

Best time to catch
Most of the year

Also known as
Bayonetfish, spindlebeak

Females can produce as many as 4 to 5 million eggs. The eggs float along with plankton until they hatch. The fry grow rapidly and can reach 4 feet in length in the first year. It can weigh as much as 70 pounds on the western Atlantic coast and exceed 9½ feet in length.

It can achieve speeds of about 65 miles per hour for short distances and will form schools from five to thirty individuals spread over a wide distance. It feeds at midwater to near surface depths on squid, mackerel, herring, mullet, and other small fish.

Sailfish is a fast, spectacular jumper and aerial fighter when hooked; it makes fast runs to the surface and can spend more time in the air than in the water. It does not usually fight at deep depths.

TARPON

Tarpon can be found in the temperate waters off Florida and as far north as Cape Hattaras, North Carolina. It is also found in the Gulf of Mexico and the Pacific Ocean (Atlantic tarpon migrated through the Panama Canal and became established in the Pacific). Tarpon is blue-gray on the back and has silver sides and large scales. It has a protruding upturned lip on its lower jaw that extends to the upper jaw, both of which have small, fine, densely packed teeth. An elongated bony plate along the upturned lower jaw is used to crush crustaceans and other prey that it doesn't consume whole. The small dorsal fin has thirteen to fifteen soft rays (no spines); the last ray is greatly elongated. The caudal fin is deeply forked and has lobes that are equal in length. The anal fin is deep and triangular in shape and has twenty-two to twenty-five soft rays; the last ray is elongated, as is the dorsal fin. The pelvic fins are large and long and have thirteen or fourteen soft rays.

Latin name
Megalops atlanticus

Best time to catch
Spring and fall

Also known as
Atlantic tarpon, cuffum, silver king, silver sides

Tarpon grow very slowly; they reach sexual maturity at about 6 or 7 years of age and about 4 feet in length. Females produce about 12 million eggs; spawning takes place as far as 125 miles offshore. The young make their way back to shallow coastal waters. Female tarpon can reach more than 8 feet in length and weigh 350 pounds, although this is rare. They usually range from 75 to 125 pounds; some fish have been caught that weighed more than 200 pounds. Males are usually smaller than females. Tarpon that weigh about 100 pounds are 13 to 16 years of age. Males can live for 30 years; females have been known to live longer.

Tarpon can tolerate a wide range of salinity and often travel upstream into fresh water. It has a swim bladder that allows it to absorb oxygen from water with almost no oxygen content, even stagnant water that is virtually depleted of oxygen. Its ability to inhabit these areas, which are mostly free from predators, protects the young.

Tarpon are primarily found in coastal waters, bays, and estuaries in subtropical, tropical, or temperate climates with a water temperature of 75 to 90°F. Because tarpon require high temperatures, they seek warmer deeper waters in cold weather, when the temperature of shallow water drops. A rapid decrease in water temperature has been known to kill a large tarpon.

Tarpon often travel in schools, and feed on midwater prey such as mullet, pinfish, Atlantic needlefish, sardines, anchovies, shrimp, sea worms, and crabs. They feed mainly during the evening hours, but also during the day.

Fishing Tips

Tarpon is not considered a food fish in the United States but is pursued by sportsmen for its fighting ability. Most tarpon are caught from March through June and during October and November; the best fishing is at night, when they are feeding. They are found in deep channels or on shallow flats; they prefer a briskly moving tide. They can be caught on saltwater flats with lures, flies, or bait.

As a game fish, tarpon have few equals. Their fighting ability is characterized by an initial hard strike followed by a series of leaps and superb runs. There is no doubt when a tarpon takes the bait. They can be caught from an anchored, drifting, or trolling boat with artificial lures or live bait. Keep your tackle box well stocked with surface plugs and deep-running, slow-sinking lures of all styles, shapes, and colors. Tarpon are very temperamental when it comes to lure type and color.

If you've never fished for tarpon, it's best to hire a guide. For your own safety, don't go alone the first time. The charter boat will be well equipped with the tackle needed to catch these excellent fighting fish.

Tarpon get spooked easily, so use common sense when fishing for them. Never run your boat through a school of tarpon or start the boat engine when a school has been spotted. Instead, stay in front of the moving school and be as quiet as possible.

If you're using live bait, place a bobber on the main line to keep the bait at the desired depth, which is usually about 6 feet.

The hook should be very sharp so it can penetrate the tarpon's hard, bony mouth. When setting the hook, try about six quick hook sets to drive the hook into the fish; otherwise, chances are the fish will easily dislodge itself from the hook during its fight.

Once you've brought the fish alongside the boat, make sure it's completely tired out before you try to bring it on board and remove the hook. These fish have been known to cause extensive damage to equipment on board the boat, not to mention injury or death to anglers because of their strong thrashing.

Gaff the fish in the mouth through the bottom lip; this will not hurt the fish. Then wet your hands or use wet gloves to remove the fish from the water. Depending on the size of the fish, two people may be needed to remove the hook and hold the fish for a photograph before releasing it.

After the photo has been taken, with wet gloves hold the fish by its lower jaw and allow water to run through the mouth and out the gills. Tarpon will be nearly spent after the fight until thus revived. Allow the fish to free itself from your grip before you release it to fight another day.

Bait

Use live shrimp, live crabs, pinfish, or dead baitfish.

Lures

When trolling, try a yellow and bright silver-sided lure, but bring along various types of lures or spoons. Also have plenty of surface plugs and deep-running, slow-sinking lures of all styles, shapes, and colors on hand.

Equipment

The type of rod depends on the size and weight of tarpon you're after, and on the technique you're using. Usually a 7- to 8-foot moderate- to extra-fast-action, medium-heavy to extra-heavy rod will work. Use a boat rod if you're fishing with a conventional bait-casting reel or when trolling. Use a spinning rod if you're using lures.

The line also depends on the weight of the fish you're seeking. About 50-pound-test or higher monofilament line will usually work. Regardless of the line used, the leader can be 80- to 100-pound-test monofilament line tied directly to a barrel swivel, which is tied to the main line.

Using fly equipment to catch tarpon makes for a memorable experience.

TAUTOG

Tautog (pronounced "TOO • tog"), or blackfish, is a popular inshore or offshore fish that resides along the Atlantic coast from Nova Scotia to South Carolina. It is most abundant from Cape Cod to Delaware Bay. It is easily identified by its dark coloration. Its leather-like skin is covered with mucous, making it slippery. It has a stout body with a blunt nose and thick lips,

Latin name
Tautoga onitis

Best time to catch
Spring and fall

Also known as
Blackfish, chub, Molly George, oysterfish, tog

which hide the large conical front teeth and the flat crushing molars. The molars grind food into dustlike bits.

Sexual maturity occurs at approximately 3 to 4 years of age. Tautog has a slow growth rate, and can live for slightly more than 15 years. Males usually outnumber females, and are usually larger and live longer than the females. The average size fish caught by anglers is 2 to 4 pounds, which is anywhere from 6 to 10 years of age. Larger tautog can be caught from late October to late November in offshore waters.

Tautog does not undertake extensive seasonal migrations, although it winters offshore at depths of 75 to 175 feet, then moves inshore to spawn in late March to early April when the water temperature reaches 40 to 50°F. When inshore, it inhabits inshore shallow areas over shell beds and around piers. Offshore it inhabits areas around structure formations—rocky bottom, artificial and natural reefs, and wrecks. Tautog feeds at dawn and dusk and is inactive at night. It eats mussels, clams, crabs, barnacles, shrimp, and small lobsters.

Fishing Tips

Tautog likes colder water, which makes early spring, late fall, and early winter the best times of year to fish. It can also be caught offshore during the winter months. It's best to board a party boat to fish for this species offshore during late fall and winter because the captain knows the locations of wrecks and reefs.

Tautog can be caught from a boat anchored right over a reef or wreck or anywhere along a rocky shoreline, such as jetties, docks, or bridge abutments in the late spring and late fall. Tautog does not roam far from structure; its diet consists of mollusks and crustaceans that frequent structure. Fishing for tautog is not for the lazy or laid-back angler. It requires a lot of knowledge and skill to hook and catch these aggressive fish.

Tautog usually shares the same areas as porgies at shallow depths, and codfish and pollock in deeper water. It likes structure where food is plentiful and can be easily found. Once hooked, tautog heads for deeper water within the structure. Try to prevent this, or your terminal tackle can become snagged on sharp rocks or other abrasive structure. Be prepared to replace it if needed. Less is best when it comes to terminal tackle.

When fishing for tautog, it's important to stay alert; the fish often hit the bait as soon as it reaches the bottom. Tautog is known for being an excellent bait stealer, so don't allow any slack in the line, so you can feel the fish below. Once the fish grabs the bait, set the hook hard by raising the rod tip high, then quickly reel up while maintaining a tight line to keep the fish from returning back down toward the structure. If you feel a tap, assume that the bait was stolen and reel up to bait the hook again.

Bait

The best bait for offshore deepwater fishing is whole or halved green crab or skimmer clams, which will often attract cod or pollock. For inshore shallow depths, use fiddler crabs, skimmer clams, or inch-long pieces of sandworms or bloodworms, although clams and worms will probably attract undesirable fish, such as bergal (cunner). Keep the bait as close to the hook as possible so it doesn't dangle too far from the barb.

Equipment

If you're fishing from a boat, use a 6- to 7-foot extra-fast-action, medium to heavy rod with a matching conventional bait-casting reel filled with 20- to 30-pound-test monofilament line. If you're fishing from shore, use a 6- to 8-foot extra-fast-action, medium to heavy spinning rod with a matching spinning reel filled with 25- to 40-pound-test monofilament line. The terminal rig hardware should consist of nothing more than a barrel swivel above the hook leader on the main line. A single-hook rig with a sinker of suitable weight will do. Hooks should range from number 6 to number 4 for offshore fishing and smaller for inshore fishing.

When fishing offshore, the sinkers should be 8 ounces or more, depending on the current below.

Carry lots of hooks and sinkers in your tackle box to replace those that are lost within the structure while fishing.

When fishing offshore in late fall and into the winter months, make sure to dress for the cold, and wear waterproof footgear.

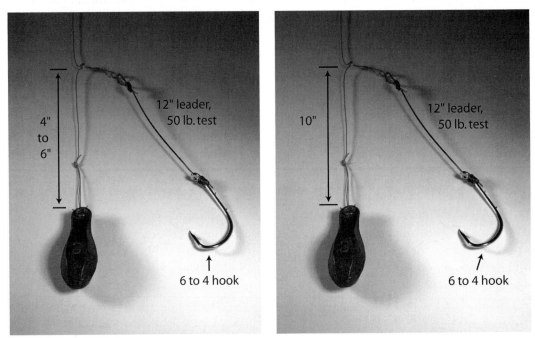

Typical terminal tackle rigs for tautog. No hardware is used on the rigs.

TILEFISH

Tilefish inhabits the outer continental shelf from Nova Scotia to South America and can be found at the bottom at about 270 feet or deeper. It can also be found off Louisiana and Texas on the continental shelf at depths that range from 500 to 1,200 feet. It is most abundant between Nantucket and Delaware and in the Gulf of Mexico. Tilefish is bluish or olive green on the back and upper part of the sides, blending to yellow or rose on the lower sides; the belly is whitish. The head is reddish on the sides and pure white below. The back and sides above the pectoral fins have small yellow spots. The dorsal fin is dusky with larger yellow spots. The anal fin is pale pink with purple and blue iridescence; the pectoral fins are pale brown with purple accents near the base.

Latin name
Lopholatilus chamaeleonticeps

Best time to catch
Winter, depending on weather conditions

Also known as
Blanquillo, golden tilefish, great northern tilefish

It sexually matures between 5 and 7 years of age. It spawns in July or August. It can weigh up to about 50 pounds but averages 10 to 25 pounds; it is about 42 inches long. It is a slow-growing fish that lives to about 30 years of age.

It lives in water temperatures of 47 to about 53°F and cannot tolerate higher temperatures. It resides over hard, muddy bottom at depths of 267 to 1,440 feet; it constructs burrows, where it spends the night. It feeds during daylight hours, most heavily between late morning and early afternoon. It moves slowly along the bottom in the subdued light around structure, feeding on crabs, lobster, squid, shrimp, starfish, sea worms, and other fish directly on the bottom or about 8 to 10 feet off it.

Do not confuse the tilefish with the sand tilefish *(Malacanthus plumieri)*, which averages about 15 inches in length and is almost eel-like in shape; it is found on reefs and sandy bottom off Florida at a maximum depth of about 50 feet.

Fishing Tips

Fishing for tilefish is not for the casual angler. This is big-time, multiday fishing that's well offshore and something that many hardcore anglers enjoy. The trip typically lasts 20 to 28 hours from port to port during the winter months, when the tilefish are closer to shore, which can be 200 miles out at sea. Only hardy anglers should consider going on these trips because the ride to the fishing area is long and can be rough.

For the most part, tilefish are fished from large party boats that venture offshore several times a year for this special trip. Tilefish occupy burrows in the sedimentary substrate around depths of 300 to more than 1,000 feet, requiring special fishing equipment. At times it requires 2 pounds of lead or more to drop and hold the bait on the bottom because of the depth of the water and the swift currents below. At these depths, electric reels are a must, along with an extra-heavy-weight rod to haul the tilefish from the bottom to the surface. The boats, which usually drift over tilefish territory, will supply all the equipment you'll need to catch these fish. You need only to dress properly and bring plenty of ice, food, and water.

Tilefish take the bait instantly when they are feeding and will fight for the first 100 feet or so. As they ascend and the water pressure changes, they succumb to the pressure changes and are less feisty until gaffed at the surface. There is no such thing as throwing back a tilefish; all are keepers, because the mortality rate from the bottom at great depths is 100 percent.

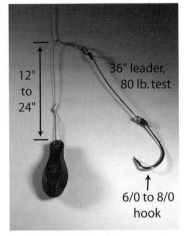

Typical single-hook bottom rig for tilefish.

Bait

Use whole squid, small fish, cut baits, whole skimmer clams, or crabs.

Equipment

The rod should be a 7- to 8-foot extra-flexible, extra-heavy-duty rod with plenty of backbone. The party boat will provide heavy-duty, deep-sea electric reels with up to 500 yards of 40-pound-test line. Most recreational anglers have no need to own an electric reel; if you're just getting started, your first introduction to this equipment will likely be on a charter boat.

Very heavy sinkers are needed to get the baited hook down and keep it on the bottom.

ATLANTIC TOMCOD

The tomcod closely resembles the Atlantic cod but is much smaller. It can be found in and around nearly every river mouth along the coast of Maine, and is frequently found off the west coast of Nova Scotia. It is plentiful along the Atlantic coast south to New Jersey and can be caught from the docks in lower New York Harbor. It has a relatively large body with an olive brown back and blotched sides. It has three dorsal fins, two anal fins with rounded tips, and a rounded caudal fin.

Latin name
Microgadus tomcod

Best time to catch
Late October to December

Also known as
Tomcod

Tomcod spawn in estuaries or at the mouths of streams in salt or brackish water. The spawning period lasts from November through February. The eggs sink and attach in a mass on stones, seaweed, or any available structure for support near the bottom. The eggs hatch about twenty days later; the fry remain in the vicinity throughout the summer. They grow to about 2½ inches by fall and begin to move into estuaries in search of food. The tomcod can reach about 15 to 18 inches in length, although few are more than 9 to 12 inches long, and weigh about 1½ pounds.

Tomcod is primarily an inshore species and rarely lives deeper than 25 to 30 feet below the surface. It frequents the mouths of streams and estuaries, shoals, muddy bottom, and brackish water and can tolerate fresh water during the winter months. It is resistant to cold temperatures. Most tomcod move to cooler waters in early spring and remain there during the summer months. They do not migrate on a regular basis.

Tomcod has small eyes and poor eyesight and relies on smell to find food. It also relies on feel, from the tips of its sensitive ventral fins along the bottom, or as it stirs up the bottom as it drags its chin barbel. It feeds on small shrimp, sandworms, bloodworms, squid, clams, and small fish.

Fishing Tips

Tomcod can be found along the shore over sand, mud, gravel, oyster beds, or rocky bottom; it is a voracious feeder. It can be caught in large numbers along the bottom at depths of less than 30 feet during the fall and early winter. The baited hook must be directly on the bottom with a suitably weighted sinker. Unlike the Atlantic cod, this scrappy little fish provides great fighting action when hooked.

Bait

Natural bait (bloodworms, sandworms, clams, mussels, and cut fish) works best, although small jigs can also be used.

Equipment

Use a 6- to 7-foot moderate- to fast-action boat rod with matching conventional bait-casting reel filled with 10- to 15-pound-test monofilament line, or a spinning rod with a matching spinning reel filled with 10- to 15-pound-test monofilament line.

The weight of the sinker is from 2 to 6 ounces depending on the current below.

Single-hook rigs are most often used, but double-hook rigs also work well.

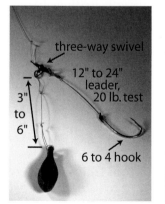

Single-hook rig for Atlantic tomcod.

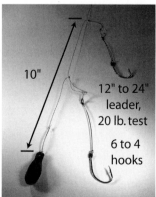

Tandem-hook rig for Atlantic tomcod.

PACIFIC TOMCOD

The Pacific tomcod ranges from the Bering Sea off Alaska to Monterey Bay, California. Its streamlined body tapers to a relatively squared caudal fin. It has an olive green back, gray sides, and white along the belly. A distinct lateral line runs from above the pectoral fin to just in front of the caudal fin. It has three dorsal fins, the last two of which resemble the two anal fins. The lower jaw has a small barbel beneath the lower jaw that is shorter than half the diameter of the eye pupil. It has a large mouth and fine teeth. Pacific tomcod is often confused with white croaker, although the Pacific tomcod has a different dorsal and anal fin arrangement.

Latin name
Microgadus proximus

Best time to catch
Most of the year

Also known as
California tomcod, piciata, tomcod, wachna

Pacific tomcod spawns from winter through spring, varying with location. Females produce as many as 2,000 eggs in a single spawn. The eggs hatch in from eight to seventeen days, depending on location and water temperature. It grows at a fast rate but lives only about five years. Because of its small size (females are about 10 inches long), it is considered a pan fish.

It is primarily a bottom dweller in nearshore environments and often schools over soft, sandy or muddy bottom, although it can be found offshore at depths up to 700 feet. It feeds on anchovies, shrimp, small crustaceans, sandworms, bloodworms, sea worms, and crabs.

Fishing Tips

Anglers can expect great action when the Pacific tomcod moves to inshore waters. It can be caught from almost all piers or docks north of Monterey Bay over sandy bottom, or from a boat. Taken with relatively light tackle, it provides fun for children.

The best method for catching Pacific tomcod is to cast out, then allow the baited hook to sink to the bottom. Start to retrieve the terminal rig as soon as it hits the bottom. Pacific tomcod often hit a baited hook from the bottom to about mid-depth as the terminal rig is being retrieved.

Bait

Use small pieces of cut sandworms or bloodworms, small strips of anchovy, or squid.

Equipment

Pacific tomcod are typically caught with light spinning tackle, such as a 6- to 7-foot moderate-action spinning rod with a matching spinning reel filled with 8- to 10-pound-test monofilament line. When fishing from a boat, you can use a 6- to 7-foot moderate- to fast-action boat rod with a matching conventional bait-casting reel filled with 10- to 15-pound-test monofilament line.

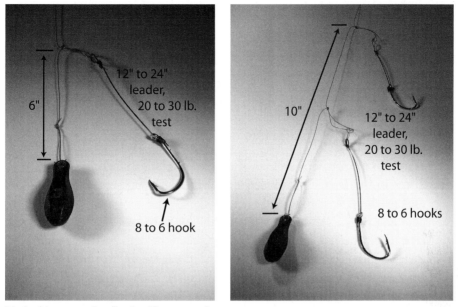

Typical bottom rigs for Pacific tomcod.

ATLANTIC BONITO

In the western Atlantic Ocean, the Atlantic bonito ranges from Nova Scotia to Argentina. In the United States it is most abundant from southern New England to New Jersey. Like other

Latin name
Sarda sarda

Best time to catch
May through October

Also known as
Belted bonito, common bonito, katonkel

fish in the mackerel family, bonito has a long, low dorsal fin, and straight horizontal stripes along its upper middle and back. It has six to eight finlets on the back and along the belly between the anal fin and tail. The small mouth has prominent needle-like teeth, and the fish feeds very cautiously.

Atlantic bonito reaches sexual maturity at age 2 and is known to live to at least 9 years of age. Spawning can take place close to shore or in offshore coastal waters from late January through July, peaking in late June depending on the location. Females spawn when they reach 17 inches in length. Each female produces about 450,000 to 3 million eggs, which are concentrated in the upper 15 feet of water.

As soon as the fry bonito are able to feed, they begin searching for prey. They are relentless, ravenous predators and will feed throughout the day, although most frequently at dusk or dawn along with adult fish. The fry feed on other fish larvae but prefer copepods. Adult bonito consume smaller mackerel, herring, menhaden, hake, mackerel, young bonito, anchovies, squid, and shrimp. At the beginning of the season, bonito weigh about 6 pounds; later in the season they average 8 to 9 pounds. They can reach about 2 feet in length.

Often confused with skipjack tuna, Atlantic bonito is a migratory species. The fish travel in large schools, inhabit tropical and temperate waters, and are strong, swift predators of the open sea. They frequently swim along with albacore and will mix in with bluefish and larger mackerel later in the season. Like albacore, bonito are aggressive surface feeders, often skipping on the surface and leaping for their food as they swim through the water at great speed. They respond to trolling, jigging, and bait.

Fishing Tips

Although considered an offshore species, bonito have been showing up in increased numbers in more inshore locations each year. They are available sooner for offshore anglers; they move inshore about mid-May in the Carolinas and work their way north to Martha's Vineyard about mid-July, and they visit more locations than do albacore. Inshore fish stay until storms and cold fronts push them offshore to deeper, warmer waters. In season they can be anywhere in pursuit of baitfish.

It's best to charter a boat when in pursuit of bonito; the captain will know where to search for fish. Starting out cold will only waste time because of the bonito's speed and many possible locations offshore. Although bonito must usually be searched for, many anglers accidentally come upon them while fishing for another species, then quickly change tackle. Bonito are an elusive and unpredictable species with regard to feeding direction. Anglers usually drift just in front of a moving school. Bonito have excellent eyesight and are wary of leaders or anything that does not appear natural. They can be considered line shy. Bonito have sharp teeth, so use caution when removing a hook.

It's best to use long-shank hooks to avoid short strikes with no hook-ups. An easy way to fish for bonito when a school is located is to troll for them just up-current of the school with shiny spoons or lures at first light or at dusk. Never cut through a school of feeding bonito. Instead, position the boat alongside them as they move, and cast into the school. Bonito are constantly on the move. Fishing action happens in isolated areas during the season. One telltale sign that bonito are in the area is seabirds frantically diving for the baitfish that are being chased by the bonito. Bonito cannot tolerate sandy or freshwater areas; they will hole up at the mouth of an inlet fed by fresh water but never enter the inlet. They prefer shoreline near deep water; unlike coastal fish, they seldom venture over shallow bars to feed near shore.

Some anglers use a fly rod and fly equipment to increase the sport of bonito fishing. However, this species packs a lot of action regardless of which type of tackle you use.

Bait

Use sand eels, spearing, small mackerel, or squid. Bonito prefer narrow-bodied bait because of their small mouth.

Lures

Chartreuse, blue, or olive-colored lures work well, as do shiny spoons weighing from ½ to 1 ounce. It's hard to know what type of baitfish to use until you reach the fishing grounds and see what the bonito are chasing.

Equipment

I recommend a 6- to 8-foot moderate-action spinning rod with a matching spinning reel that can hold at least 200 yards of 15- to 25-pound-test monofilament line.

For surf fishing, use a 10- to 12-foot moderate-action surf rod and matching spinning reel filled with 300 yards of 20- to 30-pound-test monofilament line.

Fly tackle can also be used for Atlantic bonito.

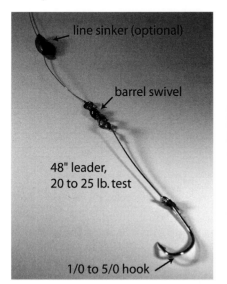

Natural bait trolling rig for bonito.

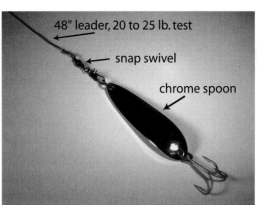

Spoon trolling rig for bonito.

PACIFIC BONITO

Pacific bonito range from Chile to the Gulf of Alaska, with the greatest number from Magdalena Bay, Baja California, to Point Conception, California. It is similar in size and color to Atlantic bonito but differs in that it does not have teeth. Pacific bonito is the only species of fish off the California coast that resembles bluefin tuna, although it is much smaller. Pacific bonito has a cigar-shaped body, a pointed nose, and a large mouth. It is dark blue on the back, with several diagonal dark stripes, and has dusky sides that graduate to silver along the belly. It has about sixteen to twenty spines on the first dorsal fin.

Pacific bonito grow quickly; they range from about 5 to 11 inches in their first year of life to about 40 inches, although this size adult is rare. Female bonito reach sexual maturity at 2 years of age and about 25 inches in length; males mature at about 1 year and about 20 inches. Most

Latin name
Sarda chiliensis

Best time to catch
Late April until the water cools

Also known as
Bonehead, boner, California bonito, eastern Pacific bonito, flasher, Laguna tuna, magneto, ocean bonito, striped tuna

spawning takes place from late January through May in inshore Southern California waters. The free-floating eggs hatch in about three days. Adults weigh about 25 pounds.

Pacific bonito form large schools of the same size fish. Schools offer protection from predators, and schools can collectively gather prey for easy consumption. Like their Atlantic cousins, Pacific bonito range primarily from the surface to the mid-depths in the open sea. They are a migratory species and are constantly moving in search of food. They are fast swimmers and can exceed 50 mph near the surface.

Pacific bonito feed primarily on anchovies and sardines, although they also eat smaller fish, squid, and shrimp. They feed throughout the day but mainly toward dawn and dusk along the surface.

Fishing Tips

Light-tackle and fly anglers eagerly await the arrival of Pacific bonito each year because they are challenging to catch and put up an excellent fight when hooked. However, they must be searched for and are constantly on the move while hunting, so they can prove elusive. They can be found within 15 miles of shore or hundreds of miles offshore.

Large numbers of bonito enter Southern California waters in early spring as the water warms (sooner in more southern waters) and remain until fall, when the water cools. They avoid cooler waters farther north. Some smaller bonito can be caught throughout the year in the warm-water discharge of electrical power plants off Southern California.

Pacific bonito take almost any type of bait or lure presented. They can be fished while trolling at or near the surface, casting and jigging, or with live bait. Schools can be located by trolling feathers or chumming squid pieces once the school has been located. They are usually fished for offshore in about 250 to 550 feet of water, and can also be found near kelp beds closer to shore.

Some anglers drift in areas that harbor bonito as well as using chumming techniques to bring them close to the boat. It's best to charter a boat; the captain will know where the bonito are at any given time, making it easier to fish for these speedsters. Fly fishing for bonito is challenging if the fish are at or near the surface.

Bait

Pacific bonito take a variety of bait (live anchovies, striped squid, shrimp).

Lures

Pacific bonito will take almost any kind of lure. Try feathers or ½- to 1-ounce shiny spoons.

Equipment

If you're trolling, use a 6- to 8-foot moderate-action boat rod with a matching conventional bait-casting reel filled with 10- to 15-pound-test monofilament line.

If you're casting lures, use a 6- to 8-foot moderate-action spinning rod with a matching spinning reel filled with 10- to 15-pound-test monofilament line.

ALBACORE

Albacore is a member of the mackerel family. It resides worldwide in temperate seas, including the Atlantic and Pacific oceans. It is most abundant in the Pacific Ocean, where it ranges

Latin name
Thunnus alalunga

Best time to catch
Late May to October

Also known as
Albacore tuna, albie, longfin, longfin tuna, pigfish

from Alaska to Mexico. (There are two populations of albacore in the Pacific Ocean—one below the equator and the other above it since albacore avoid the warm waters around the equator.) Albacore is less abundant in the Atlantic Ocean, where it ranges from Nova Scotia to Brazil, although it is rare north of New York and in the southern Gulf of Mexico. Like other tuna, it has a cigar-shaped body but is smaller and slightly thinner, with more bulk in the center. It has wavy dark lines on its back just below the dorsal fins and extending to the tail. There are no stripes or spots on the lower flanks and belly. Adult albacore have long pectoral fins, which reach to beyond the second dorsal fin and anal fin. The first dorsal fin is dark yellow and is composed of sharp spines. The rear dorsal and anal fins are soft rays. Like other tuna, albacore has large eyes and excellent eyesight, and fins that fold back into streamlined depressions, allowing high-speed travel.

Albacore become sexually mature at about 5 years of age, at which point they become more solitary and independent. Albacore spawns from July through October, reportedly offshore in the mid-Pacific and in offshore waters in the southern Atlantic, although the locations aren't known for sure. Females can release about 1 million eggs, which hatch a few days after spawning. Young albacore usually remain in the same general area for about 2 years. Albacore average about 20 pounds but can grow much larger (around 85 to 90 pounds). Most that are caught by anglers have not reached maturity. Albacore live for at least 10 years.

Two- to 5-year-old Pacific albacore travel in schools about the size of a football field and usually undertake an extensive migration in spring and early summer, ending around late fall to early winter, from Japan and across the Pacific to off the West Coast of the United States. Atlantic Ocean populations migrate along the coast from New York south to Florida.

Albacore eventually spends most of its time in loosely knit schools in deeper, cooler water, although albacore is a temperate-water species and is most often found in waters between 58 and 70°F. A migratory species, albacore travel in tight schools, consisting of several thousand fish, for protection from predators. They feed on squid, small schooling fish, crustaceans, and shrimp from mid-depths to the surface, primarily the latter. They do not have a large mouth, as do striped bass, or razor-sharp teeth, as do bluefish, both of which limit the size of the fish they feed on.

Albacore is considered the world's fastest migratory fish; due to its streamlined body, it can exceed 50 mph most of the time. Albacore is also the strongest offshore fish pound for pound.

Unlike most fish, albacore does not have a swim bladder, so it always has to be on the move to allow oxygen-rich water to flow through the gills; otherwise, it would sink and drown.

Albacore are fierce fighters when hooked. Anyone who manages to land a large albacore will need to rest after the battle.

Albacore often swim and feed with skipjack, bluefin, and bonito. When attacking, they can be as savage as bluefish but with even more speed. Albacore strike quickly when feeding and leave just as fast, frustrating anglers.

Fishing Tips

It's best to charter a boat for this type of fishing; the crew will know the best areas for albacore. (The fish can be almost anywhere close to shore or offshore.) If you plan to venture out on your own, check for possible school locations through word of mouth or at the local tackle shop.

Albacore seldom move inshore; they prefer deep, open, offshore waters, where they can be caught throughout the fishing season. In northern waters they feed until about mid-September, when storms and cold fronts push them out to deeper, warmer water. In southern waters they stay closer to shore until the first week in October, when they leave with the bonito. Atlantic albacore are mostly found off Massachusetts, Rhode Island, Montauk Point (Long Island), and the Outer Banks of the Carolinas. Pacific albacore are found from 20 to 100 miles offshore in central and Southern California. They rarely frequent nearshore locations.

The trolling speed of the boat should be no less than 7 knots; the propeller noise attracts fish toward the boat. When they investigate the surface noise, they see the lures and jump on them. Fish with as many lures as possible in the water at one time at various distances apart. The theory is to simulate a school of baitfish.

While drifting, you can chum with chunks of fresh or frozen baitfish, such as cut butterfish, whiting, smelt, herring, or squid. In most cases, when albacore are feeding on baitfish, they tend to swim in tight schools.

Albacore are primarily surface feeders, and they're selective. They have good eyesight, so study the water and match the lure or bait to that of the baitfish being chased. Because albacore are considered line shy, use 25-pound-test transparent monofilament or fluorocarbon line for the leader. Any heavier and the fish will see it and not hit the presented bait or lure. Another good method is trolling feathered jigs; use at least a 3-foot length of transparent leader.

When fighting an albacore, face the direction of the fish while reeling it in. This helps keep the line tight and prevents the fish from throwing the hook. Albacore will do anything to release itself from the hook and will put up a fantastic fight until brought on board the boat.

Bait

Natural bait is best—sand eels, spearing, smelt, butterfish, or squid cut to 4-inch lengths. Because albacore (and bonito) do not have a large mouth, they prefer thin-bodied, mouth-sized foods. Any topwater schooling bait, such as small mackerel or squid, is a good bet as well.

Lures

Use cedar plugs; feathers with the colors of red and white, blue and white, green and white, green and yellow, purple and black, or root beer. A daisy chain is also a good choice; the chain of lures simulates a small school of fleeing baitfish (although daisy chains can get tangled easily).

A daisy chain, which comes in different colors.

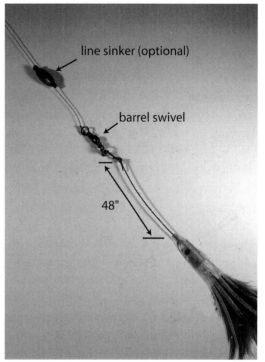

Trolling feather rig for albacore.

Equipment

A good setup is a 7- to 8-foot fast- to extra-fast-action rod with a matching conventional bait-casting reel filled with 30- to 50-pound-test monofilament line.

Use a number 2 to 3/0 hook, depending on the size of the fish you're after.

If the fish are not feeding directly on the surface, use a sliding egg sinker to get the baited hook or lure down into the main body of the school.

Fly tackle can also be used, but make sure that the flies match the size and color needed to attract these fish.

OTHER TUNA

Tuna are great game fish, and are highly sought after by anglers. Albacore and bonito are described in the previous entries; several other popular species are described below.

Bigeye Tuna

Bigeye tuna inhabits warm temperate waters and is common in the Atlantic and Pacific oceans. The first dorsal fin is yellow; the second dorsal fin is blackish brown or may be yellow, along with the anal fin. The finlets are bright yellow with black edges.

When it reaches 35 to 45 inches in length, it spawns in tropical waters about twice a year during the summer months. It averages about 15 to 68 inches in length but can grow to 75 inches.

It travels in schools during the day and feeds on squid, sardines, crustaceans, and small fish. It occasionally feeds at the surface, although it usually swims deep.

Latin name
Thunnus obesus

Best time to catch
Most of the year

Also known as
Bigeye tunny

Blackfin Tuna

Blackfin tuna resides in tropical and warm temperate waters from North Carolina south, and in the Gulf of Mexico; it is most abundant off Florida. It has uniformly shaped dusky finlets with only a trace of dark yellow and perhaps white edges. The first dorsal fin is dusky in color; the second dorsal and anal fins are dusky with a silver luster. The back is bluish black, the sides are silver-gray, and the belly is white.

It spawns offshore from Florida from April to November, and in the Gulf of Mexico from late June through September. It can grow to 40 inches in length and averages about 10 to 30 pounds.

It feeds on squid and small fish near the surface, along with skipjack.

Latin name
Thunnus atlanticus

Best time to catch
Most of the year

Also known as
Bermuda tuna, blackfinned albacore, deep-bodied tunny

Bluefin Tuna

Bluefin tuna range throughout the Atlantic and Pacific oceans, including the Gulf of Mexico and subtropical waters. It is the largest of the bony fish and is considered a prime game fish. It is in the mackerel family, as are yellowfin, bigeye, and albacore, and mackerel. These are all streamlined fish that are bulky in the middle, taper to a point at the head and tail, and have closely spaced dorsal fins. The front dorsal fin can be laid down into a groove in its back. The rear dorsal fin and anal fin resemble a sickle and do not recede. Seven to ten finlets run between the rear dorsal fin and the anal fin, and between the anal fin and the tail. Bluefin tuna has rather short pectoral fins for its size.

Latin name
Thunnus thynnus

Best time to catch
August through October

Also known as
Atlantic bluefin tuna, horse mackerel, northern bluefin tuna, tunny fish

Bluefin tuna sexually mature at about 3 to 5 years of age. They spawn from April to June off the Philippines in the Pacific, in the Gulf of Mexico, and in the Atlantic off the coast of Florida. A spawning female can deposit more than 10 million eggs, depending on her body weight. The eggs hatch about 30 to 35 hours after spawning. The fry grow rapidly and can weigh 8 pounds at 1 year of age. The young exhibit strong schooling behavior based on age and size, and often school along with albacore, bonito, yellowfin, bigeye, and yellowtail.

Bluefin tuna is categorized into four size groups: young tuna, less than 28 inches and weighing 15 pounds; school tuna, 28 to 56 inches and weighing 16 to 135 pounds; medium tuna, 57 to 75 inches and weighing 136 to 310 pounds; and giant tuna, 76 inches or more and weighing more than 310 pounds. They can weigh more than 600 pounds at about 15 years of age.

Bluefin tuna swim in schools of forty to fifty fish of the same size; they often school with several other species that are also highly migratory. They can maintain their body temperature through considerable temperature ranges. The Atlantic population of bluefin tuna migrates across the Atlantic and arrives in warmer waters off the coast of North America in June; it departs in late fall. The Pacific population migrates northward during the summer along the coast of Japan and along the Pacific coast of North America. While offshore, they feed and grow and store fat for their yearly migrations, which are tied to water temperature. Larger tuna (450 to 550 pounds) tend to be more solitary and make the longest migrations.

Known as a midwater species, inhabiting the middle to upper levels, bluefin tuna feed on herring, hake, cod, eels, crustaceans, bluefish, whiting, mackerel, smelt, and squid.

Little Tunny

Little tunny is often misidentified as being bonito or false albacore. It is found worldwide in tropical and temperate waters. In the western Atlantic Ocean it ranges from New England to Brazil. Little tunny has a torpedo-shaped body designed for speed and powerful swimming. The pectoral fins are short and pointed. It has a steel blue back with three to five broken wavy lines that do not extend below the lateral line.

Latin name
Euthynnus alletteratus

Best time to catch
Most of the year

Also known as
Atlantic little tunny, bonito, false albacore, little tuna

Males reach sexual maturity at about 15 inches in length, females at about 12 to 14 inches. They spawn from April through November; females can release as many as 1.75 million eggs in several batches. The average size is about 32 inches in length and up to 20 pounds.

Adults school according to size, and schools can be as large as 2 miles long. It feeds on small fish, squid, shrimp, and crustaceans. Little tunny is prey to dolphinfish, Atlantic sailfish, swordfish, and sharks.

Skipjack Tuna

The skipjack tuna is common in tropical waters. In the western Atlantic, it ranges from Cape Cod to Argentina. It has four to six prominent dark longitudinal stripes from its lower belly (which is silver) and sides toward the tail. Its back is a dark purple-blue.

It usually spawns throughout the year in tropical climates and from spring to fall in cooler climates. It averages from about 17 to 20 inches in length and weighs from 6 to 14 pounds.

Skipjack tuna often school with blackfin tuna; the school can exceed 30,000 individuals. Skipjack tuna is a fast-swimming fish that feeds near the surface on squid, smaller fish, shrimp, and crustaceans.

Latin name
Katsuwonus pelamis

Best time to catch
Most of the year

Also known as
Arctic bonito, ocean bonito, skipjack, striped tuna, watermelon tuna

Yellowfin Tuna

The yellowfin resides in deep, warm temperate waters worldwide and is common off Baja California. It is the most colorful of all the tuna. Its body is blue black on the back and gray or whitish below. The fins and finlets are golden yellow and the finlets have black edges.

It spawns throughout the year, peaking during the summer months. It can weigh as much as 400 pounds, although most caught fish weigh less than 100 pounds.

Younger yellowfin tuna form large schools near the surface; adults inhabit deeper water, although they frequent the surface as well. Yellowfin tuna feed on squid and small fish.

Latin name
Thunnus albacares

Best time to catch
Most of the year

Also known as
Albacore, Allison tuna, autumn albacore, yellow-finned albacore

General Fishing Tips

Laws governing recreational tuna fishing are strictly regulated by the National Marine Fisheries Service (NMFS; www.nmfs.noaa.gov) and can change daily. Check with the agency before heading out. Also, be aware that some states prohibit the sale of some larger tuna species (not albacore or bonito) by recreational sportsmen without a commercial fishing permit.

Tuna fishing is big-time sportfishing at its best. But it can be dangerous and is by no means for the novice angler. Appropriate and sophisticated equipment is needed along with a boat able to travel long distances offshore, so it's best to hire a charter boat for offshore tuna fishing.

The captain will have the equipment needed, including flies, lures, or baited hooks, will know the fish's varied locations far offshore, and will be aware of current laws regarding the size and possession limits of fish per angler and/or per boat.

Tuna is best fished by trolling, using lures or chunking with mackerel, herring, bluefish, or squid. (Chunking works best from summer through early fall at dawn and dusk.) While fishing, you need a fighting chair or fighting belt to help support the rod in the rod gimbal. With larger fish (more than 25 pounds), the fight can be hard and fatiguing.

Once hooked, tuna go on a long, fast run, so make sure the drag on the reel is set properly; otherwise, the line will snap and you'll lose the fish. The captain of the charter boat will know how to position the boat to reduce the amount of line coming off the reel and to ease the line tension. When the fish is close to the boat, it's important to keep a cool head, because this is the stage at which most tuna are lost. The fish may make a last-minute charge, and you must be ready. Always keep the line tight, and never lose track of where the fish is. The captain or mates will gaff the fish aboard the boat for you at the proper moment.

All tuna must be gaffed aboard the boat. Caution must be observed because a large tuna thrashing about on the deck can cause serious injury to anglers and/or damage to the boat's interior. Tuna must be bled and gutted soon after capture and placed on ice to preserve their freshness.

Bait

The bait varies depending on what the tuna are feeding on at the time. Natural bait, fishing lures, or flies might be used. If it's natural bait, it should be about 6 to 8 inches long and accompanied by chunking.

Lures

Artificial bait can be diamond jigs, spoons, leadhead tuna feathers, plastic squid, or daisy chains. Surface or topwater plugs will also work well if retrieved at a moderate rate when fish are on the surface.

Equipment

Use a 6- to 8-foot extra-fast-action, extra-heavy trolling rod to fight these strong fish aboard the boat.

Or you can use a conventional bait-casting reel with the highest line capacity and a reliable drag filled with 80- to 100-pound-test Dacron line. If you're fishing with natural bait, use an 8/0 to 12/0 hook.

An effective tuna feather daisy chain.

Tuna feathers and lure skirt. Most tuna will hit these types of lures when trolled.

WAHOO

Wahoo is related to mackerel and is the largest fish in the family. It resides offshore in tropical and subtropical waters in the Atlantic, Pacific, and Indian oceans. In the western Atlantic,

Latin name
Acanthocybium solandri

Best time to catch
Year-round

Also known as
Barracuda, Oahu fish, ocean barracuda, Pacific kingfish, queenfish, tigerfish

it can be found from 150 to 300 feet deep off the Carolinas. It is a slender, cigar-shaped oceanic fish with a pointed head and beak-like snout. The lower jaw is elongated and has razor-sharp teeth. Wahoo is dark blue or green along the back. It has two dorsal fins, the first being several times the length of the second. The dorsal fins are followed by eight or nine finlets, which terminate just in front of the widely forked caudal fin. The anal fin is located just below the second dorsal fin. The belly and lower sides are silver.

It reaches sexual maturity about 1 or 2 years of age. Depending on the environment, it can spawn year-round, although it usually spawns from May through August. Larger females can produce as many as 60 million eggs, which are buoyant. Young wahoo less than 20 pounds school over Pacific reefs. Wahoo can grow to about 8 feet in length and can weigh more than 180 pounds, although most individuals are from 3 to 5 feet in length and weigh 80 to 90 pounds. The average weight for wahoo caught is about 30 pounds. It can live up to about 6 years of age.

Adult wahoo tend to be solitary, although adults occasionally swim in pairs. It is rarely in nearshore waters except where deep water is close to shore. It moves with the changing seasons and travels to cooler waters during the hot summer months. It frequents reefs and ledges where warm water currents run close inshore. In the ocean, it can be located around sargassum, and logs and other debris, and on the bottom over deep reefs and holes. It feeds from a few to several feet deep on small fish, tuna, herring, and squid as well as many other species. While feeding, wahoo is aggressive and can reach speeds of 60 mph in short bursts.

Fishing Tips

Water temperature is critical; the best fishing is in water that's about 65 to 72°F. Wahoo can appear at any time, but it's generally best caught in the morning or late afternoon. You might consider fishing for wahoo five days before a new or full moon. This timing tends to spark the best action because it's when wahoo feed more actively. Most wahoo are caught offshore, or along the edges of deepwater structure or rocks closer to shore.

Wahoo will attack most any bait or lure providing that it's moving fast. Troll deep-diving lures over deep reefs, or use surface rigs. It's best to charter a boat and its crew for wahoo fishing when heading out to distant offshore locations.

Most wahoo is taken by jigging or trolling lures that contain natural bait, although natural bait alone will also work. Or you can drift while working a lure or baited hook. If you prefer trolling, let the lure or natural bait run about 30 to 50 feet below the surface. The lure's skirt color combinations that seem to work best are red/black or purple/black. You can also troll dead ballyhoo that is rigged just behind the rubber skirt and fastened to expose the back half of the bait.

Bait
Wahoo are not fussy; they will take almost any smaller fish whole or filleted.

Lures
They take shiny metal lures, and most often take feathered and skirted lures rigged with ballyhoo bait.

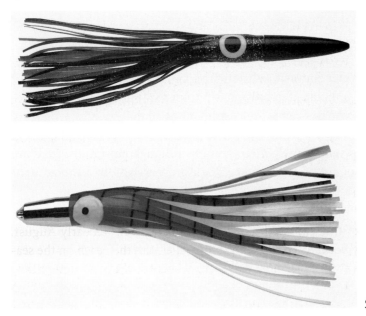

Skirted lures for wahoo.

Equipment
Use a 7- to 8-foot fast- to extra-fast-action rod with a matching conventional bait-casting reel. If you're trolling, use a trolling rod and matching conventional bait-casting reel filled with 300 yards of 50- to 80-pound-test monofilament line.

WHITING

Whiting is one of the most common species of fish in the North Atlantic. A member of the codfish family, it is a bottom-dwelling species that ranges from Maine to Florida. It is more abundant in the northern portion of this range and frequents most types of bottom formations in the Gulf of Maine, on Georges Bank and the continental shelf off New England, and in the mid-Atlantic south to Cape Hatteras. The anal fin of the whiting starts vertically

Latin name
Merlangius merlangus

Best time to catch
September through January

beneath the center of the first dorsal fin and ends at the end of the second dorsal fin. It has three dorsal fins and two anal fins that follow in close succession. The caudal fin is almost straight edged. The sides of the body are yellowish brown, dark blue, or green, and the belly is yellowish gray, white, and silver. There is often a small dark blotch at the upper base of the pectoral fins.

Whiting sexually matures at 2 years of age. Whiting spawns throughout the year, most frequently peaking in spring, in about 260 feet of water at about 55°F. A 4-year-old female, which is 11 inches long, can produce as many as 400,000 eggs during a single spawn. The eggs are deposited over a fourteen-week period and hatch in ten days. After hatching, the fry swim along with jellyfish for protection and shelter. The fry grow fast, to about 6 inches, in their first year. After that they grow relatively slowly. The fry return toward shore when they reach 1 year of age. From that point on, they live in the sediment on the bottom and consume small sea worms, sand eels, and small shrimp and other crustaceans. Whiting has a short life span; most fish caught average about 3 or 4 years of age.

Whiting feed on sand eels, young herring, smaller whiting, young cod, small haddock, sea worms, and crabs. Whiting are themselves food for larger species of fish, and small whiting are frequently used for bait.

Fishing Tips

Depending on the location, whiting can be found from late April through early August. Whiting prefer muddy or sandy bottom. They like to run parallel with the beach on the seaward side of sandbars or banks. Whiting can be fished from boats or the surf, along heavy reefs, and in the deep channels of bays and estuaries. A period of cold temperatures works in the angler's favor: whiting prefer a water temperature from 41 to 55°F; as the temperature decreases, the fish become more sluggish.

Fishing for larger whiting from a boat improves from late August through November, although most smaller whiting are taken throughout the year.

Ideal conditions for whiting are calm seas with little or no wind. They are frequently found off the beach.

Whiting are shoal fish and feed off or directly on the bottom while on the run, which requires small hooks because of their small mouth. To make a large catch, you must locate their feeding depth. Whiting is not a powerful species and often struggles against a fast-moving tide. It's best to start fishing at a higher depth during slack tide, or directly on the bottom when the tide is moving with some force.

Large whiting primarily feed at night just offshore from the beach, so surf anglers need to be at the beach by early dusk. The best time to catch whiting in bays and at the surf is during the flood tide. When fishing the flood tide at the surf, casts of 25 to 30 yards should be sufficient. (If you're fishing the ebb tide, increase the casting distance to 60 to 75 yards.)

Whiting have tiny sharp teeth, so be aware of this to prevent injury.

Bait

Use small pieces of fresh shrimp, sandworms, bloodworms, sand eels, small pieces of cut squid, or small baitfish.

Equipment

I recommend a 6- to 8-foot moderate- to fast-action spinning rod with a matching spinning reel filled with 15- to 20-pound-test monofilament line.

If you're bottom fishing from a boat, use a 6- to 7-foot moderate-action boat rod with a matching conventional bait-casting reel filled with 10- to 20-pound-test monofilament line. A suitable weight sinker is determined by the current.

If you're fishing at the surf, use a 9- to 10-foot moderate- to fast-action surf rod with a matching spinning reel filled with 10- to 20-pound-test monofilament line.

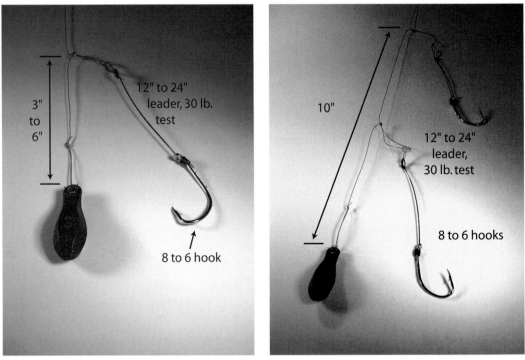

Typical bottom rigs for whiting.

CHAPTER 20

PREPARING AND COOKING YOUR CATCH

The moment a fish is caught and dies, it begins to deteriorate because of the bacteria and enzymes in its body. It's best to remove the source of bacteria as soon as possible because fish lose flavor and spoil quickly if not properly cared for.

All fish that will be kept, especially large fish, must be killed quickly and as humanely as possible—for their sake, to protect the meat, and to prevent them from thrashing about and seriously injuring people and damaging property.

To kill a large fish quickly, club it with a firm rap on the top of the head just above the eyes. Small fish may also be clubbed, or simply allowed to expire naturally.

Blood spoils faster than flesh, so bleed the fish promptly. Cut the throat crosswise just below the gills. This will sever the blood vessels, allowing the blood to flow freely. If possible, do this in a bin of ice and water to reduce blood clotting and begin cooling the fish.

Next, rapidly gut the fish to remove the digestive enzymes and bacteria in the stomach and intestines, and to retard spoilage if the fish will be kept whole.

Place a sharp knife about ½ inch into the fish's anal cavity, then move the knife toward the head, slicing open the abdomen. Make sure to center the cut along the fish's belly. Open the abdominal cavity and reach in to remove the intestines and other organs; discard them properly.

Place the fish in a plastic bag, tie the bag closed to prevent water from entering, and put the bag on ice. For larger fish, use a large plastic leaf bag. Don't allow fish to lie in ice water without first putting it in a sealed plastic bag; any water that seeps in will promote bacterial growth.

Always keep your catch cold. If there is lots of fishing action and you don't want to stop to clean the fish, at least bleed and ice them immediately. You can gut the fish later when the action slows down. **Note:** Gutting is more important with full-bodied, or "round," fish because it takes much longer for them to cool down. Flatfish cool down more quickly, so many anglers wait until they get home to gut them.

As soon as you get your catch home, wash it thoroughly in fresh water, inside and out. If you plan to freeze the fish, make a brine solution (use a ratio of 1 cup table salt to 2 cups fresh water). Allow the fish to soak in it for at least a half hour to help preserve its flavor and stop any further bacterial growth.

Fish scales are arranged like roof shingles on a house—smooth and streamlined from head to tail. Hold the fish by its tail, with the head facing away from you. Hold a knife with the blade at a 45-degree angle from vertical and the edge facing *toward* you (scraping against the grain—like stropping a straight razor). Slide the knife toward the head while applying downward pressure. This will lift and remove the scales without cutting into the flesh. Do this underwater to prevent the scales from flying all over the place. Repeat until all the scales are removed. If you prefer a bait knife, use the serrated edge to scale the fish.

There are three ways to prepare fish for cooking: keeping it whole, steaking it, and filleting it. To prepare a whole fish, start by scaling it. Remove the head, fins, and tail, if you wish, by cutting just behind the pectoral fin straight down and through the entire fish (this is called "dressing" the fish). To remove the caudal fin or tail fin, cut about ½ inch in from where the tail meets the body. Maintain a firm grip on the knife to cut through the backbone. Most whole fish are baked, broiled, or grilled with the skin on. You can remove the skin after cooking, or leave it on to serve the fish.

Most larger fish, such as cobia, cod, large bluefish, striped bass, pollock, haddock, red snapper, tuna, and weakfish, can be cut into steaks. Begin by cutting off all the fins using sharp scissors, then scale the fish. With the fish on its side, remove the head by cutting through the body just behind the gills. Cut each section thereafter to the desired thickness, up to a maximum of about 4 inches. As with whole fish, steaks may be grilled, broiled, or baked.

A fish should be at least 1½ pounds for filleting. Smaller than that and it's difficult to avoid the bone structure of the fish, so small bones remain in the meat. Make sure that your filleting knife is very sharp, and be careful when using it.

Start by snipping off the fins with shears. Rinse the fish, making sure that the abdominal cavity is clean.

To fillet a round fish, put the fish on a clean work surface, such as a wooden cutting board, that's large enough to hold the entire fish. Place a sharp filleting knife at a diagonal behind the head of the fish and cut down to the backbone; do not cut all the way through the fish (1).

Filleting knives.

Cut behind the head.

Hold the fish at the tail end with one hand and place the knife just above the bony ridge of the spine. Make a cut along the length of the backbone, about ½ inch deep, from the neck to the tail (2). This cut will serve as a guide line for filleting the fish.

Now insert the knife into the fish behind the head and cut the meat from the rib cage with short back-and-forth strokes, working toward the tail and keeping the knife horizontal and directly against the backbone. Peel back the meat with your other hand as you go until the fillet comes away in a strip. Turn the fish over with the head facing toward you, and repeat the procedure to fillet the other side.

Cut ½ inch deep along the backbone.

Removing the skin.

Next, place a fillet with the skin facing down on the work surface. Trim back a small piece of flesh from the tail end, but leave it attached. Holding on to the exposed skin, place the knife between the flesh and the skin. With the blade angled slightly downward, run the knife along the skin to remove the skin from the fillet (3).

To fillet a flatfish, rinse the fish under cold water, but do not dry it. With a filleting knife, make a V-shaped cut behind the head, cutting down to the backbone without cutting through it (1). Find the soft belly area, opposite the dorsal fin, and cut around it, taking care not to pierce the viscera.

Make a V-shaped cut behind the head.

Make a straight cut from the neck to the tail.

Position the fish on the work surface with the tail pointing toward your knife hand. Place the knife at the point of the V-shaped cut behind the head and make a straight cut along the centerline of the fish from the neck to the tail, following the ridge of the backbone (2).

Insert the knife into the cut and trim a fillet from the rib cage with short strokes, cutting parallel to the bones (3). Peel back the flesh as you go until the fillet comes away in a strip. Turn the fish over and repeat the procedure on the other side.

Remove the flesh from the rib cage with short strokes.

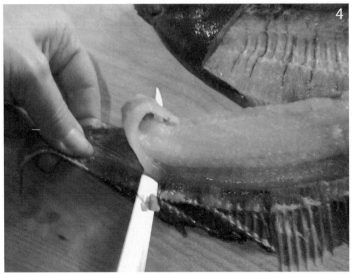

Removing the skin.

Place the fillet skin side down on the work surface. Trim back a small piece of flesh from the tail end, but leave it attached. Holding on to the exposed skin with your fingers, place the knife between the flesh and the skin. With the blade angled slightly downward, run the knife along the skin to remove it from the fillet (4).

Here are some favorite fish recipes that have been in my family for years. Most of them allow the substitution of almost any fish you choose.

Basic Fish Stock

> heads, tails, bones, skin, and backs of any saltwater fish
> 2 medium carrots, chopped
> 2 small yellow onions, peeled and chopped
> 4 stalks celery, chopped
> salt to taste
> seasonings to taste

Place all the ingredients in a large pot and add water to cover. Place a lid on the pot and simmer over low heat until the vegetables are soft. Strain, and discard everything in the strainer. Use the stock as a base for other recipes. You can add it to cooked noodles and top the dish with sour cream for a tasty fish-noodle soup.

Grouper Soup

> 1½ pounds grouper fillets or any type of fish, cut into 2-inch pieces
> 1 teaspoon paprika
> 2 15-ounce cans tomato sauce
> 8 ounces fresh mushrooms, sliced

1 teaspoon ground thyme
1 teaspoon ground marjoram
1 teaspoon ground savory
1 cup chopped green onion, for garnish

Toss the fish pieces with the paprika. Lightly coat a large skillet with nonstick cooking spray. Brown the seasoned fish over medium-high heat until it flakes easily when tested with a fork. Remove the fish from the pan and keep it warm.

In the same skillet, combine the tomato sauce, mushrooms, thyme, marjoram, and savory. Simmer over medium-low heat until the mushrooms are tender. Remove from heat and divide the mixture evenly among four soup bowls. Add the reserved fish and top with the green onion. Makes 4 servings.

Fisherman's Stew

4 strips bacon, cut into 2-inch pieces
1 large onion, chopped
2 large thin-skinned potatoes, diced
1 28-ounce can Italian-style tomatoes
1 cup dry vermouth, or $^1/_4$ cup lemon juice plus $^3/_4$ cup water
1 tablespoon Worcestershire sauce
$^1/_2$ cup pitted and chopped black olives
4 bay leaves
2 or 3 cloves garlic, minced or pressed
$^1/_2$ teaspoon ground pepper
2 pounds of 1-inch-thick fish fillets (cod, striped bass, sea bass, or a combination), cut into 2-inch pieces
salt to taste

Fisherman's stew.

In a 4- or 5-quart kettle, cook the bacon over medium heat until crisp. Add the onion and potatoes and cook, stirring frequently, until the onion is soft (about 10 minutes). Add the tomatoes (break them up with a spoon) and their liquid. Stir in the vermouth, Worcestershire sauce, olives, bay leaves, garlic, and ground pepper. Cover and simmer until the potatoes are tender (about 30 minutes).

Add the fish to the vegetable mixture as soon as the potatoes are tender. Stir gently to combine. Cover and continue simmering until the fish is just opaque when prodded with a fork (about 5 minutes). Season to taste with salt. Makes 4 to 6 servings.

Add coleslaw and hot garlic bread for a complete meal.

Fisherman's Chowder

    2 tablespoons butter or margarine
    ½ cup chopped onion
    ½ cup chopped celery
    ¾ cup chopped carrot
    2 to 3 tablespoons flour
    1 teaspoon dried thyme or Italian seasoning
    1 17-ounce can creamed corn
    2 cups milk
    ¾ to 1 pound flaked fish (any type)
    1 cup water
    1 chicken-flavored bouillon cube

In a medium saucepan, melt the butter over medium heat. Add the onion, celery, and carrot; sauté about 3 minutes. Add the flour and thyme; blend well and cook for 3 more minutes. Add the corn, milk, fish, water, and bouillon, stirring to blend. Cover and simmer for 5 minutes (do not boil) to heat through, stirring occasionally. Makes 4 servings.

This chowder is rich with chunks of your favorite fish and lots of vegetables. It's a hearty chowder for a cold winter day.

Baked Stuffed Striped Bass

    3 tablespoons butter or margarine
    ¼ cup chopped onion
    ¼ cup chopped celery
    ½ cup chopped mushrooms
    2 cups breadcrumbs
    1 teaspoon salt
    ⅛ teaspoon ground pepper
    pinch of dried tarragon
    2 pounds striped bass fillets or any type of large fish
    juice of 1 lemon or lime
    3 or 4 ripe tomatoes, peeled and sliced

Preheat the oven to 375°F. Melt the butter in a large saucepan. Add the onion, celery, and mushrooms; sauté for 5 minutes. Stir in the breadcrumbs, salt, pepper, and tarragon; set aside.

Grease a large, shallow baking dish. Arrange the fish fillets in the dish and sprinkle with the lemon or lime juice. Spread the reserved breadcrumb mixture over the fish, and cover with the tomato slices. Bake uncovered for 35 to 40 minutes. Makes 6 servings.

Baked Whole Stuffed Fish

> 2 cups Flavorful Fish Stuffing (see next recipe)
> 1 4-pound weakfish, bluefish, red drum, or any other type of large fish (dressed with the head removed, if preferred)
> $\frac{1}{8}$ teaspoon salt
> 1 slice lemon
> 1 teaspoon fish seasoning mix (or combine salt, pepper, paprika, lemon juice, parsley, and basil to taste)

Preheat the oven to 425°F. Prepare the stuffing as directed below, and set aside.

Spray a 15-by-10-by-1-inch baking dish with nonstick cooking spray and set aside.

Rinse the fish and pat dry. Sprinkle the salt inside the fish cavity, then fill the cavity with the reserved stuffing. Secure with skewers, or tie the entire fish with string. Rub the outside of the stuffed fish with the lemon slice and sprinkle with the seasoning mix. Place the fish in the prepared dish and bake until the fish flakes easily with a fork (about 30 minutes). Makes 2 to 3 servings.

Flavorful Fish Stuffing

> 2 teaspoons butter or margarine
> $\frac{1}{4}$ cup shredded carrot
> $\frac{1}{4}$ cup finely chopped celery
> 2 tablespoons finely chopped onion
> 1 teaspoon grated lemon zest
> $\frac{1}{4}$ teaspoon salt, or to taste
> $\frac{1}{8}$ teaspoon dried thyme
> dash ground pepper
> 3 tablespoons water
> 2 cups soft breadcrumbs

Melt the butter in a medium saucepan over medium heat. Add the carrot, celery, and onion. Cook, stirring, until tender. Remove from heat and stir in the remaining ingredients. Makes 2 cups. Use this to stuff fish fillets or a whole fish.

Flounder in Almond Sauce

1½ pounds flounder fillets
1 cup white wine
3 ounces canned baby shrimp
4 tablespoons butter or margarine
2 tablespoons flour
½ cup half-and-half
¼ tablespoon salt
dash ground pepper
1 4-ounce can diced tomatoes, drained
⅓ cup slivered or flaked almonds, toasted
2 ounces flaked almonds, toasted, for garnish

Preheat oven to 350°F. Spray a 13-by-9-by-2-inch baking dish with nonstick cooking spray and arrange the fillets in the dish. Pour the wine over the fish, cover, and bake until the fish flakes easily with a fork but is still moist (15 to 20 minutes). Do not overcook.

While the fish bakes, set aside ¼ cup of the shrimp, and mash the remaining shrimp with 2 tablespoons of the butter; set aside.

When the fish is cooked, remove all but 1½ cups of the cooking liquid, and keep the fish warm.

In a small saucepan, melt the remaining 2 tablespoons butter. Add the flour and cook, stirring constantly, for 2 to 3 minutes. Gradually add the half-and-half, stirring constantly, until the mixture comes to a boil. Reduce heat; add the reserved shrimp-butter mixture, the salt and pepper, and the diced tomatoes; stir until the butter melts. Stir in ¼ cup of the slivered almonds; set aside.

Transfer the fish to a heated platter (discard the cooking liquid). Pour the shrimp-tomato mixture over the fish, and garnish with the reserved ¼ cup baby shrimp and the remaining slivered almonds. Serve on a bed of rice, garnished with the toasted almonds. Makes 4 servings.

Baked Porgy with Basil

4¾ pounds dressed whole porgies
3 tablespoons minced green onion
¾ teaspoon salt
3 tablespoons chopped fresh basil (about 20 leaves), or 1½ tablespoons dried basil
1 cup dry white wine
3 tablespoons butter or margarine

Preheat the oven to 375°F. Lightly coat a large baking dish with nonstick cooking spray, or brush the bottom of the dish with olive or vegetable oil. Spread the green onion in the dish.

With a sharp knife, make several slits along the sides of each porgy. Place the fish on the bed of green onion and sprinkle with the salt and chopped basil. Set side for 5 minutes so the flavors blend. Then pour the wine over the fish and dot with the butter. Cover with aluminum foil and bake until the fish turns opaque and begins to flake (10 to 15 minutes). Makes 4 servings.

Weakfish with Tomato Sauce

> 1 3- to 4-pound weakfish or any type of fish, dressed
> 1 8-ounce can tomato sauce
> 2 tablespoons salad oil
> 1 teaspoon cheese-garlic salad dressing mix or Italian salad dressing mix
> ½ teaspoon salt
> grated Parmesan cheese

Preheat the oven to 350°F. Place the fish in a large, shallow, well-greased baking dish. Combine the tomato sauce, salad oil, dressing mix, and salt. Brush some of the mixture over the inside cavity of the fish, and pour the remaining mixture over and around the fish. Sprinkle it with the cheese, and bake until the fish flakes easily when tested with a fork (about 40 to 45 minutes). Makes 6 servings.

Atlantic Cod Fillets

> 1 tablespoon butter
> 2 8- to 16-ounce codfish or other fish fillets
> 2 large green bell peppers, sliced
> 2 large red bell peppers, sliced
> 2 green onions, chopped
> 1 tablespoon teriyaki sauce
> ½ teaspoon chopped fresh dill
> juice of 1 lime

Atlantic cod fillets.

Preheat the broiler. Remove the rack from the broiler pan and melt the butter in the pan. Place the fish fillets in the pan and set aside.

Combine the green and red bell peppers, green onion, teriyaki sauce, dill, and lime juice. Spread the mixture evenly over the fish. Broil for 6 minutes. Makes 4 servings.

Flounder and Cheese

    2 pounds flounder fillets
    2 tablespoons lemon juice
    $\frac{1}{2}$ cup grated Parmesan cheese
    $\frac{1}{4}$ cup butter, softened
    1 tablespoon mayonnaise
    3 green onions, chopped
    $\frac{1}{4}$ teaspoon salt
    1 dash hot sauce
    chopped parsley (optional)

Preheat the broiler. Place the fillets in a single layer in a greased, shallow oven-to-table broiler pan without a rack. Brush the fillets with the lemon juice. In a small bowl, combine the cheese, butter, mayonnaise, green onion, salt, and hot sauce; set aside.

Broil the fillets until the fish flakes easily when tested with a fork (4 to 6 minutes). Remove it from the broiler and spread with the reserved cheese mixture. Return the pan to the broiler and broil until the cheese is lightly browned and bubbly (an additional 30 seconds). Garnish with parsley if desired. Makes 4 servings.

Broiled Deviled Fluke

    2 pounds fresh fluke fillets
    2 tablespoons butter, melted
    salt and pepper to taste
    4 ounces cheddar cheese, grated (about 1 cup)
    $\frac{1}{4}$ cup chili sauce
    1 teaspoon prepared mustard
    $\frac{1}{2}$ teaspoon prepared horseradish
    $\frac{1}{2}$ teaspoon Worcestershire sauce

Preheat the broiler, and grease the rack of the broiler pan. Cut the fish into 6 portions; arrange them in a single layer on the greased broiler pan rack, tucking under any thin edges. Brush the fish with the melted butter and sprinkle with the salt and pepper. Broil 4 inches from the heat until the fish flakes easily when tested with a fork (about 10 to 15 minutes); do not turn over. Remove from the broiler.

Blend the cheese, chili sauce, mustard, horseradish, and Worcestershire sauce; spread it over the fillets. Return the pan to the broiler and broil until the cheese melts (about 1 to 3 minutes longer). Makes 6 servings.

APPENDIX A

FISHING AND THE LAW

When fishing in any state's jurisdiction, every saltwater recreational angler must be aware of state laws protecting saltwater fish (see pages 310–11). Contact the appropriate marine recreational fishing agency; obtain a current list of what species may be caught and kept, and under what conditions; and ask questions if you don't understand the regulations. Keep a copy of the list with you while you're fishing rather than relying on your memory. You could be subject to big fines if your memory serves you wrong.

Some states require a saltwater fishing license and/or permits for certain species of saltwater fish. Where applicable, always have a current fishing license or permit readily available for viewing by law enforcement personnel.

I haven't listed the specific regulations state by state because they change with great frequency. Don't depend on last year's list; make sure you have a current one every year. The information is usually available free of charge.

Following is contact information for all state and other agencies that regulate recreational saltwater fishing in the United States.

Alabama
Alabama Department of Conservation and
 Natural Resources
64 N. Union Street
Montgomery AL 36130
334-242-3469
www.conservation.alabama.gov/fishing
Saltwater fishing license required.

Alaska
Alaska Department of Fish and Game
Division of Wildlife Conservation
P.O. Box 25526
Juneau AK 99802-5526
907-465-4190
www.sf.adfg.state.ak.us/statewide/sf_home
 .cfm
Saltwater fishing license required.

California
California Department of Fish and Game
Licensing and Revenue Branch
3211 S Street
Sacramento CA 95816
916-227-2245
www.dfg.ca.gov/licensing
Saltwater fishing license required.

Connecticut
Connecticut Department of Environmental
 Protection
Marine Fisheries Division Headquarters
333 Ferry Road
Old Lyme CT 06371
860-434-6043
http://dep.state.ct.us/burnatr/fishing/
 fdhome.htm
Saltwater fishing license not required.

MARINE RECREATIONAL FISHING

LAWS AND REGULATIONS **2005**

Laws and regulations are frequently amended by the Legislature or DEC. You should check with the Marine Fisheries office to ensure that the requirements set forth in this notice remain in effect. ***The most recent changes to this summary are indicated by the shaded boxes and are effective as of:*** *** April 8, 2005***

For further information, visit our website at ***www.dec.state.ny.us/website/dfwmr/marine/finfish/swflaws.html***

SPECIES	MINIMUM SIZE (Total Length in Inches)	DAILY POSSESSION LIMITS (Number of Fish)	OPEN SEASONS
Summer flounder (fluke)*	17.5	5	April 29- Oct 31
Winter flounder	11	15	All state waters: 3rd Sat in March thru June 30 & Sept 15 thru Nov 30
Tautog (blackfish)	14	10	Oct 1 - May 31
Bluefish (including "snappers")	No minimum size limit for first 10 fish, 12" TL for the next 5	15 No more than 10 of which shall be less than 12" TL	All year
Weakfish	16 (10" filleted & 12" dressed)	6	All year
Atlantic cod	23	No limit	All year
Pollock	19	No limit	All year
Haddock	21	No limit	All year
Striped bass (marine waters**) Anglers aboard licensed party/charter boats	28	2***	April 15 -- Dec 15
Striped bass (marine waters**) All other anglers	28 to 40 >40	1 1	April 15 -- Dec 15
Scup (Porgy) Anglers aboard licensed party/charter boats	10.5	25 26 - 60***	July 1 - Aug 31 Sept. 1 - Oct 31***
Scup (Porgy) All other anglers	10.5	25	July 1 - Oct 31
Black Sea Bass	12	25	Jan 1 - Nov 30
Atlantic sturgeon	No possession allowed	No possession allowed	No possession allowed
Cobia	37	2	All year
Spanish mackerel	14	15	All year
King mackerel	23	3	All year
Red drum	No minimum size limit	No limit for fish less than 27" TL Fish greater than 27" TL shall not be possessed	All year

A typical state saltwater fishing regulation sheet (in this case, New York). It includes all the species that are regulated by the state and provides the size, possession limits, and season limits for each species listed. Any species that is not listed is not regulated and may be caught and kept. (Courtesy New York Department of Environmental Conservation, Bureau of Marine Resources)

SPECIES	MINIMUM SIZE (Total Length in Inches)	DAILY POSSESSION LIMITS (Number of Fish)	OPEN SEASONS
American eel	6	50	All year
Monkfish (goosefish)	21 14 tail length	No limit	All year
American shad	No size limit	5	All year
Hickory shad	No size limit	5	All year
Yellowtail flounder	13	No limit	All Year
Crabs#	No Size Limit	50	All year
American lobster# (Rec. permit required)	3¼" carapace length	6	All year

* Summer flounder may not have heads or tails removed or be otherwise cleaned, cut, filleted, or skinned until brought to shore, with the following exception: the white side fillet or white skin only of a legal size fluke may be removed to use as bait. The carcass of the fluke with dark side completely intact must be retained for inspection of size limit and counts against the possession limit.

** For striped bass only, marine waters is defined as south of George Washington Bridge.

*** Customers aboard a licensed party/charter boat who take more than 25 scup from Sept 1 - Oct 31or take two striped bass from April 15 - December 15 must possess an original dated receipt from the licensed vessel.

Lobsters and crabs in spawn (eggs visible thereon) may not be taken or possessed.

Recreational Fishing Regulations for Sharks
For further information call NMFS Fisheries
Information Line at (978) 281-9278

Category	Species	Minimum Size Limit	Daily Possession Limit
Large & Small Coastal Sharks & Pelagic Sharks	Sandbar, Silky, Tiger, Blacktip, Bull, Great Hammerhead, Lemon, Nurse, Scalloped Hammerhead, Smooth Hammerhead, Spinner, Blacknose, Bonnethead, Finetooth, Blue, Shortfin mako, Oceanic whitetip, Thresher, Porbeagle	54 inches fork length*	One shark per vessel per trip
	Atlantic sharpnose	No size limit	One Atlantic sharpnose per person per trip
Prohibited Sharks	Atlantic angel, Galapagos, Basking, Longfin mako, Bigeye Sand Tiger, Narrowtooth, Bigeye Sixgill, Night, Bigeye thresher, Sand tiger, Bignose, Sevengill, Carribean Reef, Sixgill, Carribean sharpnose, Smalltail, Dusky, Whale and White+	No possession allowed	

* Fork length means the straightline measurement of a fish from the tip of the snout to the fork of the tail. The measurement is not made along the curve of the body.

+A person may fish for white sharks with rod and reel, provided the person releases such fish immediately with a minimum of injury and that such fish may not be removed from the water.

Other provisions
▶ All landed sharks must have head, tails and fins attached
▶ No sale allowed
▶ No finning

Delaware

Delaware Department of Natural Resources
and Environmental Control
Delaware Division of Fish and Wildlife
89 Kings Highway
Dover DE 19901
302-739-9914; 800-523-3336
www.dnrec.state.de.us/fw/fishing.htm
Saltwater fishing license not required.

Florida

Florida Fish and Wildlife Conservation
Commission
Division of Marine Fisheries Management
2590 Executive Center Circle East,
Suite 201
Tallahassee FL 32301
850-487-0554; 888-FISH-FLORIDA
(888-347-4356)
http://myfwc.com/license;
http://myfwc.com/marine
Saltwater fishing license required.

Georgia

Georgia Department of Natural Resources
Coastal Resources Division
One Conservation Way
Brunswick GA 31520
912-264-7218
http://crd.dnr.state.ga.us/content/
displaynavigation.asp?/TopCategory=5
Saltwater fishing license required.

Louisiana

Louisiana Department of Wildlife and
Fisheries
Hunting, Fishing, and Boating
2000 Quail Drive
Baton Rouge, LA 70808
225-765-2800

www.wlf.louisiana.gov/apps/netgear/page39
.asp
Saltwater fishing license required.

Maine

Department of Marine Resources
21 State House Station
Augusta ME 04333
207-624-6550
www.maine.gov/dmr/recreational/
rechomepage.html
Saltwater fishing license not required.

Maryland

Maryland Department of Natural Resources
580 Taylor Avenue
Tawes State Office Building
Annapolis MD 21401
410-260-8280; 800-688-FINS (3467);
877-620-8DNR (8367)
www.dnr.state.md.us/fisheries
Saltwater fishing license required.

Massachusetts

Massachusetts Department of Fish and Game
Division of Marine Fisheries
251 Causeway Street, Suite 400
Boston MA 02114
617-626-1520
www.mass.gov/dfwele/dmf/index.html
Saltwater fishing license not required.

Mississippi

Mississippi Wildlife, Fisheries, and Parks
Department of Marine Resources
1505 Eastover Drive
Jackson MS 39211
601-432-2400
www.mdwfp.com/level1/fishing.asp
Saltwater fishing license required.

New Hampshire

New Hampshire Fish and Game
Department
11 Hazen Drive
Concord NH 03301
603-271-3421
www.wildlife.state.nh.us/Fishing/
    fishing.htm
Saltwater fishing license not required.

New Jersey

New Jersey Department of Environmental
    Protection
Division of Fish and Wildlife
P.O. Box 400
Trenton NJ 08625-0400
609-292-2083
www.state.nj.us/dep/fgw/fishing.htm
Saltwater fishing license not required.

New York

New York State Department of
Environmental Conservation
Bureau of Marine Resources
205 North Belle Mead Road, Suite 1
East Setauket NY 11733
631-444-0430
www.dec.state.ny.us/website/dfwmr/
    marine/finfish
Saltwater fishing license not required.

North Carolina

North Carolina Department of Environment
    and Natural Resources
Division of Marine Fisheries
3441 Arendell Street
Morehead City NC 28557
252-726-7021; 800-682-2632
www.ncfisheries.net
Saltwater fishing license required.

Oregon

Oregon Department of Fish and Wildlife
Fishing Resources
3406 Cherry Avenue, NE
Salem OR 97303
503-947-6200; 800-720-ODFW (6339)
www.dfw.state.or.us/resources/fishing
Saltwater fishing license required.

Rhode Island

Department of Environmental
    Management
Marine Fisheries Section
3 Fort Wetherill Road
Jamestown RI 02835
401-423-1920
www.dem.ri.gov/topics/mftopics.htm
Saltwater fishing license not required.

South Carolina

South Carolina Department of Natural
    Resources
Marine Resources Division
P.O. Box 12559
Charleston SC 29422
843-953-9031; 843-953-9300
http://saltwaterfishing.sc.gov;
    www.dnr.sc.gov/fish.html
Saltwater fishing license required.

Texas

Texas Parks and Wildlife
4200 Smith School Road
Austin TX 78744
512-389-4800; 800-792-1112
www.tpwd.state.tx.us/fishboat/fish/
    recreational
Saltwater fishing license required.

Virginia

Virginia Marine Resources Commission
2600 Washington Avenue, 3rd floor
Newport News VA 23607
757-247-2200
www.mrc.state.va.us/recreational.shtm
Saltwater fishing license required.

Washington

Washington Department of Fish and
   Wildlife
Licensing Division
600 Capital Way North
Olympia WA 98501
360-902-2464
http://wdfw.wa.gov/lic/formpage.htm
Saltwater fishing license required.

Gulf of Mexico (federal waters)

Certain waters for the five states bordering
the Gulf of Mexico fall under the jurisdiction
of federal laws and regulations concerning
recreational fishing. Federal jurisdiction begins at the following distances from shore.

State	Jurisdiction from Shore
Alabama	3 miles out
Florida	9 miles out
Louisiana	3 miles out
Mississippi	3 miles out
Texas	9 miles out

    If you plan to fish in the federal waters
of the Gulf of Mexico, contact the following
agency:
Gulf of Mexico Fishery Management
Council
2203 N. Lois Avenue, Suite 1100
Tampa FL 33607
813-348-1630; 888-833-1844
www.gulfcouncil.org
Saltwater fishing license required within
   state boundaries.

APPENDIX B

Fish Species	Minimum Water Temperature (°F)	Preferred Water Temperature (°F)	Maximum Water Temperature (°F)
Amberjack	60	65–75	80
Bass, black sea	50	64–68	78
Bass, kelp (calico)	62	64–68	74
Bass, striped	45	55–65	75
Bass, white sea	58	68	74
Bluefish	50	60–70	75
Bonefish	70	75	88
Bonito, Atlantic	55	65–75	80
Bonito, Pacific	55	70	76
Cobia	65	75	89
Cod, Atlantic	33	45	50
Corbina, California	50	60	65
Croaker, Atlantic	45	62	70
Croaker, white	58	64–68	74
Dolphin (fish)	70	72–78	82
Drum, black	52	73	86
Drum, red	52	70–90	89
Flounder, starry	48	50–55	60
Flounder, summer	50	62–66	72
Grouper	50	65	75
Haddock	35	48	55
Halibut, Atlantic	40	45	52
Halibut, California	50	55–70	77
Jack crevalle	70	75–85	91
Mackerel, Atlantic	40	45–55	70
Mackerel, Spanish	67	78	88
Marlin, Atlantic blue	65	70	86
Marlin, black	72	76	88
Marlin, white	65	55	75
Opaleye	68	75	78
Pollock	34	40–50	60
Pompano	65	70–82	87
Roosterfish	65	68	85
Sailfish	68	72–82	88
Sailfish, Atlantic	70	75	83
Sanddab, longfin	46	50	55
Scup	50	55	70
Sea trout, spotted	56	64	82
Sheephead, California	48	60–70	75
Sheepshead	55	66	75
Snapper, red	50	65	70
Snook, common	65	70	86
Spot	45	70	81
Swordfish	50	60–70	80
Tarpon	70	75–90	95+
Tautog	40	45–51	65

(continued)

Fish Species	Minimum Water Temperature (°F)	Preferred Water Temperature (°F)	Maximum Water Temperature (°F)
Tilefish	33	45	56
Tomcod, Atlantic	40	50	65
Tuna, albacore	50	62	72
Tuna, bigeye	52	62–74	80
Tuna, blackfin	65	70–75	82
Tuna, bluefin	60	70–73	84
Tuna, skipjack	62	67	78
Wahoo	70	72–77	86
Weakfish	45	56–68	78
Yellowtail	55	60	80

APPENDIX C

Every saltwater angler dreams of catching a record fish. It doesn't just happen by chance. Most of the record holders know what they're doing, do a lot of fishing, and keep at it for years. Still, good luck plays a part!

The following list was provided courtesy of the International Game Fish Association, the world-record sanctioning and registering authority. Only species common to North American waters are included.

Species	Scientific Name	Pounds, Ounces	Place	Date	Angler
Bass, black sea	*Centropristis striata*	10, 4	Virginia Beach, VA	Jan. 1, 2000	Allan P. Paschall
Bass, kelp (calico)	*Paralabrox clathratus*	5, 0	Baja, CA	June 19, 1999	Megan Burlason
Bass, striped	*Morone saxatilis*	78, 8	Atlantic City, NJ	Sept. 21, 1982	Albert R. McReynolds
Bluefish	*Pomatomus saltatrix*	31, 12	Hatteras, NC	Jan. 30, 1972	James M. Hussey
Bonito, Pacific	*Sarda chiliensis lineolatus*	23, 8	181 Spot, CA	Oct. 19, 2003	Kim Larson
Cod, Atlantic	*Gadus morhua*	98, 12	Isle of Shoals, NH	June 8, 1969	Alphonse J. Bielevich
Corbina, California	*Menticirrhus undulatus*	6, 8	Dana Harbor, CA	May 23, 1997	Scott Matthews
Croaker, spotfin	*Roncador stearnsii*	7, 10	San Onotre, CA	June 21, 2002	Matthew Learry
Drum, black	*Pogonias cromis*	113, 1	Lewes, DE	Sept. 15, 1975	Gerald M. Townsend
Drum, red	*Sciaenops ocellatus*	94, 2	Avon, NC	Nov. 7, 1984	David G. Deuel
Flounder, starry	*Platichthys stellatus*	3, 12	Gastineau Channel, AK	July 16, 2000	Mike Gallion
Flounder, summer	*Paralichthys dentatus*	22, 7	Montauk, NY	Sept. 15, 1975	Charles Nappi
Flounder, winter	*Pseudopleuronectes americanus*		Fire Island, NY	May 8, 1986	Dr. Einar F. Grell
Grouper, black	*Mycteroperca bonaci*	124, 0	Gulf of Mexico, TX	Jan. 11, 2003	Tim Oestreich II
Grouper, gag	*Mycteroperca microlepis*	80, 6	Destin, FL	Oct. 14, 1996	Bill Smith
Grouper, goliath	*Epinephelus itajara*	680, 0	Fernandina Beach, FL	May 20, 1961	Lynn Joyner
Grouper, marbled	*Dermatolepis inermis*	22, 8	Ship Shoal, LA	July 8, 2001	Daniel Landry
Grouper, red	*Epinephelus morio*	42, 4	St. Augustine, FL	Mar. 9, 1997	Del Wiseman, Jr.
Grouper, snowy	*Epinephelus niveatus*	27, 6	St. Augustine, FL	June 2, 2000	Burt Hood
Grouper, Warsaw	*Epinephelus nigritus*	436, 12	Gulf of Mexico, Destin, FL	Dec. 22, 1985	Steve Haeusler
Grouper, yellowedge	*Epinephelus flavolimbatus*	41, 1	Gulf of Mexico, Destin, FL	May 24, 1998	Christopher D. Allen
Grouper, yellowfin	*Mycteroperca venenosa*	42, 0	Cypremort Point, LA	July 26, 2002	Jim Becquet
Grouper, yellowmouth	*Mycteroperca interstitialis*	22, 8	Murrel's Inlet, SC	Sept. 2, 2001	Brian J. Ford
Halibut, Atlantic	*Hippoglossus hippoglossus*	255, 4	Gloucester, MA	July 28, 1989	Sonny Manley
Halibut, Pacific	*Hippoglossus stenolepis*	458, 0	Dutch Harbor, AK	June 11, 1996	Jack Tragis
Lingcod	*Ophiodon elongatus*	76, 9	Gulf of Alaska, AK	Aug. 11, 2001	Antwan Tinsley
Mackerel, Spanish	*Scomberomorus maculatus*	13, 0	Ocracoke Inlet, NC	Nov. 4, 1987	Robert Cranton
Marlin, blue	*Makaira nigricans*	1376, 0	Kaaiwi Point, Kona, HI	May 31, 1982	Jay de Beaubien
Pompano, African	*Alectis ciliaris*	50, 8	Daytona Beach, FL	Apr. 21, 1990	Tom Sargent
Pompano, Florida	*Trachinotus carolinus*	8, 4	Port St. Joe Bay, FL	Oct. 16, 1999	Barry Huston
Salmon, pink	*Oncorhynchus gorbuscha*	14, 13	Monroe, WA	Sept. 30, 2001	Alexander Minerich
Salmon, sockeye	*Oncorhynchus nerka*	15, 3	Kenai River, AK	Aug. 9, 1987	Stan Roach
Sargo	*Anisotremus davidsonii*	2, 0	Catalina Island, CA	July 10, 2003	Debbie Himphrey
Scup	*Stenotomus chrysops*	4, 9	Nantucket Sound, MA	June 3, 1992	Sonny Richards
Sea trout, sand	*Cynoscion arenarius*	6, 2	Dauphin Island, AL	May 24, 1997	Steve Scoggin
Sea trout, spotted	*Cynoscion nebulosus*	17, 7	Ft. Pierce, FL	May 11, 1995	Craig F. Carson

(continued)

Species	Scientific Name	Pounds, Ounces	Place	Date	Angler
Sheepshead	*Archosargus probatocephalus*	21, 4	Bayou St. John, New Orleans, LA	Apr. 16, 1982	Wayne Desselle
Snapper, red	*Lutjanus campechanus*	50, 4	Gulf of Mexico, LA	June 23, 1996	Capt. Doc Kennedy
Spot	*Leiostomus xanthurus*	1, 7	Hampton Roads Bridge-Tunnel, VA	Oct. 2, 2004	Lorraine Gousse
Sturgeon, white	*Acipenser transmontanus*	468, 0	Benicia, CA	July 9, 1983	Joey Pallotta III
Tautog	*Tautoga onitis*	25, 0	Ocean City, NJ	Jan. 20, 1998	Anthony Monica
Tilefish, great northern	*Lophalatilus chamaeleonticeps*	51, 2	Cape May, NJ	Apr. 14, 2003	Paul Brady, Jr.
Tilefish, sand	*Malacanthus plumieri*	4, 4	Oak Island, NC	Apr. 16, 2004	Eduardo Baumeier
Tuna, blackfin	*Thunnus atlanticus*	45, 8	Key West, FL	May 4, 1996	Sam Burnett
Weakfish	*Cynoscion regalis*	19, 2	Jones Beach Inlet, Long Island, NY	Oct. 11, 1984	Dennis Roger Rooney
Weakfish	*Cynoscion regalis*	19, 2	Delaware Bay, DE	May 20, 1989	William Thomas

APPENDIX D

Most fish are known by a variety of names. What you recognize as a bluefish may be known to your neighbor as an "elf," to your grandfather as a "tailor," and to your chat-room correspondents around the country as a blue, a chopper, a rock salmon, a snapper, a snapper blue, a Hatteras blue, or even a marine piranha. About the only time that the identity of a fish is not in question is when you use the Latin (scientific) name.

When fish come up in conversation and you're not sure what species is being discussed, refer to this list. Find the fish name in the left-hand column, then refer to the Common Name column to see what the fish was called in Chapter 19 and elsewhere in this book. Be aware that many of the "alternate" names are the same for different fish. For example, "amberjack" may refer to almaco jack *(Seriola rivoliana)* or yellowtail *(Seriola lalandi)*.

Alternate Name	Common Name	Latin Name
AJ	Amberjack, greater	*Seriola dumerili*
Alabato	California halibut	*Paralichthys californicus*
Albacore	Yellowfin tuna	*Thunnus albacares*
Albacore tuna	Albacore	*Thunnus alalunga*
Albie	Albacore	*Thunnus alalunga*
Allison tuna	Yellowfin tuna	*Thunnus albacares*
Amberjack	Almaco jack	*Seriola rivoliana*
Amberjack	Yellowtail	*Seriola lalandi*
American red snapper	Red snapper	*Lutjanus campechanus*
Arctic bonito	Skipjack tuna	*Katsuwonus pelamis*
Atlantic bluefin tuna	Bluefin tuna	*Thunnus thynnus*
Atlantic blue marlin	Blue marlin	*Makaira nigricans*
Atlantic little tunny	Little tunny	*Euthynnus alletteratus*
Atlantic Spanish mackerel	Spanish mackerel	*Scomberomorus maculatus*
Atlantic tarpon	Tarpon	*Megalops atlanticus*
Atlantic white marlin	White marlin	*Tetrapturus albidus*
Autumn albacore	Yellowfin tuna	*Thunnus albacares*
Autumn salmon	Chum salmon	*Oncorhynchus keta*
Banana fish	Bonefish	*Albula vulpes*
Banded drum	Black drum	*Pogonias cromis*
Barn door	California halibut	*Paralichthys californicus*
Barra	Barracuda, great	*Sphyraena barracuda*
Barracuda	Barracuda, great	*Sphyraena barracuda*
Barracuda	Barracuda, Pacific	*Sphyraena argentea*
Barracuda	Wahoo	*Acanthocybium solandri*
Barred marlin	Striped marlin	*Tetrapturus audax*
Barry	Barracuda, Pacific	*Sphyraena argentea*
Bastard halibut	California halibut	*Paralichthys californicus*
Bayonetfish	Sailfish	*Istiophorus platypterus*
Bay porgy	Scup	*Stenotomus chrysops*
Belted bonito	Atlantic bonito	*Sarda sarda*
Bermuda tuna	Blackfin tuna	*Thunnus atlanticus*
Bigeye tunny	Bigeye tuna	*Thunnus obesus*
Big redfish	Sockeye salmon	*Oncorhynchus nerka*
Billygoat	California sheephead	*Semicossyphus pulcher*
Black	Giant sea bass	*Stereolepis gigas*
Blackback	Winter flounder	*Pseudopleuronectes americanus*

(continued)

Alternate Name	Common Name	Latin Name
Black bass	Black sea bass	*Centropristis striata*
Blackfinned albacore	Blackfin tuna	*Thunnus atlanticus*
Blackfish	Black sea bass	*Centropristis striata*
Blackfish	Tautog	*Tautoga onitis*
Black flounder	Winter flounder	*Pseudopleuronectes americanus*
Black grouper	Grouper	*Mycteroperca bonaci*
Black kingfish	Cobia	*Rachycentron canadum*
Blackmouth	Chinook salmon	*Oncorhynchus tshawytscha*
Black perch	Opaleye	*Girella nigricans*
Black salmon	Cobia	*Rachycentron canadum*
Black sea bass	Black sea bass	*Centropristis striata*
Black sea bass	Giant sea bass	*Stereolepis gigas*
Black-spotted Spanish mackerel	Cero mackerel	*Scomberomorus regalis*
Black trout	Spotted sea trout	*Cynoscion nebulosus*
Black will	Black sea bass	*Centropristis striata*
Blanquillo	Tilefish	*Lopholatilus chamaeleonticeps*
Blisterback	Pollock	*Pollachius virens*
Blue	Bluefish	*Pomatomus saltatrix*
Blueback	Coho salmon	*Oncorhynchus kisutch*
Blueback salmon	Sockeye salmon	*Oncorhynchus nerka*
Blue cod	Lingcod	*Ophiodon elongatus*
Blue dolphin	Pompano dolphin	*Coryphaena equiselis*
Blue-eyed perch	Opaleye	*Girella nigricans*
Bluefish	Lingcod	*Ophiodon elongatus*
Bluefish	Opaleye	*Girella nigricans*
Bonehead	Pacific bonito	*Sarda chiliensis*
Boner	Pacific bonito	*Sarda chiliensis*
Bonito	Little tunny	*Euthynnus alletteratus*
Boston bluefish	Pollock	*Pollachius virens*
Boston mackerel	Atlantic mackerel	*Scomber scombrus*
Brill	Petrale sole	*Eopsetta jordani*
Broadbill	Swordfish	*Xiphias gladius*
Broadbill swordfish	Swordfish	*Xiphias gladius*
Buffalo cod	Lingcod	*Ophiodon elongatus*
Bull bass	Kelp bass	*Paralabrax clathratus*
Bullet mackerel	Frigate mackerel	*Auxis thazard*
Bull red	Red drum	*Sciaenops ocellatus*
Butterfly drum	Black drum	*Pogonias cromis*
Button back	Opaleye	*Girella nigricans*
Cabio	Cobia	*Rachycentron canadum*
Calico bass	Kelp bass	*Paralabrax clathratus*
Calico salmon	Chum salmon	*Oncorhynchus keta*
California barracuda	Barracuda, Pacific	*Sphyraena argentea*
California black sea bass	Giant sea bass	*Stereolepis gigas*
California bonito	Pacific bonito	*Sarda chiliensis*
California flounder	California halibut	*Paralichthys californicus*
California flounder	Starry flounder	*Platichthys stellatus*
California jewfish	Giant sea bass	*Stereolepis gigas*
California kelp bass	Kelp bass	*Paralabrax clathratus*
California king croaker	California corbina	*Menticirrhus undulatus*
California sole	Petrale sole	*Eopsetta jordani*
California tomcod	Pacific tomcod	*Microgadus proximus*
California whiting	California corbina	*Menticirrhus undulatus*
Catalina croaker	Yellowfin croaker	*Umbrina roncador*
Catalina salmon	White sea bass	*Atractoscion nobilis*

Alternate Name	Common Name	Latin Name
Catalina sanddab	Longfin sanddab	*Citharichthys xanthostigma*
Cavalla	Jack crevalle, Pacific	*Caranx caninus*
Cero	Cero mackerel	*Scomberomorus regalis*
Channel bass	Red drum	*Sciaenops ocellatus*
Chicken halibut	Atlantic halibut	*Hippoglossus hippoglossus*
Chicken halibut	California halibut	*Paralichthys californicus*
Chopper	Bluefish	*Pomatomus saltatrix*
Chub	Tautog	*Tautoga onitis*
Chum	Chum salmon	*Oncorhynchus keta*
Coalfish	Pollock	*Pollachius virens*
Cod	Atlantic cod	*Gadus morhua*
Cod	Pacific cod	*Gadus macrocephalus*
Codfish	Atlantic cod	*Gadus morhua*
Codling	Atlantic cod	*Gadus morhua*
Coley	Pollock	*Pollachius virens*
Columbia River salmon	Chinook salmon	*Oncorhynchus tshawytscha*
Columbia sturgeon	White sturgeon	*Acipenser transmontanus*
Common bonito	Atlantic bonito	*Sarda sarda*
Common drum	Black drum	*Pogonias cromis*
Common halibut	Atlantic halibut	*Hippoglossus hippoglossus*
Common jack	Jack crevalle, Atlantic	*Caranx hippos*
Common mackerel	Atlantic mackerel	*Scomber scombrus*
Common sea bass	Black sea bass	*Centropristis striata*
Common sea trout	Weakfish	*Cynoscion regalis*
Common weakfish	Weakfish	*Cynoscion regalis*
Convict fish	Sheepshead	*Archosargus probatocephalus*
Corvina blanca	White sea bass	*Atractoscion nobilis*
Crab eater	Cobia	*Rachycentron canadum*
Crevally	Jack crevalle, Atlantic	*Caranx hippos*
Crevally	Jack crevalle, Pacific	*Caranx caninus*
Croaker	Atlantic croaker	*Micropogonias undulatus*
Crocus	Atlantic croaker	*Micropogonias undulatus*
Cuban blue marlin	Blue marlin	*Makaira nigricans*
Cuban snapper	Pacific cubera snapper	*Lutjanus novemfasciatus*
Cuda	Barracuda, great	*Sphyraena barracuda*
Cuffum	Tarpon	*Megalops atlanticus*
Cultus cod	Lingcod	*Ophiodon elongatus*
Dab	Winter flounder	*Pseudopleuronectes americanus*
Deep-bodied tunny	Blackfin tuna	*Thunnus atlanticus*
Diamond back	Starry flounder	*Platichthys stellatus*
Dingo fish	Barracuda, great	*Sphyraena barracuda*
Dog salmon	Chum salmon	*Oncorhynchus keta*
Dog snapper	Pacific cubera snapper	*Lutjanus novemfasciatus*
Dolphinfish	Dolphin	*Coryphaena hippurus*
Dolphinfish	Pompano dolphin	*Coryphaena equiselis*
Doormat	Summer flounder	*Paralichthys dentatus*
Dorado	Dolphin	*Coryphaena hippurus*
Drum	Black drum	*Pogonias cromis*
Drum	Red drum	*Sciaenops ocellatus*
Eastern Pacific bonito	Pacific bonito	*Sarda chiliensis*
Elf	Bluefish	*Pomatomus saltatrix*
Emery flounder	Starry flounder	*Platichthys stellatus*
Emery wheel	Starry flounder	*Platichthys stellatus*
English whiting	Whiting	*Merlangius merlangus*

(continued)

Alternate Name	Common Name	Latin Name
Fall salmon	Chum salmon	*Oncorhynchus keta*
Fall salmon	Pink salmon	*Oncorhynchus gorbuscha*
False albacore	Little tunny	*Euthynnus alletteratus*
Fathead	California sheephead	*Semicossyphus pulcher*
Fiddler	Atlantic salmon	*Salmo salar*
Flasher	Pacific bonito	*Sarda chiliensis*
Flat croaker	Spot	*Leiostomus xanthurus*
Flatfish	Winter flounder	*Pseudopleuronectes americanus*
Flathead	Cobia	*Rachycentron canadum*
Flattie	California halibut	*Paralichthys californicus*
Flatty	California halibut	*Paralichthys californicus*
Florida pompano	Florida pompano	*Trachinotus carolinus*
Flounder	Summer flounder	*Paralichthys dentatus*
Flounder	Winter flounder	*Pseudopleuronectes americanus*
Fluke	Summer flounder	*Paralichthys dentatus*
Fly swatter	California halibut	*Paralichthys californicus*
Forktail	Yellowtail	*Seriola lalandi*
Frigate tuna	Frigate mackerel	*Auxis thazard*
Gag grouper	Grouper	*Mycteroperca microlepis*
Gator trout	Spotted sea trout	*Cynoscion nebulosus*
Genuine red snapper	Red snapper	*Lutjanus campechanus*
Giant bass	Giant sea bass	*Stereolepis gigas*
Giant black marlin	Black marlin	*Makaira indica*
Giant halibut	Atlantic halibut	*Hippoglossus hippoglossus*
Giant halibut	Pacific halibut	*Hippoglossus stenolepis*
Giant mackerel	King mackerel	*Scomberomorus cavalla*
Giant sea pike	Barracuda, great	*Sphyraena barracuda*
Goat	California sheephead	*Semicossyphus pulcher*
Gold-striped amberjack	Yellowtail	*Seriola lalandi*
Golden croaker	Atlantic croaker	*Micropogonias undulatus*
Golden croaker	Spotfin croaker	*Roncador stearnsii*
Golden croaker	Yellowfin croaker	*Umbrina roncador*
Golden tilefish	Tilefish	*Lopholatilus chamaeleonticeps*
Goldmakrele	Dolphin	*Coryphaena hippurus*
Goliath grouper	Grouper	*Epinephelus itajara*
Gray cod	Pacific cod	*Gadus macrocephalus*
Gray drum	Black drum	*Pogonias cromis*
Gray ghost	Bonefish	*Albula vulpes*
Gray trout	Weakfish	*Cynoscion regalis*
Great barracuda	Barracuda, great	*Sphyraena barracuda*
Great flounder	Starry flounder	*Platichthys stellatus*
Great northern tilefish	Tilefish	*Lopholatilus chamaeleonticeps*
Greater amberjack	Almaco jack	*Seriola rivoliana*
Greater amberjack	Amberjack, greater	*Seriola dumerili*
Green cod	Lingcod	*Ophiodon elongatus*
Green cod	Pollock	*Pollachius virens*
Greenhead	Striped bass	*Morone saxatilis*
Green perch	Opaleye	*Girella nigricans*
Grilse	Atlantic salmon	*Salmo salar*
Grilt	Atlantic salmon	*Salmo salar*
Grindstone	Starry flounder	*Platichthys stellatus*
Haddie	Haddock	*Melanogrammus aeglefinus*
Hardhead	Atlantic croaker	*Micropogonias undulatus*
Hatteras blue	Bluefish	*Pomatomus saltatrix*
Hookbill	Coho salmon	*Oncorhynchus kisutch*

Alternate Name	Common Name	Latin Name
Hooknose	Coho salmon	*Oncorhynchus kisutch*
Horse crevalle	Jack crevalle, Atlantic	*Caranx hippos*
Horse-eye bonito	Amberjack, greater	*Seriola dumerili*
Horse-eye jack	Amberjack, greater	*Seriola dumerili*
Horse mackerel	Bluefin tuna	*Thunnus thynnus*
Horse mackerel	Pacific jack mackerel	*Trachurus symmetricus*
Humpback	Black sea bass	*Centropristis striata*
Humpback	Scup	*Stenotomus chrysops*
Humpbacks	Pink salmon	*Oncorhynchus gorbuscha*
Humpback salmon	Pink salmon	*Oncorhynchus gorbuscha*
Humpy	California sheephead	*Semicossyphus pulcher*
Humpy	Pink salmon	*Oncorhynchus gorbuscha*
Jack amber	Amberjack, greater	*Seriola dumerili*
Jack Benny	Opaleye	*Girella nigricans*
Jackfish	Pacific jack mackerel	*Trachurus symmetricus*
Jack hammer	Amberjack, greater	*Seriola dumerili*
Jack mackerel	Pacific jack mackerel	*Trachurus symmetricus*
Jordan's flounder	Petrale sole	*Eopsetta jordani*
Katonkel	Atlantic bonito	*Sarda sarda*
Kelp salmon	Kelp bass	*Paralabrax clathratus*
Kennebec salmon	Atlantic salmon	*Salmo salar*
King	Atlantic salmon	*Salmo salar*
King Billy	Atlantic croaker	*Micropogonias undulatus*
King croaker	White croaker	*Genyonemus lineatus*
King croaker	White sea bass	*Atractoscion nobilis*
Kingfish	King mackerel	*Scomberomorus cavalla*
Kingfish	White croaker	*Genyonemus lineatus*
Kingfish	Yellowtail	*Seriola lalandi*
Kingie	Yellowtail	*Seriola lalandi*
King mackerel	Cero mackerel	*Scomberomorus regalis*
King salmon	Chinook salmon	*Oncorhynchus tshawytscha*
King yellowtail	Yellowtail	*Seriola lalandi*
Laguna tuna	Pacific bonito	*Sarda chiliensis*
Leadenall	Frigate mackerel	*Auxis thazard*
Leatherjacket	Starry flounder	*Platichthys stellatus*
Lemonfish	Cobia	*Rachycentron canadum*
Lemon sole	Winter flounder	*Pseudopleuronectes americanus*
Linesider	Common snook	*Centropomus undecimalis*
Linesider	Striped bass	*Morone saxatilis*
Ling	Cobia	*Rachycentron canadum*
Ling	Lingcod	*Ophiodon elongatus*
Little dolphin	Pompano dolphin	*Coryphaena equiselis*
Little tuna	Little tunny	*Euthynnus alletteratus*
Longfin	Albacore	*Thunnus alalunga*
Longfin	Almaco jack	*Seriola rivoliana*
Longfin tuna	Albacore	*Thunnus alalunga*
Mackerel	Atlantic mackerel	*Scomber scombrus*
Mackereljack	Pacific jack mackerel	*Trachurus symmetricus*
Mackerel tuna	Frigate mackerel	*Auxis thazard*
Magneto	Pacific bonito	*Sarda chiliensis*
Mahimahi	Dolphin	*Coryphaena hippurus*
Mahimahi	Pompano dolphin	*Coryphaena equiselis*
Mahi mahi	Dolphin	*Coryphaena hippurus*
Marine piranha	Bluefish	*Pomatomus saltatrix*

(continued)

Alternate Name	Common Name	Latin Name
Marlin	Striped marlin	*Tetrapturus audax*
Megrim	Pacific sanddab	*Citharichthys sordidus*
Molly George	Tautog	*Tautoga onitis*
Monterey halibut	California halibut	*Paralichthys californicus*
Mossback	Yellowtail	*Seriola lalandi*
Mottled sanddab	Pacific sanddab	*Citharichthys sordidus*
Mud dab	Winter flounder	*Pseudopleuronectes americanus*
Mutton snapper	Red snapper	*Lutjanus campechanus*
Nassau grouper	Grouper	*Epinephelus striatus*
Norfolk spot	Spot	*Leiostomus xanthurus*
Northern bluefin tuna	Bluefin tuna	*Thunnus thynnus*
Northern fluke	Summer flounder	*Paralichthys dentatus*
Northern halibut	Pacific halibut	*Hippoglossus stenolepis*
Northern red snapper	Red snapper	*Lutjanus campechanus*
Northern sea trout	Weakfish	*Cynoscion regalis*
Northern weakfish	Weakfish	*Cynoscion regalis*
Oahu fish	Wahoo	*Acanthocybium solandri*
Ocean barracuda	Wahoo	*Acanthocybium solandri*
Ocean bonito	Pacific bonito	*Sarda chiliensis*
Ocean bonito	Skipjack tuna	*Katsuwonus pelamis*
Opaleye perch	Opaleye	*Girella nigricans*
Oregon sturgeon	White sturgeon	*Acipenser transmontanus*
Oyster drum	Black drum	*Pogonias cromis*
Oysterfish	Tautog	*Tautoga onitis*
Pacific amberjack	Almaco jack	*Seriola rivoliana*
Pacific barracuda	Barracuda, Pacific	*Sphyraena argentea*
Pacific black marlin	Black marlin	*Makaira indica*
Pacific blue marlin	Blue marlin	*Makaira nigricans*
Pacific cubera	Pacific cubera snapper	*Lutjanus novemfasciatus*
Pacific dog snapper	Pacific cubera snapper	*Lutjanus novemfasciatus*
Pacific kingfish	Wahoo	*Acanthocybium solandri*
Pacific marlin	Striped marlin	*Tetrapturus audax*
Pacific red snapper	Bocaccio rockfish	*Sebastes paucispinis*
Pacific sierra	Pacific sierra mackerel	*Scomberomorus sierra*
Pacific striped marlin	Striped marlin	*Tetrapturus audax*
Pacific sturgeon	White sturgeon	*Acipenser transmontanus*
Pasadena trout	White croaker	*Genyonemus lineatus*
Phantom	Bonefish	*Albula vulpes*
Piciata	Pacific tomcod	*Microgadus proximus*
Pigfish	Albacore	*Thunnus alalunga*
Pin bass	Black sea bass	*Centropristis striata*
Pink humpback	Pink salmon	*Oncorhynchus gorbuscha*
Pinks	Pink salmon	*Oncorhynchus gorbuscha*
Pompano dolphinfish	Pompano dolphin	*Coryphaena equiselis*
Porgy	Scup	*Stenotomus chrysops*
Portsider	California halibut	*Paralichthys californicus*
Puppy drum	Red drum	*Sciaenops ocellatus*
Queenfish	Wahoo	*Acanthocybium solandri*
Quinnat	Chinook salmon	*Oncorhynchus tshawytscha*
Rat red	Red drum	*Sciaenops ocellatus*
Red bass	Red drum	*Sciaenops ocellatus*
Red fish	California sheephead	*Semicossyphus pulcher*
Redfish	Red drum	*Sciaenops ocellatus*
Red grouper	Grouper	*Epinephelus morio*
Red horse	Red drum	*Sciaenops ocellatus*

Alternate Name	Common Name	Latin Name
Red salmon	Sockeye salmon	*Oncorhynchus nerka*
Red snapper	Bocaccio rockfish	*Sebastes paucispinis*
Right-eyed flounder	Atlantic halibut	*Hippoglossus hippoglossus*
Robalo	Common snook	*Centropomus undecimalis*
Rock	Striped bass	*Morone saxatilis*
Rock bass	Black sea bass	*Centropristis striata*
Rock cod	Bocaccio rockfish	*Sebastes paucispinis*
Rockfish	Kelp bass	*Paralabrax clathratus*
Rockfish	Striped bass	*Morone saxatilis*
Rock salmon	Bluefish	*Pomatomus saltatrix*
Rock sea bass	Kelp bass	*Paralabrax clathratus*
Roosterfish	Roosterfish	*Nematistius pectoralis*
Rough jacket	Starry flounder	*Platichthys stellatus*
Roundnosed sole	Petrale sole	*Eopsetta jordani*
Runner	Cobia	*Rachycentron canadum*
Sacramento River salmon	Chinook salmon	*Oncorhynchus tshawytscha*
Sacramento sturgeon	White sturgeon	*Acipenser transmontanus*
Saithe	Pollock	*Pollachius virens*
Salmon grouper	Bocaccio rockfish	*Sebastes paucispinis*
Salmon trout	Spotted sea trout	*Cynoscion nebulosus*
Saltwater pike	Common snook	*Centropomus undecimalis*
Sand bass	Kelp bass	*Paralabrax clathratus*
Sanddab	Longfin sanddab	*Citharichthys xanthostigma*
Sanddab	Pacific sanddab	*Citharichthys sordidus*
Sand digger	Spot	*Leiostomus xanthurus*
Sandpaper flounder	Starry flounder	*Platichthys stellatus*
Sand porgy	Scup	*Stenotomus chrysops*
Scad	Pacific jack mackerel	*Trachurus symmetricus*
School drum	Red drum	*Sciaenops ocellatus*
Scoot	Barracuda, Pacific	*Sphyraena argentea*
Scooter	Barracuda, Pacific	*Sphyraena argentea*
Scrod	Atlantic cod	*Gadus morhua*
Scrod	Haddock	*Melanogrammus aeglefinus*
Sea bass	Black sea bass	*Centropristis striata*
Sea drum	Black drum	*Pogonias cromis*
Sea trout	Coho salmon	*Oncorhynchus kisutch*
Sergeant fish	Cobia	*Rachycentron canadum*
Sergeant fish	Common snook	*Centropomus undecimalis*
Sheepie	California sheephead	*Semicossyphus pulcher*
Sheepshead sea bream	Sheepshead	*Archosargus probatocephalus*
Shiira	Dolphin	*Coryphaena hippurus*
Shiner	White croaker	*Genyonemus lineatus*
Silver ghost	Bonefish	*Albula vulpes*
Silver king	Tarpon	*Megalops atlanticus*
Silver salmon	Coho salmon	*Oncorhynchus kisutch*
Silversides	Coho salmon	*Oncorhynchus kisutch*
Silver sides	Tarpon	*Megalops atlanticus*
Silver streak	Bonefish	*Albula vulpes*
Skipjack	Skipjack tuna	*Katsuwonus pelamis*
Small dolphin	Pompano dolphin	*Coryphaena equiselis*
Snake	Barracuda, Pacific	*Sphyraena argentea*
Snapper	Bluefish	*Pomatomus saltatrix*
Snapper	Pacific cubera snapper	*Lutjanus novemfasciatus*
Snapper blue	Bluefish	*Pomatomus saltatrix*

(continued)

Alternate Name	Common Name	Latin Name
Snowshoe flounder	Winter flounder	*Pseudopleuronectes americanus*
Snowy grouper	Grouper	*Epinephelus niveatus*
Soap fish	Common snook	*Centropomus undecimalis*
Sockeye	Sockeye salmon	*Oncorhynchus nerka*
Soft flounder	Longfin sanddab	*Citharichthys xanthostigma*
Soft flounder	Pacific sanddab	*Citharichthys sordidus*
Sole	Pacific sanddab	*Citharichthys sordidus*
Sole	Petrale sole	*Eopsetta jordani*
Sole	Winter flounder	*Pseudopleuronectes americanus*
Southern halibut	California halibut	*Paralichthys californicus*
Spearfish	Striped marlin	*Tetrapturus audax*
Speck	Spotted sea trout	*Cynoscion nebulosus*
Speckled trout	Spotted sea trout	*Cynoscion nebulosus*
Spikefish	Striped marlin	*Tetrapturus audax*
Spikefish	White marlin	*Tetrapturus albidus*
Spindlebeak	Sailfish	*Istiophorus platypterus*
Spot	Spotfin croaker	*Roncador stearnsii*
Spot tail bass	Red drum	*Sciaenops ocellatus*
Spotted cero	Cero mackerel	*Scomberomorus regalis*
Spotted croaker	Spot	*Leiostomus xanthurus*
Spotted squeteague	Spotted sea trout	*Cynoscion nebulosus*
Spotted weakfish	Spotted sea trout	*Cynoscion nebulosus*
Spotties	Spotfin croaker	*Roncador stearnsii*
Spring salmon	Chinook salmon	*Oncorhynchus tshawytscha*
Squeteague	Weakfish	*Cynoscion regalis*
Squid hound	Striped bass	*Morone saxatilis*
Striped drum	Black drum	*Pogonias cromis*
Striped sea bass	Striped bass	*Morone saxatilis*
Striped tuna	Pacific bonito	*Sarda chiliensis*
Striped tuna	Skipjack tuna	*Katsuwonus pelamis*
Striper	Striped bass	*Morone saxatilis*
Striper	Striped marlin	*Tetrapturus audax*
Striper bass	Striped bass	*Morone saxatilis*
Sturgeon	White sturgeon	*Acipenser transmontanus*
Summer trout	Weakfish	*Cynoscion regalis*
Surf fish	California corbina	*Menticirrhus undulatus*
Tailor	Bluefish	*Pomatomus saltatrix*
Tiderunner	Weakfish	*Cynoscion regalis*
Tigerfish	Wahoo	*Acanthocybium solandri*
Tog	Tautog	*Tautoga onitis*
Tomcod	Atlantic tomcod	*Microgadus tomcod*
Tomcod	Pacific tomcod	*Microgadus proximus*
Tommy	White croaker	*Genyonemus lineatus*
Tommy croaker	White croaker	*Genyonemus lineatus*
Toro	Jack crevalle, Atlantic	*Caranx hippos*
Toro	Jack crevalle, Pacific	*Caranx caninus*
Trevally	Jack crevalle, Atlantic	*Caranx hippos*
Trout	Spotted sea trout	*Cynoscion nebulosus*
True cod	Pacific cod	*Gadus macrocephalus*
Tule	Chinook salmon	*Oncorhynchus tshawytscha*
Tunny fish	Bluefin tuna	*Thunnus thynnus*
Tyee	Chinook salmon	*Oncorhynchus tshawytscha*
Wachna	Pacific tomcod	*Microgadus proximus*
Watermelon tuna	Skipjack tuna	*Katsuwonus pelamis*
Weakfish	White sea bass	*Atractoscion nobilis*

Alternate Name	Common Name	Latin Name
Weakie	Weakfish	*Cynoscion regalis*
White cod	Lingcod	*Ophiodon elongatus*
White corvina	White sea bass	*Atractoscion nobilis*
White weakfish	White sea bass	*Atractoscion nobilis*
Whiting	White croaker	*Genyonemus lineatus*
Whiting	Whiting	*Merlangius merlangus*
Winter trout	Spotted sea trout	*Cynoscion nebulosus*
Yellowedge grouper	Grouper	*Epinephelus flavolimbatus*
Yellowfin	Weakfish	*Cynoscion regalis*
Yellowfin drum	Yellowfin croaker	*Umbrina roncador*
Yellowfin grouper	Grouper	*Mycteroperca venenosa*
Yellow-finned albacore	Yellowfin tuna	*Thunnus albacares*
Yellow mouth	Spotted sea trout	*Cynoscion nebulosus*
Yellowmouth grouper	Grouper	*Mycteroperca interstitialis*
Yellowtail	Almaco jack	*Seriola rivoliana*
Yellowtail amberjack	Yellowtail	*Seriola lalandi*
Yellowtailed croaker	Yellowfin croaker	*Umbrina roncador*
Yellowtail kingfish	Yellowtail	*Seriola lalandi*

APPENDIX E

USEFUL FISHING WEBSITES

Electronics

Raymarine, www.raymarine.com

Lowrance Electronics, www.lowrance.com

Equipment in General

American Fishing Tackle Company, www.aftco.com

Angler Sports, www.anglersports.com

Atlantic & Gulf Fishing Supply Corporation, www.atagulf.com

Cabela's, www.cabelas.com

Calcutta, www.calcuttabaits.com

Capt. Harry's Fishing Supply, www.captharry.com

eAngler, www.eangler.com

Fisherman's Line, www.fishermansline.com

Intruder, www.intruderinc.com

KeepAlive, www.keepalive.net

Mitchell, www.fishmitchell.com

Rainbow Plastics, www.rainbowplastics.com

Sampo, www.sampoinc.com

Sea Striker, www.seastriker.com

TackleDirect, www.tackledirect.com

Fly Fishing Equipment

American Fly Fishing Company, www.americanfly.com

Fly Logic, www.flylogic.com

Griffin Enterprises, www.griffinenterprisesinc.com

Renzetti, Inc., www.renzetti.com

Hooks

Eagle Claw Fishing Tackle, www.eagleclaw.com
Owner American Corporation, www.ownerhooks.com

Line/Leader

American Fishing Wire, www.americanfishingwire.com
Ande, www.andemonofilament.com
Hi-Seas, www.hiseas.net
PowerPro, www.powerpro.com
Seaguar, www.seaguar.com
Spider, www.spiderfishing.com
Stren, www.stren.com
Sufix, www.sufix.com

Lures

Acme Tackle Company, www.acmetackle.com
Gibbs Lures, www.gibbslures.com
Hopkins, www.hopkinslures.com
Mann's Bait Company, www.mannsbait.com
Rebel Lures, www.rebellures.com
Sevenstrand, www.7strand.com
SPRO, www.spro.com
Super Strike Lures, www.superstrikelures.com
Uncle Josh Bait Company, www.unclejosh.com
Yo-Zuri, www.yo-zuri.com

Organizations

American Sportfishing Association, www.asafishing.org
Berkeley (NJ) Striper Club, www.berkeleystriperclub.org
Boynton Inlet (FL) Fishing Club, www.bifc.org

Central Connecticut Striper Club, www.striperclub.org

Coastal Flyrodders (NJ), www.coastalflyrodders.com

Fort McAllister (GA) Sport Fishing Club, www.fmsfc.com/mainpage.html

International Game Fish Association, www.igfa.org

Jersey Coast (NJ) Anglers Association, www.jcaa.org

Rhode Island Saltwater Anglers Association, www.risaa.org

Shore Fishing and Casting Club International (TX), www.sfcci.org

Sport Fisherman's Club (VA), www.sportfishermansclub.com

Reels

Abu Garcia, www.abu-garcia.com

Avet Reels, www.avetreels.com

Daiwa, www.daiwa.com

Okuma Fishing Tackle Corporation, www.okumafishing.com

Penn Fishing Tackle Manufacturing Company, www.pennreels.com

Rods

Cape Fear Rod Company, www.capefearrodcompany.com

CastAway Graphite Rods, www.castawayrods.com

Falcon Graphite Rods, www.falconrods.com

Fenwick, www.fenwickfishing.com

RodMounts, www.rodmounts.com

Shakespeare Fishing Tackle, www.shakespeare-fishing.com

Rust Inhibitor

Van Patten Industries, www.theinhibitor.com

Seasickness

Sea-Band USA, www.sea-band.com/seaband.htm

Sinkers

Bullet Weights Inc., www.bulletweights.com

Sunglasses

Fitovers Eyewear, www.fitovers.com
Flying Fisherman, www.flyingfisherman.com

Tackle Boxes

Plano, www.planomolding.com/PlanoTackleHomepage.html

Wax

Nikwax, www.nikwax-usa.com

APPENDIX F

FISHING LOG

Fishing Log Year 20____ Name of Angler: _____

Date	Species Type	Weight (lbs.)	Length (in.)	Location Fished	Tide	Water Conditions	Water Temp. (°F)	Type of Bait (natural)	Type of Lure and Color	Water Depth (ft.)	Lunar Phase	Wind Dir.	Number Caught

GLOSSARY

Air bladder: See *swim bladder*.

Anal fin: The rearmost longitudinal fin along the bottom of a fish.

Artificial bait: Man-made bait that resembles real prey. See also *lure*.

Backlash: A loose, irregular arrangement of fishing line on the spool of a conventional reel as a result of the spool overspinning, caused by improper casting.

Bail: A semicircular metal arm on an open-faced spinning reel that engages the line after the cast.

Bait: See *artificial bait; natural bait*.

Bait-casting reel: A revolving spool type of reel attached on top of a bait-casting rod.

Baited hook: A fishhook that contains live or dead (cut) bait.

Baitfish: A term used by anglers to describe any fish species used for bait.

Bait pot: A container where live bait is kept alive and stored for ready use.

Bar: An offshore ridge or mound of sand, gravel, or other unconsolidated material that is submerged at high tide and is located at the mouth of a river or an estuary or lying parallel to a beach for a short distance.

Barb: A small, sharp protrusion just below the point of a fishhook that keeps the hook embedded in the flesh of the fish's mouth.

Barbel: A whiskerlike feeler below the lower jaw of a fish used for sensing food.

Barbless hook: A hook that has no sharp point; it is used for catch-and-release fishing. This type of hook does not injure a fish when it's removed.

Beach buggy: A powered vehicle used to travel on a beach.

Bobber: A small float placed on a fishing line to hold the hook at the desired depth.

Brackish water: Slightly salty water, as found in estuaries.

Cast: The act of imparting energy to a fishing rod in such a way that the line and leader project a bait or lure to a target some distance away.

Caudal fin: The tail fin of a fish.

Charter boat: A craft, with a crew, that can be rented by one to six anglers for a day or longer.

Chum: Chopped fish, fish fluids, and other material thrown overboard as angling bait and a fish attraction.

Crustacean: A group of freshwater or saltwater animals that have a chitinous or calcereous exoskeleton (exterior skeleton), modified appendages on each segment, and two pair of antennae, such as shrimp, crabs, and lobsters.

Current: A horizontal movement of water, classified as tidal or nontidal. Tidal currents are caused by the gravitational interactions between the sun, moon, and Earth. Nontidal currents are caused by the wind or sharp changes in bottom elevation.

Custom rod: A type of fishing rod manufactured to an individual's specifications.

Depth-finder: An electronic device used to detect the geography beneath the water surface. It can also be used as a *fish-finder*.

Dock: A man-made wooden or concrete structure to which boats are secured and from which fishing lines can be cast.

Drag: A mechanism built in to a fishing reel that slows down the outward flow of line when the reel is engaged, to ease line tension and to tire a fish.

Ebb tide: The movement of the tide out to sea.

Estuary: The tidal mouth of a river, where the tide meets a river or stream.

Feathers: A lure that consists of feathers to resemble a swimming fish when moved through the water.

Fighting belt: A belt worn by anglers that has a cup to hold the butt of the fishing rod, to ease fighting and landing a large fish.

Fish-finder: A device that can detect the depth at which a school of fish is swimming, and larger individual fish. See also *depth-finder*.

Fish-finder rig: A bottom-fishing rig that consists of a sinker and a free-moving baited hook.

Fishing season: The time of year when a specific species of fish can be caught.

Fish well: See *live well*.

Flood tide: The movement of the tide toward shore.

Fluorocarbon line: A type of fishing line that is resistant to abrasion and is invisible when submerged.

Fly: A man-made lightweight fish lure specifically used with fly line and a fly rod and reel.

Fly line: A type of heavyweight line, usually 80 to 90 feet long, used specifically for fly fishing. It is cast, whipping a lightweight fly an appreciable distance.

Fly reel: The device that holds fly line to a fly rod. It gives the angler a mechanical drag system with which to exert resistance on a hooked fish.

Fly rod: A lightweight, flexible fishing rod used for fly fishing.

Fly tying: A method of making fly fishing flies.

Fry: Young fish.

Gaff: A rod that contains a large sharp hook at one end; used to bring large fish over the side of a boat.

Game fish: A large predator fish sought by anglers for sport; a fish that is regulated by law.

Gear ratio: A reference to the number of times that a reel's spool or bail rotates relative to the number of cranks on the handle.

Gill: A breathing organ of a fish that extracts oxygen from the water.

Guide foot: The base of a fishing rod guide that rests against the outside diameter of the rod blank.

Gunwale: The upper outside edge of the side of a boat.

Hit: The action of a fish attacking a baited hook or lure.

Inshore fishing: Fishing that takes place within sight of land.

Instinct: A natural or fixed pattern of behavior in animals in response to certain stimuli.

Jetty: A breakwater constructed to protect or defend a harbor; a stretch of coast or riverbank designed to protect a navigational channel.

Jig: A lure that has a hook with a lead head behind the main-line attachment eye. It's usually painted and contains hairs tied to hide the hook. Used to attract fish.

Jigging: A jerking motion with a rod and reel or hand line that moves an artificial lure through the water.

Leader: A length of monofilament, fluorocarbon, or wire line of 25-pound test or more used to snell hooks, attach a lure, or attach a sinker to a swivel.

Line friction: Friction created as the fishing line passes through the line guides located along the length of the fishing rod.

Line guide: Metal loop on one side of a fishing rod that steers the fishing line along the length of the rod. Also called "rod guide."

Live bait well: See *live well*.

Live well: A built-in compartment on a boat that can be pumped full of seawater to keep caught fish or bait alive or fresh. Some live wells for baitfish (called "live bait wells") circulate water to keep it cool and aerated.

Lure: Man-made device with hooks that imitates something that a fish would eat or is designed to catch their attention.

Main line: The line that extends from the fishing reel.

Migration: An annual journey made by certain species of fish in search of food or for propagation.

Minnow: A small baitfish used by anglers to catch other larger fish. Another name for killifish.

Monofilament: A single strand of man-made fiber, used in the manufacture of fishing line.

Moratorium: The temporary suspension of an activity, such as the taking of certain fish.

Natural bait: Live or dead bait placed on a hook to attract fish.

Neap tide: A tide just after the first or last quarter of the moon when there is the least difference between high and low tide.

Nearshore: Refers to inshore waters adjacent to the shoreline.

Offshore fishing: Fishing that takes place out of sight of land.

Outrigger: Long poles that allow the lure or hook to be placed well out to the side of the boat. They let you troll more lines and place the lure into water undisturbed by the boat's wake.

Party boat: A large seagoing vessel designed to allow large numbers of anglers to fish at the same time. Also known as a "head boat" or an "open boat."

Pectoral fin: A fin found on both sides of a fish just behind the gill opening.

Pelvic fin: Two adjoining fins located beneath the belly of a fish but ahead of the anus.

PFD: Personal floatation device, a wraparound, vested life preserver.

Pier: A structure usually of open construction that extends into the water from shore to serve as a recreational fishing facility or to secure boats.

Plug: One of many types of man-made lures made of plastic or wood that are designed to imitate baitfish.

Popper: A type of man-made fishing lure that can be pulled long distances while being worked or jigged in a steady fashion; used to attract fish.

Possession limit: The number of fish that an angler can legally keep at one time.

Predator fish: A fish that feeds on other species.

Prey: Live fish that are fed upon by larger fish.

Reef: A ridge of rock, coral, or sand (natural or man-made) above or below the water surface.

Reel: A device that is attached to a fishing rod that dispenses, retrieves, and conveniently stores fishing line.

Reel seat: A portion of the fishing rod to which the reel is fastened.

Rip: Agitation of water caused by the meeting of currents or by a rapid current moving over an irregular bottom.

Rip current: The meeting of two currents of short duration (period of time) flowing seaward from shore. They can both be surface currents, or one can be a vertical current caused by bottom formations.

Rod: A long, slender, lightweight, hollow tube made of fiberglass, graphite, or composite materials used for fishing; it usually has line guides to steer the fishing line along its length.

Rod blank: The rod itself, without any line guides.

Rod guide: See *line guide*.

Rod holder: A tube-like device designed to support a fishing rod.

Roller guide: A heavy-duty line guide with an internal bearing system that eliminates heat and abrasion on fishing line when the line is under heavy stress.

Runabout: A small motorboat used for short trips.

Sandbar: A long, narrow raised area of sand below the surface of the water, especially where a river enters the sea or at the surf, usually formed by moving currents.

Sand spike: A long, hollow tube with a pin that is pushed deep into the sand to support a surf rod vertically on a beach. The surf rod is suspended from the pin.

School: A closely spaced collection of fish that swim in association with one another. Fish in a school are usually of the same species and of similar size, although species may intermingle.

Sharpening stone: An artificial or natural stone used to sharpen knives or fishhooks. Also called a hook hone.

Shucked clam: A clam from which the shell has been removed.

Sinker: A weight that is attached to the end of fishing line to keep the baited hook(s) on the bottom.

Skiff: A shallow-draft, open boat with a sharp bow and square stern. Can be rowed, but is most often powered.

Slack tide: A tide that is neither ebbing nor flooding.

Slip sinker: A lead weight with a hole through its center that slides freely up and down the fishing line unless altered by a swivel.

Snelled hook: A hook purchased with line already attached.

Spawn: The act of fish reproduction. Also, the eggs themselves.

Spinner: A fishing lure with thin metal blades that revolve around a wire shaft to attract fish.

Spoon: A thin metal fishing lure that wobbles from side to side in the water when retrieved; used to attract fish.

Sportfishing boat: A type of fishing boat that is 23 feet or longer and is used for offshore fishing.

Spring tide: A tide just after a new or full moon, causing higher high tides and lower low tides.

Strike: The action of a fish hitting a baited hook or an artificial lure.

Structure: Underwater rocks, shells, debris, or shipwrecks to which fish are attracted for shelter and feeding.

Substrate: Sea bottom configuration.

Surf casting: Fishing from the surf with a specially designed rod that has a long handle, which allows the angler to make long, precise casts.

Swim bladder: A thin-walled sac that may function as a buoyant float, a sound producer and receptor, and/or a respiratory organ. It allows fish to move up and down through the water. Fish with an open swim bladder (connected to the digestive tract) can let air escape through the mouth. Fish with a closed swim bladder depend on gas diffusion through the blood vessels in the bladder walls: when gas is added, the fish becomes less dense, allowing it to rise; when gas is removed, the fish becomes more dense, allowing it to sink. If a fish with a closed swim bladder is brought to the surface from deep water very quickly, its swim bladder can explode.

Swivel: A coupling between two sections of fishing line, enabling one section to revolve without turning the other.

Tackle: Term used for all the equipment required for sportfishing.

Tackle shop: A store where fishing tackle and bait are sold.

Terminal tackle: Hooks, sinkers, snaps, and swivels that are at the end of the fishing line.

Tippet: The thin end of a tapered leader.

Tip-top: The rod guide located at the tip of a fishing rod.

Trolling: Fishing while dragging artificial lures or live or dead bait behind a slow-moving boat under power; used to entice game fish to strike.

Trolling rod: A specially designed rod used to drag small or large lures or live or dead bait behind a boat while in motion. These rods usually have a roller guide.

Undertow: Current below the surface of the sea moving in the opposite direction to the surface current.

Wire leader: A short or long piece of specially designed small-diameter wire line that is attached between the main fishing line and the hook to prevent fish from biting through the line.

Wire line: Fishing line made of wire for strength and sinking ability.

Work hardened: Metal bent to the point where it weakens or breaks.

Worm weight: Lead weight that is bullet shaped and placed on the leader ahead of a plastic or jelly worm.

ABOUT THE AUTHOR

Martin Pollizotto has been fishing for more than 40 years. He's fished from party, charter, and private sportfishing boats and has fished numerous bays, estuaries, harbors, and the surf along the Atlantic and Pacific coasts and in the Gulf of Mexico. Experienced in all fishing methods, he enjoys offshore deepwater and surf fishing the most. His boat, *Five Joys,* is frequently seen heading to offshore fishing grounds, or along the shore while drifting or bottom fishing.

Martin recently retired after teaching aviation maintenance technology at the vocational high school level for 30 years—a career that provided the spare time to visit fishing locations all over North America. His teaching propensities extend to fishing. As a member of local angling clubs and the International Game Fish Association, he frequently teaches saltwater fishing in his community and is actively involved in youth fishing derbies. He has helped hundreds of saltwater anglers improve their proficiency and increase their enjoyment of the sport. An advocate of hook and release, Martin believes that most fish caught should be safely returned to ensure the viability of saltwater stocks in the future.

Martin has been married for 38 years. His wife often accompanies him on fishing trips, as do their three children, all of whom enjoy saltwater fishing.

INDEX

Numbers in **bold** refer to pages with illustrations.